Lecture Notes in Computer Science   7195

Commenced Publication in 1973
Founding and Former Series Editors:
Gerhard Goos, Juris Hartmanis, and Jan van Leeuwen

Björn Regnell   Daniela Damian (Eds.)

Requirements Engineering: Foundation for Software Quality

18th International Working Conference, REFSQ 2012
Essen, Germany, March 19-22, 2012
Proceedings

 Springer

Volume Editors

Björn Regnell
Lund University
Department of Computer Science
221 00 Lund, Sweden
E-mail: bjorn.regnell@cs.lth.se

Daniela Damian
University of Victoria
Department of Computer Science
P.O. Box 3055, Victoria, BC, V8W 3P6 Canada
E-mail: danielad@cs.uvic.ca

ISSN 0302-9743   e-ISSN 1611-3349
ISBN 978-3-642-28713-8   e-ISBN 978-3-642-28714-5
DOI 10.1007/978-3-642-28714-5
Springer Heidelberg Dordrecht London New York

Library of Congress Control Number: Applied for

CR Subject Classification (1998): D.2, C.2, H.4, F.3, K.6.5, D.4.6

LNCS Sublibrary: SL 2 – Programming and Software Engineering

Typesetting: Camera-ready by author, data conversion by Scientific Publishing Services, Chennai, India

Printed on acid-free paper

Springer is part of Springer Science+Business Media (www.springer.com)

Preface

This LNCS volume contains the papers accepted for presentation at the 18th Working Conference on Requirements Engineering: Foundation for Software Quality (REFSQ 2012), held in Essen, Germany, during March 19–22, 2012.

Requirements engineering (RE) has long been recognized as a major factor for achieving high-quality software-intensive, computer-based systems and services. REFSQ seeks reports of novel ideas and techniques that enhance RE processes and artifacts as well as reflections on current research and industrial practice about and in RE. In proudly presenting this program of 2012, we are confident that the REFSQ motto "I heard it first at REFSQ!" will be agreed upon by the conference participants.

REFSQ, in this 18th incarnation, provided a well-established, leading international forum with its special working conference format that promotes intensive interaction and hands-on research work involving both academics and practitioners. In particular, the appreciated REFSQ format involves, unlike many conferences and workshops, a discussion time following a paper's presentation that is (at least) as long as the presentation.

A total of 103 submissions were received, of which 84 papers entered the review process (after rejecting those papers that were late, oversized, or clearly out of scope). Each paper received reviews by three different members of the Program Committee. Whenever the reviews for a paper showed any divergence, the reviewers were asked to conduct a discussion electronically with the aim of reaching a consensus. Eleven members of our Program Committee met in person in Essen on December 2 to discuss the reviews of all papers and to agree on the papers to be presented at the conference and included in the proceedings. Out of the 84 peer-reviewed submissions, a total of 27 papers were accepted (14 long papers, including 10 Full Research papers and 4 Experience Report papers; as well as 13 short papers, including 9 Research Preview papers, 1 Vision paper, and 3 Problem Statement papers). This yields an 18% acceptance rate for long papers, and a 32% overall acceptance rate.

As in previous years, these proceedings serve not only as the record of one meeting of REFSQ, but also as a snapshot of the state of research and practice about and in RE. Therefore, these proceedings are of interest to the whole RE community, ranging from students beginning their PhD studies, through experienced scholars doing sustained RE research, novice requirements analysts, to experienced practitioners interested in emerging knowledge.

Anyone interested in an account of the discussions that took place during the working conference should consult the post-conference summary published, as is usual, in ACM SIGSOFT's *Software Engineering Notes*.

Above all, REFSQ is a collaborative effort. First, we thank Klaus Pohl for his continuing work as General Chair of the working conference. We would also give our sincerest thanks to Vanessa Stricker, who very ably served as Organization Chair. We thank the Steering Committee, listed here, consisting of past REFSQ Program Committee and General Chairs, for their seasoned advice.

We thank also the organizers of the four workshops held on the day before the conference and Samuel Fricker for chairing the workshop selection process. We thank Barbara Paech for organizing the Doctoral Symposium for the second time, Neil Maiden for organizing the Industry Track, and Richard Berntsson Svensson for serving as Publication Chair.

For the second year, REFSQ 2012 had two innovative events: (1) the Empirical Fair organized by Joerg Dorr, Norbert Seyff and Daniel Berry, in which practitioners and researchers propose empirical studies sought by their organizations or which they would like to conduct in such organizations, and (2) the Empirical Studies at REFSQ in which practitioners and academics are given the opportunity to conduct empirical studies during the working conference itself. Both of these activities are designed to bring together the community of researchers and practitioners who are interested in empirical studies.

As the Program Committee Co-chairs for REFSQ 2012, we thank especially the members of the Program Committee, listed here, for their careful, thorough, and timely reviews and for their lively consensus e-discussions. We thank in particular those of the Program Committee who attended the Program Committee meeting and those who volunteered to serve as anonymous gatekeepers for conditional accepts. Finally, we thank all the sponsors, also listed, who contributed generously to this edition of the REFSQ working conference.

January 2012   Björn Regnell
                                                                      Daniela Damian

Conference Organization

General Chair

Klaus Pohl   University of Duisburg-Essen, Germany

Program Co-chairs

Daniela Damian   University of Victoria, Canada
Björn Regnell   Lund University, Sweden

Workshops Chair

Samuel Fricker   Blekinge Institute of Technology, Sweden

Empirical Track Chair

Jörg Dörr   Fraunhofer-IESE, Germany

Industry Chair

Neil Maiden   City University London, UK

Doctoral Consortium Chair

Barbara Paech   University of Heidelberg, Germany

Organization Chair

Vanessa Stricker   University of Duisburg-Essen, Germany

Publication Chair

Richard Berntsson Svensson   Lund University, Sweden

Program Committee

Aybuke Aurum	University of New South Wales, Australia
Brian Berenbach	Siemens Corporate Research, USA
Daniel Berry	University of Waterloo, Canada
Sjaak Brinkkemper	Utrecht University, The Netherlands
David Callele	University of Saskatchewan, Canada
Jane Cleland-Huang	DePaul University, USA
Eric Dubois	CRP Henri Tudor, Luxembourg
Jörg Dörr	Fraunhofer-IESE, Germany
Armin Eberlein	American University of Sharjah, United Arab Emirates
Xavier Franch	Technical University of Catalonia, Spain
Samuel Fricker	Blekinge Institute of Technology, Sweden
Donald Gause	Binghamton University, USA
Vincenzo Gervasi	University of Pisa, Italy
Martin Glinz	University of Zurich, Switzerland
Tony Gorschek	Blekinge Institute of Technology, Sweden
Olly Gotel	Independent Researcher, USA
Paul Gruenbacher	Johannes Kepler University Linz, Austria
Peter Haumer	IBM Rational, USA
Mats Heimdahl	University of Minnesota, USA
Patrick Heymans	University of Namur, Belgium
Matthias Jarke	RWTH Aachen University, Germany
Natalia Juristo	Polytechnic University of Madrid, Spain
Erik Kamsties	University of Applied Sciences and Arts Dortmund, Germany
Marjo Kauppinen	Aalto University, Finland
Kim Lauenroth	University of Duisburg-Essen, Germany
Soren Lauesen	IT University of Copenhagen, Denmark
Pericles Loucopoulos	Loughborough University, UK
Nazim Madhavji	University of Western Ontario, Canada
Sabrina Marczak	PUCRS, Brazil
Raimundas Matulevicius	University of Tartu, Estonia
Ana Moreira	New University of Lisbon, Portugal
John Mylopoulos	University of Toronto, Canada
Cornelius Ncube	Bournemouth University, UK
Andreas L. Opdahl	University of Bergen, Norway
Barbara Paech	University of Heidelberg, Germany

Oscar Pastor Lopez	Polytechnic University of Valencia, Spain
Anne Persson	University of Skövde, Sweden
Jolita Ralyte	University of Geneva, Switzerland
Gil Regev	Federal Polytechnic University of Lausanne, Switzerland
Colette Rolland	University of Paris 1, Panthéon Sorbonne, France
Camille Salinesi	University of Paris 1, Panthéon Sorbonne, France
Kristian Sandahl	Linköping University, Sweden
Pete Sawyer	University of Lancaster, UK
Kurt Schneider	University of Hannover, Germany
Norbert Seyff	University of Zurich, Switzerland
Guttorm Sindre	Norwegian University of Science and Technology, Norway
Janis Stirna	Royal Institute of Technology, Sweden
Christer Thörn	Jönköping University, Sweden
Inge Van De Weerd	Utrecht University, The Netherlands
Roel Wieringa	University of Twente, The Netherlands
Eric Yu	University of Toronto, Canada
Konstantinos Zachos	City University London, UK
Didar Zowghi	University of Technology Sydney, Australia

External Reviewers

Abelein, Ulrike	Merten, Thorsten
Acher, Mathieu	Myllärniemi, Varvana
Barnes, Raymond	Naab, Matthias
Barney, Sebastian	Raspotnig, Christian
Bos, Rik	Rifaut, Andre
Carrizo Moreno, Dante	Solari, Martin
Daneva, Maya	Spruit, Marco R
Delater, Alexander	Stoiber, Reinhard
Galster, Matthias	Todoran, Irina
Gross, Anne	Torkar, Richard
Jansen, Slinger	Unterkalmsteiner, Michael
Jeanneret Wueest, Cdric Dustin	Vlaanderen, Kevin
Jung, Christian	Vriezekolk, Eelco
Koziolek, Anne	Zikra, Iyad
Mahaux, Martin	Zorn-Pauli, Gabriele

Steering Committee

Dan Berry	University of Waterloo, Canada
Daniela Damian	University of Victoria, Canada
Jörg Dörr	Fraunhofer-IESE, Germany
Xavier Franch	Technical University of Catalonia, Spain
Vincenzo Gervasi	University of Pisa, Italy
Martin Glinz	University of Zurich, Switzerland
Patrick Heymans (Chair)	University of Namur, Belgium
Andreas Opdahl	University of Bergen, Norway
Barbara Paech	University of Heidelberg, Germany
Anne Persson	University of Skövde, Sweden
Björn Regnell	Lund University, Sweden
Camille Salinesi	University of Paris 1, Panthéon Sorbonne, France
Pete Sawyer (Vice-Chair)	University of Lancaster, UK
Roel Wieringa	University of Twente, The Netherlands

Requirements Engineering for Enterprise Systems: A Keynote to the REFSQ'2012 Conference

Ian Sommerville

St Andrews University, United Kingdom
ian.sommerville@st-andrews.ac.uk

Abstract. Many approaches to requirements engineering are behavioural and attempt to define required system features and functionality. They, typically, have a 'single system' focus. In this talk, I will argue that this approach to requirements engineering is inappropriate for extending 'enterprise systems' - systems of systems that support many different operations in an organization. I will discuss an approach to requirements engineering which moves away from the behavioural approach to requirements engineering to focus on the information requirements of stakeholders in the enterprise. Information requirements are concerned with the information needed by stakeholders, the channels used to deliver that information and the issues and problems that arise if the information is not delivered in a timely manner. I will propose that a model of stakeholder responsibilities is an effective way of understanding and analyzing these information requirements.

Biography

Ian Sommerville is a Professor of Computer Science at the University of St Andrews, Scotland and was previously Professor of Software Engineering at Lancaster University. He is currently a principal investigator in the UK's Large Scale Complex IT Systems research and training programme with interests in modeling complex systems of systems and in cloud computing. He has published extensively in software and requirements engineering and is the author of a widely-used software engineering textbook. He was awarded the 2011 ACM SIGSOFT Outstanding Educator award for his work in software and requirements engineering education.

Sponsors

Platinum Level Sponsors

Gold Level Sponsors

Silver Level Sponsors

Table of Contents

Session 4: Requirements Analysis

Session 5: Templates and Heuristics

Session 6: Requirements Traceability

Session 7: Tools and Quality

Session 8: Services and Clouds

Session 9: Self-adaptivity

Session 10: Industrial Case Studies

Why the Electronic Land Registry Failed

Soren Lauesen

IT University of Copenhagen, Denmark
slauesen@itu.dk

Abstract. **[Context and motivation]** In 2009 Denmark got a compulsory IT system for Land Registration of ownership. It soon created a national disaster because selling houses and getting mortgages might take months, rather than a couple of days. In this period, house owners had to pay a much higher interest rate. **[Question/problem]** The press claimed it was yet another IT failure, but actually the IT system worked as intended. What was the real cause? **[Principal ideas/results]** The visible problem was overloaded staff in the Registry Office, but behind this were optimistic estimates of human performance, lack of usability, insufficient user interface requirements, unrealistic SOA requirements, immature risk analysis, and other factors. **[Contribution]** This paper shows details of the requirements, what went wrong, and what could have been done, e.g. early design of the user interface and giving the supplier more influence on the architecture.

Keywords: information system failures, software failures, public software acquisition, organizational implementation, usability, user interface requirements, SOA architecture, risk analysis.

1 Background

In September 2009 Denmark got an Electronic Land Registry system (e-LR) that overnight became the only way to register ownership of land and mortgage deeds. All registrations had to be entered online or through system-to-system interfaces to financial IT systems. It was planned that 30% of the registrations should be selected for manual checking based on confidential criteria. All stakeholders had known about the new system for a long time and had been advised to prepare for the change.

Figure 1 shows the system and its context. Real-estate agents, lawyers and ordinary citizens were expected to use a web interface (the *external portal*), the registry staff used an internal user interface (the *internal portal*). The e-LR system integrated to several government systems, e.g. the national digital signature (DanID), the civil registration system, the business registry, one of the tax systems (for collecting the registration fee) and the land plot registry.

Based on historical data, it was estimated that 5 million registrations would be handled per year, corresponding to about 2 per second during peak load in daytime. (Denmark has around 5 million inhabitants). The customer (the Land Registry) had carefully estimated the number of employees needed to support this load, but the estimate turned out to be far too small.

B. Regnell and D. Damian (Eds.): REFSQ 2012, LNCS 7195, pp. 1–15, 2012.

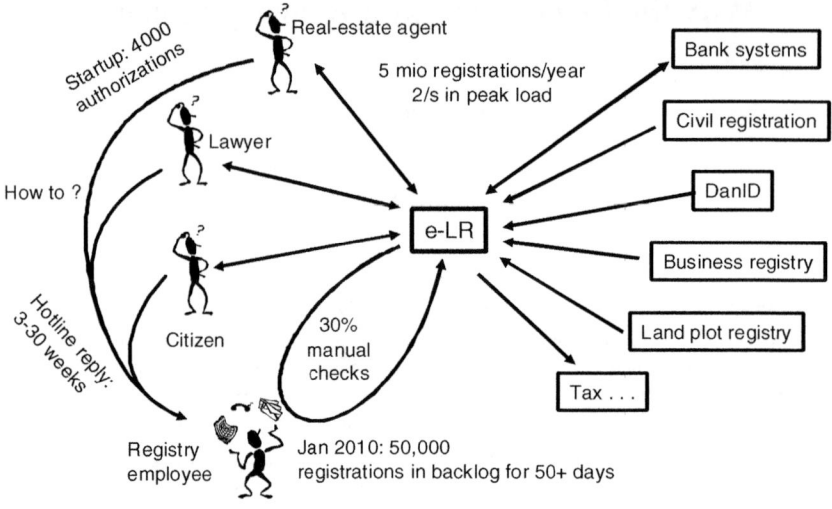

Fig. 1. Electronic Land Registry – Big-Bang Sept 2009

Technically the system worked as intended, but the staff immediately became overloaded. Early 2010, more than 50,000 registrations were waiting for manual checking with a delay of 50 days. The lucky 70% who were not selected for manual checking, got their registration within a minute.

The unfortunate 30% lost money because they had to pay a much higher interest rate in these 50 days. Since selling and buying real-estate is financially stressful to an ordinary family, this loss could have serious consequences.

The situation could have been much worse. Due to the financial crisis in 2009, there were only half as many registrations as expected. If the expected number had occurred, the situation had become a true disaster.

This paper reports on how the overload could happen. There are many studies on systems that fail or vastly exceed the budget and deadline [1, 2, 3, 4, 5, 6, 7, 17], but the explanations are usually on a high level, such as poor project management, lack of senior management support, or lack of user involvement. Poor project management doesn't directly create a disaster. It is created through many specific flaws, such as ignoring certain risks or not watching what the system supplier is doing. These specific flaws are rarely reported, and probably vary a lot from project to project. However, one study goes into detail: Leveson & Turner's investigation of the Therac-25 accidents, where patients were seriously harmed when treated by an electron beam [11]. The cause was believed to be operator mistakes or faulty switches, but turned out to be an error in the central real-time software where concurrent activities communicated through shared memory locations without proper synchronization.

In this paper we start with the visible problem - the overloaded staff - and identify the main causes behind it. Some of the root causes are well known factors such as poor project management, but some other causes are not covered by literature.

Unfortunately, in complex systems the network of causes is not a precise concept. Several factors contribute in each link of the chain [5, 11, 16]. All we can do is try to identify the major ones and their approximate relationships.

2   Project History

The e-LR system was developed and operated by a large software house that won the contract after a tender process. The customer was the Danish Courts. Denmark has around 30 courts and most of them operated a land registration office for properties in their own district. The plan was to locate the electronic land registration in only one of the courts, in that way saving around 220 staff.

The history was as follows.

- Early 2005. A consultancy company had made a business case that showed that the registration office could save around $20 M a year, and citizens and the financial sector around $80 M. (For simplicity, we have defined 1 USD = 5 DKK.)
- June 2006. The customer and his consultant had developed tender material (including the requirements specification) and made a request for proposals.
- December 2006. The customer selected one of the suppliers and they signed the contract. Expected deployment of the system was March 2008.
- 2007. It became obvious that the system couldn't be delivered on time. The new deployment time was changed several times.
- 2007-2008. The huge archives of existing registered documents (40 million pages) were scanned and filed, ready for the new system.
- Early 2009. The 220 staff were dismissed with the standard notice time of around 6 months. It was planned to be around three months after deployment, but the schedule slipped once more, and as a result these employees had left when the system was deployed.
- September 2009. The system was deployed as a big-bang. The registry office soon became the overloaded bottleneck.
- Late 2010. The registration office managed to get rid of the backlog, and from the end of 2010, 99% of the manual checks were handled within 15 days. The remaining cases were the very complex ones.

The development time had increased from the planned 18 months to 36 months. The software cost had increased from the budgeted $15 M to $21 M (+40%).

Today the system is a definitive success. As an example, a citizen can walk into his bank, and in less than an hour get a mortgage and $200,000 on his bank account.

3   Method

Late 2009, the Danish State Auditors (*Statsrevisorerne,* members of the parliament) asked the National Auditors (*Rigsrevisionen*) to audit the project. They contracted with Lauesen to help them with the IT aspects. The team agreed that an important aspect of the audit was to identify issues that other IT projects could learn from.

The team gathered information in several ways. We read the existing documents about the system. From an IT perspective, the most interesting ones were:

1. The requirements specification (406 pages with 413 requirements).
2. The supplier's proposal (600 pages).
3. The contract (32 pages with requirements and proposal as appendices).
4. Design specification, change specifications, etc. (more than 2000 pages).

We interviewed real-estate staff and lawyer staff to hear about the system and the problems it caused. They also showed us how the system worked and how they used it.

We conducted a focus group with senior representatives for the stakeholders: the financial sector, the land surveyors, the lawyers, the real-estate agents, the customer (the Land Registry) and the customer's consultant. We asked about good and bad points in the system, and the stakeholders' priorities for improvements.

We had expected that the ordinary staff member's opinion differed from the senior representative's opinion, and that stakeholders disagreed with each other. This turned out to be wrong. Everybody agreed on good and bad points, although they gave them somewhat different priorities.

We met with experts from the financial institutions to hear about their experiences with the system-to-system integration, and with senior representatives for the customer and his consultant.

Later we met with the supplier's senior staff and developers to discuss our findings and the relationship between supplier, customer, and the customer's consultant. This brought a quite different perspective to what had happened and why.

We wrote our findings as a preliminary report and submitted it to the customer for review, discussed disagreements, and published the final report [15].

Later, Lauesen interviewed and exchanged mails with the president of the Danish Courts and the supplier in order to get further insight into the overload and related issues.

4   What Caused the Overload?

Why did the registry become overloaded? We found several reasons, but the most important were these:

Cause 1: An unexpected number of requests for authorization. It was expected that citizens would sign the various registrations digitally, using DanID, but few did. Although DanID had been operational for several years, few citizens used it. It was far too complex to install and maintain. (In contrast, most citizens used the bank's shared digital signature without trouble.) The result was that lawyers and real-estate agents needed to digitally sign on behalf of their clients, but to do so required authorization from the Registry. The Registry was surprised to get 4000 authorization requests, and handling them caused much trouble.

Cause 2: An unexpected, huge number of requests to the Registry's hotline. The requests came from lawyers and real-estate agents who couldn't figure out how to use the system.

Cause 3: Registry staff was much less productive than expected. They were not comfortable with the user interface, although they had received training.

Cause 4: Mistakes in recent registrations. Since the old registry staff had been dismissed, registrations until the big-bang were done by temporary staff, who made many mistakes. After the big bang, many of these mistakes were revealed during the manual checks and caused further delays.

Cause 5: Big-bang without a pilot test. Could the causes above have been anticipated? In hindsight it looks possible, but systems of this kind are so complex that there always are surprises. One way to detect them is by running a pilot test, for instance deploying the system in only one of the 30 Danish courts. This would have revealed all the causes above, and it would have been far easier to deal with them.

Below we will discuss the secondary causes, e.g. why the customer (the Land Registry) didn't ensure proper usability, which would have reduced cause 2 and 3.

5   Usability and User Interface Requirements

Cause 2 and 3 above are consequences of low usability, so we will look at the usability and how it was handled in the project. By definition we have a usability problem if the system can support the user's tasks, but the user is unable to find out how or unable to perform the tasks efficiently [10, 12, 13].

There are some examples in literature where low usability seems to be the root cause of the system failure, e.g. the London Ambulance [1], the FAA Air Traffic Control System [5] and the Sydney health record system [16].

Here are four of the many usability problems real-estate agents and lawyers told us about in the e-LR system:

1. *How do you register a condominium deed? There were several options in the menu: Single-family housing, cooperative apartment, farm – but no condominiums.*

The professionals were stuck and called the e-LR hotline. It was busy, so they might wait for an hour and then try the next day at a different time. It might take three weeks to succeed. Once they got through, there was an immediate reply: Select single-family housing – it includes condominiums. Since hotline had got this question frequently, one might wonder why developers didn't change the menu. The reason was that the judge in charge of the entire project refused: the law was clear and the term single-family housing covered also condominiums.

Amazingly, the Land Registry was not aware that the essential waiting time was three weeks. To his staff, it looked as nobody waited for more than an hour.

2. *Is it free to make a trial registration? And how much does it test?*

The user interface offered *trial registration*, but there was no hint at what it did and whether there was a fee. Professionals knew that there was a fee (a tax) for registering a mortgage, but would they be charged already at the trial? They had also experienced that a registration was accepted in trial mode, but rejected when they tried to make it final. So what was checked? Again it would take a long time to get a reply from hotline.

3. "Registration rejected". But why? Just try again?
When a registration was rejected, there was no explanation of the cause. Professionals experimented wildly to find out why.

4. When are requests selected for manual checking?
The system told you that your request had been picked for manual check, but professionals had no idea why. When time approached Xmas, some professionals wrote "Merry Xmas" in the field "message to the registry staff" - just to show sympathy with the Registry staff. They didn't realize that the result was that the registration was picked for manual checking (otherwise the staff couldn't see the message). The consequence was a delay of two months.

Usability Testing
How could these usability problems have been avoided? Usability specialists recommend that you make usability tests where potential users try to perform realistic tasks with the system [10, 12, 13, 14]. They are given the same help as they would have in real life. One or two usability specialists or developers observe what the user does and record the problems. To help them understand the problems, the users are asked to think aloud. Next the development team tries to remedy the serious problems, and then run the test again until the result is acceptable.

With this approach, all four usability problems above would have been easy to detect. The first two usability problems would also have been easy to repair even a few days before the big-bang. The last two problems are harder to deal with. They might require much programming. The last problem would even need some strategic rethinking, because some rules for picking a registration were measures against tax evasion, etc. So these rules had to be secret. But others could be open to help the users.

Usability experts also recommend that designers make an early prototype or mockup of the user interface. It is used for testing and improving the user interface. In this way, it would also have been possible to deal with the last two problems.

Usability Requirements
What did the requirements say about usability? The main requirement was this:
Req. 153: The supplier must during development test the usability of the external portal. The bidder must describe how.

This is actually a great usability requirement, compared to what most requirements say about usability. The supplier's reply to this requirement is also great:
Reply to req. 153: [We will test with] Rolf Molich's principles from his book . . .
Molich is a Danish usability specialist and he too recommends thinking aloud with early prototypes [12, 14]. However, the supplier's reply to appendix 21 about quality assurance interprets Molich's approach in a different way:
Reply to app. 21, quality assurance: . . . this means that the test manager guides the test participants through the tasks, asks explorative questions, and helps as needed.

This completely ruins the approach because the help available in real life is very different from this test approach. In real life nobody is available for guiding the user and helping as needed.

Apparently, none of these approaches were carried out in the project. Five months before the big bang, we find this change note among several others:

Change 32, 30-03-2009: Usability tests are replaced by a very close dialog between [a supplier expert and a land registry expert]

This means that a domain expert (a land registration judge) and the supplier's designer defined the user interface, but didn't do any usability testing. Usability experts know that a user interface designed in this way is only understandable to a domain expert. And this turned out to be the case also in this project. The lawyers and real-estate agents didn't understand.

During our interview with 10 key participants on the supplier's team, they admitted that they didn't know what usability testing was and hadn't done any. They had made some *user testing*, which seemed to be more like the procedure suggested in the reply about quality assurance.

The information we gathered from the customer (the land registry) showed that usability testing was considered a nice thing to do at the end - if time allowed, but it didn't. The attitude was that it was the professional user's own problem to learn about the system. They had not taken the opportunity to make courses, etc. The customer (and the supplier) used as an excuse that the system was not intended for the ordinary citizen. It was hard to make them realize that the problems we reported were experienced by professionals, not by the ordinary citizen.

Concerning usability, the Danish Tax authorities are strikingly different. Tax rules are very complex, yet the Tax authorities have very successful web sites for reporting your actual income and your expected income. These sites are not compulsory, but the Tax authorities measure their success by how many citizens use the sites. In principle, the e-LR could have been launched the same way.

User Interface Requirements

While usability requirements specify the *quality* of the user interface, user interface requirements specify the *functionality* of the user interface. This can be done in several ways, for instance listing the functions that should be available or describing situations where the user will use the system. Both approaches were used in the e-LR requirements. *Use cases* served as a list of functions and *user stories* as descriptions of situations. Use cases as well as user stories come in many versions, but the versions used in the e-LR were not effective.

Fig. 2 shows part of a user story from the requirements specification. The full user story is 5 pages and in the story the user has to click a lot of buttons. It is a vivid scenario where you as a reader can imagine the situation. It is obvious that the writer has imagined a very concrete user interface with screens, pictures, menus and buttons to click. There are a total of 7 user stories for the external portal and 11 for the internal.

Are these user stories requirements? This would mean that the final system should have screens and buttons as described here. This would give the supplier little freedom and would mean that the customer had taken responsibility for usability. Fortunately, the specification says that these user stories are not requirements.

Notification of division of property

Hansel and Gretel got married in 1989, but now they will divorce. Throughout the marriage they have lived in Hansel's house and they have agreed that Gretel stays.

Hansel logs on to www.landregistry.dk. A welcome text appears. There is text and picture for land registry of *real estate, car mortgage* . . . He can see an icon for *Information Center* . . .

Hansel clicks on the text *real estate*. Then he is shown a login picture . . . Hansel has his digital signature stored on his PC . . . He is asked whether he wants to register or ask about real estate . . . and his e-mail address . . . and whether he will work with information on ownership, mortgages, easements or other.

He selects ownership and is asked whether it is
  - Final deed
  - Final deed on several properties
  - Deed upon purchase price payment
  - (And four other options, including division of property)

In total 5 pages for this user story. The spec says it isn't requirements.

Fig. 2. From the requirements: User stories

However, the main idea of a long sequence of clicks, questions and screens to fill, is visible in the final system. For instance it takes 22 screens to specify ownership of a property.

Fig. 3 shows a use case that describes how the user can make a test registration. It is a typical use case with an elaborate template with goal, precondition, post condition and exceptions. In this example it is just a lengthy way of writing this:

Use case A.5: Test registration
1. The user chooses a filled out registration.
2. The system performs a test registration.
3. The user gets the result.

An even shorter version is a requirement in traditional IEEE-830 style:
Requirement A.5: The system must provide a function for test registration.

USE CASE

Name: Test registration	Actor: External user	Ver: 1.0 ID: A.5
Goal:	It must be possible to perform a test registration of a deed that has been filled out in the portal, in order that the user gets a quick reply whether the deed can be registered.	
Precondition:	The user has filled out a registration and wants to check it against the Land Registry	

Step:	Actor:	System:	Proposer's solution:
1.	Select the registration	The user must select the registration to be tested.	
2.	Test register	The system performs a test registration of the selected item.	Context missing
Exceptions:			
Post condition:	The user gets the result of the test.		

Fig. 3. From the requirements: Use cases

The main problem is that in the e-LR use cases we see too little of the context. Although use cases are supposed to explain the context, they rarely do in practice. Some of the user-story aspects are missing. When would the user do this? And what will he do afterwards? Notice that a system that just reports *Registration rejected* fully meets the requirement expressed by the use case.

The specification contained 23 similar use cases for the external portal, for instance *fill out registration, attach file, sign digitally*. The internal portal had 31 use cases. A note added that the use cases were not a full list of the user interface requirements.

Although these specifications go too far in the design direction (the user stories) or don't cover the context of use (the use cases), they are actually quite good compared to average requirement specifications. Most requirements deal poorly with the user interface, and the traditional techniques offer no help.

Task descriptions are an alternative that combines the best parts of user stories and use cases [9, 10]. Fig. 4 shows user interface requirements for registration of ownership, expressed as a task description. Based on the interviews with the professionals, the author wrote this task description in half an hour.

The left part of the task description lists what user and computer have to do together to register ownership. During a physical session on the web site, the user may do some of the steps, preferably in a free order. He should be able to park the case, for instance waiting for other persons to sign the registration. In this example, the system must enforce some preconditions between the steps. For instance it must not be possible to modify the registration without getting new sign offs. In order not to obscure the user's picture of the process, these preconditions need not be part of the task description.

The left part also mentions problems the user may have, for instance whether a test registration costs something.

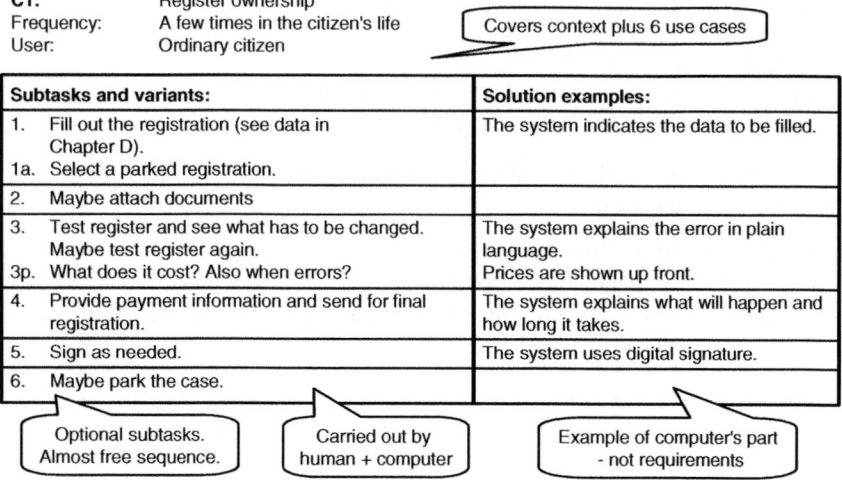

C1:	Register ownership	
Frequency:	A few times in the citizen's life	Covers context plus 6 use cases
User:	Ordinary citizen	

Subtasks and variants:	Solution examples:
1. Fill out the registration (see data in Chapter D). 1a. Select a parked registration.	The system indicates the data to be filled.
2. Maybe attach documents	
3. Test register and see what has to be changed. Maybe test register again. 3p. What does it cost? Also when errors?	The system explains the error in plain language. Prices are shown up front.
4. Provide payment information and send for final registration.	The system explains what will happen and how long it takes.
5. Sign as needed.	The system uses digital signature.
6. Maybe park the case.	

Optional subtasks. Almost free sequence.   Carried out by human + computer   Example of computer's part - not requirements

Fig. 4. Task descriptions: The system must support C1 . . .

The right part of the task description gives examples of what the system could do to support the user, for instance inform about the prices and what is wrong. The right-hand side is not requirements, but just examples. The true requirement is that the system must support this task (and maybe 20 other tasks).

Compared to the other approaches, this single task description covers the context, six use cases, and several usability problems. The description has not been carefully reviewed by domain experts, but the immediate reaction has been: *yes, we could have done it this way.*

6   Architecture and SOA Integration

One of the secondary causes of the staff overload was that development was late, so there was no time for a pilot test. This again had several causes, one of them being that there were time-consuming, unnecessary requirements in the architectural area. We will look at some of the causes here.

Availability and Open Target
The customer (and his consultant) had specified that the system had to be available 99.9% of the time. It is easy to ask for this, but customers don't think about the consequences. Experienced system operators can meet this requirement, but it is expensive. The system must run in several copies distributed geographically, maintenance and upgrades are complex, etc. If the customer had asked for 99.5%, it would be a routine matter.

In the e-LR case, the cost of operating the system with 99.5 availability is around $1 M per year. A 99.9% availability costs around $3 M per year. Is it worth it? In the old system, the availability was 25% because the Registry office was open 8 hours every weekday. Going for 99.9% in the future seems hard to justify.

The basic issue is that the customer may not be aware of the technical possibilities and their costs. This can be remedied by requirements with a more open target, such as this:
Req. 120: The customer expects availability around 99.8%.

The supplier could then offer two alternatives:
Req 120, alternative 1: 99.5% at 1M $ per year.
Req 120, alternative 2: 99.9% at 3M $ per year.

Such requirements and alternatives must be supported by rules in the contract, for instance as shown in [8]

Service-Oriented Architecture (SOA)
The customer (or rather his consultant) had suggested an advanced service-oriented architecture, and this was what the requirements asked for. We have summarized the requirements in this area as follows:

R1. The system must consist of modules connected with XML-services and a service broker. Each possible check of a registration must be a separate service.

R2. The system must connect to the external systems with XML-services. The data must always be retrieved from the external systems and not stored as a local copy.

A note added that all the external systems were stable and had well-defined XML interfaces.

These requirements sounded okay, but they caused many problems in practice. Here are some of them:

SOA Eats Computer Power. Using an XML-interface requires 10-50 times more computer power (CPU time) than traditional approaches. With the high demand at peek load, this might become a problem. The supplier knew about this, but if he made reservations in his proposal, he ran a risk of being non-compliant. He ended up saying that he could make it as the customer asked for, but that he strongly suggested the traditional approach being used for the internal interfaces.

Not surprisingly, in the final system, the traditional approach is used internally.

Always Getting Data from the Source Degrades Availability and Response Time. The reason is that if the external system is out of service, the e-LR system will essentially be out of service too. A similar argument holds for response time.

In this case the supplier made reservations in his proposal. The availability and response times in the external systems had to be "deducted" from the availability and response times of the e-LR system. The supplier also explained that he would construct the system so that it would be easy to change each external connection to a local copy with nightly synchronization.

Not surprisingly, the final system has a local copy of all the external data with nightly synchronization of changes. The only exception is the digital signatures in DanID. Here a high data actuality is justified, so that theft and other abuse can be stopped immediately.

In general, instead of asking for a specific architecture, the customer should ask for a specific data actuality, i.e. how old the data may be [8]. As an example, it is not a problem if a citizen's address is a few days old. This allows the supplier to come up with a suitable architecture.

The External Systems Were Not Stable. The customer's consultant's dream of stable external systems was just a dream. All of these systems (except the civil registration system) were under major revision. Furthermore, all of the systems had to accommodate changes made specifically for the e-LR system. These issues were very costly and time consuming to deal with for the supplier.

The supplier was lucky not to be judged non-compliant. Lauesen has seen some public acquisitions with unrealistic requirements such as 100% availability. All bidders except one made reservations. As a result the customer judged all of them non-compliant except the unrealistic one. Later in the project it turned out, of course, that the supplier couldn't meet the requirements, but the parties kept this confidential.

The ambitious SOA requirements were not really the customer's needs, but an idealistic concept enforced by the customer's consultant's IT architect. It took a long time to replace these ideals with something pragmatic.

7   Risk Analysis

Several of the causes above could have been prevented with proper risk management. During the project the parties made regular risk analyses, but they seemed to be used mainly for arguing that the risk wasn't important. Most of the bad things that actually happened had been identified as a risk, but no action was taken. As an example, we find these risks early 2007 (abbreviated):

ID	Risk	Level: 5 highest	Consequence	Status/comment
1	SOA is immature	1		Tax uses SOA
2	Has the customer low IT experience?	1		Has much experience
3	Supplier staff leaves	3	Less time for test	Tight project management
4	Interfaces to many systems	3		The systems are stable

Comments:

Risk 1: The Tax department actually used SOA, but the large projects were not successful or not yet completed.

Risk 2: The customer (the Danish Courts) had experience with IT systems for internal use, but had not made a system for public use. With internal systems, they could easily support the users, but a system for large-scale public use was very different.

Risk 3: The supplier had planned to use a team with strong expertise in this kind of projects. However, the entire team was bought by Google. This stalled the project for a year, but the customer didn't notice. He just expected that the system would be delivered according to the contract. When the customer found out, he asked his consultant to manage the project. Together they succeeded making the supplier give the project a high priority.

Risk 4: As explained above, the systems were not stable.

Five days before the big bang, this risk analysis was made:

ID	Risk	Level	Consequence	Status/comment
5	Low usability shows up at deployment	[none stated]	Lack of usability	The case is closed. Probability reduced.
6	Lack of staff at customer site	4	Long delays	The customer assesses the situation.

Comments:

Risk 5: The status "the case is closed" refers to the agreement four months earlier about usability being replaced with a close dialog between customer and supplier. It is scaring that the consequence of low usability wasn't understood: high load on hotline and low productivity in the Registry office, causing further delay.

Risk 6: This is a clear statement that the risk is high, but the supplier will not take responsibility for the consequences. Earlier the supplier had recommended a pilot test and on-line help, but the customer claimed it was impossible.

It should be obvious that the risk analysis was not used correctly. There were no safeguards and nobody took action for the high risks.

8   Discussion and Conclusion

Above we have identified many causes on various levels. Fig. 5 gives a graphical overview of them. We can see the network of causes and effects that resulted in low usability. We can also see the causes that made it impossible to run a pilot test. Notice that some causes have effect on several other causes, and some are caused by several lower-level causes in combination.

Cause 17 (staff fired and funding cut too early) has not been mentioned above. When a project like e-LR is funded by the government, the expected benefits are part of the project plan. Once the decision is made, the government cuts the funding according to the project plan. When the project becomes delayed, it is extremely hard to get the funding back. Further, if the customer waits too long to dismiss the redundant staff, he has to pay several months salary for no good. In the e-LR case, staff was dismissed so early and the project delayed so much that there was no time for pilot testing.

The figure also shows some broad root causes that were clearly in play here: Poor understanding of user capabilities and needs, poor use of established usability techniques, poor risk analysis, and poor project management. More surprisingly, a major root cause was that state-of-the-art in user interface requirements is insufficient.

Conclusion
The table below compares the findings in the e-LR project with the root causes reported by others. The list of root causes is compiled from Glass [5, 1998], Ewusi-Mensah [4, 2003] and Charette [2, 2005]. If we ignore the somewhat different wordings, there is a large overlap between these lists. From the comparison, we can conclude this:

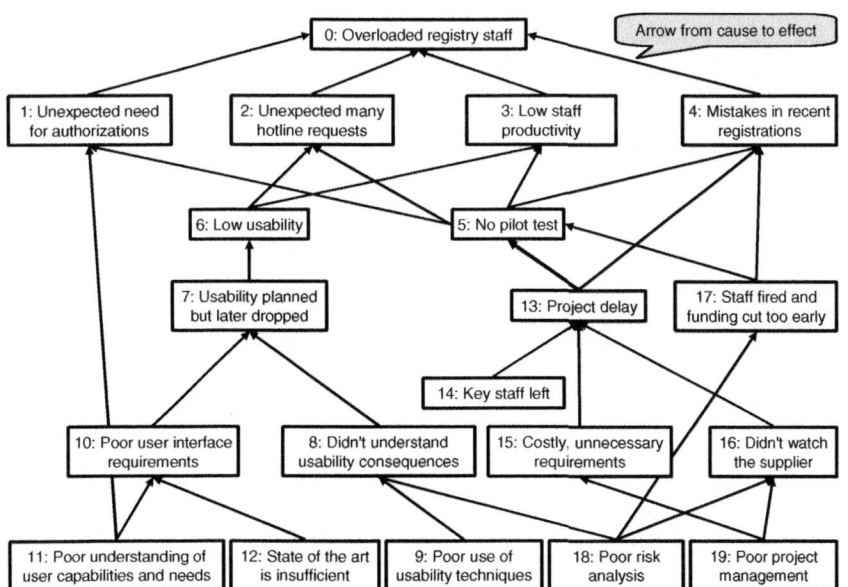

Fig. 5. Causes and effects

Human-Performance Causes Are Not Covered by the Literature: Most of the causes that directly related to the long delays are not covered by root causes from literature (causes 0, 2, 3, 4, 6). Although it seems obvious in hindsight, none of the authors suggest that you should estimate and test user performance, and that usability is a key factor for human performance.

Practices beyond State-of-the-Art Are Needed: *Poor development practice (D)* and *poor requirements (B)* do in principle cover the issues about low usability and poor user interface requirements, but unfortunately the relevant techniques are not widely known. They are beyond state-of-the-art in software engineering.

Customers State Ambitious Requirements without Caring about the Cost: Although good requirements practice would guard against this, it doesn't happen in public acquisitions. It is all too easy for the customer to state very ambitious requirements, and in the tender process it is dangerous for a supplier to reply with an adequate, but less ambitious proposal. He might be deemed non-conforming.

The remaining causes are covered in principle, meaning that if project management, risk analysis, etc. had been carried out perfectly according to state-of-the-art, these causes should not occur.

Root causes from literature	Causes found in e-LR
A. Too ambitious project	15 (costly unnecessary requirements)
B. Poor requirements	10 (poor user interface requirements), 15 (costly unnecessary requirements)
C. Technology new to the organization	
D. Poor development practices	8 (didn't understand usability consequences), 9 (didn't master usability techniques), 12 (state-of-the-art is insufficient)
E. Inability to handle the project's complexity	
F. Poor performance by hardware/software suppliers	14 (key staff left)
G. Poor system performance	
H. Poor project management	5 (no pilot test), 16 (didn't watch the supplier)
I. Bad planning and estimating	13 (project delay)
J. Poor status reporting	
K. Poor risk management	7 (usability planned but later dropped)
L. Poor communication between customers, developers and users	1 (unexpected need for authorizations), 11 (poor understanding of user capabilities and needs)
M. Insufficient senior management involvement	
N. Stakeholder politics	17 (staff fired and funding cut too early)
O. Commercial pressures	
P. Causes not covered	0, 2, 3, 4, 6 (human performance)

Implications for Requirements Research and Practice: There is a large gap between best practice in requirements and best practice in usability. As an example, early mockups of the user interface combined with usability tests of the mockups are not considered a crucial technique in requirements. It should be a standard approach.

Further, current practice is inadequate for specifying requirements to the user interface. Neither traditional shall-requirements, nor user stories or use cases are adequate. Task descriptions [9] cover much better and should be widely used.

Finally, there is a need to include user performance and organizational implementation in requirements. Little has been done in this area and literature is weak.

References

1. Beynon-Davies, P.: Human error and information systems failure: the case of the London ambulance service computer-aided despatch system project. Interacting with Computers 11(6), 699–720 (1999)
2. Charette, R.N.: Why software fails. IEEE Spectrum (September 2005) (Lists 31 failed US projects from 1992 to 2005)
3. Emam, K.E., Koru, A.G.: A replicated survey of IT software project failures. IEEE Software (September/October 2008)
4. Ewusi-Mensah, K.: Software development failures. The MIT press (2003)
5. Glass, R.L.: Software runaways. Prentice Hall (1998)
6. Jones, C.: Patterns of large software systems: failure and success. IEEE Computer (March 1995)
7. Keil, M., Rai, A., Mann, J.E.C., Zhang, P.: Why software projects escalate: The importance of project management constructs. IEEE Transactions on Engineering Management 50(3) (August 2003)
8. Lauesen, S.: Guide to Requirements SL-07 - Template with Examples (2007), http://www.itu.dk/people/slauesen/SorenReqs.html#SL-07 ISBN: 978-87-992344-0-0
9. Lauesen, S., Kuhail, M.: Task descriptions versus use cases. Requirements Engineering Journal (2011), doi:10.1007/s00766-011-0140-1
10. Lauesen, S.: User Interface Design - A Software Engineering Perspective. Addison-Wesley (2005)
11. Leveson, N.G., Turner, C.S.: An investigation of the Therac-25 accidents. IEEE Computer (July 1993)
12. Molich, M.: Usable Web Design. Nyt Teknisk Forlag, Denmark (2007)
13. Preece, J., Rogers, Y., Sharp, H.: Interaction Design – Beyond Human–Computer Interaction. John Wiley & Sons, New York (2002)
14. Redish, J., Molich, R., Bias, R.G., Dumas, J., Bailey, R., Spool, J.M.: Usability in Practice: Formative Usability Evaluations — Evolution and Revolution. In: CHI 2002, Minneapolis, USA, April 20-25 (2002)
15. Rigsrevisonen: Beretning til Statsrevisorerne om det digitale tinglysningsprojekt (in Danish) (August 2010), http://www.rigsrevisionen.dk/media(1610,1030)/14-2009.pdf
16. Southon, G., Sauer, C., Dampney, K.: Lessons from a Failed Information Systems Initiative: Issues for complex organisations. In: APAMI/HIC 1997, Sydney (August 1997)
17. Wallace, L., Keil, M.: Software project risks and their effect on outcomes. Communications of the ACM (April 2004)

Answering a Request for Proposal –
Challenges and Proposed Solutions

Barbara Paech[1], Robert Heinrich[1], Gabriele Zorn-Pauli[1]
Andreas Jung[2], and Siamak Tadjiky[2]

[1] University of Heidelberg, Im Neuenheimer Feld 326, 69120 Heidelberg, Germany
{paech,heinrich,zorn-pauli}@informatik.uni-heidelberg.de
[2] S4M - Solutions for Media GmbH - Broadcast Management Systems.
Am Coloneum 3, 50829 Köln, Germany
{andreas.jung,siamak.tadjiky}@s4m.com

Abstract. **[Context and motivation]** The tender process is a special requirements engineering process. The customer provides a request for proposal (RFP) with requirements of varying detail. Several software companies answer with a solution proposal. The customer chooses the supplier according to the price and the quality of the proposed solution. So far very little has been published on how the requirements engineering process of the suppliers in producing the solution proposal should be performed. **[Question/problem]** The main challenges of the tender process for the supplier are that the RFP is very big and the solution proposal has to be produced in a very tight time frame. Furthermore, there is typically very little direct communication between customer and supplier, which is needed to clarify the requirements in the RFP. So, the supplier needs to guess the meaning of the requirements. **[Principal ideas/results]** The main idea to overcome these challenges is to produce a structured documentation of available solutions and typical risks experienced in former tender processes. This documentation can be used to identify the most important risks of the current tender process and to efficiently produce a viable solution proposal. **[Contribution]** In this paper we report on the experiences of a supplier company with tender processes. We summarize the challenges of the requirements engineering for tender processes from the viewpoint of the supplier and we describe the solutions envisaged by this company for these challenges.

Keywords: Tender process, requirements engineering, request for proposal, risk assessment, knowledge management.

1   Introduction

In the area of requirements engineering (RE) very often continuous communication between customer and supplier is assumed. In practice this is often not the case. In market-driven development the supplier produces software for a vast number of unknown customers [8]. Another situation where such communication is not possible is a tender process. The customer provides a request for proposal (RFP) with a big

B. Regnell and D. Damian (Eds.): REFSQ 2012, LNCS 7195, pp. 16–29, 2012.
© Springer-Verlag Berlin Heidelberg 2012

number of requirements of varying detail. Several software companies answer with a solution proposal. The customer chooses the supplier according to price and quality of the proposed solution. The main problem of such a tender process for the supplier is that the RFP is very big and the solution proposal has to be produced in a very tight time frame. Furthermore, there is typically no direct communication between customer and supplier, which is needed to clarify the requirements in the RFP. So the supplier needs to guess the meaning of the requirements. Very few papers have been published dealing with RE for tender processes. Lauesen [2] is one of the few exceptions. He provides guidelines for the creation of the RFP by the customer. These guidelines could also support the suppliers. However, experience of the authors of this paper shows that they are not applied by the customers. We did not find specific guidelines for the suppliers in the literature.

In this paper we report on the experiences of a supplier company with tender processes. This company has 15 years of experience. Most of the supplier's projects are acquired by proposal submission.. The supplier has been continuously improving their software engineering processes and the RFP phase.

In the following we summarize the challenges of RE during the tender process from the viewpoint of the supplier and we describe the solutions envisaged by this company for these challenges. We only refer to the RE process after the tender has been won, if it is important to understand the RE during the tender process. In Section 2 we discuss related work and introduce Lauesen's guidelines. Section 3 describes the situation of the supplier and the resulting challenges. Company-specific details are left out on purpose. The solutions for these challenges have been developed in several internal workshops at the supplier company and in one workshop moderated by the first author of this paper. The last workshop is sketched out in Section 4. The outcome of the last workshop – guidelines on how to improve the RE process of the supplier – is summarized in Section 5. Section 6 concludes the paper and proposes future research work on this topic.

2   Related Work

A literature search concerning RFP (or call for tender) surfaced a paper about an agile RFP process [1]. It advocates a careful RE process from the customer based on user stories of different detail. RE for tender processes is also discussed in the area of COTS selection e.g. [5], but again there the focus is on the customer view. Similarly, in [9] the customer RE process is targeted by re-using former requirements through patterns. In [6] requirements interchange in complex customer supplier relationships, such as in the car industry, is discussed. This also includes a tender process, but because of long-term relationships, a collaborative communication is advocated. This is not the case in most other domains. The consultant Tom Searcy published a book on RFP from the supplier viewpoint [10]. This book provides guidance on the decision whether to get involved in a tender process or not, and how to organize a response to the RFP. It does not comprise guidelines on the elicitation and management of the system features to be included in the response.

Most detailed are the mentioned guidelines by Lauesen. He discusses the tender process for public organizations in the EU from the viewpoint of the customer [2].

The processes have to follow strict rules to protect against corruption. Private RFPs do not have to follow these rules, but often adapt them.

Lauesen's guidelines are based on his Task and Support approach [4]. In his *Guide to Requirements SL-07* he provides a template for a better handling of requirements by the customer within a tender process [3]. It is aimed at coping with the major challenges such as risk balance between customer and supplier, solution-focused customer requirements or requirements which do not cover important customer demands. The approach provides two main artifacts which are explained in the following:

- *Task descriptions* to illustrate customer demands and to differentiate them from solution specifications.
- A *template* for associating customer requirements with proposed solutions that also provides information about gaps by using codes to categorize solution specifications.

Tasks

In Lauesen's approach user tasks capture customer requirements as shown in Table 1.

> *"A user task is something user and computer do together from start to end without essential interruptions. A good start point is something that happens in the user's world, for instance that a client calls. A good end point is that nothing more can be done about the case right now - the user deserves a "coffee break" (task closure)." [3]*

Table 1. Requirement Template SL-07 Used for RFP (taken from [3])

Task: Handle request	
Subtasks and variants:	**Example solutions:**
1. Receive the request through phone or email. Or look at the pending requests.	
2. Record the request, particularly the user's phone, email and the cause of the request.	In case of an email request, the system automatically transfers data from the email.
2p. **Problem**: Cumbersome to record, particularly when it is an on-the-spot solution.	
2a. It may be an update of an existing request. Find it.	The system shows possible matches with the caller's name or parts of it.

Table 1 is taken from an example Hotline development project. It describes the first part of the main hotline task of handling requests. The first column of the table lists the subtasks. Subtasks can also capture variants. The user decides which subtasks are done in which sequence. The advantage of using task descriptions is to be able to state problems (see Table 1, row 2p.) without specifying how to cope with the problem. Additionally, further context information related to a task can be captured, such as the actors (users) or the environment where the task is performed. Tasks which are related to the same environment can be bundled into work areas. A work area provides information about the user profiles (roles) and the environment.

Requirement Template

The template, as illustrated in Table 1, provides two columns. In column 1 the customer´s demands are shown and column 2 presents solution possibilities regarding specific needs. This could be used to capture specific requirements in the RFP by the customer. In the example there are two subtasks (receiving the request and recording the request). R 2a indicates a variant for the subtask 2. Row 2p captures a specific problem when performing subtask 2. Column 2 indicates two example solutions proposed by the customer. The supplier, however, is free to provide a different solution for the subtask or problem.

Table 2. Requirement SL-07 Template Used as RFP Response (taken from [3], example codes are from an earlier version)

Task: Handle request		
Subtasks and variants:	**Example solutions:**	**Code**
1. Receive the request through phone or email. Or look at the pending requests.		5
2. Record the request, particularly the user's phone, email and the cause of the request.	~~In case of an email request, the system automatically transfers data from the email.~~ (The system has a semi-automatic capture of email. The user must initiate the recording.)	1
2p. **Problem**: Cumbersome to record, particularly when it is an on-the-spot solution.	A. The present version records the caller based on the email. B. Release 18 will provide buttons for easy recording of the most frequent causes	4.18
2a. It may be an update of an existing request. Find it.	The system shows possible matches with the caller's name or parts of it. The system also provides phonetic search. See screen 12 in App. x.	1

The supplier could use the provided template for the response to detail the solution by filling column 2 in accordance with the supplier's system. The supplier may indicate alternative solutions or deviations from solutions proposed by the customer as shown in Table 2 (row 2). For subtask 2, the solution proposed by the customer is cancelled and another solution mentioned. For the problem 2p, two new solutions are proposed.

In addition, a further column can be added to capture further information depending on the nature of the project. The customer may specify priorities of the requirements, or give a score for the supplier's solution. Another possibility is that the supplier fills in column 3 with a code that specifies the delivery (see Table 3) to support effort and time estimations. Example applications are shown in Table 2.

Table 3. Codes for Solution Specifications (taken from [3])

Code	Description
1	Part of the supplier's system
2.x	An extension of the supplier's system, but the extension is covered by the ordinary maintenance agreement. Will be available from delivery stage x.
3.x	Custom-made software or an extension of the supplier's system that is *not* covered by the ordinary maintenance agreement. Will be available from delivery stage x.
4.y	Part of a future release that will be supplied under the ordinary maintenance agreement. Will be available from release y.
5	No solution is offered for this requirement.
alt.z	Alternative solutions are offered. This solution is part of alternative z.

3   Being a Supplier in a Tender Process

The situation of the supplier is as follows: a customer has provided a list of requirements – often phrased as questions – and the supplier is requested to detail which requirements can be met and how the solution could look like. Often the RFP is made available via a web portal for online editing or with sophisticated Excel-sheets where each requirement has a specific identification key. This key is used for tracing by the customer, but also by the supplier. The answers to the questions have to be provided in the same manner as the questions. The supplier derives the answers to the questions from *existing systems* which have been developed earlier for other customers. During this phase (which we call *RFP phase* in the following) the supplier has to make difficult decisions as to which kinds of *gaps* exist between the request and the existing systems and how much effort it is to develop a system filling these gaps. In particular, it is important that the sketched solution system and the estimated cost are competitive compared to other suppliers.

In the following, we sketch the roles involved on the supplier's side in producing the response to the RFP and their information responsibilities. Based on this, we explain the challenges of this process.

3.1   Roles

Several roles need to be involved to create a response to an RFP. This includes RE experts, who have worked in former tender processes and who also have been involved in the projects following a successful tender process, as well as development experts, who have been involved in the creation of previous systems.

In detail, the following roles are important:

Consultants are responsible for the elicitation and specification of the requirements during the RE phase after the proposal has been won. As experts for the customer view, they are involved during the RFP phase. They do not have detailed technical knowledge and contact the module specialists when needed during RE. Their work during the RE phase is based on the outcome of the RFP phase. Thus, they are very interested in producing a good response during the RFP phase.

Management makes the main decisions regarding the price offered to the customer and the internal resources.

Module specialists are responsible for one or more modules which are used in the different existing systems. They know the technical details of the modules and how the modules interact with one another. They know when to consult the software architects. During the response creation they are important to decide on the detailed technical risks of the envisioned system.

Sales specialists are the persons mainly responsible during the RFP phase. They talk to the customer and answer the RFP. Therefore, they have to decide about the features to be offered to the customers. This decision is based on existing systems from the supplier. They delegate some of the work to answer the questions to consultants.

Software architects are responsible for the architecture of the system delivered to the customer. They know how the different modules work together. During the RFP phase they are involved as experts for the architecture-related technical risks of the envisioned system.

3.2   Information Responsibilities

The purpose of this subsection is to characterize the RE process of the supplier for the response to the RFP. As described in [7] we prefer to characterize a process by an **information model** instead of a process model. It would involve too much detail to describe all the activities of the roles. Furthermore, one would need to describe a control flow between the activities, which cannot be given in general. An information model answers the following questions:

- Which *viewpoints* (the level of technical detail and intended audience) are captured, and in which documents?
- Who creates which information, and for which audience?
- Who approves the documents?
- Who reviews the documents?
- Who checks consistency?
- Who approves and propagates change?

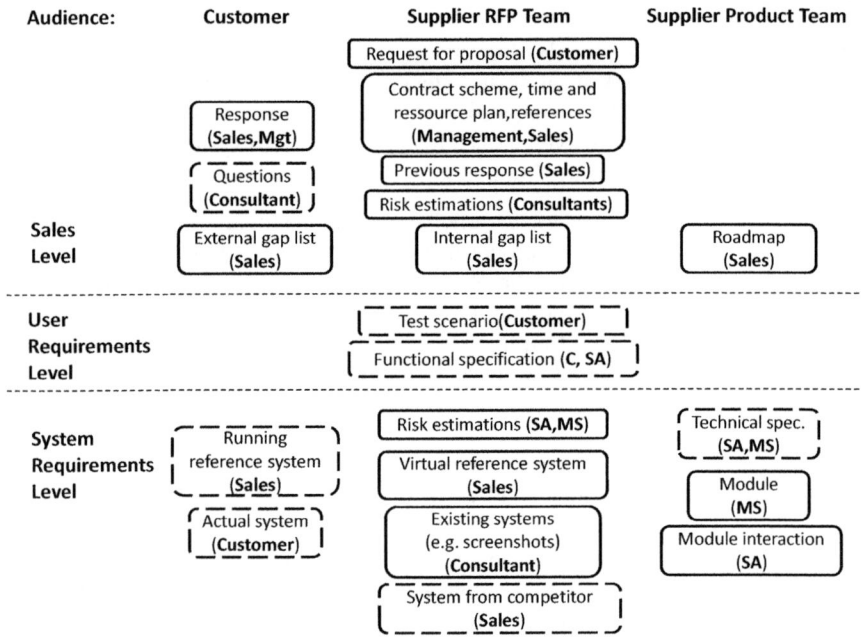

Fig. 1. Information Model

For the purpose of this paper we focus on the first two questions. In Figure 1 the information model is depicted. It shows the information (which is documented or just in the head of some person) currently used for RFP phase decisions. Each information item is represented by a box. Information which is only sometimes available is indicated with a dotted line. The information is categorized with respect to the creator (who creates the document or who is responsible for the information). The creator is shown in brackets in the box. The information is also categorized with respect to the audience (who is the intended reader of the document or the intended receiver of the information – shown in the upmost row) and the level of technical detail (shown in the left column). Three levels are distinguished:

Sales Level: This is the level used by the customer in the RFP and by the supplier in the response. It describes the system in terms of features (represented in the response to the RFP questions). On this level sometimes technical details are involved, but they are not backed up by a detailed understanding of the user requirements.

User Requirements Level: This level captures the business processes and use cases from the viewpoint of the user. It details the features and thus makes clear how the features support the user.

System Requirements Level: This level captures the functionality and quality characteristics of the system. It details the user requirements and thus makes clear which system functions and data and qualities are needed to realize the user requirements.

The audience can be the customer or the supplier team involved in the RFP phase. Furthermore, for the supplier,   the product development team providing the products (in part by adapting existing systems) is involved as well.

The following can be seen from Figure 1:

Sales Level

- The customer provides the *RFP*
- The customer answers *questions* by the consultants (sometimes).
- Sales provide the *response* to the customer. This includes cost and project resources.
- Sales create a *roadmap*. This is a list of features which are to be developed in following releases, but which are included in the cost to the customer.
- Sales use *previous responses* to identify features which can be offered.
- Management provides constraints for the *contract, time and resource planning* as well as *references* to be included in the response.
- Consultants provide *estimations of risks* for selected features (as requested by sales).
- Sales create a list describing the *gaps* between the requested requirements and existing systems (for internal purposes and with adaptations also for the customer).

User Requirements Level

- The customer provides *test scenarios* describing business processes and use cases (sometimes). The supplier has to demonstrate that they can satisfy these scenarios.
- Sales use *functional specification* documents describing use cases for parts of existing systems (sometimes).

System Level

- The customer requests a *running reference system* (sometimes).
- The customer provides information on their *actual system* (sometimes).
- Software architects and module specialists provide *estimations of technical risks* for selected features (as requested by sales or consultants).
- Sales base their response on a *reference system*. This system is mostly *virtual*, that means it combines features of different existing systems, but this combination is not yet implemented at the time   the response is created.
- Sales (with the help of consultants) use *knowledge about the supplier's existing systems*.
- Sales use knowledge about the *systems of the competitors* (sometimes).
- Module specialists and software architects use *technical specifications* of existing modules (sometimes).
- Module specialists provide knowledge about *the modules and their dependencies and conflicts* with one another.
- Software architects provide knowledge about *the interaction* of the modules.

3.3   Challenges

This section describes the main challenges for the supplier. They are clustered into two categories: the first category comprises challenges incurred by the behavior of the customer. Typically, it is not possible to alter this behavior. So the supplier has to develop countermeasures to deal with this behavior. In the second category are problems relating to RFP phase communication and decision making within the supplier.

Customer-Incurred Challenges

- The RFP is of low quality so that many questions are difficult to understand.
- The customer requests specific solutions. It would be helpful to understand the business processes and user requirements behind these solutions, because sometimes the supplier could offer a (better) realization of the user requirements, but not of the specific RFP requirements.
- Very rarely a direct communication with the customer is possible to clarify the requirements. Sometimes questions from the supplier to the customer are possible, but mostly the answers do not give much further insight. Furthermore, often answers to these questions are made available also to the competitors so that through questions supplier-specific features can become public. Therefore, the supplier has to decide very carefully which question to pose how.
- The supplier RFP team must estimate cost and effort without a detailed understanding of the requirements.
- The customer not always answers questions timely. This slows down the creation of the response.
- The time for response creation is very short.

Internal Challenges with RFP Handling

- The following challenges are typical for any offer. They are particularly difficult in the RFP process, because of the customer-incurred challenges mentioned above:
    o The decisions about what to offer to what price are high risk decisions. Wrong decisions induce high cost.
    o Effort estimation is difficult.
    o The balance between customer satisfaction and cost is difficult.
- It is dangerous to include screenshots in the response as the customer might get too focused on this exact solution.
- Communication between sales and consultants on the one side and module specialists and software architects on the other side must be very efficient.
- Gaps and risks are not always identified correctly: Often they can only be recognized by looking at the whole reference system. Individual systems or modules may offer solutions which are incompatible.
- A reliable basis for the creation of the response is not always given, as some knowledge regarding the existing systems is implicit. This knowledge is often captured in responses to previous RFPs, but not consolidated to be reusable in other responses or projects.

- The identification of experts and generalists who can provide important information is not easy.
- The response creation process is slowed down because experts are busy with other projects.

4   The Workshop

The supplier had discussed the challenges in internal workshops, but then decided to have one more workshop with an external moderator. In preparation of the workshop a one-day meeting was held with the first author and two representatives of the supplier. During this meeting the roles involved in the RFP phase, documents created and activities performed during these phases were discussed. In addition, also a preliminary list of challenges was identified and the goals for the workshop were determined. The latter were:

- To make clear the complexity of the RFP RE process and of the involved decisions, as well as the challenges faced during and after the decisions.
- To motivate the whole team for the importance of these decisions.
- To learn about existing techniques to support these decisions.
- To create a common view of the current processes and their challenges.
- To create a common view of possible solutions and a vision of applying the solutions.

Thus, the agenda of the workshop comprised the following topics:

- General introduction of participants, terminology and RE basics (including the template by Lauesen)
- Brainstorming of typical challenges of the RFP phase
- Creation of an information model for the current RFP process
- Discussion of solutions for particular challenges in two groups and presentation of group work results
- Discussion of workshop results, identification of next steps and feedback on the workshop

In addition to three members of the Heidelberg Software Engineering group, there were 10 participants from the supplier side comprising representatives of the different roles. The outcome of the workshop is presented in the next section.

5   Proposed Solutions for the Challenges

The following three main solutions for the challenges emerged during the workshop:

1. Development of a risk classification checklist for customer-incurred risks
2. Improved documentation of knowledge about existing systems
3. Improved documentation of knowledge from the RFP process.

These solutions are detailed in the following three sub-sections.

5.1   Risk Assessment Checklist

The first group identified types and indicators for customer incurred risks. These types and indicators deal with the specification and communication problems (the first three customer incurred challenges described in subsection 3.3), as the time constraints cannot be influenced. They should provide a checklist to review the RFP with respect to important risks. Examples are the following:

Type 1: Incomplete Customer Requirements
Many times the customers are influenced by the functionality of the actual system or an ideal system they have in mind. Therefore, the set of requirements contains often requirements to extend the functionality of the actual system. A lot of information or knowledge about customer needs or processes is available only implicitly. Additionally, interface requirements are often neglected, but they potentially involve risks and problems.
Indicators:
- Customer references a running or hypothetic system.
- Customer business processes or system interfaces are not transparent.

Type 2: Customer Requirements Are Specified on the Solution Level
If the customers specify requirements on a solution level, the solution alternatives are unnecessarily constrained.
Indicators:
- Customer references a running or hypothetic system.
- Customer requirements do not describe *What* is required of the new system, but *How* this should be implemented instead.
- Attachments such as screenshots, reference to interfaces, provided technical data suggest requirements on solution level.

Type 3: Customer Requirements Are Too Generic (e.g. Non-functional Requirements)
Every requirement that is specified in a vague manner poses potential risks. For example, "The system must provide filter functionality as in Excel".
Indicator:
- Requirements are specified in a way, that they are not testable.

Type 4: Customer Requirements Specification Is Very Domain-specific
Depending on the customer context specific domain knowledge is necessary to understand customer needs. Missing joint understanding of terminology involves potential risks.
Indicator:
- A comprehensive glossary is absent.

Type 5: Customer Requirements Contain Conflicts
To identify conflicts within customer requirements, a link to business processes or workflows, which provide additional context information, would be helpful.

Conflicts will only become apparent if viewed in the context, but there are difficulties of an end-to-end view for requirements that span multiple systems or processes.

Indicators:
- Requirements could not be assigned to already known workflows or use cases.
- Customer business processes are not transparent.

Type 6: Customer Requirements Are Not Realizable
Every "must have"-statement in the RFP involves potential risks, because this specification represents non-negotiable requirements which must be provided by the solution. Additionally, technology-specific requirements also involve potential risks related to the technical realization possibilities.

Indicator:
- Requirements specification contains "must have"-statements.
- Data migration needs
- New technologies involved
- Interfaces to other systems are needed.

This preliminary list developed in the workshop should be consolidated by looking at previous tender processes. Furthermore, it should be continuously updated. Related to the approach of Lauesen (see Section 2) a tagging approach for requirements in the RFP could be developed. Codes corresponding to the risk types could be used to tag every requirement. This provides a better overview of the risk level of the whole RFP.

5.2. Documentation of the Existing System

As can be seen from the previously presented list of internal challenges (see sub-section 3.3.), knowledge capture and communication are very critical. To be prepared for a quick assessment of the RFP the following knowledge should be readily available:

- Which existing system uses which module?
- Which module supports which features?
- Which feature is in conflict with which other feature? A conflict occurs when two features cannot be realized in the same system.

This knowledge should thus be documented compactly. The conflicts could be documented between modules or features. A conflict matrix between modules would describe which modules exclude one another. Similarly conflicts between features could be captured (which are typically induced by conflicts between the modules implementing the features). In both cases only the indication of the conflicts would not be enough, because it is not clear why this conflict exists. Thus, descriptions of the conflicts need to be captured as well.

Based on this documented knowledge it can easily be documented

- which feature (and thus which module) is used in the reference system and
- which known conflicts are contained in the proposed reference system?

The main effort for such documentation is to come up with a good set of features (not too detailed) and to find good representations for conflict relationships. In the long run visualizations of the conflict relationships will be helpful to get a quick overview. However, this requires high maintenance effort. Depending on the numbers of features, modules and systems, a database or an Excel sheet is sufficient. In both cases it is necessary to analyze which information is used when (e.g. when and how often does someone want to know which features a module has and when and how often does someone want to know which modules or systems are used for a feature). Then a format should be chosen according to these usages. This also applies to the definition of the conflict representation.

This documentation should be updated during development. New conflicts detected during the RFP phase or implementation of an offered system should be captured.

5.2   Documentation of the RFP Knowledge

As many people are involved in response creation at different times, as much knowledge as possible on assumptions and decisions made should be documented.

Such knowledge includes

- the features and modules of existing systems used for the reference system together with cost estimations and development risk estimations.
- the external and internal gaps. It should be clearly documented when a gap is identified. This applies when the gap is communicated to the customer (external), but also when the gap is closed in the response by a hypothetical feature in the reference system (internal). As described in Lauesen's approach (see Table 2) a gap should be treated as a feature (whose realization has to be paid by the customer or by the supplier in a future release).
- the lessons learned from the RFP negotiations.

The first two bullets correspond to a draft response consisting of a list of features which are tagged as external gap or as internal gap or as existing features. Each feature is also tagged with cost and development risk estimates. Clearly, only part of this information is passed on to the customer.

6   Conclusion

In this paper we have presented challenges and proposed solutions for the RE of the supplier in a tender process. To our knowledge this is the first description of the supplier view. The solutions have not yet been fully applied in practice. The company reviewed the workshop results one month after the workshop and decided to start implementing the proposed solutions. They will be applied in the next RFP phase.

Currently the company is consolidating the description of the conflicts and of the gaps identified in previous responses. Furthermore, they are refining the risk list and improving means to cope with these risks.

From the research view it seems interesting to study the following questions:

- What is a good way to document existing systems so that they can easily be compared with a RFP? For the documentation of features and their relationships product line approaches could be relevant. However, there is not that much overlap between the systems offered to different customers. Thus, product line approaches need to be adapted for efficient use in the tender process.

- What is a good way to document gaps between requirements and system descriptions on different levels? So far the literature mainly concentrates on the refinement of high-level descriptions to low-level descriptions and on the capturing of traces of these refinements. However, in the RFP context a pure top-down process is not possible. High-level requirements of the RFP have to be mapped to low-level descriptions of features of the existing systems. A list of features necessary for the RFP but not yet provided is a first idea of such a gap description. However, it bears the risk that the features are very specific to the given RFP. Thus, from several RFPs a huge list of small gaps would be collected. Also, the organization of the list for efficient search is a problem.

Acknowledgements. We thank all the participants of the workshop for the stimulating discussions and their commitment during the group work.

References

1. Andrea, J.: An Agile Request for Proposal (RFP) Process. In: Agile Development Conference, pp. 152–161. IEEE (2003)
2. Lauesen, S.: COTS Tender and Integration Requirements. Requirements Engineering Journal 11(2), 111–122 (2006)
3. Lauesen S.: Guide to Requirements SL-07: Template with Examples, version 4 (2011), http://www.itu.dk/~slauesen/SorenReqs.html
4. Lauesen, S., Kuhail, M.A.: Use Cases versus Task Descriptions. In: Berry, D., Franch, X. (eds.) REFSQ 2011. LNCS, vol. 6606, pp. 106–120. Springer, Heidelberg (2011)
5. Maiden, N.A., NCube, C.: Acquiring COTS Selection Criteria. IEEE Software, 46–56 (March 1998)
6. Monteiro, M.R., Ebert, C., Recknagel, M.: Improving the Exchange of Requirements and Specifications between Business Partners. In: Int. Conf. Requirements Engineering, pp. 253–260. IEEE (2009)
7. Paech, B., Doerr, J., Köhler, M.: Improving Requirements Engineering Communication in Multi-project Contexts. IEEE Software 22(1), 40–47 (2005)
8. Regnell, B., Brinkkemper, S.: Market-Driven Requirements Engineering for Software Products. In: Aurum, A., Wohlin, C. (eds.) Engineering and Managing Software Requirements, pp. 287–308. Springer, Heidelberg (2005)
9. Renault, S., Mendez, O., Franch, X., Quer, C.: A pattern-based method for building requirements documents in call-for-tender processes. Int. Journal of Computer Science and Applications 6(5), 175–202 (2009)
10. Searcy, T.: RFPs Suck! Channel V Books (2009)

Impediments to Requirements-Compliance

Md. Rashed Iqbal Nekvi[1], Nazim H. Madhavji[1],
Remo Ferrari[2], and Brian Berenbach[2]

[1] University of Western Ontario, London, Canada
[2] Siemens Corporate Research
mnekvi@csd.uwo.ca, madhavji@gmail.com,
{remo.ferrari,brian.berenbach}@siemens.com

Abstract. **[Context & motivation]** Large contractual projects often have to comply against government regulations and standards. **[Question/problem]** In such a context, the contractual document can be voluminous, and there can be a large number of standards and regulations to follow. These documents typically form a complex interrelationship network. This means that in the requirements engineering (RE) process, this network needs to be analysed for deriving project requirements to be implemented. A key activity of this RE process is to demonstrate compliance by showing, through appropriate traces, that all relevant requirements have been elicited from the regulatory documents. **[Principal ideas/results]** **[Contribution]** In this problem-statement paper, we describe some key impediments to achieving requirements-compliance that we have identified in a large systems engineering project.

Keywords: requirements-compliance, systems engineering, impediments.

1   Introduction and Overview of Related Work

Large systems engineering projects, involving a multitude of technical domains, typically have to comply with governmental regulations and standards. A railway infrastructure upgrade project, for example, could involve various technical domains (such as software, hardware, networks, communications, power, signalling and others), requiring the upgraded system to comply with regulations and standards to do with public safety, railway system, electrical devices, underlying operating system interfaces, etc.

The requirements engineering (RE) process in such a project is fundamental to ensuring the system's compliance, not only because it is a foundation for quality for downstream development and the resultant system [8], but also because requirements are a core part of the project's contract (in contractual projects) and of the applicable standards. It is unimaginable how one could attain compliance without explicitly dealing with the system's requirements and the regulatory documents.

In a large-scale systems engineering project, however, the number and sizes of the various regulatory and contractual documents, and their inter-relationships, is mind-boggling. As will be shown later in the paper, there can be hundreds of documents to contend with and many are thousands of pages long with countless cross-references, making RE quite a mountain to climb.

B. Regnell and D. Damian (Eds.): REFSQ 2012, LNCS 7195, pp. 30–36, 2012.

Related work on compliance-challenges describes experiences with, and opinions about, ambiguity [5] and domain specific terms [1] in regulatory text; cross-referencing among regulatory documents [1, 2, 3]; legislative conflicts [2, 5]; the changing nature of the applicable laws [2, 4, 5]; complexity in a distributed environment [4]; and contractual specification practices [6]. Typically, these are based on the analysis of one regulatory document, e.g., Federal Regulations (CFR 40) [1] and HIPAA [3].

This paper, however, differs from previous research on at least three fronts:

(i) *context of the investigation*:   an actual case study we are currently conducting on a multi-domain, systems engineering contractual project that aims to upgrade a railway infrastructure;

(ii) *quantitative insight into certain impediments*[1], e.g.: size of regulatory documents, the spread of regulatory requirements in the contract, and spread of regulatory documents across various legislature authorities; and

(iii) *impediments due to large-scale project, e.g.*: the large number and size of the documents, contractual complexity, and complexity of the system to be developed.

The observed impediments are new and add to the growing body of knowledge on how to possibly design RE processes that ensure system compliance against regulations and standards. It is important to note, nevertheless, that this is a "problem statement" paper; the results are still emerging and they await further analysis in the on-going empirical study.

2   Study Overview

The studied case is a RE project, a sub-project within a large-scale development project that aims to upgrade a rail corridor infrastructure system. The RE project is steered by a contract (over 1000 pages) made between the company and the customer organization. The contract outlines high-level requirements and contains regulatory requirements referencing to approximately 300 engineering standards and 30 regulations to which the project is expected to demonstrate compliance. Typically, a regulation is denoted by a specific document representing a legislated act, a law, and is legally binding on the population affected.

The RE project used DOORS (www-01.ibm.com/software/awdtools/doors) to capture the project requirements and establish traceability among the various artefacts (such as the contract, project requirements specifications, standards and regulations, etc.). The requirements management tool was populated with information by the organisation in charge of the project.

Ethnographically, we identified regulatory requirements from the recognised documents, often involving clarification sessions with appropriate domain experts. We also attended two workshops where we learnt about, amongst other things, the types of different documents that describe regulatory requirements, the role of domain experts in the RE process, and the difficulties the organisation was facing in tracing contractual requirements to standards and regulations.

---

[1] An impediment (in this project) is a hindrance or obstruction in achieving compliance of system requirements against regulations and standards.

Based on the gained understanding, we are analyzing project data such as the project contract, relevant regulations and standards, and requirements documents in order to yield a quantitative and qualitative understanding of the impediments. Analysis thus far has led to the identification of artefact types and their compliance-oriented inter-relationships [7]. In [7], however, we only cursorily mention some impediments related to these artefacts and inter-relationships; the current paper takes a significant step forward in describing many other impediments, quantitatively, and in much greater detail.

3   Impediments to Requirements-Compliance

Below, we describe a few impediments due to size and nature of regulatory text, contractual complexity, and large-scale system development. We also describe the impact of the impediments on the RE process.

3.1   Size and Nature of Regulatory Text

In the project under study, as described in Section 2, over 300 distinct standards and regulations (each one a separate document) are referenced from the contract (through the contained approx. 12,000 requirements). Complex as this already is, the situation is in fact more daunting. That is, the contract also mentions: "The list [for standards and regulations] is provided as a convenience only, and is not considered exhaustive." The implication of this is that: (a) the number of regulatory documents in the project scope is not clear; (b) it can be higher than that specified in the contract; and (c) the analysts need to circumspectively map out the project scope in terms of the applicable regulatory documents in the project.

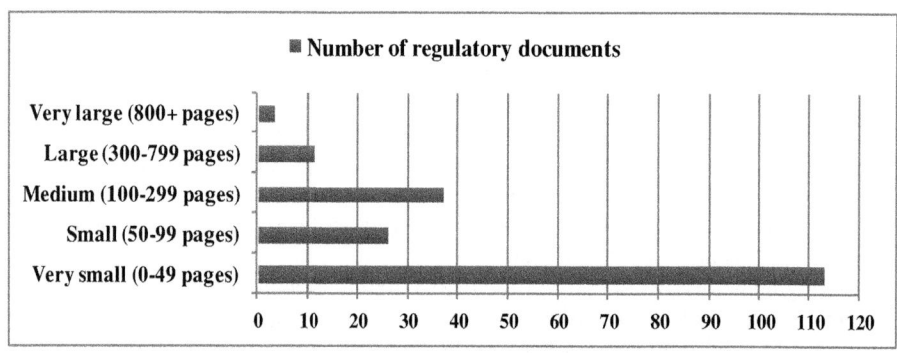

(We analysed the 190 available standards and regulations in the project)

Fig. 1. Size of regulatory documents

Not only is the number of regulatory documents huge, the sizes of some of these documents are substantial too; see Figure 1.   Examples of large-to-very large documents include: CSA A23.1-09/A23.2-09 for Concrete materials and methods (573 pages), IEEE Std. 1003.1 for IT--Portable O/S Interface (3,760 pages), and AREMA for American railway standard (2,049 pages). Such sizes add to the impediments in the compliance project.

Concurring to the findings reported in [1, 2, 3], our cursory analysis of the project documents suggests existence of cross-references among the documents and use of domain specific terms. Without appropriate support tools and domain knowledge, these characteristics can also add to the impediments in the compliance project.

3.2   Contractual Complexity

The contract is in excess of 1,000 pages, and contains (as mentioned earlier) approx. 12,000 (regulatory and non-regulatory) requirements referred to as contractual requirements which encompass both functional and quality aspects. Regulatory requirements are specified non-contiguously in the contract (see Figure 2 for a sample view).

Now, the contractual document is organized into ten domain-specific "divisions" (such as electrical, mechanical, doors and windows, metals, etc.) and so when identifying regulatory requirements for a particular sub-system from the contract, one needs to go through all the divisions carefully to identify the applicable ones in the mixed set of requirements. There is no straightforward predictability as to when next to expect a regulatory requirement (as can be seen from Figure 2), which makes the identification task manual, extremely slow and arduous.

Thus far, we have identified approximately 600 regulatory requirements in the contractual document, giving an overall ratio of regulatory to non-regulatory requirements as 1:19. Note that this is twice the ratio of the chunk of pages (1:10) in Figure 2, implying that identifying the regulatory requirements in the overall contractual document is more difficult than in the chunk in Figure 2.

Also, this level of complexity is dilute when one considers the 300-odd regulatory documents (see Section 3.1) to be examined for regulatory requirements. For example, with reference to Figure 2, the following two requirements: (i) p. 622: *"All (switch clearing device) products shall comply with CSA B149"*, and (ii) p.629: *"Provide all materials and installation to ground the switch clearing devices housing including rods and conductors in accordance with Division 16 of AREMA"* – (which are from the same system component – "switch clearing device") refer to two different standards (CSA and AREMA), complicating the elicitation of requirements (because it may need different domain experts to comprehend the requirements).

The complexity of identifying regulatory requirements from the contract translates into difficulties in other project tasks, for example: (a) deriving project requirements (i.e., those actually used for system implementation) from the contract, ensuring consistency and style; (b) creating traces for the derived requirements to/fro the sources in the contract; and (c) monitoring progress of the degree of requirements-compliance attained at any given time in the project life-cycle.

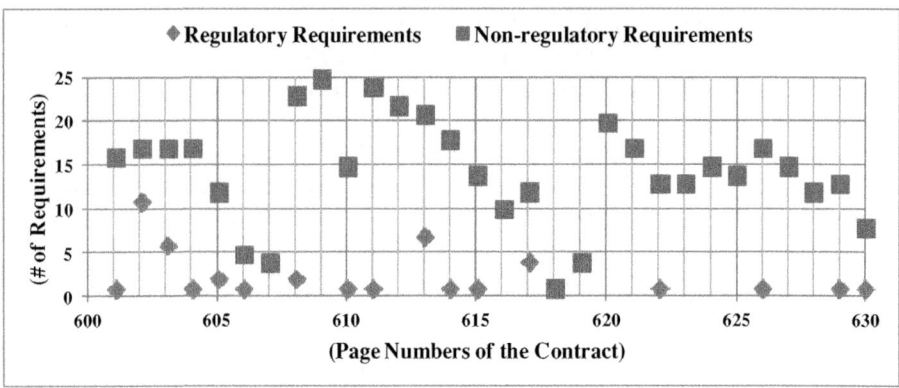

(We selected randomly a 30 page-chunk of the contract (using the avarage of 10 random numbers between 1 and 1086 pages of the contract as a starting page. Ratio of regulatory to non-regulatory requirements in this chunk is 1:10)

Fig. 2. Non-contiguous requirements in the contract

Also, we have noticed that standards and regulations are referenced by the contract in several principal ways, for example: (i) through the customer's high-level requirements specified in the contract (e.g., *the **depth of buried gas supply pipe** shall be in accordance with CSA B149.1*); (ii) through the overall system requirement (e.g., *the **system** shall comply with the requirements of AREMA*); and (iii) through a reference to a particular part of the standard or regulatory document (e.g., *nuts and washers shall be in conformance with the AREMA, **Part 14.1.11***), or to the entire document (e.g., *the wayside track circuits shall be furnished in accordance with (the applicable sections) of the AREMA*). The above permutations suggest further complications in conducting and managing system requirements and to demonstrate system compliance.

We also noticed in our project that approximately 50% of the standards and regulations are referenced at a high level from the contract to some arbitrary part of the system -- as described in (i) above); whereas, the rest are referenced at even higher-level (i.e., system level, without denoting any particular part of the system -- as described in (ii) above). The latter is quite staggering because it suggests that in order to elicit concrete project requirements (for a particular part of the system) the set of standards and regulatory documents referenced in (ii) above must be analysed (by relevant domain experts).

3.3   'Large-Scale' System

The studied system has planned seven major sub-systems (civil structures, network management, communication, power supply, signalling, switch clearing device, and building services) consisting of thirty six components. For example, the signalling sub-system consists of the components: signals, switch, cables, circuits, relay and six others. Table 1 shows the distribution of requirements. From the compliance point of view, we can see that the three-level hierarchy (system, sub-system and component) and the cross-cutting requirements at each of these levels suggest a need for lateral and vertical compliance-related communications among the personnel responsible. Currently, we are still analysing this aspect.

Table 1. Distribution of requirements (regulatory and non-regulatory)

Requirements Type	# of Requirements (all)	# of Regulatory Requirements
System Level	1221	12
Project Execution	1185	62
Cross-cutting	1911	240
Switch clearing device subsystem	360	29
Building service subsystem	928	32
Civil structures subsystem	165	46
Communication subsystem	328	10
Network management subsystem	3799	6
Power supply subsystem	1146	97
Signalling subsystem	767	60
Total	11,810	594

Further complications stem from "cross-cutting" requirements – those that span multiple sub-systems or components. We noted that approximately 40% of the regulatory requirements from the contract were cross-cutting requirements (see Table 1 – 240 v. 594). These requirements do not mention explicitly where in the system or subsystem(s) or component(s) they span. Furthermore, in most cases, they are not detailed (see Section 3.2 – (i) to (iii)), meaning that the referenced sections of the regulatory documents need to be understood and interpreted to yield detailed cross-cutting requirements that address the need of the relevant planned subsystems or components. Given that many domain experts are assigned to the sub-systems and components, it is important that they interpret the numerous contractual sections similarly (semantically) so that uniformity of associating regulatory requirements to the various sub-systems and components is maintained. As can be appreciated, this is quite complicated and error-prone.

In the case study RE project, the organisation used tracing technology[2] to attempt to cope partially with this complexity. For this purpose, they define tracing requirements, such as: (i) the contract links to standards and regulations (without giving any more details than this); (ii) project requirements should be traced to relevant standards and regulations; and (iii) project requirements should be traced to their respective contractual requirements. However, the tracing technology used by the organisation, by itself, would not be adequate in dealing with the fundamental problems inherent in large requirements-compliance projects. For example, recognising where in the multi-level system hierarchy the cross-cutting regulatory requirements exist requires human expertise on the domain issues in the contract, various standards and regulations, and the railway system so that: (i) one can identify the relevant regulatory documents, (ii) determine the requirements therein, and (iii) recognise precisely the locations in the system or subsystem(s) or component(s) where the regulatory requirements apply.

---

[2] This technology resembles the tracing models described in the literature (e.g., Ramesh et al. [9] and Zhenyu et al. [10] that indicate, for example, how requirements, assumptions, decisions, rationale, source, etc., are inter-connected).

4   Conclusions, Implications and Future Work

In compliance-oriented projects, there are specific impediments in the RE process some of which are cited in the literature (see Section 1). In contrast, through a case study of a large-scale systems engineering project, we have identified, quantitatively and qualitatively, numerous managerial and technical impediments to achieving requirements-compliance. Section 3 describes three clusters of impediments: size and nature of regulatory text; contractual complexity; and the large-scale of the system. The sheer scale of the impediments and their associated quantitative figures is new knowledge, and provides much-needed details on requirements-compliance issues faced in industry. However, note that this is still preliminary work.

Future work includes two primary areas: (i) investigating the contract-writing process to gain an improved insight into the problems injected during this process for the development project; and (ii) determining technological support (e.g., methods, processes, tools, techniques) for the RE process to handle impediments in large, compliance-oriented, contractual projects - not only in the systems engineering domain but other domains such as healthcare, automobile, finance, etc.

Acknowledgments. Our sincere thanks to the reviewers for their excellent and encouraging comments.

References

1. Kerrigan, S., Law, K.H.: Logic-based Regulation Compliance-Assistance. In: 9th Int. Conf. on AI and Law, pp. 126–135. ACM, Scotland (2003)
2. Otto, P.N., Antón, A.I.: Addressing Legal Requirements in Requirements Engineering, pp. 5–14. IEEE Computer Society, CA (2007)
3. Breaux, T.D., et al.: Towards Regulatory Compliance: Extracting Rights and Obligations to Align Requirements with Regulations. In: 14th IEEE Int. RE Conf., pp. 49–58. IEEE Computer Society, Minnesota (2006)
4. Penzenstadler, B., et al.: Complying with Law for RE in the Automotive Domain. In: 1st Int. Workshop on RELAW, pp. 11–15. IEEE Computer Society, Barcelona (2008)
5. Kiyavitskaya, N., et al.: Why Eliciting and Managing Legal Requirements is Hard. In: 1st Int. Workshop on RELAW, pp. 26–30. IEEE Computer Society, Barcelona (2008)
6. Berenbach, B., Lo, R., Sherman, B.: Contract-based Requirements Engineering. In: 3rd Int. Workshop on RELAW, pp. 27–33. IEEE Computer Society, Sydney (2010)
7. Nekvi, R.I., Ferrari, R., Berenbach, B., Madhavji, N.H.: Towards a Compliance Meta-model for System Requirements in Contractual Projects. In: 4th Int. Workshop on RELAW, pp. 74–77. IEEE Computer Society, Trento (2011)
8. Damian, D., et al.: Requirements Engineering and Downstream Software Development: Findings from a Case Study. Empirical Software Engineering 10(3), 255–283 (2005)
9. Ramesh, B., Jarke, M.: Towards Reference Models for Requirements Traceability. IEEE Trans. Software Eng. 27(1), 58–93 (2001)
10. Wang, Z., et al.: ACCA: An Architecture-Centric Concern Analysis Method. In: 5th Work. IEEE/IFIP Conf. on WICSA, pp. 99–108. IEEE Comp. Soc., Pennsylvania (2005)

How Architects See Non-Functional Requirements: Beware of Modifiability

Eltjo R. Poort[1], Nick Martens[2], Inge van de Weerd[2], and Hans van Vliet[3]

[1] Logica, Amstelveen, The Netherlands
eltjo.poort@logica.com
[2] Utrecht University, The Netherlands
namartens@gmail.com, i.vandeweerd@cs.uu.nl
[3] VU University, Amsterdam, The Netherlands
hans@cs.vu.nl

Abstract. This paper presents the analysis and key findings of a survey about dealing with non-functional requirements (NFRs) among architects. We find that, as long as the architect is aware of the importance of NFRs, they do not adversely affect project success, with one exception: highly business critical modifiability tends to be detrimental to project success, even when the architect is aware of it. IT projects where modifiability is perceived to have low business criticality lead to consistently high customer satisfaction. Our conclusion is that modifiability deserves more attention than it is getting now, especially because in general it is quantified and verified considerably less than other NFRs. Furthermore, IT projects that applied NFR verification techniques relatively early in development were more successful on average than IT projects that did not apply verification techniques (or applied it relatively late in development).

Keywords: Software Architecture, Requirements Management, Software Project Management, NFR, Modifiability, Empirical Software Engineering.

1 Introduction

Organizations are investing heavily in Information Technology (IT) in order to stay competitive [3]. For many of those organizations, improving IT project success rates is critical for their survival. Failure of IT projects is often linked to shortcomings in the requirements phase [12, 19]. Especially dealing with non-functional requirements[1] (NFRs), requirements that represent quality characteristics, is a promising area for improvement, because dealing with NFRs is viewed as a particularly difficult part of requirements engineering [2]. Not properly taking NFRs into account is considered to be among the most expensive and difficult of errors to correct once an information system is completed [16] and it is rated as one of the ten biggest risks in requirements engineering [11]. NFRs are widely seen as the driving force for shaping IT systems'

---

[1] The term "non-functional requirements" is widely disparaged, many prefer "quality attribute requirements" or "extra-functional requirements". However, because in the survey target audience the term is much better established and understood than its alternatives, we have chosen to maintain it throughout the survey and in this paper.

B. Regnell and D. Damian (Eds.): REFSQ 2012, LNCS 7195, pp. 37–51, 2012.
© Springer-Verlag Berlin Heidelberg 2012

architectures [1, 4, 15, 17]. According to [8], "there is a unanimous consensus that non-functional requirements are important and can be critical for the success of a project".

One could say that architects are responsible for facilitating and realizing NFRs during software development; they are the population that has to "deal" with NFRs. Knowledge about how architects perceive and address NFRs can help IT organizations improve their architecting practices and project success rates. Therefore, we set up a survey among the members of the architecture community of practice in a major Dutch IT services company[2] to gather such knowledge. The survey was aimed at investigating how architects perceive the importance of NFRs, and which approaches they use to deal with them. We were also interested to see whether we could link these findings with IT project success.

1.1   Conceptual Model

The context of this study is bespoke software development in ABC, a major Dutch IT services company. More specifically, it is about IT Development Projects, defined as *a project where an IT system (application, software, infrastructure or other IT system) is designed, constructed and implemented.*

The focus of the survey is on investigating the two relationships depicted in the conceptual model, shown in Fig. 1, within the context of bespoke software development, and from the perspective of the architects. On the one hand, the more important non-functional requirements are, the greater the implied risk to IT project success if they are not fulfilled. On the other hand, several NFR approaches could help an IT project deal with NFRs. To put it another way, the assumption is that IT project success depends on the importance of the NFRs and the application of approaches for dealing with NFRs. We are interested in the following questions:

1. How do architects perceive the importance of non-functional requirements?
2. Is there a significant relationship between the perceived importance of non-functional requirements and IT project success?
3. What approaches for dealing with non-functional requirements do practitioners apply?
4. Is there a significant relationship between applying approaches for dealing with non-functional requirements and IT project success?

A complicating factor in this model is the fact that we are by necessity looking at all this through the architect's eyes. Since the measuring instrument is a survey among architects, we are not actually measuring the importance of NFRs, but rather the *architect's awareness* of their importance. Architecture is a risk driven discipline [7]. Awareness of a risk is a prerequisite to dealing with it. The more an architect is aware of the importance of a requirement and its implicit risk of not being fulfilled, the better he is able to address it. This mechanism works against the expected negative impact of NFR importance on project success; it can even completely negate it when the architect is fully successful in addressing the NFRs he is aware of.

---

[2] In this paper, this company will be identified as ABC.

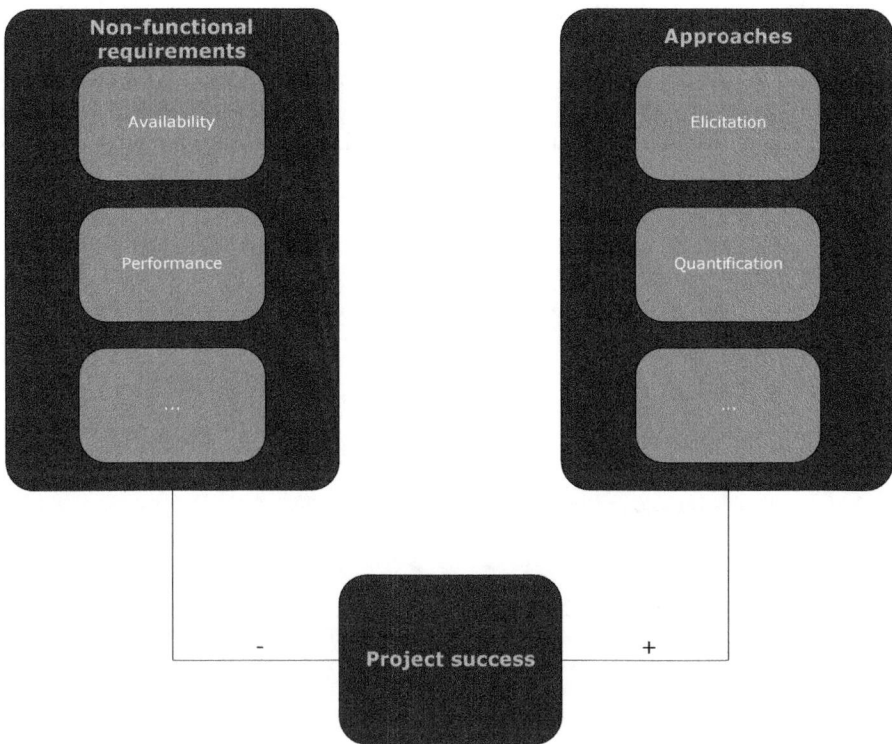

Fig. 1. Conceptual model

2 Survey Description

The core of this study is an on-line survey that was conducted in 2010 among practicing architects. In addition to the survey itself, we organized two expert workshops, consisting of a guided discussion with a select group of architecture experts in the ABC company. One workshop was held prior to the survey itself, and its prime objective was to align the survey's contents with the vocabulary and way of working within ABC. The second workshop was held after the survey, and its purpose was to enrich the initial quantitative analysis results with qualitative knowledge from practicing architects.

The invitation to participate in the survey was sent out by e-mail to around 350 members of the Netherlands (NL) Architecture Community of Practice (ACoP) of the ABC company. The ACoP consists of experienced professionals practicing architecture at various levels (business, enterprise, IT, software, and systems architecture) in project or consultancy assignments. The survey was closed after 16 days. By that time, 133 responses were collected. After elimination of duplicates (1), incomplete responses (51) and responses from respondents that indicated they had not fulfilled the role of architect on their latest project (41), 39 responses remained.

The survey consists of 23 questions divided over four sections. The first section consists of questions that are related to the general characteristics of the latest completed project of the respondent. The second section asks the respondent to evaluate the success of his or her latest completed project from a number of perspectives. Respondents were asked to characterize their latest completed project in terms of NFRs in the third section of the survey. The fourth section evaluates the approaches deployed for managing and dealing with NFRs in their latest completed project. The survey concludes by presenting a number of statements about NFRs to the respondent. Examples of what the survey questions looked like are shown in Fig. 2.

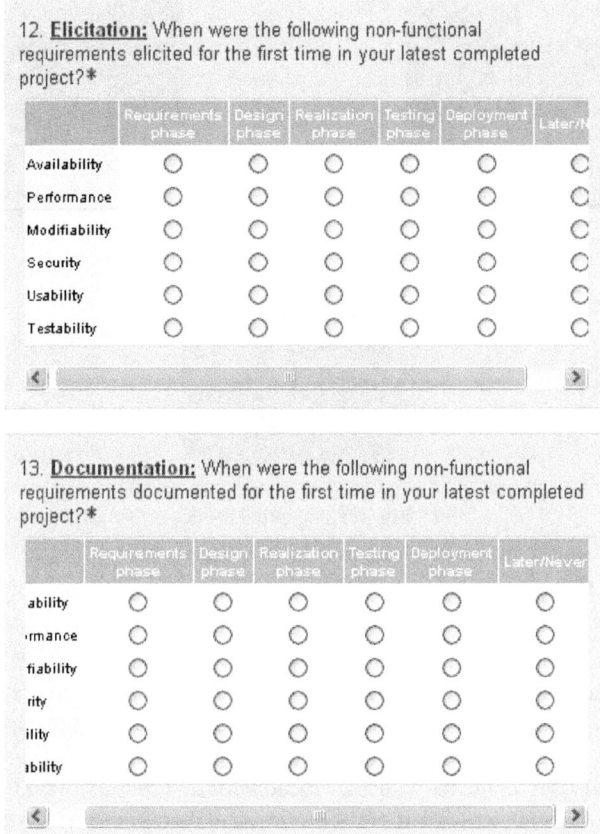

Fig. 2. Example survey questions

2.1   Constructs

Considerable time and effort was spent on translating the key concepts of the conceptual model into operationalized constructs for use in the survey. The four key concepts were *Non-Functional Requirements, NFR importance, project success* and *NFR approach*. Each of these concepts was first operationalized by looking for useful descriptions and classifications in literature, which resulted in a draft survey. The draft survey was then the subject of an expert workshop, in which it was discussed by eight architecture experts from ABC's central technical unit (a kind of architecture board). The constructs were the main topic of the workshop discussion - especially the use of terms and models that would be commonly understood by the ABC company's architecture community. The workshop outcome led to a modified, final version of the survey.

Non-Functional Requirements The Non-Functional Requirements concept had to be made more specific. To be able to analyze the impact of different NFRs, the NFR concept had to be classified into subtypes. The problem of choosing a specific scheme to sub-classify NFRs lies in the observation that even well-known classification schemes are terminologically and categorically inconsistent with each other [4]. Many of the published classifications and definitions of NFRs have their own communities in science and practice [1]. Since a significant number of architects of ABC had been trained in the software architecture practices of the Software Engineering Institute, the six most common and important types of NFRs distinguished by those practices were used in the survey. Their basic descriptions were taken from [1], and were slightly enhanced with examples by the pre-survey expert workshop to increase understandability in the ABC architecture community context:

Availability concerns system failure and its associated consequences. A system failure occurs when the system no longer delivers a service consistent with its specification. Such a failure is observable by the system's users (either humans or other systems). Reliability and recoverability are examples that belong to this type.

Performance events (interrupts, messages, requests from users, or the passage of time) occur, and the system must respond to them. Performance is concerned with how long it takes the system to respond when an event occurs. Efficiency and throughput are examples that belong to performance.

Modifiability considers how the system can accommodate anticipated and unanticipated changes and is largely a measure of how changes can be made locally, with little ripple effect on the system at large. Adaptability, maintainability and compatibility are examples that belong to this type.

Security is a measure of the system's ability to resist unauthorized usage while still providing its services to legitimate users. An attempt to breach security is called an attack and can take a number of forms. It may be an unauthorized attempt to access data or services or to modify data, or it may be intended to deny services to legitimate users.

Usability is concerned with how easy it is for the user to accomplish a desired task and the kind of user support the system provides. It can be broken down into the following areas: learning system features, using a system efficiently, minimizing the impact of errors, adapting the system to user needs, increasing confidence and satisfaction.

Testability refers to the ease with which software can be made to demonstrate its faults through (typically execution-based) testing.

NFR Importance. How does one measure the importance of each type of NFR for a project? The experts in the pre-survey workshop agreed that simply asking for the number of requirements for each type of NFR is not valid. Intuitively, a project could have only a few performance requirements that are nevertheless critical for the system. Conversely, it could have more requirements of another type that are not critical. Furthermore, when you measure the number of requirements for each type of NFR, you are only measuring NFRs that were documented or elicited. The problem with NFRs often is that certain NFRs are *not* documented or elicited. Therefore, the suggestion of the experts was to use the concept of *business criticality*: a certain type of NFR is more important if it is relatively more critical for the system and the business of the customer. This is a concept that can be judged by the respondent in hindsight and is more valid than a simple requirement count. An NFR is considered business critical when it is vital to the customer's business. The measure in which highly business critical NFRs are fulfilled has a high impact on the system's business value, and vice versa. Respondents were asked to rate the business criticality of each of the six types of NFRs on a 5-point Likert-scale (very low, low, medium, high, very high).

Project Success. The project success construct consists of five dimensions, that are designed to reflect the interests of the three main stakeholders (cf. [6]). Meeting time and budget corresponds to project success from a managerial perspective, as does efficient use of resources. Customer satisfaction is included to reflect the perspective of the customers, and solution quality is the dimension that measures the success from the perspective of the development team. Respondents are asked to rate the success of their latest completed project in terms of these dimensions on a 5-point Likert-scale (very unsuccessful, unsuccessful, neutral, successful, very successful). The overall project success parameter is the sum of the responses for the 5 values. Cronbach's α [5] was used as a reliability test to assess internal consistency of this construct; at $\alpha = .858$, the construct proves to be valid ($> .8$).

NFR Approach. The survey asks the respondents to indicate what approaches were applied for dealing with NFRs during their latest completed IT project. Practitioners find dealing with NFRs the most difficult part of requirements engineering [2]. The need for ways to manage NFRs has led several researchers to propose methods and techniques for dealing with NFRs. A set of similar methods and techniques, related to the same requirements engineering activity, that can be used to deal with or manage NFRs (or requirements in general) is defined as an *NFR approach*.

Svensson [2] and Paech [18] both provide classifications of activities aimed at dealing with NFRs. After merging these two classifications and discussing the result in the pre-survey expert workshop, the following approaches were included in the survey:

Elicitation interacting with stakeholders (customers, users) of a system to discover, reveal, articulate, and understand their requirements.

Documentation requirements are written down in order to communicate them to stakeholders (designers, developers, testers, customers).

Quantification NFRs are made explicit by giving them numbers on a measurable scale. This makes the NFRs verifiable.

Prioritization assigning priorities among the different NFRs on the basis of their relative importance.

Conflict analysis identifying the interdependencies and conflicts among the NFRs.

Verification verifying that a system fulfills requirements, e.g. by prototyping, simulation, analysis, testing or other means.

For a full operationalization of the NFR Approach construct, we not only need a classification of sub-types, but also a way to measure their usage in the projects. The simplest way to determine which of the approaches were applied would be to ask respondents using a yes/no format. However, this is not sufficient. We want to be able to distinguish between situations where the approaches were used early on in the project ("on time") and late in the project ("after the fact"). Several studies [9, 20] have pointed out that the relative costs of correcting (requirements) errors increases during the development life cycle. In line with these findings, one may expect that applying an approach later in the development life cycle is less effective; in other words, the earlier an approach for dealing with NFRs is applied, the stronger its positive impact on project success is expected to be. Therefore, respondents are asked to indicate *when* the approaches were applied during the development life cycle for each type of NFR on a 6-point Likert-scale. The Likert-scale represents five phases of a generic systems development life cycle (requirements phase, design phase, realization phase, testing phase, deployment phase) and a later/never option.

3 Analysis

In this section, we present the most interesting results of the quantitative analysis of the survey responses. The outcome of this quantitative analysis was discussed by a post-survey workshop with architecture experts in the ABC company. The results of this post-survey workshop will be presented in the Discussion section of this paper.

In Fig. 3, an overview is given of how the software architects rated the business criticalities of the NFRs.

Availability and (to a slightly lesser degree) usability are generally considered highly business critical, while modifiability and testability score relatively low. Performance and security are somewhere in the middle.

Overall, the types of NFRs are almost never unimportant: very few respondents rated the business criticality of any type of NFR as very low or low. This suggests that each type of NFR has at least some basic level of business criticality in every project. Therefore, each project involves dealing with every type of NFR at least to some degree.

Figure 4 shows how many of the 39 architects applied each of the approaches, differentiated per NFR. Again, modifiability scores low: almost all approaches are applied less for modification than for other NFRs, especially quantification and verification.

3.1 Non-Functional Requirements and Project Success

Based on the theory described earlier, the expectation is that the business criticality of NFRs is negatively correlated with IT project success, but that this effect may be

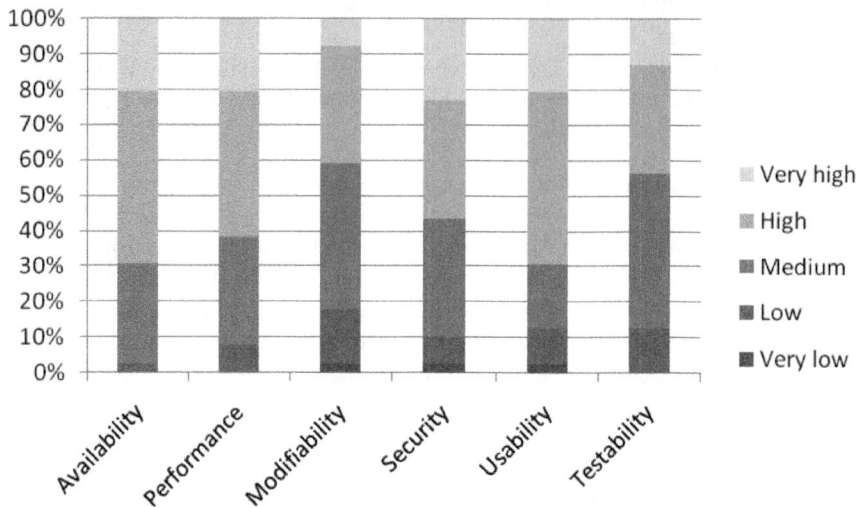

Fig. 3. Perceived business criticality of NFRs

	availability	performance	modifiability	security	usability	testability	Total
elicitation	37	37	32	37	35	34	212
documentation	32	30	25	32	25	26	170
quantification	32	29	16	30	20	21	148
prioritization	26	27	18	24	19	17	131
conflict analysis	22	24	15	20	18	16	115
verification	29	33	18	33	28	30	171
TOTAL	**178**	**180**	**124**	**176**	**145**	**144**	

Fig. 4. Application of approaches per NFR

dampened by the architect's awareness bias. For each NFR category, this hypothesis is tested using Kendall's τ (one-tailed) and the level of statistical significance is .05 (α = .05). The value of Kendall's τ ranges between -1 (perfect negative correlation) and +1 (perfect positive correlation).

A summary of the results is presented in Table 1. Statistically, we should ignore correlation coefficients where the significance $Sig. > .05$, which are indicated by "ns" (not significant) in the table. Only Modifiability shows a significant correlation between its perceived business criticality and project success. In other words, *projects where modifiability is highly business critical tend to be less successful than projects where modifiability is less important.*

Further analysis in Table 2 shows that this correlation can be attributed largely to one project success factor: customer satisfaction. This result is visualized in Fig. 5. The figure shows a remarkably consistent level of customer satisfaction for all projects

Table 1. NFRs, correlation coefficient with IT project success

Type of NFR	Kendall's τ	Sig. (1-tailed)
Availability	.086	ns
Performance	-.181	ns
Modifiability	-.257	.023
Security	.078	ns
Usability	-.102	ns
Testability	.095	ns

Table 2. IT project success factors, correlation with perceived business criticality of modifiability

Success Factor	Kendall's τ	Sig. (1-tailed)
Time	-.212	ns
Budget	-.219	ns
Efficient use of resources	-.207	ns
Customer satisfaction	-.324	.010
Solution quality	-.233	ns

where the architect judged business criticality of modifiability to be low or very low. As business criticality of modifiability grows, customer satisfaction ratings are spread over a wider range, and decrease on average.

3.2 Approaches and Project Success

The six requirements engineering approaches we consolidated from literature are expected to have a positive correlation with IT project success. For each identified approach, respondents had to indicate if it was applied and when it was applied during their latest completed project. The earlier the application of an approach in the systems development life cycle the higher the score, measured on a 6-point Likert-scale where each rating represents a project phase (requirements phase, design phase, realization phase, testing phase, deployment phase, later/never). The rationale behind this argument was described earlier. Statistical techniques are used to test the hypotheses and the results are presented in this section.

A summary of the results is presented in Table 3.

As seen from the table, only applying verification is positively correlated with IT project success.

Count		Criticality modifiability				
		Very Low	Low	Medium	High	Very high
Customer satisfaction	Very Successful			3		1
	Successful	1	6	6	6	
	Neutral			6	4	
	Unsuccessful			1	2	
	Very Unsuccessful				1	2

Fig. 5. Cross-table of business criticality of modifiability and customer satisfaction

Table 3. NFR Approaches and their correlation coefficient with IT project success

NFR Approach	Kendall's τ	Sig. (1-tailed)
Elicitation	.054	ns
Documentation	.065	ns
Quantification	.024	ns
Prioritization	.057	ns
Conflict analysis	-.128	ns
Verification	.256	.014

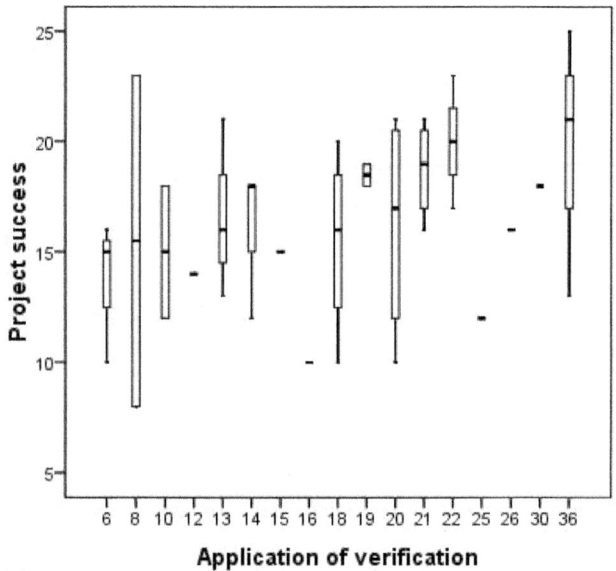

Fig. 6. Boxplot of the correlation between the application of verification and project success

The correlation between verification and project success is visualized in Fig. 6. The horizontal axis in this figure represents a score based on when verification was applied, accumulated for all NFRs listed in 2.1: the higher the score, the earlier in the project verification was applied. There is a significant positive relationship between applying verification and IT project success, $\tau = .256$, p (one-tailed) $< .05$. In other words, we find that *projects where NFRs are verified in an early stage tend to be more successful than projects where NFRs are not verified or only at a later stage in the project.*

4   Discussion and Related Work

In this section, we further discuss the results found above, and share the key contributions from the post-survey analysis expert workshop. We will also discuss threats to validity, and relate our work to additional material found in literature.

4.1 Availability Most Business Critical

In the perception of architects, on average the business criticality of availability is highest. Earlier studies found similar results. For instance, in [10] reliability was identified as the most important type of NFR in software platform development. Furthermore, in [13] reliability was ranked as the most important NFR and availability was ranked as the most important sub-characteristic for intranet applications. These studies used the six quality characteristics from the ISO/IEC 9126 standard as types of NFRs, where availability is a sub-characteristic of reliability. Furthermore, their definition of reliability is very similar to the definition of availability used in this research.

4.2 Non-Functional Requirements and Project Success

The results show that the perceived business criticality of modifiability is negatively correlated with IT project success. In other words: on average, IT projects where modifiability is seen as relatively important are significantly less successful than IT projects where modifiability is considered to be relatively unimportant. This correlation is largely due to the level of customer satisfaction.

The following three possible explanations for this phenomenon were generated by the post-survey workshop with architecture experts:

1. A high demand for modifiability might be an indication that the **customer does not know what he wants**. This means that a customer that demands high modifiability, is a customer that is more likely to change his requirements later on. A development team is trying to hit a moving target in such a situation. This explanation is in line with the leading role of customer satisfaction in the correlation.
2. Modifiability **leads to complexity**. Known techniques to realize high modifiability (such as layering, late binding and parameterizing) quickly lead to increasing complexity, with an adverse effect on budget and timescale. If this were the case, projects where modifiability is highly business critical would be expected not only to be less successful, but also larger and more prone to budget and schedule overruns. Thus, one would expect significant correlations between modifiability and project size, time and budget success factors. None of these correlations were found; in fact, some of the respondents that indicated low criticality for modifiability were working in some of the larger projects compared to other respondents. Thus, the survey yields no evidence supporting this theory.
3. Modifiability gets **too little attention**. This explanation appears to be confirmed by the relatively low scoring of modifiability in terms of perceived business criticality and application of techniques reported above. Expert workshop members experienced multiple reasons for "underappreciation" of modifiability:

   – modifiability is harder to quantify or measure, less "mathematical" than other NFRs; even though there are well known modifiability related code analysis metrics like cyclomatic complexity [14], such metrics are seen as only indirectly related to the actual modifiability business goals, and easily "cheated"

  – other NFRs have a more direct effect on the project's business stakeholders (end-users, managers), while modifiability is sometimes perceived to become important only after the project is over - a dangerous view in light of the research presented here

No correlation is found between the business criticality of the other types of NFRs (availability, performance, security, usability and testability) and IT project success. This can either mean that the negative impact of NFRs is too small to be measured in a population this size, or that the dampening effect discussed before is in play: architects can only respond that NFRs are highly business critical if they are *aware* of this business criticality at the time of the survey. If an architect is aware of an NFR's business criticality at the time of creating the architecture, this awareness normally leads to addressing of the NFR in the architecture, thus reducing the risk to project success. The expert workshop produced anecdotal evidence confirming the second theory. For example, the ABC company has a project unit that is specialized in highly reliable system construction. Projects where availability is highly business critical get assigned to this unit. This leads to economies of learning and thus more successful projects.

All this leads to the following conclusion regarding the link between NFRs and project success:

As long as the architect is aware of the business criticality of NFRs, they do not adversely affect project success, with one exception: highly business critical modifiability tends to be detrimental to project success, even when the architect is aware of it.

4.3   Approaches and Project Success

The application of verification is positively correlated with IT project success. More specifically: IT projects that apply verification early in the development life cycle are significantly more successful than IT projects that apply verification late in the development life cycle. Verification was defined earlier as: verifying that a system fulfills NFRs, e.g. by prototyping, simulation, analysis, testing or other means. Although it is quite trivial that verification techniques reduce errors, there are apparently obstacles that prevent early verification of NFRs. This result indicates that practitioners should spend effort to overcome those obstacles.

It is surprising that none of the other approaches were found to have a significant effect on project success. After all, to be able to apply verification, shouldn't one at least have elicited and quantified the NFRs first? When evaluating the operationalization of the questions, some limitations come to mind. First, it might be more meaningful to measure *how* a certain approach was applied instead of measuring *when* it was applied. In the current situation, IT projects that very carefully elicited NFRs with multiple stakeholders using a formal method are not necessarily discriminated from IT projects where elicitation is informally applied in an ad-hoc fashion by a single stakeholder; moreover, the approaches are not really orthogonal with respect to the development phases. Second, the 6-point Likert-scale used is based on a general waterfall systems development life cycle and does not map very well unto iterative development methodologies. During the validation session, the experts judged that they were sufficiently aligned with the majority of the projects carried out by ABC. However, at least one respondent had trouble answering the questions about the application of the approaches, because his projects always use iterative development. These limitations mean we have to be careful interpreting this result, beyond that it is good to have some statistical evidence that early NFR verification is correlated with successful projects in at least one company.

4.4   Threats to Validity and Opportunities for Further Research

A few important limitations of this survey have to do with generalizability. First, the context of the research is architecture, since it has such a strong link with dealing with NFRs. This was a conscious choice, but it does mean that all results are subject to the perception of the projects' architects. It would be interesting to also investigate the impact of NFRs from other perspectives and compare the results. In particular, a study that would be able to distinguish between NFRs' business criticality and the architect's awareness of that criticality might shed more light on the material.

Second, the data was collected using respondents from a single organization. A cross-organizational approach would have been preferred, but this was not feasible due to practical limitations. Strictly speaking, the results are valid only in the context of this single organization. However, the IT services company where this research was carried out has many similarities with other similar companies. Moreover, from other surveys we know that over half of the ACoP architects fulfil their roles on-site in customer organizations; so the results represent a mix of experiences in ABC and its customer base in the government, utilities, financial and other industrial sectors. Nevertheless, some results could be specific to the ABC company, and cannot be generalized without further research.

The measurement of the applied approaches was already mentioned as a limitation of this study. This could be a reason why no significant relationships were found between applying the approaches and IT project success except for verification. A study that focuses on measuring maturity of the applied approaches might be better capable to differentiate successful IT projects from unsuccessful ones. Another recommendation for future research would be to use a different kind of measurement for project success, e.g. including the actual customer and his evaluation of a project's success.

Other suggested extensions to future versions of this research are:

- extend the definition of business criticality (see Section 2.1) to the company developing the software, rather than only its customers, which might yield a more balanced view on e.g. testability
- include *Designing for NFRs* in the list of approaches; this key activity of architects is left implicit in this survey, but making it explicit may yield additional interesting results
- ask the architects *when* they became aware of the business criticality of NFRs, to validate the conclusion at the end of Section 4.2.

5   Conclusions

We set out on this survey with the goal to investigate the awareness and handling of non-functional requirements among architects, and their effect on IT project success.

The first part focused on trying to identify if certain types of NFRs have a relationship with IT project success. In other words, are there under-performing IT projects based on the types of NFRs they deal with? A significant negative relationship between the business criticality of modifiability and IT project success was found. Therefore, it can be concluded that IT projects where modifiability is relatively business critical perform significantly worse on average. Even though this result might be local to the ABC company, it provides a warning to all practitioners dealing with IT projects with a strong focus on modifiability. Aspects like quantification, verification and managing customer expectations around modifiability might require additional attention, because it seems that customer satisfaction especially is significantly lower on average in this type of IT projects.

The second part views the research question from another perspective: do approaches for dealing with NFRs have a positive influence on IT project success? From the results it can be concluded that the application of verification (starting as early as possible during the software development life cycle) has a positive influence on IT project success. In other words: IT projects that applied verification techniques relatively early in development were more successful on average, than IT projects that did not apply verification techniques (or applied it relatively late in development). As said earlier, practitioners should be aware that the long term benefits of verification outweigh the short term extra costs.

References

1. Bass, L., Clements, P., Kazman, R.: Software Architecture in Practice, 2nd edn. Addison Wesley (2003)
2. Berntsson Svensson, R.: Managing Quality Requirements in Software Product Development. PhD thesis, Department of Computer Science, Lund University (2009)
3. Centraal Bureau voor de Statistiek. Nationale rekeningen 2006 (2007)
4. Chung, L., Nixon, B., Yu, E.S., Mylopoulos, J.: Non-Functional Requirements in Software Engineering. Kluwer Academic (1999)
5. Cronbach, L.J.: Coefficient alpha and the internal structure of tests. Psychometrika 16(3), 297–334 (1951)
6. Dvir, D., Raz, T., Shenhar, A.J.: An empirical analysis of the relationship between project planning and project success. International Journal of Project Management 21, 89–95 (2003)
7. Fairbanks, G.: Just Enough Architecture: The Risk-Driven Model. Crosstalk (November/December 2010)
8. Glinz, M.: On non-functional requirements. In: 15th IEEE International Requirements Engineering Conference RE 2007, pp. 21–26. IEEE (2007)
9. Grady, R.B.: An economic release decision model: Insights into software project management. In: Proceedings of the Applications of Software Measurement Conference, Orange Park, Software Quality Engineering, pp. 227–239 (1999)

10. Johansson, E., Wesslén, A., Bratthall, L., Höst, M.: The importance of quality requirements in software platform development - a survey. In: HICSS 2001: Proceedings of the 34th Annual Hawaii International Conference on System Sciences, vol. 9, p. 9057. IEEE Computer Society, Washington, DC (2001)
11. Lawrence, B., Wiegers, K., Ebert, C.: The top risks of requirements engineering. IEEE Softw. 18(6), 62–63 (2001)
12. Leffingwell, D.: Calculating your return on investment from more effective requirements management. American Programmer 10(4), 13–16 (1997)
13. Leung, H.K.N.: Quality metrics for intranet applications. Information and Management 38(3), 137–152 (2001)
14. McCabe, T.: A complexity measure. IEEE Transactions on Software Engineering 2, 308–320 (1976)
15. Mylopoulos, J.: Goal-oriented requirements engineering, part ii. In: RE 2006: Proceedings of the 14th IEEE International Requirements Engineering Conference, IEEE Computer Society, Washington, DC (2006)
16. Mylopoulos, J., Chung, L., Nixon, B.: Representing and using nonfunctional requirements: A process-oriented approach. IEEE Trans. Softw. Eng. 18(6), 483–497 (1992)
17. Paech, B., Detroit, A., Kerkow, D., von Knethen, A.: Functional requirements, non-functional requirements, and architecture should not be separated - a position paper. In: REFSQ, Essen, Germany (September 2002)
18. Paech, B., Kerkow, D.: Non-functional requirements engineering - quality is essential. In: 10th Anniversary International Workshop on Requirements Engineering: Foundation for Software Quality (2004)
19. Sheldon, F.T., Kavi, K.M., Tausworth, R.C., Yu, J.T., Brettschneider, R., Everett, W.W.: Reliability measurement: From theory to practice. IEEE Software 9(4), 13–20 (1992)
20. Westland, J.C.: The cost of errors in software development: evidence from industry. Journal of Systems and Software 62(1), 1–9 (2002)

Research Preview:
Prioritizing Quality Requirements Based on Software Architecture Evaluation Feedback

Anne Koziolek

Department of Informatics, University of Zurich, Switzerland
`koziolek@ifi.uzh.ch`

Abstract. [**Context and motivation**] Quality requirements are a main driver for architectural decisions of software systems. Although the need for iterative handling of requirements and architecture has been identified, current architecture design processes do not provide systematic, quantitative feedback for the prioritization and cost/benefit considerations for quality requirements. [**Question/problem**] Thus, in practice stakeholders still often state and prioritize quality requirements before knowing the software architecture, i.e. without knowledge about the quality dependencies, conflicts, incurred costs, and technical feasibility. However, as quality properties usually are cross-cutting architecture concerns, estimating the effects of design decisions is difficult. Thus, stakeholders cannot reliably know the appropriate required level of quality. [**Principal ideas/results**] In this research proposal, we suggest an approach to generate feedback from quantitative architecture evaluation to requirements engineering, in particular to requirements prioritization. We propose to use automated design space exploration techniques to generate information about available trade-offs. Final quality requirement prioritization is deferred until first feedback from architecture evaluation is available. [**Contribution**] In this paper, we present the process model of our approach enabling feedback to requirement prioritization and describe application scenarios and an example.

1 Introduction

Quality attributes such as performance, reliability, and maintainability, are crucial for the success of any software system. The software architecture largely influences the quality properties a software system will exhibit.

However, while quality requirements are defined in many companies mainly upfront, they are not systematically incorporated during development and thus are often dismissed later [2,3]. In particular, interdependencies and trade-offs among quality requirements often remain unclear. Major difficulties complicate quality requirements prioritization tasks: First, quality attributes are often pervasive, so that their effect and costs are difficult to estimate in advance [2, pp. 3,9]. Second, for many types of quality requirements, a value on a continuous scale, such as a response time of 5 seconds, needs to be defined. Choosing

B. Regnell and D. Damian (Eds.): REFSQ 2012, LNCS 7195, pp. 52–58, 2012.

the right required value (i.e. the required *level* of quality, which is a subtask of requirements prioritization) is difficult for managers [3, p. 74].

Although the need for iterative handling of requirements and architecture has been identified decades ago, and several processes have been proposed [13,14], no approaches provide *systematic and quantitative feedback* from software architecture design to support quality requirement prioritization.

Quantitative architecture evaluation approaches allow to predict quality properties (such as performance [10] and reliability [9]) based on models of the software architecture and underlying theories (such as queueing networks or Markov chains). They improve design decisions with respect to quality attributes and help to understand the incurred costs. However, these approaches assume fixed quality requirements and thus try to help the software architect to achieve these requirements, thus not reflecting the iterative nature of the development process.

As the contribution of this paper, we propose a new approach to prioritize quality requirements, relying on feedback from architecture evaluation and automated design space exploration. The approach requires identification of relevant quality attributes upfront but defers the decision for required quality levels. Only after initial architecture evaluation and design space exploration, the trade-off between quality attributes and the costs for achieving quality levels can be reliably estimated. To validate our research idea, we will (1) extend the existing design space exploration tool PerOpteryx [11] to explicitly support quality requirements prioritization and (2) evaluate its benefits in empirical studies, which include business reporting and industrial automation systems. The expected results of our approach are (1) better informed quality level definition, (2) guidance in quality requirement prioritization, and, as a result, (3) higher trust in quality requirements during the development process. Ultimately, our approach shall enable iterative handling of quality requirements and architecture.

The remainder of this paper is organized as follows. In Sec. 2, we discuss the current state and related approaches in more detail. Then, Sec. 3 describes our idea how to bring quality requirements and software architecture closer together and enable feedback. Finally, Sec. 4 concludes.

2   Related Work

The need for iterative handling of requirements and architecture has been identified decades ago [5]. The Twin Peaks model [13] suggests to concurrently develop requirements specification and architecture by using insight from one activity in the other. Woods and Rozanski [14] describe how insight from software architecture design can frame and inspire requirements specification. However, while both methods describe a mindset for software architects, they do not provide concrete methods and tool support to combine the two worlds.

2.1   Quality Requirements in Software Architecture Evaluation

Most approaches for quantitative software architecture evaluation only focus on one quality attributes (e.g. performance [10] or reliability [9]). Some qualitative approaches such as ATAM specifically trade off quality attributes based on architecture insights.

In ATAM, the main steps with respect to quality requirement prioritization are the following. In step 2, the business drivers, among them main quality attributes, are discussed and defined. In step 5, a utility tree is defined for quality attributes which capture the importance of quality requirements and the value of achieving a certain level of quality. Thus, the utility tree is a form of quality requirements prioritization. Then, in step 6, possible architectural approaches are evaluated with respect to this utility tree, e.g. by using performance prediction techniques based on queuing networks. Trade-off points where quality attributes conflict with each other are highlighted. However, ATAM does not explicitly support the architect and stakeholders to question and revise the previously defined utility tree based on the evaluation results, but rather focuses on the effects of architecture decisions to find a combination of decisions that together optimize the given utility tree. Our approach complements ATAM by enabling *systematic* feedback for revising the utility tree after architecture evaluation.

Recently, approaches to help the software architect to improve a given software architecture model have been proposed (e.g. PerOpteryx, ArchE, Performance Booster, Archeopteryx [11]). Such approaches automatically vary a given architectural model based on predefined degrees of freedom, such as component allocation to servers, component selection, change of hardware and software parameters, or other, custom defined design decisions expressed as simple model transformations. The reached variants of the architecture are called architecture candidates and are evaluated using multiple quantitative quality prediction techniques. Thus, the approaches explore a part of the design space. Still, so far these approaches only provide feedback to the software architect, and their connection to decisions on the requirements side remains unexplored. In this work, we address the question how to feed the gained information back to the requirements engineering phase.

2.2 Quality Requirements Prioritization in Research

While numerous approaches to handle quality requirements have been suggested [6], few approaches address the prioritization of quality requirements. A survey from 2008 on quality requirements prioritization [8] found that many approaches rely on converting quality requirements into functional requirements first for cost estimation. For example, a security requirement is operationalized to a requirement for a login functionality first.

However, operationalization does not reflect the pervasive nature of such quality requirements as performance or reliability. Furthermore, quality requirements often have the before-mentioned continuous scale, trade-offs among each other, and effect on the utility of each other and the utility of functional requirements [1]. Thus, prioritization techniques for functional requirements are not properly applicable to quality requirements [1,3].

As an exception, the QUPER approach [4] specifically supports to prioritize quality requirements and supports analysts to define appropriate quality levels.

However, reasoning in QUPER is qualitative and relies on estimating quality costs. Our proposed approach is complementary and could be used to determine QUPER costs barriers and also trade-offs among quality attributes based on quality prediction.

3   Prioritization by Architecture Feedback

Our planned approach provides feedback for requirements prioritization (Fig. 1). Because an initial understanding of quality requirements is required for architecture design, the process starts with the requirements engineering activities and with the design of an initial architecture as before. Compared to previous approaches, more information is collected (design space exploration and analysis of trade-off and dependencies) and a feedback loop from architecture evaluation to requirements prioritization is introduced.

Note that according to Berntsson Svensson et al. [2,3], the definition of required quality levels is a subtask of requirements prioritization. Quality requirements elicitation is concerned with identifying relevant quality attributes and quality requirements specification is concerned with defining how to measure (or, more generally, test) the quality requirements[1].

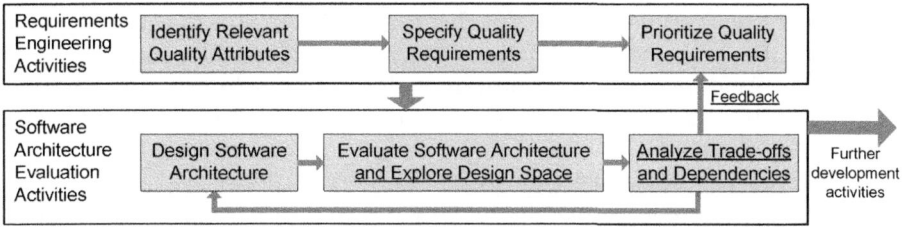

Fig. 1. Prioritizing Quality Requirements using Software Architecture Evaluation (new activities are underlined)

This process can for example be instantiated for a business reporting system (BRS). Only quality requirements are discussed in the following, functional requirements and project requirements are neglected here.

Step 1: Identify relevant quality attributes (stakeholders and requirements engineers): Performance, reliability, and operating costs are relevant for the BRS.

Step 2: Specify quality requirements (stakeholders and requirements engineers): For performance, a response time requirement is defined for the "reporting" use case. For reliability, the up-time of "reporting" per month is defined. The operating costs are hardware (servers, network, etc.) and maintenance costs.

---

[1] That is, a quality requirement specification thus only specifies the quality to measure with all its details and environmental conditions (e.g. "the response time of service X must be low under workload Y"), but does not yet define a level of quality (here e.g. "lower than 5 seconds"). If we understood quality level definition as a subactivity of requirements specification instead, Fig. 1 would be changed accordingly and also provide some feedback into the requirements specification phase.

Step 3: Prioritize quality requirements (stakeholders and requirements engineers): Initially, stakeholders agree that reliability and costs are more relevant than performance. The required quality levels are only roughly defined at this point: The up-time should be as high as economically sensible, while the response time should be low enough that users do not notice waiting times.

Step 4: Design initial architecture (software architect): Based on the initially prioritized quality requirements, the software architect designs an initial architecture and creates an architecture model with quality annotations required for evaluation.

Step 5: Evaluate software architecture and explore design space (software architect and tools): Based on the defined architecture model and existing model-based quality prediction techniques, a design space exploration tool such as PerOpteryx [11] automatically searches the design space for optimal architecture candidates, e.g. by varying component allocation to servers, by changing the hardware to procure, by adding load-balancing or redundancy measures, and by selecting from several available third-party components. Complex architecture models can be handled by such tools, as shown in several case studies [11,12,7]. The result is a set of architecture candidates with optimal trade-off between the quality attributes (i.e. *Pareto-optimal* candidates), as shown in Fig. 2. Each point represents a Pareto-optimal architecture candidate and is plotted for the predicted response time and costs of this candidate. Architects can inspect further properties of each found candidate, such as the allocation, with the tool.

Step 6: Analyze trade-offs (software architect): Based on the design space exploration results (Fig. 2), the software architect notes that all three quality attributes are in conflict. Optimal response time and costs form a typical trade-off curve ($\diamond$), but these architecture candidates have a lower availability of 98% per year. To achieve an availability of 99% per year ($\times$), sacrifices for response time and/or costs need to be made. As a result of this step, the discovered quality dependencies and insights are fed back into the requirements prioritization. If more quality attributes are analyzed, advanced tool support from multi-criteria decision support research is required to efficiently explore the found trade-offs.

Step 7: Re-prioritize quality requirements (stakeholders and requirements engineers): Based on the results by the software architect, stakeholders discuss and negotiate on the required quality levels. Finally, they agree that 98% availability is actually sufficient and allows them to achieve a response time of 3 seconds while having low operating costs of less than 500 T EUR

Step 8: Re-design software architecture (software architect): The software architect updates the architecture accordingly by selecting the found optimal architecture candidates just below 500 T EUR. Alternatively, if the stakeholders would not have come to an agreement yet, the software architects could try to make high-level, manual changes to the architecture (e.g. changing the architecture style), and rerun the design space exploration (indicated by the backward arrow to design in Fig. 1).

Step 9: Further development: The architecture design is used to implement the system. The architecture model should be continuously updated, especially with insights for quality properties. For example, the model should be updated by continuous performance measurements of prototypes and first versions of the system. If the quality properties change, the steps above may be revisited.

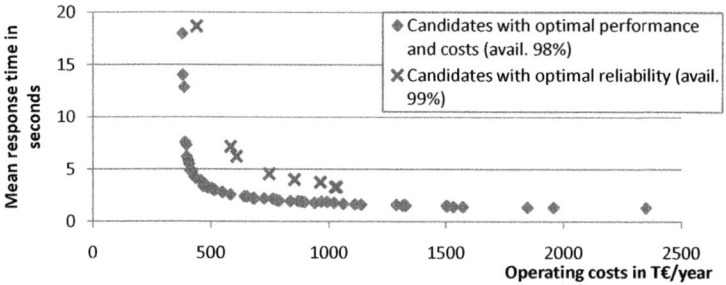

Fig. 2. PerOpteryx Results of BRS Design Space Exploration

As a result, our process supports the iterative and deferred definition of quality requirements, and thus provides a structured approach for stakeholders and software architects to revisit requirements engineering activities after software architecture design.

The design space exploration itself is already realized in the PerOpteryx tool [11] (cf. Sec. 2.1), but no support for interpreting the results (Fig. 2) is available so far. Thus, to support our new process, we will investigate the new step of trade-off and dependency analysis based on design space exploration results as next steps in this research. Here, the main research question is how to extract and represent quality dependencies relevant to stakeholders and requirements engineers, such as conflicts and necessary trade-offs, to support prioritization.

Prioritization by architecture feedback could be applied in more scenarios than the described development process. The prerequisites are (1) that an architecture model of a system is available, and (2) that several quantifiable quality attributes are relevant and can be predicted based on the available architecture model. The architecture model can be (a) an initial architecture model based on initial quality requirements as described above, (b) an initial architecture model based on functional requirements only, (c) a reference architecture for the target domain which is to be adjusted, or (d) the architecture of an existing system which is to be extended or maintained.

4   Conclusion

We present an approach to support quality requirements prioritization by providing feedback from quantitative architecture evaluation and design space exploration. Applying our approach, stakeholders, requirements engineers, and software architects gain a better understanding of the dependencies of quality attributes and the effects of achieving certain quality values. Thus, it helps them to prioritize quality requirements and decide for an optimal trade-off. However, the approach is currently limited to quantitatively evaluated quality properties.

As next steps, we will investigate how the dependencies of quality properties can best be extracted from design space exploration results and how the insight can best be presented to the stakeholders, especially if more than three quality requirements are present.

References

1. Berander, P., Andrews, A.: Requirements prioritization. In: Aurum, A., Wohlin, C. (eds.) Engineering and Managing Software Requirements, pp. 69–94. Springer, Heidelberg (2005)
2. Berntsson Svensson, R., Gorschek, T., Regnell, B., Torkar, R., Shahrokni, A., Feldt, R.: Quality requirements in industrial practice – an extended interview study at eleven companies. IEEE Trans. on Software Engineering (preprint:1, 2011)
3. Berntsson Svensson, R., Gorschek, T., Regnell, B., Torkar, R., Shahrokni, A., Feldt, R., Aurum, A.: Prioritization of quality requirements state of practice in eleven companies. In: RE 2011, pp. 69–78. IEEE (2011)
4. Berntsson Svensson, R., Sprockel, Y., Regnell, B., Brinkkemper, S.: Setting quality targets for coming releases with QUPER: an industrial case study. In: Requirements Engineering, pp. 1–16
5. Boehm, B.W.: A spiral model of software development and enhancement. Computer 21(5), 61–72 (1988)
6. Chung, L., do Prado Leite, J.C.S.: On Non-Functional Requirements in Software Engineering. In: Borgida, A.T., Chaudhri, V.K., Giorgini, P., Yu, E.S. (eds.) Mylopoulos Festschrift. LNCS, vol. 5600, pp. 363–379. Springer, Heidelberg (2009)
7. de Gooijer, T., Jansen, A., Koziolek, H., Koziolek, A.: An industrial case study of performance and cost design space exploration. In: ICPE 2012 , Boston, USA (to appear, 2012)
8. Herrmann, A., Daneva, M.: Requirements prioritization based on benefit and cost prediction: An agenda for future research. In: RE 2008, pp. 125–134. IEEE (2008)
9. Immonen, A., Niemelä, E.: Survey of reliability and availability prediction methods from the viewpoint of software architecture. Software and System Modeling 7(1), 49–65 (2008)
10. Koziolek, H.: Performance evaluation of component-based software systems: A survey. Performance Evaluation 67(8), 634–658 (2010)
11. Martens, A., Koziolek, H., Becker, S., Reussner, R.H.: Automatically improve software models for performance, reliability and cost using genetic algorithms. In: WOSP/SIPEW 2010, pp. 105–116. ACM, New York (2010)
12. Meedeniya, I., Buhnova, B., Aleti, A., Grunske, L.: Reliability-driven deployment optimization for embedded systems. Journal of Systems and Software 84(5), 835–846 (2011)
13. Nuseibeh, B.: Weaving together requirements and architectures. IEEE Computer 34(3), 115–117 (2001)
14. Woods, E., Rozanski, N.: How software architecture can frame, constrain and inspire system requirements. In: Avgeriou, P., Grundy, J., Hall, J.G., Lago, P., Mistrk, I. (eds.) Relating Software Requirements and Architectures, pp. 333–352. Springer, Heidelberg (2011), doi:10.1007/978-3-642-21001-3_19

A Simulation Approach for Impact Analysis of Requirement Volatility Considering Dependency Change

Junjie Wang[1,2], Juan Li[1], Qing Wang[1], He Zhang[3], and Haitao Wang[1,4]

[1] Laboratory for Internet Software Technologies, Institute of Software
Chinese Academy of Sciences, Beijing 100190, China
[2] Graduate University of Chinese Academy of Sciences, Beijing 100039, China
[3] National ICT Australia, University of New South Wales, Sydney, Australia
[4] nfschina Inc, Beijing
{wangjunjie,lijuan,wq,wanghaitao}@itechs.iscas.ac.cn,
he.zhang@nicta.com.au

Abstract. Requirement volatility is a common and inevitable project risk which has severe consequences on software projects. When requirement change occurs, a project manager wants to analyze its impact so as to better cope with it. As the modification to one requirement can cause changes in its dependent requirements and its dependency relationship, the impact analysis can be very complex. This paper proposes a simulation approach DepRVSim (Requirement Volatility Simulation considering Dependency relationship) to assessing this sort of impact. We abstract the general patterns of the influence mechanism, which may trigger modification in its dependency relationship and bring changes in other requirements through dependency. DepRVSim can generate such information as the probability distribution of effort deviation and schedule deviation. As a proof-of-concept, the applicability of DepRVSim is demonstrated with an illustrative case study of a real software project. Results indicate that DepRVSim is able to provide experimental evidence for decision making when requirement changes.

Keywords: Requirement Volatility, Requirement Dependency, Software Process Simulation.

1 Introduction

It is widely reported that requirements often change during the software/system development process. These changes are caused by several factors, such as evolving customer needs, errors in original requirements, technological changes, and changes in the business environment or organization policy. Requirements volatility often results in cost and schedule overruns, unmet functions and, at times, cancelled projects [1, 2]. Houston et al. [3] described an approach to modeling risk factors and simulating their effects. The effects of six common and significant software development risk factors were studied, including inaccurate cost estimation, staffing attrition and turnover, etc. Simulation results reflected that requirements volatility is the most significant risk factor modeled.

B. Regnell and D. Damian (Eds.): REFSQ 2012, LNCS 7195, pp. 59–76, 2012.
© Springer-Verlag Berlin Heidelberg 2012

Most requirements cannot be treated independently, since they are related to and affect each other in complex manners [4, 5]. When a certain requirement changes, other requirements would be influenced through dependency relationship in ways not intended or not even anticipated. Apart from that, the requirement dependency relationship would not remain the same when requirement changes happen. Hence, during the impact analysis of requirement changes, dependency relationship is one of the important factors need to be carefully considered.

Several simulation approaches have emerged to assessing the impact of requirement volatility on project performance. Pfahl et al. [6] built a system dynamic simulation model for Siemens Corporate Technology to demonstrate the impact of requirement volatility on project duration and effort. His work modeled the relationship between unstable definition of requirements and rework cycles, rework cycles and development productivity, development productivity and project duration, and so on. This model captured a specific real-world development process in sufficient detail, but was not easily adaptable to new application contexts. Ferreira et al. [7] utilized empirical survey results and built an executable system dynamics model to demonstrate the impact of requirement volatility on cost, schedule and quality. These studies are conducted applying system dynamics simulation approach. This type of research focuses on phenomenological observations of external behaviors of process, such as job size, overall project effort, requirement defects and so on [8].

Compared with system dynamics, discrete-event simulation allows more detailed descriptions of activity, resource and work product and more suitable for building fine-grained software process simulation models [8]. Liu et al. [9] proposed a simulation approach to predict the impact of requirement volatility on software project plans. This discrete-event simulation model can capture internal behaviors of software process, such as traceability and dependency relationship. But his approach did not consider dependency relationship in sufficient detail and did not model the changes in dependency relationship.

In this paper, we propose a simulation approach named DepRVSim (Requirements Volatility Simulation considering Dependency relationship) to analyze the impact of requirement volatility on project plan. In DepRVSim, we model the dependency relationship and traceability relationship, as well as the changes in dependency relationship. We abstract the general patterns of the influence mechanism, which may trigger modification in its dependency relationship and bring changes in other requirements through dependency. DepRVSim can generate such information as the probability distribution of schedule deviation.

Among previous studies, only a part of the simulation approaches were validated in industrial settings. Others just used industrial context as simulation inputs. We not only base our validation on real industrial context, but also compare model outputs with actual process data and obtain statistical results. Simulation results indicate that for 10 man hours offset from real effort deviation and 10 hours offset from real schedule deviation, DepRVSim can reach a correct rate of approximately 45% and 70% respectively. DepRVSim can assist project managers in decision making process and help understand the impact of requirement volatility in depth.

Note that, there is no standard definition of requirements volatility. Usually it expresses the changing nature of requirements over the system development life cycle

[10, 11]. Here we use these two terms – requirements volatility and requirements change – interchangeably in this paper.

The remainder of the paper is structured as follows. Section 2 describes mechanism of DepRVSim in detail. Section 3 illustrates the applicability and usefulness of DepRVSim with the help of a case study. Section 4 discusses threats to validity. Section 5 discusses related work. Finally, Section 6 concludes the paper and gives directions of our future work.

2   The DepRVSim Approach

DepRVSim is a discrete-event simulation approach, which adopts the framework of RVSim [9]. There are four components in DepRVSim as shown in Figure 1.

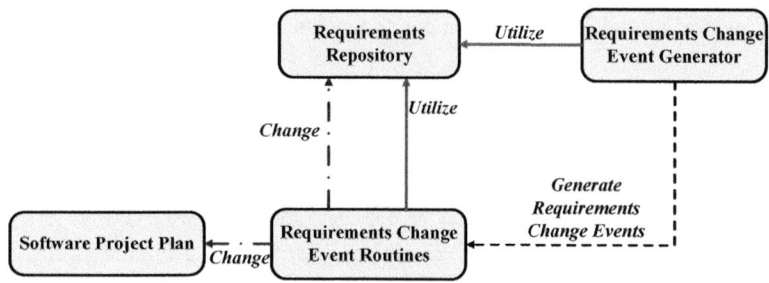

Fig. 1. DepRVSim structure

Requirements Repository stores description for requirements attributes, including requirements' traceability information and dependency information. Requirements traceability is concerned with tracing information between requirements and its related tasks, while requirements dependency deals with the relationship between requirements. One change on a certain requirement not only influences its related tasks through traceability, but also probably impacts other requirements through dependency, furthermore the dependency relationship can go through changes.

Requirements Change Event Generator generates events which represent requirements changes in simulation. There are three kinds of events in DepRVSim: Requirements Addition, Requirements Deletion and Requirements Modification.

Requirements Change Event Routines includes three routines responsible for handling the three kinds of events respectively in simulation.

Software Project Plan is the plan of the software project which is analyzed by DepRVSim.

Firstly, Requirements Change Event Generator generates requirements change events and sends them to Requirements Change Event Routines. Secondly, the corresponding routines are started to deal with these events in order utilizing the information in Requirements Repository. Thirdly, the routines analyze the effects of these events, and then change the related part in Software Project Plan and Requirements Repository, so users can easily see how requirements volatility impacts on project plan.

In the following section, we will first present an overview about how we model the dependency and traceability relationship, then give a detailed description of the simulation process.

2.1   Requirements Dependency/Traceability Relationship

We assume a set of requirements Req_1, Req_2, ... , Req_N will be developed. We use ReqId to distinguish these requirements.

Requirements relate to each other and these relationships are called dependency. Researches on it have different classification of dependency [12, 13]. Dahlstedt et al. compiled these different classifications into an integrated view and developed "an overall, neutral model of requirement dependencies" [14].

Table 1. Dependency classification [14]

Category	Description	Type
STRUCTURAL	The structure of the requirement set	Requires, Explains, Similar_to, Conflict_with, Influences
COST/VALUE	The cost and value of realizing requirement	Increase/Decrease_cost_of, Increase/Decrease_value_of

Since the purpose of our approach is to estimate the impact of requirements change, we apply a general representation to model the dependency relationship, in which we focus on the similar influence of different types of dependencies.

DependencySet denotes the set of dependencies. Each item in DependencySet is represented as follows: (ReqId, DepDirection, DepStrength). DepDirection specifies the dependency direction, which is IN or OUT. The IN direction denotes that other requirements depend on this one, while the OUT direction denotes that this requirement depends on others. DepStrength specifies the degree of the dependency relationship, which is STRONG or WEAK.

As the COST/VALUE category has little relevance to this paper, we only handle the STRUCTURAL category of dependencies. Table 2 shows how to transform the detailed dependency to our general representation.

Table 2. Rule for transforming detailed dependency to general representation

Original Dependency	General representation	
	R_A's dependency	R_B's dependency
R_A Requires R_B	(R_B, OUT, strength)	(R_A, IN, strength)
R_A Explains R_B	(R_B, OUT, strength)	(R_A, IN, strength)
R_A Similar_to R_B	Do not consider it because of its little relevance to impact analysis.	
R_A Conflict_with R_B	Suppose this type of dependency has been resolved before using this approach.	
R_A Influences R_B	(R_B, IN, strength)	(R_A, OUT, strength)

Requirements traceability refers to the ability to describe and follow the life of a requirement [15]. This is done mainly by establishing the traces from the requirement to other artifacts. As our method supports the impact analysis before coding begins, we utilize the software project plan to construct the traceability relationship. So, the traceability in this paper refers to the relationship between a requirement and the corresponding tasks for realizing the requirement.

RelatedTaskSet denotes the set of traceability relationship. Each item in Related-TaskSet is one of the related tasks for realizing the requirement and is represented as follows: (TaskId, Type, Effort). Typical task types are design, code and test. Effort denotes the estimated effort needed to fulfill a task. Note that certain dependency relationships between tasks are applied, e.g., test cannot be started before some or all of the code has been finished.

2.2   Requirements Change Event Generator

The first step of the simulation process is to generate requirements change events by Requirements Change Event Generator. Change event is described as a tuple: (ReqId, RChangeType, RChangeTime, ModifyLevel).

ReqId corresponds to the requirement which is added, modified or deleted.

RChangeType defines the type of requirements change event, which are Requirements Addition, Requirements Modification and Requirements Deletion.

RChangeTime is the time when requirements change event happens.

ModifyLevel specifies the degree to which one requirement is modified for the change type Requirements Modification. Possible values of ModifyLevel are MAJOR, MODERATE and MINOR, which are calibrated based on historical project data and expert judgement.

DepRVSim allows users to specify how Requirements Change Event is generated. There are two modes for generating events: definite events inputted by users and automatically generated events according to user-defined rules. Rules can be obtained by analyzing historical project data (like [16, 17]) or by expert experience. Users can also do "what-if" analysis by setting up different rules.

2.3   Requirements Change Event Routines

The second and third step of the simulation process is to handle the generated change events and change related parts of Software Project Plan and Requirements Repository. This is done by Requirements Change Event Routines. There are three general routines for the three types of requirements change events in simulation, which is represented as follows. Assume the changed requirement is R_i, the requirement that R_i depends on is R_{out}, the requirement that depends on R_i is R_{in}.

Requirements Addition Event Routine
This routine has three steps as follows:

♦   **Step1:** Add R_i to Requirements Repository with related tasks

♦   **Step2:** Generate R_i.DependencySet

Assume the total number of requirements is N, the parameter dper (dependency percent) of R_i is defined as follows: $dper = (N_d / N) * 100$.

N_d can be calculated easily by N and dper. dper is generated based on the uniform distribution of the type UNIFORM (dperMin, dperMax), with two user-input parameters. Choose N_d requirements as ones with which R_i has dependency relationship. Randomly generate DepDirection and DepStrength.

♦   **Step3:** Rearrange tasks properly in Software Project Plan.

In DepRVSim, overlapping of the phases for one requirement is not allowed. Design tasks have precedence relationship the same as the dependency of requirements related to them. In code and test phases, tasks do not have such precedence relationship and can be parallel.

Requirements Deletion Event Routine

This routine has three different steps from addition routine, which is shown as follows:

♦   **Step1:** Delete R_i from Requirements Repository

♦   **Step2:** Modify the influenced requirements

When deleting R_i from current project plan, the requirements with which R_i has dependency relationship might be influenced. The ModifyLevel of these requirements is shown in Table 3, where "none" indicates that the requirement is not influenced.

Table 3. Rule for ModifyLevel of R_{out} and R_{in} in deletion routine

R_i's ModifyLevel	DepStrength	R_{in}'s ModifyLevel	R_{out}'s ModifyLevel
delete	STRONG	delete	none
delete	WEAK	major	none

♦   **Step3**: Adjust the Software Project Plan.

Requirements deletion may cause idle time between tasks, so the Software Project Plan needs to be adjusted.

Requirements Modification Event Routine

There are four steps in the routines:

♦   **Step1**: Modify corresponding tasks' effort of R_i

Set up a parameter emp (effort modified percent). DepRVSim distinguish the variant effort for the situation that a task has not been started and the situation that a task has been finished, which is signified by RChangeTime. Suppose the original task effort is Eff_i. If the task has not been started, the effort after modification is $Eff_i*(1+emp)$. If the task has been finished, apply the parameter reworkRate to signify this difference. The rework effort is $Eff_i*emp*reworkRate$. If the task has been started but not finished, divide the task into two parts and calculate new effort respectively.

The parameter emp is generated based on uniform distribution, parameters of which are determined based on ModifyLevel. The reworkRate is an input parameter calibrate based on particular project.

♦   **Step2:** Modify the dependency relationship of R_i

Experiences from software development show that requirement dependency relationship would not remain unchanged when the certain requirement is modified. DepRVSim model this situation. When analyzing the changes in dependency relationship, we distinguish adding content and deleting content of certain requirements, as well as the direction of the dependency relationship. Detailed rules are described as follows:

Rule1: When the modification to R_i is adding its content, R_i might newly depend on other requirements.

Set up a parameter dperAdd to represent the dependency percent of newly added dependency relationship. We generate dperAdd based on the same uniform distribution as emp. We also apply an input parameter fAdd to revise the generated dperAdd. The parameter fAdd is different among software projects and can be decided based on expert judgement.

The number of newly added dependency relationship can be calculated using dperAdd, fAdd and N. Randomly choose requirements and generate the dependency relationship for R_i where DepDirection is OUT.

Rule2: When the modification to R_i is adding its content, for the dependency relationship that R_i depends on others, current dependency might be strengthened.

We apply a parameter dpermp to represent the modified percent of dper. Generate dpermp based on the same uniform distribution as emp. The number of changed dependency relationship can be calculated by N * dper * dpermp.

Randomly choose the influenced relationship. If current DepStrength is WEAK, change it to STRONG. If current DepStrength is STRONG, keep it unchanged.

Rule3: When the modification to R_i is deleting its content, for the two kinds of dependency relationship, current dependency relationship is weakened or disappears.

Apply the parameter dpermp to decide the number of changed relationship as Rule2. Randomly choose the influenced dependency relationship. Change the STRONG strength to WEAK, and delete the WEAK relationship.

◆   **Step3:** Modify the influenced requirements

When modification to R_i happens, the requirements with which R_i has dependency relationship might be influenced. The ModifyLevel of these requirements is shown in Table 4.

Table 4. Rule for ModifyLevel of R_{out} and R_{in} in modification routine

R_i's ModifyLevel	DepStrength	R_{in}'s ModifyLevel	R_{out}'s ModifyLevel
major	STRONG	major	none
major	WEAK	moderate	none
moderate	STRONG	moderate	none
moderate	WEAK	minor	none
minor	STRONG	minor	none
minor	WEAK	none	none

◆   **Step4:** Adjust the Software Project Plan

Requirement modification may change duration and precedence relationship of related project tasks, or cause idle time between tasks, so the Software Project Plan needs to be adjusted.

3   Case Study

The method in this paper is mainly applied to the matured software organizations, such as the ones which have achieved CMMI (Capability Maturity Model Integration) maturity level 4 or higher. Such organizations have stable development and maintenance processes. After a long-period accumulation of process execution data, they can analyze and determine the dependency strength, the modification level and other parameters with sufficient data.

We utilized a real software project – Qone [18] in such an organization to demonstrate the applicability of the proposed approach. With more than 600 thousand source lines of code, this product has been developed and maintained for more than 7 years. More than 300 Chinese software organizations are using this tool to manage their projects.

The whole project was developed in iterative process. This case study was conducted applying the real development data of one release – Qone 5.1. During the development phase, change request were forwarded to project manager. For example, changes in business environment might require a certain requirement to be enhanced. These changes made the schedule prolonged and one or several weeks' delay was the common case.

We have developed a tool named DepRVSimulator which implements the DepRVSim model. DepRVSimulator is developed based on an open source simulation package SimJava [19]. It has a user-friendly graphical interface which can display the adjusted software project plan evolved due to requirements volatility.

The preparation for this simulation concerns collecting the requirements related information and deciding the model parameters' values. For requirements related data, we developed a questionnaire and asked the project manager to complete it utilizing the stored process data. For parameters' values, we conducted a semi-structured interview with the project manager, a requirement analyst and a programmer. These values were determined according to the stored empirical data and the interviewees' experience.

3.1   Project Introduction

There are 24 requirements (R_1~R_{24}) generated through the requirement phase in this release. Table 5 shows the requirement-related information, including ReqId, requirement name and the estimated task-specific efforts per requirement.

Table 6 presents the estimated task-specific productivities per developer. Productivity represents the amount of work done per hours. Figure 2 shows the requirements' dependency information. For example, the dependency relationship between R_1 and R_2 is that R_2 strongly depends on R_1.

Table 5. Requirements information of Qone 5.1

ReqId	Requirement name	Design (man hour)	Code (man hour)	Test (man hour)	Total (man hour)
R_1	Generate new PIIDS table	48	104	90	242
R_2	Search PIIDS related in-	48	104	90	242
R_3	Maintain PIIDS table	48	104	90	242
R_4	Export PIIDS table	48	104	90	242
R_5	Import evaluation tools	48	104	90	243
R_6	Approve change request	44	56	73	173
R_7	Timing task notification	44	56	73	173
R_8	Table handling notification	44	56	73	173
R_9	Table selection conflict	44	56	73	173
R_{10}	Project problem submission notification	44	56	73	173
R_{11}	Identity authenticate	23	18	72	113
R_{12}	Access control	20	21	72	113
R_{13}	Data security	16	18	72	106
R_{14}	Import and export file	16	40	122	178
R_{15}	Import and export project	20	37	122	179
R_{16}	Project data matching	18	37	122	177
R_{17}	Import and export failure handling	18	43	122	183
R_{18}	Import and export information modification	18	38	122	178
R_{19}	Related project handling	16	40	110	166
R_{20}	Department report import and export	16	40	110	166
R_{21}	Add configuration files	4	3	1	8
R_{22}	Bug comment	4	3	1	8
R_{23}	Size restriction of change	4	3	1	8
R_{24}	Add links for project	4	3	1	8

Table 6. Estimated productivity of developers for different task types

Developers	Design (dimensionless)	Code (dimensionless)	Test (dimensionless)
Dev_1	2	1	1
Dev_2	1	0	2
Dev_3	1.2	2	1.4
Dev_4	1	1.5	2

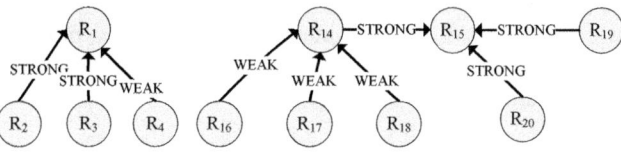

Fig. 2. Dependency relationship between requirements of Qone 5.1

Software project plan specifies the planned start time and end time for each task, as well as the allocated developer for the task. Due to the limited space, we do not present the whole plan here. Part of it is shown in Figure 3.

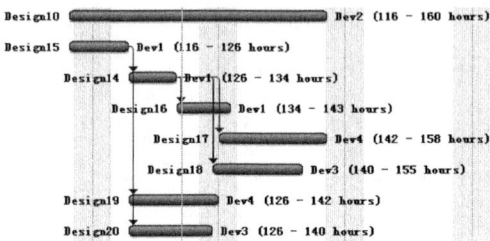

Fig. 3. Part of the initial software project plan

We collected the change data of Qone 5.1, as summarized in Table 7. It has 10 requirement changes. Effort deviation and schedule deviation information was also recorded in change database. Effort deviation denotes the difference between the new total effort under requirement changes and the planned total effort. Schedule deviation is the difference between the new project duration after changes and the planned project duration. The ModifyLevel is obtained based on the actual change degree and expert judgement.

Table 7. Change data of Qone 5.1

ReqId	ModifyLevel	Effort deviation (man hour)	Schedule deviation (hour)
R_{14}	MAJOR	176	49
R_{15}	MAJOR	176	49
R_{16}	MAJOR	176	49
R_{17}	MAJOR	176	49
R_{18}	MAJOR	176	49
R_{19}	MAJOR	176	49
R_{20}	MAJOR	176	49
R_{11}	MODERATE	115	38
R_{12}	MODERATE	115	38
R_{13}	MODERATE	115	38

The parameters defined in Section 2 are set as follows: dperMin =0, dperMax = 0.4; major = 0.45, moderate = 0.3, minor = 0.15; reworkRate = 0.5; fAdd = 0.15. These parameters are determined by the semi-structure interview. Take reworkRate as an example, this parameter works in Step 1 of modification routine. Together with the parameter emp, this parameter decides the rework effort for the finished tasks. The interviewees can refer to similar circumstances of historical projects to obtain such information as the added workload of rework task. This parameter can then be determined through statistical techniques utilizing these project data.

3.2 Simulation Scenario and Impact Analysis

Due to limit space, we only demonstrate how Requirements Modification Event Routine works. This scenario is based on actual change data in Table 7. During project development, customers requested the requirement "import and export project" to be enhanced and refined. Hence, the modification to R_{15} is adding its content. The change time is 130 hours and ModifyLevel for R_{15} is MAJOR, which is obtained in the change databases.

Note that, many of the parameters below are just random values generated based on certain distribution during this certain simulation scenario. We applied these parameters to illustrate how DepRVSim works. The ultimate simulation outcome is based on 10000 simulation scenarios of this kind, in which these parameters might differ among simulation scenarios.

According to Requirement Modification Event Routine, there are four steps to handle this change event.

- **Step1:** Modify corresponding tasks' effort of R_{15}

R_{15} has three tasks, respectively $Desing_{15}$, $Code_{15}$ and $Test_{15}$. When this change event happens at 130 hours, $Design_{15}$ has been finished, as Figure3 shows, and the other two tasks have not been started. The original effort for $Design_{15}$ is 20 hours, as Table 5 shows. The rework effort for $Design_{15}$ is 20*emp*reworkRate. Suppose the randomly generated emp is 0.38 in this simulation scenario based on UNIFORM(0.3, 0.45). The reworkRate is 0.5, so the rework effort for $Design_{15}$ is 4 hours. The new effort for $Code_{15}$ and $Test_{15}$ can be calculated in the similar way, which is not shown due to space limit.

- **Step2:** Modify the dependency relationship of R_{15}

Current dependency relationship of R_{15} is {(R_{14}, IN, WEAK), (R_{19}, IN, WEAK), (R_{20}, IN, STRONG)} as Figure 2 shows. DepRVSim would utilize Rule1 and Rule2 to handle dependency change of R_{15}.

According to Rule1, R_{15} might newly depend on other requirements. Suppose the generated dperAdd is 0.32 in this simulation scenario based on UNIFORM(0.3, 0.45). The input parameter fAdd is 0.15. So the number of newly added dependency is 24*0.32*0.15 ≈ 1. Suppose the newly added dependency is (R_{10}, OUT, WEAK) in this simulation scenario.

According to Rule2, the current dependency relationship of DepDirection = IN is strengthened. dper for R_{15} is 3/24 = 0.125, suppose the generated dpermp is 0.36 in this simulation scenario, the number of changed dependency is 24*0.125*0.36 ≈1. Suppose the randomly chosen dependency is (R_{14}, IN, WEAK), change it to (R_{14}, IN, STRONG). The dependency relationship of R_{15} after change happens is {(R_{10}, OUT, WEAK), (R_{14}, IN, STRONG), (R_{19}, IN, WEAK), (R_{20}, IN, STRONG)}.

- **Step3:** Modify the influenced requirements

There are requirement changes in these requirements that depend on R_{15}, which are R_{14}, R_{19} and R_{20}. These requirement changes are reflected through the changes in corresponding tasks' effort. When this change event happens at 130 hours, $Design_{14}$, $Design_{19}$ and $Design_{20}$ are all on-going tasks, as Figure 3 shows. The effort after modification can be calculated similar with Step1.

- **Step4:** Adjust the Software Project Plan

The adjusted project plan of Figure 3 is shown in Figure 4. The red box denotes the rework for finished tasks, while the green box denotes the modification for unfinished tasks. The purple box denotes the tasks which are indirectly influenced. We can see from Figure 4 that due to the postponement of $Design_{14}$ and rework of $Design_{15}$, Dev_1 is late for conducting $Design_{16}$. And the follow-up tasks would be influenced.

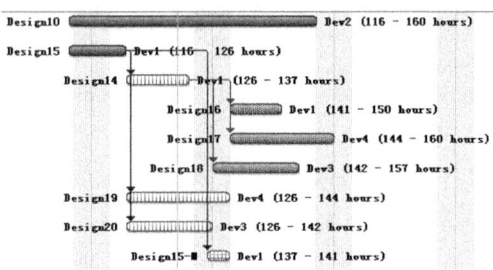

Fig. 4. Part of the adjusted software project plan

To avoid the influence of exceptional values on outcomes, we simulated 10000 times for this change event. The simulated effort deviation and schedule deviation are shown in Figure 5 and Figure 6.

The real development data in Table 7 showed that the effort deviation and schedule deviation for this requirement change are respectively 176 man hours and 49 hours. From Figure 5 and Figure 6, the probability that the simulated effort deviation has 10 man hours offset with real project data is 41.7%, while the probability for 10 hours offset of schedule deviation is 65.6%.

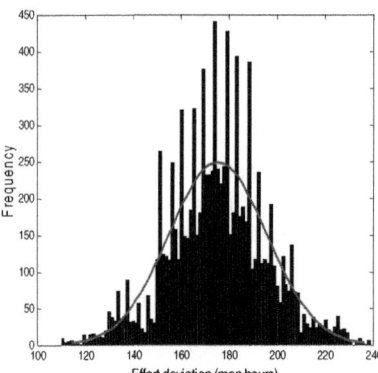

Fig. 5. Simulation results of effort deviation

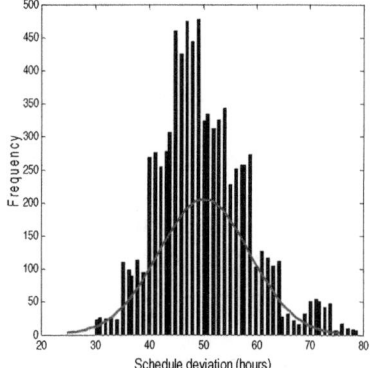

Fig. 6. Simulation results of schedule deviation

3.3   Evaluation of DepRVSim

We utilize the change data in Table 7 to carry out the evaluation of DepRVSim. We simulate these requirement change events and generate the effort deviation and schedule deviation information. Our work obtains the minimum, maximum and average value, as well as the probability of offset with real project data. These results are listed in Table 8 and Table 9.

Table 8. Effort deviation information of DepRVSim

ReqId	Minimum effort deviation	Maximum effort deviation	Average effort deviation	Effort deviation±10	Effort deviation±20
R_{14}	110	238	172	42.6%	67.5%
R_{15}	110	235	174	41.7%	66.5%
R_{16}	110	232	172	42.9%	67.2%
R_{17}	105	212	166	41.3%	66.0%
R_{18}	105	218	168	42.1%	68.2%
R_{19}	102	215	172	43.3%	69.2%
R_{20}	102	214	172	43.4%	69.2%
R_{11}	67	155	110	45.0%	63.6%
R_{12}	68	156	110	46.7%	65.5%
R_{13}	57	145	99	49.2%	64.7%

Effort deviation±K signify the probability that simulation results have K man hours offset from real effort deviation. Take R_{14} as an example, Table 7 shows that the real effort deviation is 176 man hours, so effort deviation±10 means the probability that the simulated effort deviation falls into the interval from 166 man hours to 186 man hours. The results in Table 8 show that for 10 and 20 man hours offset from real effort deviation, DepRVSim can predict correctly in the probability of around 45% and approximately 70%.

Table 9. Schedule deviation information of DepRVSim

ReqId	Minimum schedule deviation	Maximum schedule deviation	Average schedule deviation	Schedule deviation ±5	Schedule deviation ±10
R_{14}	34	75	52	40.2%	68.5%
R_{15}	34	77	52	37.9%	65.6%
R_{16}	34	76	54	37.8%	64.0%
R_{17}	35	73	54	39.7%	63.9%
R_{18}	36	76	54	40.9%	66.4%
R_{19}	33	74	50	41.1%	68.9%
R_{20}	33	73	51	41.3%	68.7%
R_{11}	32	58	42	45.2%	69.2%
R_{12}	29	58	43	48.8%	67.4%
R_{13}	32	55	40	46.3%	64.4%

Similar with effort deviation information, the results in Table 9 show that for 5 and 10 hours offset from real schedule deviation, DepRVSim can reach a correct rate of 49% and 70%.

We can notice that the simulated schedule deviation is often bigger than the actual project data. Through interviews with the project manger of this project, we found that there is rescheduling process to better utilize the human resources during requirement changes in real software project. However, in our work, the added task effort caused by changes is assigned to the original developer. Even so, the simulation results accord well with the real effort deviation and schedule deviation. Project manager can refer to these simulation results to decide whether to accept a particular change request or not.

The previous discussion showed what can be benefited from interpreting the simulation outcome. When it comes to the cost to prepare the simulation, the main work is to collect the requirements related information and decide the model parameters' values. This is done by the project manger, a requirement analyst and a programmer in our study. As the organization has a stable development process and long-period accumulation of process execution data, the preparation only takes 14 person hours. From this point, we can expect this simulation approach is a beneficial one.

4   Threats to Validity

From running a series of simulation scenarios we have gained additional insight into the nature of requirement volatility. The results from our case study provide an indication that there is a good chance to support project managers in decision making about requirement change request. In order to better judge the meaningfulness and applicability of the results, we have to carefully check their validity status.

Construct validity: a central construct in our work is the mechanism for impact of requirement volatility. Since no generally accepted mechanism for requirement change, we had to base our routines on empirical study and real software development process. We assume that this impact can be model through dependency relationship and traceability relationship. Another construct in our work is the mechanism for changes in dependency relationship. We assume that deleting requirement content might weaken its current dependency, while adding requirement content might strengthen its dependency generally. We also distinguish the direction of these dependency relationships. It is shown that the applied routines work well in general. However, as is the case for routines in general, we cannot precisely evaluate the quality of the solution for other particular project process. This might also impact the comparability between the different projects slightly.

Internal validity concerns the extent to which observed differences can be attributed to an experimental manipulation. Since our work heavily relies on a computerized simulation model, in principle, this should be one of the easiest types of validity to maximize. The simulated environment offers the experimenter a sterile setting in which entities adhere strictly to whatever routines they are assigned and within selected parameter bounds.

External validity is the degree to which the findings in a local setting, containing a single set of sampling units, are applicable to the population of sampling units as well as other setting. In our particular case, external validity is enhanced in many ways. First of all, we base our study on real software project and apply real project change data to do the evaluation. Apart from that, we provide customizable parameters in our model and users can assign their own value according to their specific software projects. These all increase the external validity of our results. However, to further prove external validity, we need to conduct our evaluation on more software projects.

While stressing the limitations of the applicability of the results, we also want to emphasize that the overall methodology is applicable more broadly in the context of simulation-based analysis. The only difference would be the adjustment of the simulation model and the inherent heuristics.

5   Related Work

The idea of using software process simulation for predicting project performance or evaluating processes is not new. Beginning with pioneers like Abdel-Hamid [20], Bandinelli [21], Gruhn [22], Kellner [23], Scacchi [24], dozens of process simulation models have been developed for various purposes. The primary purposes of simulation models are summarized as: strategic management, planning, control and operational management, process improvement and technology adoption, as well as training and learning [25].

Planning involves the prediction of project effort, cost, schedule, quality, and so on. The impact analysis of requirement volatility is among this purpose. Pfahl et al. [6] built a simulation model for Siemens Corporate Technology to demonstrate the impact of requirement volatility on project cost and effort. Ferreira et al. [7] derived related factors from empirical survey and built a system dynamic simulation model to demonstrate the impact of requirement volatility on cost, schedule and quality.

Control and operational management involves project tracking and oversight. Project can be monitored and compared against planned values computed by simulation, to help determine when corrective action may be needed. The management of software development risks is within this purpose. Houston et al. [5] described an approach to modeling risk factors and simulating their effects as a means of supporting certain software development risk management activities. His approach considered requirements volatility as one of the six risk factors and simulated its influence on project cost and duration.

Apart from software process simulation, empirical study is often applied in the impact analysis of requirement volatility on development productivity [26], project cost [27], defect density [28], project effort [27], project schedule [10] and change effort [30]. Zowghi et al. [26] conducted a survey of 430 software development companies in Australia, and the results showed that over 80% projects were late because of requirement volatility. Stark et al. [10] developed a regression analysis model to predict the schedule change percent due to requirements volatility. These empirical studies can serve as the basis for parameter calibration and general mechanism of simulation model.

The simulation method presented above focus on phenomenological observations of external behaviors of software process. Our model focused on the study of the internal details and working of process. We modeled the changes in dependency relationship when requirement changes occur. This is common in software development and a key factor for impact analysis of requirement volatility, but is not well explored yet. We abstracted the general patterns of dependency changes and provided customizable parameters for users' own process models.

6   Conclusions and Future Work

In this paper, we presented a simulation approach DepRVSim which can predict the impact of requirement volatility on software project plans. DepRVSim adopts discrete-event simulation which is able to provide many kinds of project data for users besides the project effort and schedule in the case study.

Our primary contribution is modeling the dependency relationship to assist the impact analysis of requirement volatility. Besides, we evaluate the effectiveness and applicability of DepRVSim applying the real software development data.

One significant feature of DepRVSim is that it supports fine-grained requirement change and detail change impact analysis. This feature not only provides users with such information as probability distribution of effort deviation and schedule deviation, but also assists project managers to understand the impact of requirements volatility deeply.

It should be pointed out, however, that the presented material is just the starting point of the work in progress. Future work will focus on calibration of model parameters applying data mining techniques. Another enhancement aims at validation of the proposed approach in more industrial environment, quantitative cost-benefit analysis, improvement of model usability, and – more importantly – enhancement of the DepRVSim model. Enhancement of DepRVSim will in particular aim at distinguishing specific dependency types when conducting the impact analysis and adding a heuristic that takes manpower resources into consideration.

Acknowledgment. This work is supported by the National Natural Science Foundation of China under grant No.60803023, No.60873072 and No.60903050, the National Basic Research Program (973 Program) of China under grant No.2007CB310802.

References

1. Boehm, B.W.: Software Risk Management: Principles and Practices. IEEE Software 8(1), 32–41 (1991)
2. Kotonys, G., Sommerville, I.: Requirements Engineering Process & Techniques. John Wiley & Sons (2002)
3. Houston, D.X., Mackulak, G.T., Collofello, J.S.: Stochastic simulation of risk factor potential effects for software development risk management. JSS 59(3), 247–257 (2001)
4. Dahlstedt, Å., Persson, A.: Requirements interdependencies - Moulding the State of Research into a Research Agenda. In: The Ninth International Workshop on Requirements Engineering: Foundation for Software Quality (REFSQ 2003), Klagenfurt/Velden, Austria, pp. 71–80 (2003)
5. Wohlin, C., Aurum, A.: What is important when deciding to include a software requirement in a project or a release? In: Fourth International Symposium on Empirical Software Engineering, Noosa Heads, Australia, November 17–18 (2005)
6. Pfahl, D., Lebsanft, K.: Using Simulation to Analyze the Impact of Software Requirements Volatility on Project Performance. Information and Software Technology 42(14), 1001–1008 (2000)

7. Ferreira, S., Collofello, S.J., Shunk, D., Mackulak, G.: Understanding the Effects of Requirements Volatility in Software Engineering by Using Analytical Modeling and Software Process Simulation. The Journal of Systems and Software 82, 1568–1577 (2009)
8. Zhang, H., Kitchenham, B., Pfahl, D.: Software Process Simulation Modeling: An Extended Systematic Review. In: Münch, J., Yang, Y., Schäfer, W. (eds.) ICSP 2010. LNCS, vol. 6195, pp. 309–320. Springer, Heidelberg (2010)
9. Liu, D., Wang, Q., Xiao, J., Li, J., Li, H.: RVSim: A Simulation Approach to Predict the Impact of Requirements Volatility on Software Project Plans. In: Wang, Q., Pfahl, D., Raffo, D.M. (eds.) ICSP 2008. LNCS, vol. 5007, pp. 307–319. Springer, Heidelberg (2008)
10. Stark, G., Skillicorn, A., Ameele, R.: An Examination of the Effects of Requirements Changes on Software Releases. CROSSTALK. The Journal of Defense Software Engineering, 11–16 (December 1998)
11. Al-Emran, A., Pfahl, D., Ruhe, G.: Decision Support for Product Release Planning based on Robustness Analysis. In: Proc. IEEE International Requirements Engineering Conference (RE), pp. 157–166 (2010)
12. Ramesh, B., Jarke, M.: Toward Reference Models for Requirements Traceability. IEEE Transactions on Software Engineering 27(1), 58–93 (2001)
13. Robinson, W.N., Pawlowski, S.D., Volkov, V.: Requirements Interaction Management, GSU CIS Working Paper 99-7, Department of Computer Information Systems, Georgia State of University, Atlanta (1999)
14. Dahlstedt, A.G., Persson, A.: Requirements Interdependencies - Moulding the State of Research into a Research Agenda. In: Ninth International Workshop on Requirements Engineering: Foundation for Software Quality in Conjunction with CAiSE 2003 (2003)
15. Gotel, O., Finkelstein, A.: An Analysis of the Requirements Traceability Problem. In: Proc. IEEE International Requirements Engineering Conference (RE 1994), pp. 94–101 (1994)
16. Nurmuliani, N., Zowghi, D., Powell, S.: Analysis of Requirements Volatility During Software Development Life Cycle. In: Proceedings of the 2004 Australian Software Engineering Conference (ASWEC 2004), Melbourne, Australia (2004)
17. Nurmuliani, N., Zowghi, D., Williams, S.P.: Characterising Requirements Volatility: An Empirical Analysis. In: Proceedings of the 4th International Symposium on Empirical Software Engineering (ISESE 2005), Noosa, Australia (2005)
18. http://qone.nfschina.com/qone/
19. http://www.icsa.inf.ed.ac.uk/research/groups/hase/simjava/
20. Abdel-Hamid, T.K., Madnick, S.E.: Software Projects Dynamics – an Integrated Approach. Prentice-Hall, Englewood Cliffs (1991)
21. Bandinelli, S., Fuggetta, A., Lavazza, L., Loi, M., Picco, G.P.: Modeling and Improving an Industrial Software Process. IEEE Trans. on Soft. Eng. 21(5), 440–453 (1995)
22. Gruhn, V., Saalmann, A.: Software Process Validation Based on FUNSOFT Nets. In: Derniame, J.-C. (ed.) EWSPT 1992. LNCS, vol. 635, pp. 223–226. Springer, Heidelberg (1992)
23. Kellner, M.I., Hansen, G.A.: Software Process Modeling: A Case Study. In: Proc. AHICSS 1989, vol. II - Software Track, pp. 175–188 (1989)
24. Mi, P., Scacchi, W.: A knowledge-based environment for modeling and simulating software engineering processes. IEEE Trans. on Know. and Data Eng. 2(3), 283–294 (1990)
25. Kellner, M.I., Madachy, R.J., Raffo, D.M.: Software process simulation modeling: Why? What? How? The Journal of Systems and Software 46(2/3), 91–105 (1999)

26. Zowghi, D., Offen, R., Nurmuliani, N.: The Impact of Requirements Volatility on the Software Development Lifecycle. In: Proc. International Conference on Software Theory and Practice (IFIP World Computer Congress) (2000)
27. Zowghi, D., Nurmuliani, N.: A Study of the Impact of Requirements Volatility on Software Project Performance. In: Proc. Asia-Pacific Software Engineering Conference (APSEC 2002), Gold Coast, Australia, pp. 3–11 (2002)
28. Malaiya, Y.K., Denton, J.: Requirements Volatility and Defect Density. In: Proc. International Symposium on Software Reliability Engineering (ISSRE 1999), pp. 285–294 (1999)
29. Nurmuliani, N., Zowghi, D., Williams, S.: Requirements Volatility and Its Impact on Change Effort: Evidence Based Research in Software Development Projects. In: Proc. Australian Workshop on Requirements Engineering (AWRE 2006), Adelaide, Australia (2006)
30. Ferreira, S., Collofello, J., Shunk, D., Mackulak, G., Wolfe, P.: Utilization of Process Modeling and Simulation in Understanding the Effects of requirements volatility in Software Development. In: International Workshop on software process Simulation and Modeling (proSim 2003), Portland, Oregon, USA, May 3-4 (2003)

Collaborative Resolution of Requirements Mismatches When Adopting Open Source Components

Nguyen Duc Anh[1], Daniela S. Cruzes[1], Reidar Conradi[1],
Martin Höst[2], Xavier Franch[3], and Claudia Ayala[3]

[1] Norwegian University of Science and Technology,
Department of Computer and Information Science, Trondheim, Norway
{anhn,dcruzes,Reidar.Conradi@idi.ntnu.no}
[2] Lund University, Department of Computer Science, Lund, Sweden
martin.host@cs.1th.se
[3] Technical University of Catalunya, Department of Service Engineering
and Information Systems, Barcelona, Spain
{franch,cayala@essi.upc.edu}

Abstract. [**Context and motivation**] There is considerable flexibility in requirements specifications (both functional and non-functional), as well as in the
features of available OSS components. This allows a collaborative matching and
negotiation process between stakeholders such as: customers, software contractors
and OSS communities, regarding desired requirements versus available and thus
reusable OSS components. [**Problem**] However, inconclusive research exists on
such cooperative processes. Not much empirical data exists supporting the conduction of such research based on observation of industrial OSS adoption
projects. This paper investigates how functional and non-functional requirement
mismatches are handled in practice. [**Results**] We found two common approaches
to handle functional mismatches. The main resolution approach is to get the components changed by the development team, OSS community or commercial
vendor. The other resolution approach is to influence requirements, often by postponing requirements. Overall, non-functional requirements are satisfactorily
achieved by using OSS components. Last but not least, we found that the customer involvement could enhance functional mismatch resolution while OSS
community involvement could improve non-functional mismatch resolution.
[**Contribution**] Our data suggests that the selecting components should be done
iteratively with close collaboration with stakeholders. Improvement in requirement mismatch resolution to requirements could be achieved by careful consideration of mismatches size, requirements flexibility and components quality.

Keywords: Requirements elicitation; Requirement mismatches; Open source
software; Collaboration; Empirical study.

1   Introduction

The rapid growth in scale and complexity of software systems, together with the
availability of third party software components, such as Commercial Off-The-Shelf

B. Regnell and D. Damian (Eds.): REFSQ 2012, LNCS 7195, pp. 77–93, 2012.

(COTS) or Open Source Software (OSS) components, increase the adoption of component-based software development (CBSD) in software industry [1]. This adoption demands specialized software development processes that aim at supporting Off-The-Shelf (OTS, including both COTS and OSS) component acquisition, especially Requirements Engineering (RE) processes.

Traditional RE basically consists of eliciting stakeholder's needs, refining the acquired goals into non-conflicting requirements statements, and finally validating these requirements with stakeholders [2].The RE process for OSS based development is quite different from this traditional one since integration with third party components is the essential part of software development. It is an intertwined process between requirements engineering activities and OTS component selection to select the best-matched set of components and requirements. Therefore, requirements elicitation and negotiation becomes more likely a collaborative activity, which involves customers, software suppliers and third party vendors/communities. This collaborative process closely relates to the OSS component identification and selection processes [3]. The main challenge comes from the dynamic nature of requirements and evolution of OSS components [4, 5]. The continuously evolved requirements and updated versions of chosen components could make the component features differ from the requirements in post-selection phases. These mismatches between components and requirements are unavoidable and need to be resolved during the project lifetime.

Since the process of matching requirements and selected components is crucial for a successful adoption of OSS components in software projects, it is necessary to explore the relevant industrial collaboration practices, such as requirement elicitation, component selection and mismatch handling [4, 6]. Several studies have focused on the COTS component selection processes [6, 7]. However, less effort has been allocated to the investigation RE practices in the context of OSS component adoption and even less to empirical studies in this topic.

In this paper, we present a mixed quantitative and qualitative survey of how such requirement/OSS component selection and requirements mismatches are handled in fifteen European software-intensive companies in Norway, Sweden and Spain. The main purpose of the study is to explore the requirements and component selection practices and their relationships to the requirement-component mismatch resolution.

The remainder of the paper is organized as follows: Section 2 presents previous RE studies on OTS-based development. Section 3 describes our research approach. The results are provided in Section 4 and discussed in Section 5. The threats to validity and conclusions are given in Section 6 and Section 7.

2   Research Background

2.1   Requirements-Components Matching Processes

Requirement - component matching and mismatch resolving process are overlapping activities but occurs in different phases of CBSD. While component matching consists of eliciting requirements and finding matching components in early development phase [7, 8], mismatch resolution concerns about detecting the problems with selected components and resolving it in later development [9].

Literature reveals a significant amount of research on matching process [7, 10, 11, 12, 13]. Mohamed et al. summarized the evolution of COTS selection practices in 18 COTS selection approaches [7]. The common steps include defining the evaluation criteria using requirements, COTS search, filter search results, evaluation of COTS components, and selection of best-fit COTS. Stol et al. summarized 20 different initiatives for OSS component selection and evaluation [10]. Morisio et al. surveyed 15 COTS adoption projects and characterize the COTS adoption process [11]. The common steps for the requirement phase are requirement analysis, system requirements review, COTS identification and selection, glueware and integration requirement identification. The authors also found two major issues, namely dependence on the vendor and flexibility in requirements. Paech and Reuschenbach [13] present a requirements engineering process for OSS selection. In this process, the choice of product is based on a comparison of prioritized requirements from the stakeholders and evaluation results for candidate products. Höst et al. summarize experience from a set of organizations on how to select open source components in software projects, and observe for example that it is important to understand the requirements for the identified components [12].

These studies, nevertheless do not consider the dynamic nature of requirements as well as OSS components, which lead to the issues of requirement mismatches after selecting the best-fit component at the mentioned time.

2.2   Requirements-Components Mismatches Resolution Process

Since component features are predetermined when selecting components, the changes in requirements introduce challenges to adoption of the components. A requirement-component mismatch is a difference in functional feature or non-functional quality attributes from a given component and a desired requirement.

On one hand, some studies see requirement negotiation as an approach to resolve the mismatches [2, 4, 8, 9, 14, 15]. In these cases, the component is fixed beforehand and requirements are the target of changes [8]. Maiden and Ncube observed that this process is iterative: from an initial stage with all the customer wish-list and the full market-place available, mismatches progressively force requirements negotiation and candidate filtering until the final COTS component is selected [14]. Rolland proposed a goal-oriented approach for considering mismatches at the business level and then defined goal matching as the conceptual framework for resolving them [8]. Other approaches focused on lower level but highly challenging requirement problems, with integration requirements in call-for-tender processes [15].

On the other hand, a mismatch can be solved by modifying or adapting the selected components to fit to the requirements [4, 9, 16]. The components are modified when it takes a long time for external support [4] or when there is a need to adapt to new changes in requirement [9].

There is although a lack of empirical investigations of industrial practices on mismatch resolution. Consequently, there is no attempt to explore which approach is conducted in which scenario.

3   Research Approach

3.1   Research Questions

It is important to understand industrial practices on both requirement and component perspectives in order to investigate the mismatches between them in the later phases. The source of requirements and how they are described could infer how flexible the requirements can be. Besides, the component search and selection process could indicate potential problems with components while implementing requirements. The understanding of both perspectives leads to a comprehension of factors that influence requirement-component mismatches. This argument leads us to RQ1:

RQ1: What are the general practices of requirement elicitations and OSS component selection in OSS adoption software projects?
Secondly, we distinguish the concepts of functional and non-functional requirements with regarding to requirement mismatches. In this study, we define functional mismatches as the differences between functional requirements and features provided by the components. These functional mismatches are investigated in the component level. Since the functional requirements are often explicitly described, it is not problematic to identify the functional mismatches when they occur. We are interested in investigating how the functional mismatch between a requirement and a component is handled by project stakeholders. It is hypothesized as an intertwined process of negotiation and technical resolution that involve customer, developers and OSS community. To investigate this scenario in industry, we propose the RQ2:

RQ2: How are the functional mismatches between requirements and OSS components collaboratively managed in OSS adoption software projects?
Thirdly, in addition to discovering what functionalities are important to users at the system level, qualities associated with particular functionality/user goals should be elicited. The qualities may need to be translated by developers from user-level objectives, values and concerns into specific technical quality requirements, though non-functional requirements are often not well-described and poorly understood [17, 18], hence the mismatches between non-functional requirements and components are hard to investigate and assess. Besides, non-functional requirements are normally system characteristics. Therefore, they are often verified in the later phases of system development, when the modules are integrated and tested. Consequently, instead of investigating the mismatches between non-functional requirements and components, we investigated which and how non-functional requirements are fulfilled by using OSS components. This rationale leads to RQ3:

RQ3: How are non-functional requirements fulfilled by using OSS components in OSS adoption software projects?

3.2   Data Collection and Analysis

The study was performed in the period between September 2010 and September 2011, including study design, piloting, data collection and analysis.

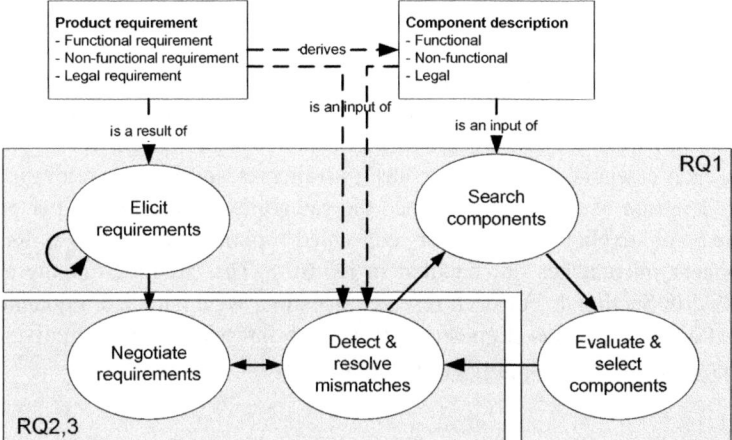

Fig. 1. Research questions mapping

Population: Our target is software-intensive organizations that adopt OSS in producing software product. This population includes organizations with different sizes and in different application domains. 64 companies from our contact list were selected and contacted by phone call and email, in which fifteen stakeholders (developers or project leaders), who represented for 15 projects, agreed to participate in the survey. Some of the contacts were not eligible for participating due to several reasons, such as lack of adoption of OSS components in the projects, the companies changed the OSS adoption policy or the adoption strategy was not publishable.

Interview Guide (Survey): The method used in this study is semi-structured interviews. The interview guide was adjusted after three pilot interviews. The purpose of the survey is to discover the practices in OSS adoption, such as Requirements elicitation, Component selection, Requirement mismatch resolution and Collaboration process in adopting OSS components. In the scope of this study we focused on results extracted on RE practices. The survey was designed as a 5-section survey, with both closed and open questions. The closed questions were used to solicit information on interviewee and project context. The open questions were used to gather information on component-requirement mismatches resolution practices and communication to the community. The survey also included explanation for important terminology and description of context background in order to offer a common understanding for all participants. The relevant survey questions are given in the Appendix.

Data Collection Procedure: The interview survey was sent to all participants some days before the interview meeting. In this way, the participants could be well-prepared for the interview. The participants were asked to fill in the first two parts of the survey and give back to us before hand. The next three parts of the survey were asked directly to the participant during the interview. Each interview session lasted between 40 to 75 minutes. Interviews were attended by one to three interviewers. The conversations were recorded and transcribed for posterior analysis. The transcripts vary from 13 to 21 pages in size.

Analysis Procedure: We analyzed the filled-in questions and transcripts using a qualitative research tool NVIVO. The approach is a tailored thematic synthesis [19]. The analysis consists of four steps: extracting data from the interview transcription; grouping data into fundamental groups based on the structure of the survey; coding data within each category; translating codes into themes and linking relevant themes together. The first two authors examined the categories from different perspectives and searched for explicitly stated or concealed opinions about how Requirement-Component mismatches are handled in industry. The results from the analysis are described in Section 4. For each research question, we conducted a quantitative summary of answers on closed questions from each interview and qualitative analysis of taped conversations to support the quantitative part.

4   Results

4.1   Projects Description

We surveyed the requirement mismatch resolution process in fifteen projects from Norway, Sweden and Spain. Table 1 shows some of the projects characteristics of the surveyed projects. The team size ranges from two to 250 people. The project life cycles include ad hoc development, waterfall, iterative development and agile, with a prevalence of the agile model in seven projects. The adoption of lightweight development life cycles, such as Agile or Scrum, introduces flexibility in requirements elicitation and component selection. The application domain covers a wide variety of domains, including Communication system, Information system, Web application and Public-sector support, with a dominant of Public sector support in five cases.

The OSS components portion represents the interviewees' estimation about the proposition of actual use part of OSS components in total product size in LOC. The OSS portion ranges from 10 to 90%. In one project, the interviewee could not provide a percentage due to absent information about the total product size. The large portion of OSS shows the importance of OSS components in the software, which could influence the priority of components during the mismatch resolution process.

The "Selection in RE" column indicates whether the component selection is decided in the RE phase or not. Interestingly, in seven projects, the components selection is not considered in the RE phase. In projects 5, 6, 13 and 15, the requirements are predetermined (i.e. subcontract or outsourcing) and selecting components are considered and design or coding level as an approach to implement given requirements. In Project 9, the company provides services to customers and selection of components is transient in RE phase.

Table 1. Projects characteristics

ID	Team size	Development process	Application domain	OSS portion	Selection in RE?	Req. source
P1	20-25	Iterative	Communication system	90%	Yes	External
P2	4	UNK	Audio/ Video processing	10%	Yes	Internal
P3	2	Agile	Search engine	80%	Yes	Internal
P4	18	Waterfall + Scrum	Embedded system	ca. 17000 KLOC	Yes	Internal
P5	2	Iterative	Oil/gas support product	77%	No	Internal
P6	200	Scrum	Public sector support	75%	No	External
P7	4	Scrum	Document processing	10%	Yes	External
P8	20	Agile	Public sector support	66%	Yes	External
P9	2	Agile	Information system	90%	No	External
P10	2	Iterative	Public sector support	60%	Yes	External
P11	250	Agile	Telecommunication	90%	No	External
P12	3	Ad-hoc, requirement-driven	University	90%	No	External
P13	3	Ad-hoc	Information system	5%	No	Internal
P14	5	Tailored waterfall	Public sector support	80%	Yes	External
P15	6	Iterative	Public sector support	20%	No	External

4.2   RQ1: What Are the General Practices of Requirements Elicitation and OSS Component Selection in OSS Adoption Software Projects?

4.2.1 Requirements Elicitation Practices

Source of Requirements: In eight projects, requirements come from external customers, and in one of the cases, managed by an external consulting company, as shown in Table 1. In one project the requirements come from both external customers and internal development team since customers required a system with similar functionalities of existing system. In this project, the requirements are flexible since the customers require the product to confront a predetermined standard and development team has to find out the detail requirements themselves.

In five projects, requirements are market-driven, coming from an internal development team. In three of them, developers also play the role of customers. Moreover, in the fourth one, they consulted other development teams that deployed similar systems, whilst in the fifth case the marketing department also had a stake. Another project's requirements come solely from the marketing department. In this project, the software is a part of an embedded system to sale.

Requirement Description Level: Figure 2 shows that among investigated projects, seven projects have requirements coarsely described. We categorize the requirement specification according to three categories: coarsely, medium and detail based on requirement description and notation. The detail level of requirement specification infers the flexibility of the requirements since the coarser one is probably the more flexible one. The coarse description of requirements in major projects is probably caused by the adoption of agile methodology. Only three projects have requirements described in detail and three in-between. Concerning specification notations, free text is used as much as structured text. Both of these requirement notations are used in seven projects. Use cases and test cases are used in three projects each, and one case used "informal" flow diagrams for expressing navigational-related requirements in a web application.

4.2.2 Component Identification and Selection Practices

Component Identification: Figure 3 describes the approaches to identify the OSS components in company's projects. Projects often used more than one approach. The most common approach is based on previous experiences without formal search and evaluation processes, which are used by ten out of fifteen interviewees. The second option (8 out of 15 interviewees) is either to use a search engine or to ask friends, colleagues or someone that has experience from before with the component. Both of these options were six interviewees mentioned about peer-review or grey literature as another source to find components. Only two projects contact customers during component identification process. One of the interviewees could not provide details in this questions nor the rest of this subsection since the selection process was entirely run by a team of software architects.

Component Selection Process: none of the interviewees reported the usage of formal evaluation processes, which are abundant in literature [7, 10], in their projects. This observation is similar to findings from a previous study [20]. The evaluation activity is normally undertaken in ad hoc manner. For small components, reading the documents or looking into the code is probably sufficient. For the more significant components, a survey may be conducted to search for alternative options. A short trial with the goal to "try to get it work as a proof-of-concept" is also one possibility.

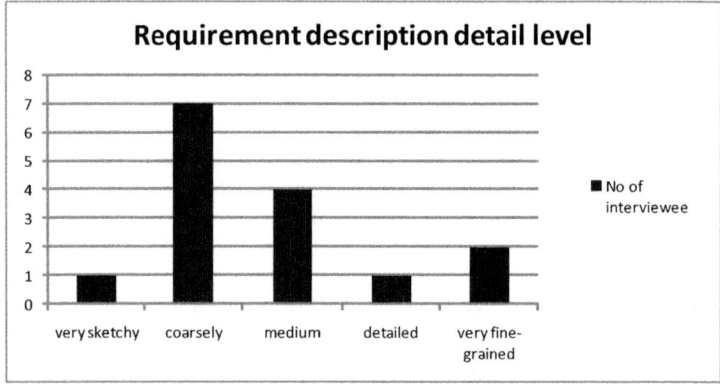

Fig. 2. Requirement description detail level

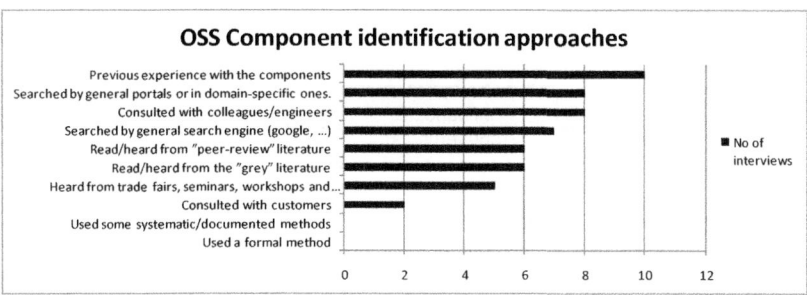

Fig. 3. OSS Component - Requirement identification approaches

4.3 RQ2: How Are the Functional Mismatches Between Requirements and OSS Components Collaboratively Managed in OSS Adoption Software Projects?

4.3.1 Functional Mismatches Identification

Grounded from interview's conversation, there are three main criteria used to decide on a mismatch between a requirement and an open source component, namely fit to functional requirements, fit to non-functional requirement and fit to legal requirement. As the basic purpose of using external components, the OSS components should have the basic functionalities that fit to the requirements. The functional mismatch is the ratio between part of the component that satisfies the requirement and the full set of requirement features. In case of small or fine-grained requirement (as in Figure 4a), the mismatch appears when there is a relative small portion of overlap functionality between the requirement and component. In case of large or coarse-grained requirement or product feature (as in Figure 4b), the mismatch happens when the component only provide part of required requirements.

With respect to non-functional requirements, reliability of the components is a highly cited criteria, and concerns the number of defects in the component; if the component is functionally fit to the requirement, but it contains many bugs then it would take a time and effort to use the components.

Last but not least, third criteria concern about component license issue. OSS components employ different types of licenses that would be taken into consideration, as one interviewee mentioned: "a lot of GPL license components cannot be used ... doing a mistake like shipping a GPL license component in a commercial product is very bad PR, and kind of legal problem ...".

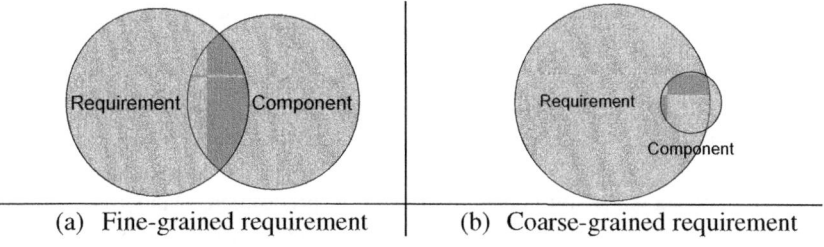

| (a) Fine-grained requirement | (b) Coarse-grained requirement |

Fig. 4. Functional mismatch type

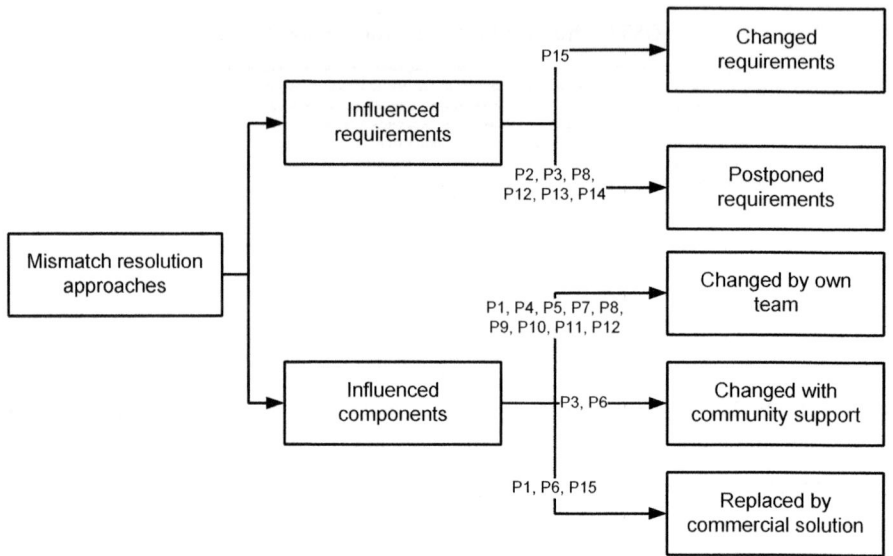

Fig. 5. Requirement - component mismatch resolution approaches

4.3.2 Mismatches Resolution Approaches

Figure **5 Requirement - component mismatch resolution approaches** provides the scenarios in which mismatches are handled. The majority answered that they change the components in some way, such as creating a glueware or addware, modifying the components and replacing the components, rather than get requirements affected. Nine interviewees said to modify or add adjustments to the OSS components by themselves. Six of them chose to make the changes globally, and send it back to the OSS community. Three interviewees make the changes locally, which are reserved for internal use only. Only two interviewees utilize community support for adapting the components while three interviewees chose commercial vendors instead.

4.3.3 When Are Requirements Changed?

In most of the cases, the requirement is not a subject to change or relax as it is often at the higher priority over components. Some interviewees said: *"... there is no case giving up on the requirements. Requirements are usually at first priority"*, *"... selecting an OSS component does not impact the requirement so much. It is not so much you can relax your requirement a bit or replace five hour of coding with existing component, it is not possible." "... normally requirement is not in the position to relax it a lot.", "... requirements were not negotiated because the project was about reengineering a legacy system into a web application; the requirements were the ones for the departing system"*.

In three projects, requirements come from predefined standards, government reform and they are not possible to negotiated or modified. In some other projects, the adopted components are of small to moderate size, and are implemented by domain specific libraries or as part of a framework. Since the integrated components serve for small and fine-grained functional requirement, it does not affect much on the overall requirements of the system. Some interviewees said: *"requirements usually do not really affect choice of components that much, as most components we use are small and not visible to the customer"*, *"... we use smaller components rather than larger sort of application server or something, the customer doesn't really see the component as a separate components, it is a part of the product"*.

Besides, OSS components offer an opportunity to modify/adjust the components upon the mismatches. This flexibility of OSS components gives more chances to satisfy the requirements, as some interviewees said: *"If there is a partial mismatch, I think we just use it for what we could use it for."*, *"...was quite simple to extend the open source project to get the functionality we needed ..."*, *"... one of the reasons to select one of the components was that it provides a proprietary script language that allows specifying its behavior when starting the system"*. Particularly, in one project, the mismatched component was rewritten from the scratch since it was a small library.

We found only one case where the option of relaxing requirements was selectively taken. The development team adopted a compensatory strategy: whilst explaining to the customer which (non-critical) requirements were not satisfied, they emphasized additional functionalities that the OSS component was covering and could be incorporated into the delivered system. It was also helpful that the customer had a very technical profile and was able to understand the consequences (in terms of cost) of not relaxing the requirements.

4.3.4 When Are Requirements Postponed?

While there is only one case where requirements is relaxed or modified, it is worth-noticed that seven interviewees mention scenarios where some requirements were postponed. The requirements were postponed in some critical cases. In one case, requirements were postponed due to the quality of components: *"... we have postponed the project because there are a lot of bugs in [Component name]. We have to look for a new library"*. In the other case, the customer accepted to postpone some non-essential requirements, the strategy followed by the development team to convince the client was to highlight those features that were not required by the customer and were offered by the component.

4.4   RQ3: How Are Non-functional Requirements Fulfilled by Using OSS Components in OSS Adoption Software Projects?

Figure 6 shows the perceptions of interviewee about non-functional requirements achieved by using OSS components. For each of non-functional requirement attribute, the grey column represents for the number of interviewees that mentioned about it. The black column shows the number of interviewees that satisfy with the quality attribute of the OSS component. The most concerned non-functional requirements regard to OSS components are performance, reliability, maintainability and cost.

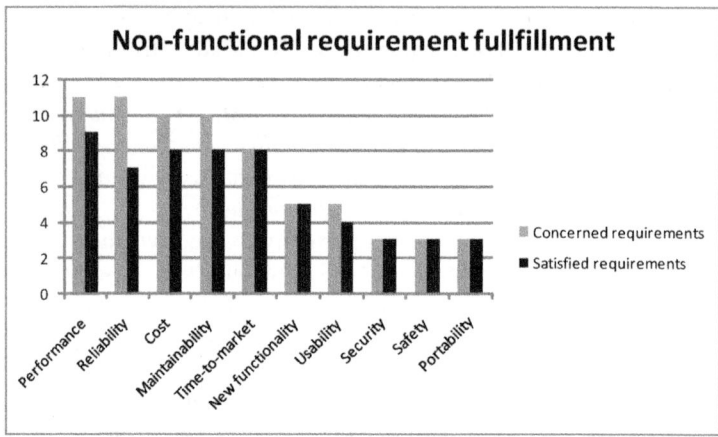

Fig. 6. Non-functional requirement fulfillment by OSS components

The list of concerned non-functional requirements in our study is different from the most concerned requirements in Berntsson Svensson et al., namely usability, performance and flexibility [21]. Their context was limited to the embedded system and market-driven projects and it may be the reason for the conflicting results.

4.4.1 Performance
Performance is satisfied by using OSS components in nine out of eleven interviews. The performance is perceived as sufficient or at least not affecting much the overall performance of the system. Some interviewees mention the problem with performance problems but these mainly come from hardware and infrastructure issues.

4.4.2 Reliability
There are contradictory opinions about reliability of OSS component. Seven interviewees experienced good reliability, with little or few bugs, with the correctness of the system exceeding expectation. Four interviewees had experiences with both reliable and unreliable OSS components. There is a misunderstanding during the conversations with some interviewees between Reliability and Maintainability. Some people said the OSS component turned out to have sufficient reliability because the code is available and then it is easy to fix the bug.

4.4.3 Maintainability
Maintainability is an important feature for OSS components. Eight out of ten interviewees are satisfied with the maintainability of the components. The factors that that contribute positively to the maintainability of OSS components are:

- The openness of the code, that allows developers to "dive into the code" to fix bugs.

- Synchronization with the upstream development: the OSS community offer a chance for the company to escape from the burden of maintenance since the components can be synchronized with the upstream development, contact with the OSS community (in comparison with a commercial component), significantly influence the maintainability of the components.
- Documentation of the code that facilitate understanding and using components.

As maintainability is as important as reliability for selecting suitable OSS components, practitioners should look for components that are not only reliable but also has a high bug fixing rate.

4.4.4 Time and Cost
Concerning time and cost, all of the interviewees are happy with the reduction of deliver time by using OSS components. Eight out of ten interviewees are happy with the cost due to the saving of licensing and implementation. There are two cases where cost is not satisfied. In one project, a lot of problems were reported due to the technical misuse of OSS component. At the end the team had governance problems that resulted in higher costs and poor reliability, performance and particularly maintainability, because the team in charge was not very big and the learning curve too steep.

5   Discussion

Our observations from fifteen projects with different context settings and requirement practices offer some implications for improvements in requirement mismatch handing process. The findings are consolidated in five propositions.

Proposition 1: market driven requirements are more flexible than bespoken requirements while resolving functional mismatches in OTS based development.

The result suggests that the choice of requirement mismatch handling approaches varies across projects and most likely do not depend on project context factors, such as: team size, application domain, development life cycle, portion of OSS components and component selection phase. Therefore, the decision whether to modify OSS components or influence requirements is influenced by the nature of requirements and components themselves, e.g. type of requirement source. Among five projects with requirements from internal development teams, four of them have requirements postponed. The requirements from internal teams (or market-driven type of requirement) would be more flexible due to consideration of given functionality and implementation effort. The requirements from external customers (or bespoken type of requirement) are less flexible due to contractual predetermination in required functionality.

Proposition 2: A functional mismatch with a flexible requirement is resolved by postponing the requirement, rarely by changing it.

Although flexibility of requirement does not hinder the requirement priority, it is beneficial for mismatch resolution by extending the resolution time. Regardless of requirement source type, requirement is normally in the first priority. Therefore, the definition of requirement flexibility is associated with the ability to postpone requirements, rather than with the ability to change or give up on the requirements [11]. Postponing requirements often occurs with customer negotiation and debugging process.

Proposition 3: A small functional mismatch is resolved by modifying OSS component while a large functional mismatch is resolved by replacing it by another OSS component or a COTS one.

Our data suggests that the detail level of requirement and the size of components influence how mismatches are resolved. Given the flexibility of OSS components, the small mismatch (a fine-grained requirement with small component) require less effort to modify or rewrite while a large mismatch take much more effort to close the gap by adapting the components. This observation recommends that component selection in early phase, such as requirement elicitation, would be risky when the requirement is not clear enough and in general level. However, selecting components for fine-grained requirements in later phase, such as design or implementation also have threats of extra cost in integrating small components.

Proposition 4: Component reliability issues lead to postponed requirements by fixing the component or replacing it.

Reliability is one of the most concerned non-functional attributes while adopting OSS component. It also receive contradict perception from interviewees. It is difficult to correctly evaluate component reliability in component selection phases. The information that are used as early quality indicators and selection criteria, such as number of fixed bugs, component reputation and project roadmap, is not sufficient. The problem in this non-functional attributes would influence functional requirements by delaying the accomplishment of these requirements. The fewer bugs in components would take more time to fix while many bugs in components would require for the replacement. In later case, the selection and matching process will be conducted again, which cost much more time and effort. This suggests a better care of non-functional requirements of OSS components when selecting components.

Proposition 5: A functional mismatch that gets support from the OSS community is associated with a perceived increase in satisfaction regarding component maintainability.

Three collaborative resolving requirement mismatch involve customers, OSS community and commercial vendor, alternatively. Keeping changes in components synchronized with OSS community is beneficial for fixing and maintaining these components. In resolving requirement mismatch, community involvement would not only reduce the developer's effort in maintaining the components but also bringing more confidence on component quality as "given enough eyeballs, all bugs are shallow". As maintainability is as important as reliability for selecting suitable OSS components, practitioners should look for components that are not only reliable but also has a high bug fixing rate.

6   Threats to Validity

In this study, most variables are taken directly, or with little modification, from the existing literatures. To ensure that the given concepts are understood correctly by the interviewees, we sent the interview guide with a detailed description of the survey to the interviewee beforehand. One of the possible threats to the internal validity is our misunderstanding of respondents' answers. Although at least two interviewers carried out the interviews and there was only one interviewee in each interview, we taped all interviews. Listening to the tape helped to ensure correct interpretation of answers and comments. However, having an independent (third) person to listen to the tape might increase data quality. During the interview, we tried to ensure the interviewee understand what they are asked. The primary threat to external validity is that the study is based on few and possibly not typical projects. In general, most empirical studies in industry suffer from non-representative participation. In the data sampling step, we tried to have projects with all sizes, from various domain application and have different portion of OSS adoption in the projects. Besides, this study is still a preliminary study. Future studies with more interviews will be implemented to give more statistically significant results.

7   Summary and Future Works

The main purpose of this study is to gain understanding of how requirements mismatches are collaboratively handled in OSS adoption projects. We found two scenarios in solving functional mismatches. The main resolution approach is to get the components changed by the development team themselves, OSS community or commercial vendor. The choice of adapting or replacing components depends on the mismatch size, component reliability and level of community support. The other resolution approach is to influence requirements, often by postponing requirements. This scenario is associated with issues of component reliability and maintainability. Non-functional requirements are satisfactorily achieved by using OSS components in general. Finally, we found that the customer involvement enhance functional mismatch resolution while OSS community collaboration could improve non-functional mismatch resolution.

The study identifies topics for future research on the requirement mismatches handling process. One of the potential future extensions of the study is a supporting framework for OSS component selection decision-making. The main purpose of the framework is to find out indicators of components reliability and maintainability from the OSS component community. Besides, some of the context factors show potential impact on requirement mismatch resolution decision, such as source of requirement or reliability of components. However, we do not have enough data to conduct a quantitative analysis on these factors. In future studies with more data points, a more quantitative analysis of impacting factors could be implemented. Last but not least, we highlighted the importance of stakeholder involvement in mismatch resolving process. The deeper understanding of stakeholder involvement would help to improve the matching process.

Acknowledgements. This work has been supported by the Spanish project TIN2010-19130-C02-01 and partly funded by the Industrial Excellence Center EASE - Embedded Applications Software Engineering, (http://ease.cs.lth.se).

References

1. Hauge, Ø., Ayala, C.P., Conradi, R.: Adoption of Open Source Software in Software-Intensive Industry - A Systematic Literature Review. Information and Software Technology 52(11), 1133–1154 (2010)
2. Alves, C.: COTS-Based Requirements Engineering. In: Cechich, A., Piattini, M., Vallecillo, A. (eds.) Component-Based Software Quality. LNCS, vol. 2693, pp. 21–39. Springer, Heidelberg (2003)
3. Parra, A., Seaman, C., Basili, V., Kraft, S., Condon, S., Burke, S., Yakimovich, D.: The Package-Based Development Process in the Flight Dynamics Division. In: 22nd Software Engineering Workshop, NASA/Goddard Space Flight Center, pp. 21–56 (1997)
4. Alves, C., Finkelstein, A.: Negotiating Requirements for COTS-Based Systems. In: 8th Int. Workshop on Requirements Engineering: Foundation for Software Quality, Essen (2002)
5. Li, J., Conradi, R., Bunse, C., Torchiano, M., Slyngstad, O., Morisio, M.: Development with Off-the-Shelf Components: 10 Facts. IEEE Software 26(2), 80–87 (2009)
6. Morisio, M., Seaman, C.B., Basili, V.R., Parra, A.T., Kraft, S.E., Condon, S.E.: COTS-based software development: processes and open issues. Journal of System and Software 61(3), 189–189 (2002)
7. Mohamed, A., Ruhe, G., Eberlein, A.: COTS Selection: Past, Present, and Future. In: 14th IEEE Int. Conf. on the Engineering of Computer-Based Systems, Tucson, pp. 103–114 (2007)
8. Rolland, C.: Requirements Engineering for COTS based Systems. Information and Software Technology 41, 985–990 (1999)
9. Mohamed, A., Ruhe, G., Eberlein, A.: MiHOS: an approach to support handling the mismatches between system requirements and COTS products. Requirement Engineering 12(3), 127–143 (2007)
10. Stol, K.-J., Ali Babar, M.: A Comparison Framework for Open Source Software Evaluation Methods. In: Ågerfalk, P., Boldyreff, C., González-Barahona, J.M., Madey, G.R., Noll, J. (eds.) OSS 2010. IFIP AICT, vol. 319, pp. 389–394. Springer, Heidelberg (2010)
11. Morisio, M., Seaman, C.B., Parra, A.T., Basili, V.R., Kraft, S.E., Condon, S.E.: Investigating and improving a COTS-based software development. In: 22nd International Conference on Software Engineering, Limerick, pp. 32–41 (2000)
12. Höst, M., Oručević-Alagić, A., Runeson, P.: Usage of Open Source in Commercial Software Product Development – Findings from a Focus Group Meeting. In: Caivano, D., Oivo, M., Baldassarre, M.T., Visaggio, G. (eds.) PROFES 2011. LNCS, vol. 6759, pp. 143–155. Springer, Heidelberg (2011)
13. Peach, B., Reuschenbach, B.: Open Source Requirements Engineering. In: 14th International Requirements Engineering Conference, Minnesota, pp. 252–259 (2006)
14. Maiden, N.A.M., Ncube, C.: Acquiring Requirements for Commercial Off-The-Shelf Package Selection. IEEE Software 15(2), 46–56 (1998)
15. Lauesen, S.: COTS tenders and integration requirements. Requirements Engineering 11(2), 111–122 (2006)
16. Li, J., Conradi, R., Slyngstad, O.P.N., Bunse, C., Torchiano, C.M., Morisio, M.: An Empirical Study on Decision Making in Off-the-shelf Component-based Development. In: Proc. 28th International Conference on Software Engineering, Shanghai, pp. 897–900 (May 2006)

17. Chung, L., Nixon, B.A., Yu, E., Mylopoulos, J.: Non-Functional Requirements in Software Engineering. Kluwer Academic Publishers, Norwell (2000)
18. Jacobs, S.: Introducing Measurable Quality Requirements: A Case Study. In: 4th ISRE 1999, pp. 172–179. IEEE Comput. Soc. (1999)
19. Cruzes, D.S., Dybå, T.: Recommended Steps for Thematic Synthesis in Software Engineering. In: 5th Empirical Software Engineering and Measurement, Banff (2011)
20. Ayala, C.P., Hauge, Ø., Conradi, R., Franch, X., Li, J.: Selection of Third Party Software in Off-The-Shelf-Based Software Development - An Interview Study with Industrial Practitioners. Journal of Systems and Software 84, 620–637 (2011)
21. Berntsson Svensson, R., Gorschek, T., Regnell, B.: Quality Requirements in Practice: An Interview Study in Requirements Engineering for Embedded Systems. In: Glinz, M., Heymans, P. (eds.) REFSQ 2009. LNCS, vol. 5512, pp. 218–232. Springer, Heidelberg (2009)

Appendix

Part 1: Background Questions on Project and System (to be filled up prior to the meeting)

1.1 What was the mean annual staff-size of the project (both full- and part-time employees)?

1.2 What part of the staff had previous experience with OSS-based development?

1.3 Did you have previous experience with OSS-based development before joining the project?

1.4 What was the total effort of the project?

1.5 What was (roughly) the starting time of the project?

1.6 What was the time of the first complete delivery from the project?

1.7 What were the major application domain(s) of the system?

1.8 Where did the requirements come from?

1.9 How were the functional Requirements described with regard to level of detail?

1.10 What was the overall, software development process/environment of the project?

Part 2: Identify initially some OSS Component candidates that may satisfy the Requirements

2.1 In which lifecycle phases were such OSS Components selected?

2.2 How was the search process and initial evaluation for such OSS Components done?

2.3 What were the main information sources in deciding whether the OSS Component candidates from point 2.2 could (partly) match your functional Requirements?

Part 3: Final evaluation and decision process to resolve possible Requirements mismatches vs. OSS Components

3.1 What did you do when the functional Requirements could not be sufficiently matched by OSS Component candidates?

3.2 How well were the major non-functional Requirements ("quality attributes") achieved?

3.3 Focusing on the 5 most important functionalities from the Requirements, can you name and explain the matching OSS Components that you finally integrated into your system?

3.4 How big part of the system do the OSS Components now occupy?

High-Level Requirements Management and Complexity Costs in Automotive Development Projects: A Problem Statement

Tim Gülke[1], Bernhard Rumpe[1], Martin Jansen[2], and Joachim Axmann[2]

[1] Software Engineering, RWTH Aachen University
[2] Volkswagen AG, Wolfsburg

Abstract. Effective requirements management plays an important role when it comes to the support of product development teams in the automotive industry. A precise positioning of new cars in the market is based on features and characteristics described as requirements as well as on costs and profits. [Question/problem] However, introducing or changing requirements does not only impact the product and its parts, but may lead to overhead costs in the OEM due to increased complexity. The raised overhead costs may well exceed expected gains or costs from the changed requirements. [Principal ideas/results] By connecting requirements with direct and overhead costs, decision making based on requirements could become more valuable. [Contribution] This problem statement results from a detailed examination of the effects of requirements management practices on process complexity and vice versa as well as on how today's requirements management tools assist in this respect. We present findings from a joined research project of RWTH Aachen University and Volkswagen.

Keywords: requirements management, complexity costs, automotive, product development.

1 Today's Requirements Management in Automotive Practice

The automotive industry is facing several challenges ranging from entirely new engine concepts to customer-configurable infotainment systems and networks of computers and infrastructure. The trend of increasing product complexity has not yet been stopped and is still gaining speed [9], which also leads to growing complex structures within the companies [12]. For the automotive industry, Schleich et al. [16] already linked increasing numbers of variants with rising complexity and overhead costs.

Requirements management plays a vital role by providing supportive processes and tools for the employees engaged in development activities [8,13]. Particularly in the process of defining a product's characteristics – e.g., what infotainment features will be available to the customer, how many different types of engines for which sort of fuels, or how many passengers the car will be designed

B. Regnell and D. Damian (Eds.): REFSQ 2012, LNCS 7195, pp. 94–100, 2012.

for – and later changes to those, requirements management aids in the engineers day to day work. For the last few years, ideas which have been developed in theory have proven themselves functional in practice, although much work still remains to be done [18]. This refers, e.g., to the application of templates in requirements elicitation, the usage of clear and non-ambiguous words, traceability in general and the inclusion of suppliers into the requirements work [6,15]. When two or three decades ago a single group of employees was able to keep track of the requirements for a car with pen and paper and in their heads, nowadays collected information is spread through countless documents, systems, and people. The evolutionary step from vehicle platforms to modules and modular toolkits makes it even more difficult, since now links between requirements and parts are not limited to one vehicle anymore. Requirements management can therefore be seen as a measure to handle the increasing complexity by providing a way of keeping all necessary information connected. It enables engineers to estimate the impact of proposed changes and equips the project leaders with powerful tools to track status.

The underlying concept of requirements management is traceability, which means the connection of different artifacts throughout one or multiple projects. Therefore, a requirements management tool can only be as good as the level of traceability it operates on when it comes to impact analysis of changes or additional requirements. So far, traceability connects most product-related things like parts, functions, all kind of documents and specifications, scenarios and tests with requirements. The amount to which this is done differs in companies and also in projects. The complexity of electronic systems in vehicles forces the automotive industry to maintain a high level of traceability within their projects [7]. This is why it is current practice to be able to estimate the costs of changes on a very detailed level, knowing the impact of a proposed change by tracing all connected artifacts.

Today, there are several programs available on the market supporting development teams in eliciting, organizing, tracing, linking, and generally managing requirements. Tools like IBM DOORS, Borland CaliberRM, Jama Contour, and others provide the ability to describe requirements in a specific way, implement hierarchies and most possess modeling-functionality for the underlying structure [5]. However, they're all limited to product-centric models and do not provide any way of including costs originating in processes far from the product (or even costs at all).

2   Requirements and Costs

Changes in requirements or the introduction of new requirements (regardless in what stage the current project is in) lead to three different types of costs:

1. **Investment Costs:** Costs originate from necessary investments into the development of a product and its parts. This includes, e.g., the purchase of tools and machines as well as the production of prototypes.

2. **Direct Costs:** These are the later internal "pricetags" on parts or whole systems, whether they're bought from a supplier or made in-house when it comes to the production of the car. There are usually targets defined for every individual part or function to stay within a defined price-range for the whole car with which it is placed on the market.

3. **Overhead/Indirect Costs:** Overhead costs are costs which occur in the production-phase of the car that cannot be related to a definite cost object (i.e. a vehicle sold on the market). They're generated by employees filling out excel-sheets, making phone-calls, etc.

If a requirement is added or changed, two things happen: First, additional investment costs are generated because a new or different feature is included into the car. Reasons behind the requirement can be manifold and range from competitors providing a new function with their vehicles that has to be matched to regulatory/legal problems. Second, overhead costs may rise due to an increased complexity in the processes of the company [16]. The estimation of investment costs for a proposed change is done very accurately, but mostly relies on the knowledge of the engineers regarding the type of the change. This slows down the decision process which then again slows down the early phases of a vehicle development project. Decision-makers are left with three choices when it comes to predicting the overall costs caused by a requirement:

1. Huge manual effort can be put into figuring out which departments are affected by a change (purchasing department? engineering? marketing? which ones exactly?) and then ask each of those to estimate the amount of work needed. These two steps are time- and cost-intensive and the results are not guaranteed to be exact.

2. Another way is to use a fixed amount of money based on prior experiences with similar changes. This might cause problems, since it's unclear whether this amount is accurate to the actual costs, but it's quick and feasible.

3. Last, those costs can simply be added to the affected departments overhead costs and not be counted against a project's budget.

While investment costs can at least be estimated, the prediction of the change of complexity in OEMs (and suppliers) is difficult and rarely done. A new variant, caused by a changed requirement, leaves only small traces in the company – e.g., one more line to be added to an MS Excel sheet, one more item to be synchronized between two systems, one more line in a report, etc. – and mostly causes administrative work [4]. It is estimated though, that if the number of variants are doubled, overhead costs rise 20%-30% because of increased complexity [19]. Strikingly it is the combined number of small steps that can cause this increase, but they are not part of the decision process, since it is difficult to predict where exactly what amount of additional work is caused [16].

Complexity's impact on products is currently under research and approaches are being proposed [11], some work is done with regard to complexity [12] and of course many new developments in the field of requirements management are being published [10], although many focus on software-only projects [14]. It seems promising to combine these different areas of research for practical use and extend the current focus of the product in requirements management to processes and their complexity. Almefelt et al. [2] for example already recommend the conduction of a cost/benefit-analysis for requirements changes.

3   Example

Automotive OEMs follow a combined sequential/iterative process-model during the development of a new vehicle. This leads to an early declaration of requirements in a so-called *product definition phase*, where different business units collect, exchange and adjust their requirements for the new car. Based on an early bill of materials, costs are estimated for the realization of the requirements. These costs include necessary investment costs and expected direct costs of the car in later production. Requirements may lead to a decrease of direct costs, e.g., by making a single part of the car available in two or more different variants, some applying inexpensive materials, the others with the standard ones and using these accordingly in different variants of the car (e.g., in different "lines" or brands). If the installation rate of the lower-cost part is high enough, revenues will be raised.

However, the new variant of the part has not only to be constructed or programmed, bought from suppliers, stored in factories, databases, etc. but to be maintained in different systems and processes as an artifact – and these make up of most for the overhead costs. It has already been published in Schleich et al. [16] that with an increased variability, overhead costs rise in the field of production and logistics, but the figures of how this rising variability combined with construction kits and platforms affects costs in product development and change processes cannot yet be answered. It is therefore to be suspected that changed or new requirements might partially lead to costs that exceed revenues gained from them. If an accepted methodology and software were available that estimated how a requirement affects the companies complexity, the raise of overhead costs could at least be controlled. It can be assumed that certain topics might be decided differently, if complexity costs were considered in the decision-making process. Last, the approach would allow a cleanup of variants with complexity costs that are significantly higher than their revenues and thus lower a company's overhead costs.

4   Extending Traceability

Today's automotive companies are confronted with increasing complexity not only in it's products, but also in their internal organizations. This is seldom considered when it comes to requirements changes during vehicle development projects. Doing this manually for each change is error-prone and cost-intensive. Requirements management tools should widen their focus from a straight product view towards a process view that includes all aspect of a company since very few tools provide the ability to model processes at all or they do only focus on automating simple tasks and routines.

The key to this problem might be the thorough modeling of corporate structures and artifacts. Making knowledge of this kind available to software will enable it to consider far more aspects of decisions than it does now. But so far, the creation of models from a company's artifacts decoupled from a concrete software project is seldom done, since the benefit is not immediately visible. Even the formal description of processes will only be done if the need arises to automate some parts of the process or in optimization projects.

But first of all, requirements management tools need to implement cost-structures (e.g., from product data management systems) and connect them with their data models. This will enable decision-makers to anticipate how a certain change would affect direct costs. Afterwards, process-engineering tools like ARIS [1] can be connected to extend the decision-process by the inclusion of the affected processes. Once all this data is present, modeling of artifacts inside the processes can begin, providing an even deeper insight into how, e.g., a new variant will be processed throughout the whole company.

The mentioned topics can be seen as an extension to the already powerful concept of traceability. Making not only parts or documents, but all artifacts of a company traceable, will enable decision-makers to estimate investment costs faster and predict the change of complexity. This can only be done if tools are available that have the ability to include these artifacts or at least be able to communicate with systems that do.

A company-wide repository for models of artifacts like processes or documents would need a standardized description language, which is able to both capture the models and set them into context with each other. Efficient modeling tools need to be available as well that support model developers in creating those models fast enough to keep up with the pace of change in a company. Next, requirements management tools would need to use the available models and their contexts and wave them into their own traceability model – and maybe even provide a way other tools could reuse those models.

The research area of semantic networks already provides languages and concepts to capture information as described above. Connecting these with the powerful tools available in the requirements management world might prove valuable. Languages like OWL/RDFS which are thoroughly documented [3] could be used to construct a knowledge repository that requirements management tools could use. Approaches providing a way of automated ontology creation for the gathering of this semantic data might be helpful [17].

Knowing the financial benefit beforehand is difficult, since the costs that are going to be addressed are not traceable so far – otherwise this problem would not exist. Therefore, only the careful introduction of an approach like this will definitely show its benefits. But since the automotive world is getting more complex every day with a widened portfolio in brands and products and more detailed markets being all deeply connected, it needs the ideas and concepts traceability and requirements management provide.

There is no denying that more research is needed on how requirements and costs play together. Also, a solution for the efficient and easy modeling of process artifacts is necessary, as well as how to use that knowledge in a requirements management tool. To come to an end, not only might this problem be an automotive-industry specific one, but it could also be extended into other domains.

References

1. ARIS, ARIS Platform, http://www.softwareag.com/de/products/aris_platform/default.asp (visited 2011-12-14)
2. Almefelt, L., Berglund, F., Nilsson, P., Malmqvist, J.: Requirements management in practice: findings from an empirical study in the automotive industry. Research in Engineering Design 17(3), 113–134 (2006)
3. Antoniou, G., van Harmelen, F.: A Semantic Web Primer, 2nd edn. Cooperative Information Systems series. The MIT Press (2008)
4. Bensberg, F., vom Brocke, J., Schultz, M.B.: Trendberichte zum Controlling: Festschrift für Heinz Lothar Grob (German Edition), 1st edn. Physica-Verlag HD (2004)
5. Bühne, S., Lauenroth, K., Pohl, K.: Anforderungsmanagement in der Automobilindustrie: Variabilität in Zielen, Szenarien und Anforderungen. In: Dadam, P., Reichert, M. (eds.) Beiträge der 34. Jahrestagung der Gesellschaft für Informatik e.V (GI). GI-Edition - Lecture Notes in Informatics (LNI), vol. 2, pp. 23–27 (2004)
6. Fricker, S.: Pragmatic Requirements Communication: The Handshaking Approach. Ph.D. thesis, Universität Zürich (2009)
7. Gladigau, J.: Anforderungsmanagement - Vom Anfänger zum Profi. OBJEKTspektrum RE/2010 (2010)
8. Hood, C., Wiedemann, S., Fichtinger, S., Pautz, U.: Introduction to Requirements Management. In: Requirements Management, pp. 59–78. Springer, Heidelberg (2008)
9. Houdek, F.: Requirements Engineering Erfahrungen in Projekten der Automobilindustrie. Softwaretechnik-Trend 23 (2003)
10. Langer, B., Tautschnig, M.: Navigating the Requirements Jungle. In: Leveraging Applications of Formal Methods, Verification and Validation, pp. 354–368 (2009)
11. Lindemann, U., Maurer, M.: Facing Multi-Domain Complexity in Product Development The Future of Product Development. In: Krause, F.-L. (ed.) The Future of Product Development, ch.35, pp. 351–361. Springer, Heidelberg (2007)
12. Lindemann, U., Maurer, M., Braun, T.: Structural Complexity Management: An Approach for the Field of Product Design, 1st edn. Springer, Heidelberg (2008)
13. Luhmann, J., Langenheim, F., Hofmann, P.M.: Herausforderungen eines Anforderungsmanagement im Automotivbereich. In: ReConf. 2007, HOOD Group, Munich, Germany (2007)
14. Pohl, K.: Requirements Engineering. Dpunkt.Verlag GmbH, 2., korrigierte Auflage. edn. (2007)
15. Roy, R., Kerr, C., Sackett, P.: Requirements Management for the Extended Automotive Enterprise. In: ElMaraghy, H.A., ElMaraghy, W.H. (eds.) Advances in Design. Springer Series in Advanced Manufacturing, ch. 22, pp. 269–279. Springer, London (2006)
16. Schleich, H., Schaffer, J., Scavard, L.F.: Managing complexity in automotive production. In: 19th International Conference on Production Research (2007)

17. Wang, Y., Völker, J., Haase, P.: Towards Semi-automatic Ontology Building Supported by Large-scale Knowledge Acquisition. In: AAAI Fall Symposium On Semantic Web for Collaborative Knowledge Acquisition. vol. FS-06-06, pp. 70–77. AAAI Press, Arlington (2006)

18. Weber, M., Weisbrod, J.: Requirements engineering in automotive development-experiences and challenges. In: Proceedings of IEEE Joint International Conference on Requirements Engineering, pp. 331–340 (2002)

19. Wirtz, B.W.: Komplexitätsmanagement. In: Multi-Channel-Marketing, pp. 354–362. Gabler (2008)

Choose Your Creativity: Why and How Creativity in Requirements Engineering Means Different Things to Different People

Martin Mahaux[1], Alistair Mavin[2], and Patrick Heymans[1,3]

[1] PReCISE Research Centre, University of Namur, Belgium
{Martin.Mahaux,Patrick.Heymans}@fundp.ac.be
[2] Rolls-Royce PLC, Derby, UK
Alistair.Mavin@rolls-royce.com
[3] INRIA Lille-Nord Europe, Université de Lille 1 – LIFL – CNRS, France

Abstract. [**Context and Motivation**] The word "creativity" is used widely in business and academia, but its meaning may differ greatly depending on context. This may cause confusion in the minds of requirements engineers who have to determine which kinds of creativity are relevant to their project and which creativity tools to use. [**Question/Problem**] The main goal of this work is to understand why and how the meaning of the word "creativity" varies, and study the impacts of these variations on requirements engineering. [**Principal ideas / results**]. A comparative review of creativity-related literature from Social Sciences and Requirements Engineering was performed. [**Contributions**] This study results in a new framework for understanding the precise local meaning of creativity used in a specific context, before deciding on the adequate support for it. Since creativity in RE is still a relatively new topic, research directions are also proposed.

1   Introduction

Creativity is now recognised as an important topic in Requirements Engineering (RE) [1]. However, it is still a fuzzy concept for the Requirements Engineer (REer). Consider, for example, that at the kick-off meeting of a new development project, the sponsor emphasised the importance of creativity. Now, as the REer on this project, you feel in trouble: are you supposed to get together in a funny workshop using sticky notes? Or are you supposed to use new technology? Do you have to make a revolution in your product line? Or do you have to find new ways of collaborating? Are you supposed to take risks? Should you challenge the very problems you are asked to solve?

As this story indicates, there are many ways one could be creative during the development of a socio-technical system, and many ways one could support creativity during the project. In its early phases, the REer will manage an important part of the creativity on the project. So the REer has to choose a certain creativity, and find ways to support it. The Research Question of this paper can be formulated this way:

B. Regnell and D. Damian (Eds.): REFSQ 2012, LNCS 7195, pp. 101–116, 2012.
© Springer-Verlag Berlin Heidelberg 2012

RQ: How can we help the REer to find the adequate creativity for a project?

To address this question, this paper proposes an actionable framework that the REer can use to guide interviews with projects sponsors, and to structure the results in a way that a specific creativity is determined.

After a brief description of the method (Section 2) and related work (Section 3), the rest of this paper summarises the history of the understanding of creativity in the Social Sciences (Section 4). It then reviews the definitions of creativity in RE (Section 5), and introduces a two-dimensional framework meant to explain *why* and *how* the meaning of creativity varies in RE (Section 6). Concrete usage of the framework in practice is also discussed (Section 7). Finally, creativity in RE is re-examined in the light of the proposed framework, which triggers various questions and new research directions (Section 8).

2   Method

In order to grasp what was lacking in REer's understanding of creativity in general (a pre-requisite to understanding the creativity needed on his specific project), a comparative literature review on creativity in RE and in other fields was performed. Doing so, the authors realized that bringing a summary of the understanding of creativity in social sciences would benefit to the RE community. During the review, the authors also gathered elements that had an influence on creativity, as well as elements characterizing creativity itself, and analyzed which of these would apply to RE. The first were called *contextual factors,* and the latter *dimensions,* and were summarized in the framework described below.

The comparative review involved selecting appropriate papers in many disciplines. RE literature was initially collected from reference databases (DBLP [3], Google Scholar [4]) using keyword searches. These initial results were manually filtered from an analysis of the abstracts. Snowballing (discovery of new papers through analysis of a paper's references) was then applied until no new significant reference could be found.

For the other disciplines, the sheer volume of multi-disciplinary creativity-related literature made rigorous analysis impractical. For the Social Sciences, Keith Sawyer's book "Explaining Creativity" [5] was used as a guide. This recent book, rich with approximately 500 references, sets out to be a summary of what is known in the field about creativity. This prominent source introduces bias in this study. It was however judged preferable to be biased by a recognised figure in the field than by the inevitably superficial analysis that would have otherwise been made. The survey was complemented by literature from Design, Management Sciences and the Arts.

3   Related Work

This work builds on existing work, which is referenced throughout the report, so citing all sources here would be redundant. However, the relationship with Nguyen and Shanks' framework for understanding creativity in RE [6] merits specific explanation. The two studies share initial goals (understanding creativity in RE) and many opinions, but also partly diverge in their results. This work uses different sources, leading to a separate model and new research directions. Although there are significant overlaps with Nguyen and Shanks, the architecture and formulation of the frameworks are quite distinct. They suggest creativity can be understood by analysing in turn the creative *product*, the *process* leading to that product, the *people* behind that process, the *domain of application* and the *context* surrounding the project. In contrast, the present study structures its framework in such a way that contextual factors and creativity dimensions are distinguished, and the interactions between factors and dimensions are emphasized. This study does not claim more validity than Nguyen and Shanks' study, but rather suggests another viewpoint that is likely to be complementary. An empirical comparison would be helpful to assess the applicability of each of these frameworks in specific situations.

4 A Brief History of Creativity in the Social Sciences

In his book *Explaining Creativity* [5], Sawyer describes the history of the understanding of creativity. Starting in the 1950's, psychologists tried to define creativity as a personality trait. Consequently they attempted to measure it, similarly to using an IQ test to measure intelligence. By the 1970's, their failure was clear, and it convinced many psychologists that creativity is not a distinct personality trait or mental process, but a combination of everyday cognitive processes [5]. Studies that tried to relate creativity to mental illness or to explain creativity based on the brain's biological components failed for the same reasons; that creativity is not a personality trait. Another reason for psychologists' failure to define creativity is that creativity is a culturally and historically specific idea that changes from one country to another, and from one century to another (as noted by Sawyer [5]).

Understanding that creativity was a combination of more basic cognitive processes, cognitive psychologists studied and analysed creativity as a process. Major contributions include those from Wallas [7] and Hadamard [8], who argued that creativity involved four main phases: *preparation* (accumulation of knowledge), *incubation* (cognitive release), *illumination* (the "aha", or "eureka" moment) and *verification* (evaluation and elaboration of ideas). Boden [9] explained three possible phases that the human brain experiences during a creative problem solving process: *exploration* of a possible solution space, *combination* of two or more existing ideas, and *transformation* of the solution space to make previously impossible things possible. More pragmatic contributions include those from Osborn (Brainstorming, Creative Problem Solving (CPS)) [10] and Gordon (Synectics) [11] who developed processes for creative problem solving.

While cognitivist models have proven useful, criticisms exist, in particular towards the sequential nature of the aforementioned creativity process. Some researchers (such as Rothenberg and Vinacke in [5]) argue that Wallas' phases are not easy to distinguish from one another in practice, and adopt an approach where all the steps are quasi-concurrent in the creative person's head, describing very short cycles. The single important illumination moment is also replaced by many mini-insights, supported by hard work (Weisberg in [5]). To illustrate this, they take the example of a painter, whose creativity is developed as a back-and-forth movement from an idea in the head to its elaboration as a set of brushstrokes, and the immediate evaluation (judging the observable result) that will lead to the next idea. Cycles are very short, so that the elaboration and evaluation instantly feed back into the preparation process. This is similar to the work of Philosopher John Dewey [12], who suggested in 1910 that human thought is a continual repeating cycle of problem, solution and evaluation.

By the 1980's, psychologists started to think that they needed the help of other social sciences (such as sociology, anthropology and history) to understand creativity. This lead to the adoption of a sociocultural approach, defined as follows [5]: creativity is specific to a *domain*, of which the existing artefacts and conventions are the input to the creative *person*'s own work; the latter will then be judged as creative or not by influential people: the *field*. The creative artefact, new in its domain and judged valuable by the field, is then added to the domain. The creative person is one that is able to come up with such artefacts. Research, artistic disciplines and business all require an explanation of the sociocultural approach to creativity [5]. Many authors share this view, but fail to emphasize the importance of domain and field, and rather add an emphasis on *surprisingness*. For example, Boden suggests that creativity is the ability to come up with ideas or artefacts that are new, surprising and valuable [9]. Similarly, Sternberg and Lubart define creativity as the ability to produce work that is both novel (original and unexpected) and appropriate [13].

In the sociocultural view, the short creative cycles in the creator's head are embedded in a macro-cycle at the level of the sociocultural entity formed by the person, domain and field [5]. As in a fractal, the small follows the same pattern as the large. For example, in painting, each brushstroke entails preparation, incubation, illumination and verification. The final painting follows the same cycle. Indeed, the artist lives in a society that possesses a culture, is aware of centuries of painting tradition, and continuously exchanges with peers in one way or another (*preparation* and *incubation*). Then, once the canvas is painted (*illumination*), gallerists evaluate it and chose to promote it. This selection provides feedback on what is valuable, which is complemented by the public choices (*verification*). This endorses the view that, even in disciplines like painting that are known to be solitary, no creative work exists in isolation, as our interactions with the field and the domain are important contributors to the creative process [14]. Collaboration is absolutely central to creativity in the sociocultural view [5], [15]. As Graham Bell stated: *"Great discoveries and improvements invariably involve the cooperation of many minds!"* (cited in [5]).

These advances led some researchers to focus on group creativity while their predecessors had mainly focused on the individual [5]. Their use of the sociocultural model challenged one of the main western myths about creativity: that it is the result of an unconscious dream of a lone unrecognized genius having a sudden burst of insight [5]. The sociocultural view argues that creativity is a collaborative, social phenomenon that requires hard work and is made of many mini-insights [5], [15]. It suggests that group creativity is qualitatively different from individual creativity, and it must be analysed as a collective social phenomenon, incorporating concepts from sociology, communication and organizational behaviour [15].

5   A Review of Creativity Definitions in RE Literature

The DBLP [3] database returns around 700 publications for the main RE source, the IEEE "RE" conference series. Selecting papers using the search query "creativ" OR "invent" OR "innovat" in the title returns only 13 papers. As a comparison, the word "goal" yields 45 references, and the word "scenario" yields 39 references. This gives a crude indication of the maturity of the creativity sub-field within RE.

Many of the RE authors have chosen a simple interpretation of the sociocultural definition for creativity; that creativity is something novel and valuable. However, they frequently omit definitions of the terms *novel* and *valuable*, and rarely mention the *person-domain-field* triad. Consequently, the emphasis on collaboration that the sociocultural approach suggests is also neglected in most cases. For example Jones *et al.* [16] cite [9] and [13] above, while Nguyen and Shanks [6] chose *novelty*, *value* and *surprisingness* as three characteristics of the creative outcome in RE. Mich *et al.* [17] also insist on surprisingness, Regev *et al.* use the sociocultural *person-domain-field* model, and add this intuitive formulation: *"Creative as the contrary of usual, obvious, i.e. unexpected, unusual, new. Independent thinking. Taking distances from the rules. Breaking the norms (...)"* [18]. Pennel and Maiden formulate this practical definition: *"From a practical point of view, generating genuinely creative ideas was less important than to enable participants to produce ideas for requirements that would not normally have been elicited."* [19].

Maiden *et al.* [1] resolve the creativity definition problem by using the proxy of the Creative Problem Solving (CPS) process [10], a framework that suggests a series of steps to follow in order to be creative. Taking this view, any discipline that follows the CPS is likely to be a creative discipline. Therefore, if a software development project follows the CPS in the earlier stages corresponding to RE, then the project must be creative. They propose a way to measure the novelty of requirements, by computing dissimilarity between new requirements documents and existing ones. This ongoing research is expected to help define what *novelty* means for requirements.

Nguyen and Cybulski [20] chose an alternate view of creativity. They see it as an act of constructivist learning; an authentic and (inter-)personal construction of knowledge. Their model involves three dimensions: *endogenous* (learning from the inner self), *exogenous* (from others) and *dialectic* (with others). They argue that in order to be creative, both analysts and developers must become learners in their application domain and in the domain of general problem solving.

Nguyen and Shanks [6] argue that *"Creativity in problem solving involves individuals engaged in a cognitive and social collaborative process to produce a novel and valuable outcome, which will be subject to evaluation within a specific domain and social context."* This perspective is clearly indebted to the sociocultural definition of creativity, by acknowledging the importance of collaboration and the *de facto* situated character of creativity. Ocker focused on the development of distributed computer systems to support group interaction. Consequently, his definition of creativity looks at the collaborative side of creativity: *"Creativity is a complex interaction of person and situation that takes place at both the individual and group levels."* [21].

6   Why and How the Meaning of Creativity Changes

Creativity is all about bringing something new in a domain, which will be judged valuable by a field. However, the breadth of discussion on this simple definition in the Social Sciences suggests that creativity cannot be reduced to a single clear concept. For a REer, it is important to define creativity for a particular organisation, or for a particular project within that organisation, or even for a particular moment within a project. Indeed, within each project, combinations of different creativities appear to be the most likely reality.

This section reports three *contextual factors* that explain *why* creativity can be understood differently in RE, and five *dimensions* that explain qualitatively *how* creativity's meaning can vary in RE. Together they form a conceptual framework for choosing and defining a project-specific creativity, which is represented graphically on Figure 1. For each of the fifteen combinations of contextual factor and dimension, there are possibly two important questions to ask. The first assumes a given context: *"In what context am I working, and how does that impact this dimension of creativity for me?"*. The second goes in the reverse direction, and assumes that one has specific goals for creativity: *"What is my desired value for this dimension, and how should I change my context consequently?"*. In practice, both context and goals are likely to be partly given and partly free to define. In any case, both have to be discovered in order to choose a specific creativity. Consequently, we expect that the practitioner will at times ask the first question, at other times the second, and frequently both.

Below, each of the contextual factors and dimensions are presented and discussed in detail. As for now, this study only points the practitioner to good questions he should ask. It illustrates the relevance of these questions by briefly discussing the likely interactions between contextual factors and dimensions (labelled with *"Interactions:"* at the end of each of the sub-sections in section 6.2). It must be understood that these questions may be extremely difficult to answer. For example, the contextual factor "culture" is probably an even broader concept than creativity is. So understanding the interactions between both can be a very tricky job, and certainly is for a REer who is not a specialist of these questions. In the future, it is hoped that research can help in giving good answers to these good questions. To this end, this paper systematically suggests appropriate Research Agenda items (numbered with *"RAx:"* at the end of each of the sub-sections in sections 6.1 and 6.2).

6.1 Contextual Factors

Culture. Culture is the set of shared values, goals, attitudes, and practices that characterises a group of people. Culture is subject to changes over time. As mentioned above, the notion of creativity depends on culture and history [5]. For example, before the Renaissance, a creative painter was one who was able to accurately reproduce nature. In traditional cultures, artistic creativity was linked with the ability to communicate with superior spirits. In modern western cultures, an artist's creativity is often seen as the exteriorisation of their unique inner self.

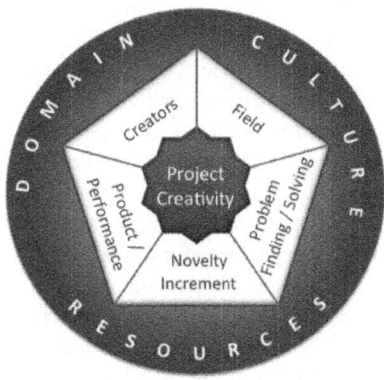

Fig. 1. Three contextual factors and five dimensions for creativity in RE

In recent years, the way organizations undertake creative efforts has changed, including in the software industry, and consequently in RE. For example, Yilmaz discusses modern conceptions of creativity in Software Engineering, such as collaborative creativity, open innovation and socio-technical ecologies [22]. The creativity that REers must consider on a project is likely to be very different today than five or ten years ago. Additionally, not only does each organization have a unique culture, but each of its sites might have a different way of implementing that culture, and each project will have its own "local" culture. For these reasons, cultural impacts ensure that no two RE projects ever have the same relation to creativity.

All the definitions of creativity used in RE literature assume a modern, western vision of creativity. This is implicit and most likely due to the fact RE research essentially exists in the modern western culture. Sawyer argues that a characteristic of the modern western vision of creativity is its focus on originality, in the sense of "uncommon" or "surprising" [5]. Originality is also a key requirement for academic excellence, and industry sometime argues that originality must precede value. In the RE literature, creativity definitions emphasise words like "surprising" and "not normal". What is not clear, however, is why RE creativity is so interested in surprise. Is it rational to have a preference for *unexpected* value (surprise) over *expected* value (no surprise)? Surprise is a scary word for some managers [18]. Some of them even reject creativity upfront as they think it is *novel and surprising* instead of *novel and valuable,* as defined in the sociocultural definition of creativity above. It appears that cultural bias might play an important hidden role here.

This discussion leads us to identify the following research agenda (RA) items:

RA1. Explore the relationship between culture and creativity in RE.
RA2. Is RE research biased towards surprisingness? If so, what are the positive and negative consequences of this bias?

Application Domain. Authors like Baer and Kaufman [23] suggest that creativity entails both domain-independent and domain-specific elements. Domain-independent factors include characteristics and skills such as intelligence, motivation and openness. These imply that some personality traits will help you to be creative in more than one domain.

On the other hand, domain-specific factors are things that must be known about a domain in order to bring something new and valuable to it. These imply that a creative cook is not necessarily creative in science or music. This is consistent with the sociocultural view of creativity that requires a domain to define creativity. Consequently, when REers change their application domain, they change the nature of creativity. Furthermore, all application domains (video game industry or medical software, for example) have their own characteristics, including: a unique culture; a specific way to interact with a market; a level of competition; an innovation rate; an acceptable risk level. All of these factors, and more, drive different kinds of creativity for the REer to consider.

The application domain has an important influence on the whole software development process, including RE [24]. REers should be able to tailor RE processes to specific projects and situations. As soon as a project is different from the previous one to some degree, the RE process might also have to be novel to some degree, and hopefully be as valuable as possible. Building the right RE process is perhaps the first creative task for the REer. Some might argue that this is the most important, or even the *only*, place where the REer is responsible for the content of a creative artefact. This view is consistent with the Participatory Design view where requirements are the collective responsibility of the stakeholders, including the REer as a facilitator [25]. In this view, the REer should be as neutral as possible in terms of content, but as active as possible in the role of catalyst for value creation. This initiates discussion on the role of the REer who is, depending on the point of view, a translator, a discoverer, a business expert, a learner, an inventor, a facilitator, or some combination of these. The broader understanding of creativity reopens this important discussion, and offers a new point of view. In the RE literature, only Cybulski *et al.* [26] explicitly distinguish between the domain-specific and general abilities needed to be creative. They argue that research should clarify the distinctions, and education should support both explicitly.

RA3: Explore the relationship between Application Domain and creativity.

RA4: Explore the role of the REer in the creative process.

RA5: Clarify the distinction between general and domain-specific creative abilities in RE.

Resources (time, money, skills). The amount of resources available for a project will inevitably influence creativity. However, this relationship is certainly not as simple as "no money, no creativity". Indeed, money and time-pressure could be factors, or even triggers, for certain kinds of creativity. Studies have shown that recent movies budgets had no correlation with best picture awards and were negatively correlated with critical acclaim [27]. Cowen and Tabarrok [28] discuss how money and other resources lead artists to adopt different creative styles. In terms of human resources, it is implicit that group creativity can only be used when there is more than one participant available, and that any creative effort relies on suitable skills.

Lack of resources is a major factor preventing REers from producing good quality work in general [29]. Research on more resource-efficient RE techniques is in progress [30]. However, RE authors have different opinions on the impact of resources on creativity. Maiden *et al.* [1] recall that incubation requires time and that external consultants cost money, so lack of resources is a barrier to creativity in their view. While Gorshek *et al.* [31] recognise that innovation-driven requirements compete for resources with the day-to-day urgent requirements, they propose a lightweight creativity style to deal with that barrier. Finally, Regev *et al.* [18] take an opposite stance and claim that ample resources may not encourage creativity at all. Fricker and Seyff [30] suggest that smart collaboration processes and novel ways of doing RE can be the basis for increasing the productivity of requirements engineering, while reducing the required effort. Given these issues, it seems logical that RE should follow other disciplines and recognise that different quantities and types of resources will lead to different forms of creativity.

RA6: Explore the relationship between resources and creativity in RE.

6.2 Dimensions

The Creative Group. There is a qualitative difference between individual and group creativity [15]. The creative process in a person's head has only little similarity to the creative process within a group. Activities and outcomes are different. The relationship between creative individuals and creative teams is not simple; for example, the fact that brainstorming is usually inefficient [32] shows that it is not enough to put creative people together to have a creative team. The size of the group matters, as well as the way the members interact. Is the group a small informal group, a company, a community of interest, or the human society as a whole? Each group will have its own understanding of creativity and its own way to handle it.

Many authors claim that RE is essentially a collaborative social endeavour. For example, according to Arias *et al.* [33] and Boehm *et al.* [34], requirements emerge from the interactions, sometimes the conflicts, in the stakeholders group. Coughlan and Macredie [35] therefore adopt a more collaborative and emergent view of requirements elicitation. Holtzblatt and Beyer state: "*All aspects of Requirements definition ultimately succeed or fail based on how well people work together*" [36]. Having studied creativity workshops in some depth (see [37], for example), Maiden and colleagues also argue that collaboration is key in RE creativity. Maiden *et al.* [1] suggest tools and trainings to support collaboration, a research track that they continue to pursue. Through the constructivist learning framework, Nguyen and Cybulski [20] clearly distinguish between individual and collaborative creativity, and suggest that specific support is required for each. Innovative research in this direction was recently showcased at the RE conference [38].

The arguments above suggest that this dimension deserves particular attention in the RE domain. However, Nguyen and Shanks [6] stress the particularly low level of understanding of collaboration-centric processes. They identify this topic as a major research challenge, a view that is shared by the authors. Group creativity theories already exist [15] and could be transferred to RE to address this challenge.

Interactions: Some cultures promote individuality, some actively foster collaboration, others will be in between. In some domains, the complexity of interdependent systems will leave no other choice than explicit company-wide or even inter-company collaboration. In other domains, it will be possible to innovate alone. Collaboration is likely to require both time and skilled people, but in the appropriate circumstances, collaboration could be a way to save resources.

RA7: Explore how to support collaborative creativity in RE.

The Field. Authors see different types of creativity depending on the scale of the social recognition of the creative work [9], [39], [40]. The literature discusses the *field* and its *size*. Creativity ranges from everyday insights that an individual experiences (the field is just the creator); through hobby-level creativity (the field is a small local group of pairs); the creativity of the talented professional (the field is a set of important people working in an area); to creativity that leaves the creator's name in history (the field consists of thousands of people). For the socio-culturalists, creativity is by definition always relative to its field. For example, the fact that a movie can be a box office success while not being acclaimed by the critics [27] is a sign that creativity is specific to its field.

The size of the field is discussed by a number of RE authors. Maiden *et al.* [1] and Nguyen and Shanks [6], for example, use Sosa's *situated* creativity [39]. Some authors ([18], [19]) perceive that the typical RE project's *field* is made of the project stakeholders, and the *domain* is restricted to the existing ideas and products in the company. This is perhaps more likely to be the case for the development of bespoke products and services. In market-driven contexts, the domain corresponds to the products already on the market, and the field is made of the many people in the market, from a small number of big clients to many thousands of retailers and end-users. Neither is more genuinely creative than the other, but they require different strategies towards creativity.

Interactions: Most application domains have a particular market structure. However, in many cases a project/organisation can choose the target market, for example choosing a specific niche versus going worldwide. Large field innovation is likely to require more resources, and culture will play an important role in such choices.

RA8: Explore how to support creativity in RE depending on the size of the field (for example in custom versus market driven contexts).

The Size of the Novelty Increment. Many authors of business-oriented creativity research make a distinction between creativity leading to *incremental* innovation ("evolution"), and creativity leading to *radical* innovation ("revolution") [41–43]. The difference is that, in radical innovation, there is a major break with the domain's current conventions. This intuitively suggests that the risk of non-acceptance is higher, but the potential pay-off is higher, too. Management Sciences acknowledge the need for a balance between exploration and exploitation [43], and stress that both are needed for creativity [42].

Regev *et al.* [18] discuss innovation in the light of the change it causes for adopters. They stress the need to control the size of the increment to balance novelty and stability in the adopting organisation. They argue that an idea will be accepted if and only if the risk of accepting it is less than, or equal to, the risk of rejecting it. Mich *et al.* [17] suggest that creativity can be seen as a threat too, and Dallman [44] experimentally analysed willingness to take risk and conformism as factors influencing the creative process. However, the authors are not aware of any study that compares RE creativity support for evolution versus revolution.

Interactions: Culture is likely to have a significant impact on the novelty increment. Some organisations define themselves as "big innovators" while others find a way to make products cheaper. Innovation must not always be seen as desirable, and creativity might then simply be a question of having the right mindset to solve conflicts more efficiently. More mature application domains may make revolution harder, while newer market segments might see revolutionary shifts every week. All else being equal, bigger novelty increments are likely to require more resources.

RA9: Explore creativity support depending on the size of the novelty increment.
RA10: Explore how to define the ideal balance of evolution/revolution on a project.

Performance and Product-Orientation. Sawyer [15] studied the difference between *performance-oriented* creativity and *product-oriented* creativity. In performance-oriented creativity, there is no tangible product at the end of the creation process, since the process itself *is* the deliverable. A jazz concert is an example of performance-oriented creativity, while writing a book is an example of a product-oriented creative process. Sawyer argues that most creative genres use a combination of both.

There appear to be no RE authors who explicitly make the above distinction. Perhaps under the influence of the prevailing business culture, RE has implicitly focused on product-related creativity. However, requirements workshops can certainly be considered as a group performance, just like a musical or theatre show [15], [45]. Ellen Gottesdiener [46] advises on how to run requirements workshops. Although she does not refer to the work on group creativity discussed above, her advice is largely consistent with it. Workshops are an important technique in RE [46], together with other human-interaction intensive techniques like interviews. Consequently, there are good reasons to be interested in performance-related creativity. Depending on one's RE process or methodology, there will be more or less performance moments. REers have to choose the right mix of performance-oriented and product-oriented collaboration moments.

In his study of group performances [15], Sawyer suggested that any performance relies on some structure, but is also inherently partly chaotic. The goal for the REer is then to find the right amount of structure for the project. This must be done in parallel with considerations for the level of agility of the development process as a whole. Maiden *et al.* [1], suggest that the increasing importance of the Agile paradigm is seen as a driver for creativity. This is due to Agile's emphasis on collaboration, parallel work and shortened iteration cycles. Agility, structure and performance-oriented creativity seem to be strongly related.

Sawyer noted that *"group creative performance could be viewed as the creative process in microcosm"* and concluded that *"observation of group creativity could provide valuable insights into creative fields in which the creative process takes too long to observe directly"* [15]. This is another argument for further research into group performance creativity.

Interactions: Culture, as well as skills, influence the number of performance-oriented moments during RE projects. Performance-related moments are likely to require more openness and more experience, both of which are cultural factors. Performance moments like effective workshops can save time, but are likely to cost more money.

RA11: Explore the amount of structure needed to support creativity on a project.
RA12: Explore the relationship between agile processes and creativity in RE.
RA13: Explore how artistic performance can inform group work in RE.
RA14: Explore how to determine the ideal balance of performance- and product- oriented creativity moments for a specific project.

Problem-Finding and Problem-Solving Orientation. Another dimension identified by Sawyer is the difference between *problem-finding* and *problem-solving* creativity. Problem-finding is an emergent and divergent form of creativity. Problem-solving is a well planned and convergent form of creativity, that aims to lead from a known problem to a solution. For example, an abstract painter who does not know what a painting will look like until it is completed is engaged in a problem-finding activity. In contrast, a painter who faithfully reproduces a photograph is engaged in problem-solving. The two are likely to work in a fundamentally different way. Sawyer explains that in most creative genres, *"the creative process is a constant balance between finding a problem and solving that problem, and then finding a new problem during the solving of the last one"* [5].

Visser suggests that RE requires both problem understanding and problem solving [47]. There is, however, less consensus on whether RE follows a constant movement between problem-finding and problem-solving, or a more CPS-like process where problem-finding and problem-solving are sequential steps. Maiden *et al.* [1] explicitly compare RE to CPS, while Nguyen *et al.* suggest that RE processes involve oscillations of complexity, described by the "catastrophe-cycle model" [48]. They showed how the intertwining of problem understanding and solving is reflected in the incremental structuring and occasional restructuring of the requirements model during the requirements process. Meanwhile, Jones *et al.* [16] have been experimenting with divergent and convergent creativity techniques during requirements workshops. Maiden *et al.* [1] have argued that problem finding in RE was extensively supported by goal-oriented approaches. Authors agree that creativity in RE should be supported by rational and structured processes as well as by emergent and more chaotic processes, and by more collaboration-centric processes [1], [6].

Interactions: Whether a company favours emergence or structured processes is likely to strongly depend on its culture. Emerging processes may seem to involve more risk. Risk, in turn, has an impact on project resources. Safety-critical application domains, for example, are likely to be reluctant to take risks during their creativity process.

RA15: Explore how to support problem solving and problem finding creativity in RE.
RA16: Explore how to define the right interactions between problem finding and problem solving on a specific project.

7   Using the Framework

To make things more concrete, we provide below an example of how the framework could be used to engineer creativity support on a project.

BankMessages is a company that offers messaging services to banks. It establishes messaging standards so that banks can communicate with each other. Recently the company has committed a small multidisciplinary team (16 highly skilled, experienced people) to develop a new product, supposed to enhance the service to a level that is above what clients expect. Figure 2 summarizes the creativity analysis that one could do for their case. On the left column are the contextual factors, as well as the main goals for being creative on the project. On the right, one can see the corresponding discussion for each dimension of creativity. The lines in the middle (better seen in color) give an idea of the complex interactions that link contextual factors and creativity dimensions. This one-hour work made with, and validated by, key stakeholders helps us decide about the support we need to give to this specific creativity. In this example, one might want to support creativity with an agile development method, including numerous workshops with clients to discover and validate requirements (e.g. through prototyping) and maybe some specific creativity techniques.

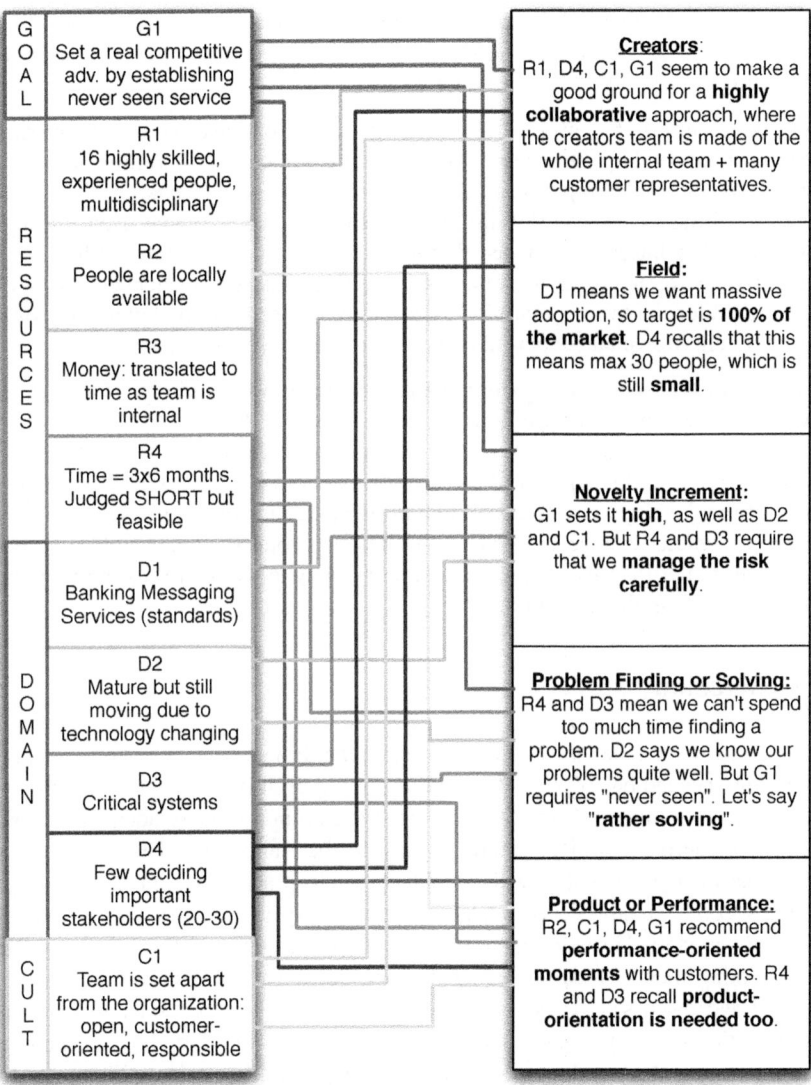

Fig. 2. BankMessage creativity analysis

8   Discussion

Partial Analysis and Validation. During the literature review, the identification of the contextual factors and dimensions was based on the authors' analytical sense. This work would probably benefit from a more systematic way of deriving a framework, and empirical validation would be useful in strengthening the framework. Moreover, as suggested earlier, creativity is a relatively immature topic in RE. Other research disciplines are more mature in their study of creativity, but include a great many references, that are only partially covered by this analysis. This study therefore presents an initial framework proposal, which may not be complete. There may be more contextual factors and dimensions, which it is hoped will be uncovered as this work continues beyond that reported here.

Innovation versus Creativity. Innovation and creativity are two overlapping concepts. The boudary between both is not very clear. A common view is that creativity is about having ideas, and innovation is about making them real, in particular selling them. The definitions of creativity that we have used through this work reject this interpretation, as elaboration is part of creativity. While the term "innovation" is frequently used in management sciences, social sciences almost do not use it; the prefer the term "creativity". Our study focused on this latter body of work, and might benefit from a deeper investigation of the innovation literature.

Creativity in RE versus in Systems Engineering. In this study, we focused on RE. However, as we have shown, the modern understanding of creativity blurs the boundary between an idea and its execution, and shows how both are really part of the creative process. In this context, the RE effort cannot be considered in isolation from the rest of the development. Hence, a natural next step for this work would be to study how far its results can be applied in the broader context of software and systems engineering rather than RE. Studying creativity in agile teams, for example, would be a good candidate in this direction.

9   Conclusion

RE strives to create a new (version of a) system that brings *value*. Creativity is therefore by definition needed on 100% of RE projects. However, it is not always the same type of creativity that is required. Consequently, the first step in providing adequate support for creativity is defining which creativity has to be supported. This study lays the foundations of a method that will eventually guide practitioners in determining their situation-specific creativity needs and choosing adequate support. In this paper, this endeavour was started by studying the creativity literature in Social Sciences and RE, and by confronting them. Three contextual factors and five dimensions of creativity were identified and discussed. These can readily be used by a practitioner to structure the analysis of the creativity needed on a project, for example by asking how each contextual factor interacts with each dimension. The reasoning can flow in both directions: from a given context to dimensions, or from given dimensions to context. This study also highlights that a significant amount of research is needed in exploring, comparing and combining the various creativity situations uncovered, in order to help the practitioner answer these complex questions and choose an adequate support accordingly.

Acknowledgments. This work is sponsored by (1) the Interuniversity Attraction Poles Programme of the Belgian State, Belgian Science Policy, under the MoVES project, (2) the Walloon Region under the European Regional Development Fund (ERDF) and (3) the FNRS.

References

[1] Maiden, N., Jones, S., Karlsen, K., Neill, R., Zachos, K., Milne, A.: Requirements Engineering as Creative Problem Solving: A Research Agenda for Idea Finding. In: IEEE RE 2010, Sydney, Australia, pp. 57–66 (2010)

[2] Deming, W.E.: Out of the crisis, Massachusetts Institute of Technology (1986)

[3] Ley, M., Bast, H.: Computer Science Bibliography, http://www.dblp.org

[4] Google Scholar, http://scholar.google.be/ (accessed: October 8, 2011)

[5] Sawyer, R.K.: Explaining Creativity: The Science of Human Innovation, 1st edn. Oxford University Press, USA (2006)

[6] Nguyen, L., Shanks, G.: A framework for understanding creativity in requirements engineering. Information and Software Technology 51(3), 655–662 (2009)

[7] Wallas, G.: The Art of Thought, Abridged ed. Watts and Co. (1949)

[8] Hadamard, J.: An essay on the psychology of invention in the mathematical field. Courier Dover Publications (1954)

[9] Boden, M.: The creative mind: myths & mechanisms, 2nd edn. Routledge, London (2004)

[10] Osborn, A.F.: Principles and procedures of creative problem-solving. Scribner (1963)

[11] Gordon, W.J.J.: Synectics: the development of creative capacity. Collier Books (1961)

[12] Dewey, J.: How We Think. Dover Publications (1997)

[13] Sternberg, R.J., Lubart, T.I.: Investing in creativity. American psychologist 51(7) (1996)

[14] Fischer, G.: Social creativity: turning barriers into opportunities for collaborative design. In: Procs. 8th Conference on Participatory Design, vol. 1, pp. 152–161 (2004)

[15] Sawyer, R.K.: Group genius: the creative power of collaboration. Basic Books (2007)

[16] Jones, S., Lynch, P., Maiden, N.A.M., Lindstaedt, S.N.: Use and Influence of Creative Ideas and Requirements for a Work-Integrated Learning System. In: RE, pp. 289–294 (2008)

[17] Mich, L., Anesi, C., Berry, D.M.: Requirements engineering and creativity: An innovative approach based on a model of the pragmatics of communication. In: Proc. REFSQ, pp. 3–922602 (2004)

[18] Regev, G., Cause, D.C., Wegmann, A.: Creativity and the Age-Old Resistance to Change Problem in RE. In: Procs. IEEE RE 2006, pp. 291–296 (2006)

[19] Pennel, L., Maiden, N.A.M.: Creating Requirements – Techniques and Experiences in the Policing Domain

[20] Nguyen, L., Cybulski, J.: Into the future: inspiring and stimulating users' creativity. In: Proceedings of the Pacific Asia Conference on Information Systems PACIS (2008)

[21] Ocker, R.J.: Promoting Group Creativity in Upstreal Requirements Engineering. In: The Right Concepts for the Right Problems, p. 55 (2010)

[22] Yilmaz, L.: On the Synergy of Conflict and Collective Creativity in Open Innovation Socio-technical Ecologies. In: Procs. CSE 2009., vol. 4, pp. 502–508 (2009)

[23] Baer, J., Kaufman, J.C.: Bridging Generality and Specificity: The Amusement Park Theoretical Model of Creativity. Roeper Review: A Journal on Gifted Education (2005)

[24] Glass, R.L., Vessey, I.: Contemporary application-domain taxonomies. IEEE Software 12, 63–76 (1995)
[25] Vaajakallio, K., Mattelmäki, T.: Collaborative design exploration, p. 223 (2007)
[26] Cybulski, J., Nguyen, L.: Learning to Become a Creative Systems Analyst. In: The PSI Handbook of Virtual Environments for Training and Education (2008)
[27] Simonton, D.K.: Cinematic creativity and production budgets: Does money make the movie? The Journal of Creative Behavior 39(1), 1–15 (2005)
[28] Cowen, T., Tabarrok, A.: An Economic Theory of Avant-Garde and Popular Art, or High and Low Culture. Southern Economic Journal 67(2), 232–253 (2000)
[29] Wever, A., Maiden, N.A.M.: The day-to-day factors that are preventing business analysts from effective business analysis. In: Procs IEEE RE 2011, Trento, Italy (2011)
[30] Fricker, S., Seyff, N.: 1st international requirements engineering efficiency workshop. ACM SIGSOFT Software Engineering Notes 36, 26 (2011)
[31] Gorschek, T., Fricker, S., Palm, K., Kunsman, S.: A Lightweight Innovation Process for Software-Intensive Product Development. IEEE Software 27(1), 37–45 (2010)
[32] Mullen, B., Johnson, C., Salas, E.: Productivity loss in brainstorming groups: A meta-analytic integration. Basic and Applied Social Psychology (1991)
[33] Arias, E., Eden, H., Fischer, G., Gorman, A., Scharff, E.: Transcending the individual human mind. ACM TOCHI 7(1), 84–113 (2000)
[34] Boehm, B., Grunbacher, P., Briggs, R.O.: Developing groupware for requirements negotiation: lessons learned. IEEE Software 18(3), 46–55 (2001)
[35] Coughlan, J., Macredie, R.D.: Effective communication in requirements elicitation: A comparison of methodologies. Requirements Engineering 7(2), 47–60 (2002)
[36] Holtzblatt, K., Beyer, H.R.: Requirements gathering: the human factor. Communications of the ACM 38(5), 31–32 (1995)
[37] Maiden, N., Robertson, S.: Integrating creativity into requirements processes: Experiences with an air traffic management system (2005)
[38] Mahaux, M., Maiden, N.A.M., Heymans, P.: Making it all up: getting on the act to improvise creative requirements. In: IEEE RE 2010, Sydney, Australia (2010)
[39] Sosa, R., Gero, J.: Design and change: a model of situated creativity, Sydney (2003)
[40] Kaufman, J.C., Beghetto, R.A., Baer, J., Ivcevic, Z.: Creativity polymathy: What Benjamin Franklin can teach your kindergartener. Learning and Individual Differences 20(4) (2010)
[41] Vera, D., Crossan, M.: Improvisation and innovative performance in teams. Organization Science 16(3), 203–224 (2005)
[42] Castiaux, A.: Radical innovation in established organizations: Being a knowledge predator. JETM 24(1-2), 36–52 (2007)
[43] March, J.G.: Exploration and exploitation in organizational learning. Organization Science 2(1), 71–87 (1991)
[44] Dallman, S., Nguyen, L., Lamp, J., Cybulski, J.: Contextual factors which influence creativity in requirements engineering. In: Procs. ECIS (2005)
[45] Mahaux, M., Maiden, N.: Theater Improvisers Know the Requirements Game. IEEE Software 25(5), 68–69 (2008)
[46] Gottesdiener, E.: Requirements by Collaboration: Workshops for Defining Needs. Addison-Wesley Professional (2002)
[47] Visser, W.: Designers' activities examined at three levels: organization, strategies and problem-solving processes. Knowledge-Based Systems 5(1), 92–104 (1992)
[48] Nguyen, L., Carroll, J., Swatman, P.A.: Supporting and monitoring the creativity of IS personnel during the requirements engineering process. In: HICSS, p. 7008 (2000)

Supporting Failure Mode and Effect Analysis:
A Case Study with Failure Sequence Diagrams

Christian Raspotnig and Andreas Opdahl

Department of Information Science and Media Studies, University of Bergen
NO-5020 Bergen, Norway
{Christian.Raspotnig,Andreas.Opdahl}@uib.no

Abstract. **[Context and motivation]** In air traffic management (ATM) safety assessments are performed with traditional techniques such as failure mode and effect analysis (FMEA). **[Question/problem]** As system modelling is becoming an increasingly important part of developing ATM systems, techniques that integrate safety aspects and modelling are needed. **[Principal ideas/results]** This paper proposes an approach for thorough failure analysis of ATM systems that consist of several interacting components and similar systems. The new technique is called failure sequence diagrams (FSD) and supports FMEA in modelling failures and their effects through interactions between system components. FSD has been used in a case study by safety and system engineers in three different ways. **[Contribution]** The study suggests that FSD was easy to use and supported FMEA well, but did not cover its weakness in analysing multiple failures.

Keywords: Failure analysis, safety, sequence diagrams.

1 Introduction

Air traffic management (ATM) in Europe is about to undergo the most extensive technological change in its history through the Single European ATM Research (SESAR) program [1]. A part of the change is describing the current and future systems of ATM, where modelling is becoming crucial. Modelling languages such as UML [2] are widely used in many domains, and the ATM community in Europe is becoming increasingly interested in using modelling for systems development.

The current safety assessments conducted in the European ATM community are following methods such as Eurocontrol's Safety Assessment Methodology [3], which includes the Functional Hazard Analysis [4]. This method can include traditional techniques, such as Hazard and Operability studies (HazOp) and Failure Mode and Effect Analysis (FMEA) [5], which are used at lower abstraction levels. While these techniques sometimes use models as an input, they typically use worksheets to discuss and document the hazards and failures. However, using models more actively in safety assessments can give benefits, such as better discussions and understanding of the system under assessment, along with integration of model-based system engineering. For ATM systems that consist of several interacting components, there is a need for a thorough failure analysis of the interactions, which are not easily analysed with the traditional techniques.

B. Regnell and D. Damian (Eds.): REFSQ 2012, LNCS 7195, pp. 117–131, 2012.
© Springer-Verlag Berlin Heidelberg 2012

The purpose of this industry case study is to obtain real experiences on combining FMEA with Failure Sequence Diagrams (FSD), a specialized version of Misuse Sequence Diagrams (MUSD) [6] from the security field. FSD is a new technique in the safety field and in this paper the technique and the results obtained when combining the technique with FMEA in a safety assessment are presented.

The paper is structured as follows; in section 2 the background for the research is described along with the relevant work. Section 3 describes the research method used for obtaining the results presented in section 4, which are analysed in section 5 and further discussed in section 6. Finally, in section 7, we conclude upon the research and look ahead at further work, before we direct our acknowledgements.

2   Background

A system failure is defined as "an event that occurs when the delivered service deviates from the correct service" [7]. The relationship between fault, error and failure is described together with how it relates to interacting system components in [7]. FMEA is not only used for identifying the failure modes of system components and their effects, but also for finding the causal factors causing the failure to occur and thereby follows the idea with respect to faults, errors and failures. Although FMEA relates failure modes to system components and to the complete system, it does not address interactions between components. Most FMEA worksheets contain information about local or immediate effect and system effect, where the latter is a description of the failure propagated to system level. However, there is no support by FMEA to investigate failure propagation, except reasoning about the local and system effect of a failure mode.

FSD addresses failures and propagation between the interacting components. In Fig. 1 the notation for the FSD is presented, showing how the notation extends UML sequence diagrams. The notation includes current control and recommended action (indicated by dashed/green symbols), also referred to as mitigations. FSD also includes a notation for indicating component failure that can be used to differentiate whether a component fails (indicated by red/dashed symbols) to deliver its service, or if the failure only propagates through the component (indicated by a black/solid component symbols) without causing it to fail.

In Fig. 2 the use of FSD is presented by an example that is similar to the system that was analysed in the case study with FMEA. It shows that a corrupted flight coordination message, indicated by a red/dashed arrow, is sent into the system and not detected by the router or the LAN. When the corrupted message is received by the flight processor (FP) component, it causes the FP to crash and the FP is not able to send an alert to the monitoring system (MON). The MON continuously sends heartbeat messages to FP as current control. It registers that no response is given by the FP. Although the MON has a current control of sending an alert message (last message in the diagram) to the supervisor (SUP), a recommended action is to include new messages through the flight display (FD) to alert the air traffic control officer (ATCO) of the failure of the FP.

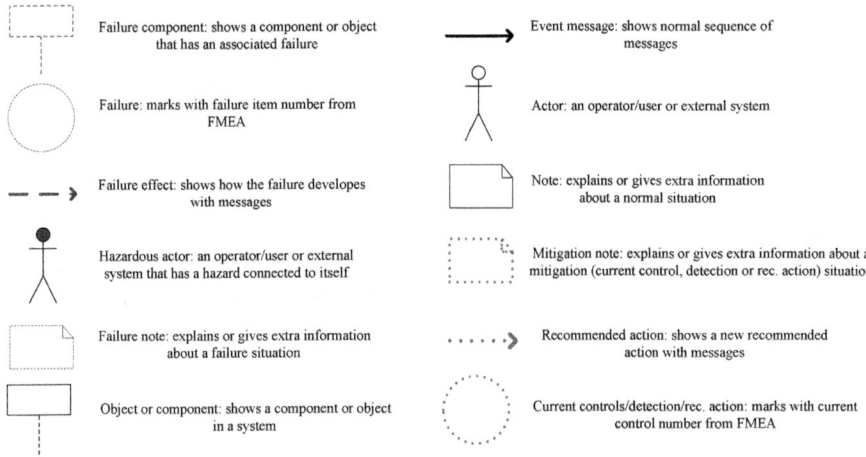

Fig. 1. Notation for the Failure Sequence Diagrams

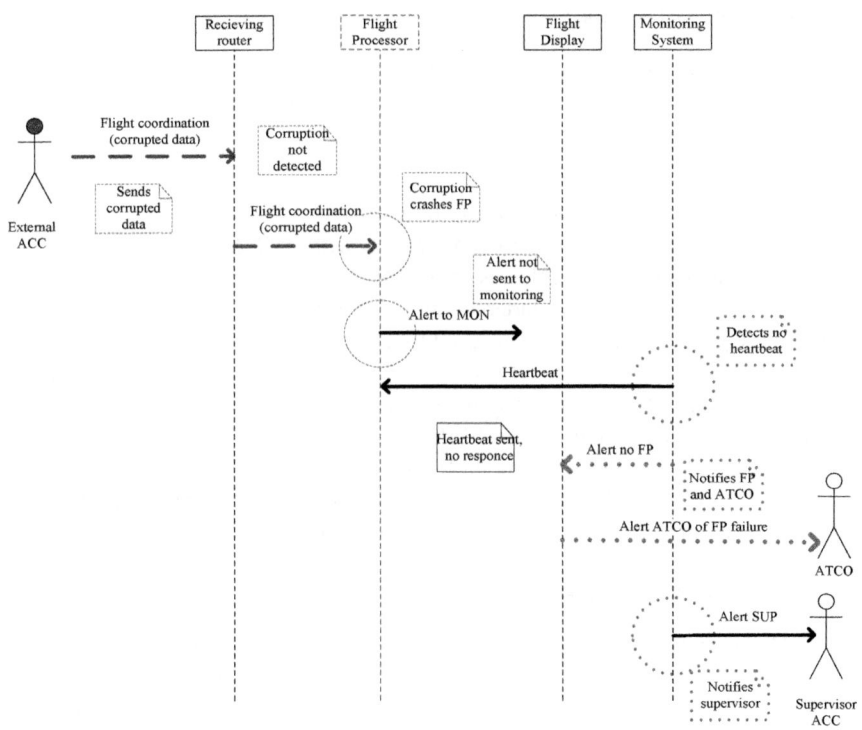

Fig. 2. Example in the use of the FSD

There are several related works to ours: on combining UML and failure identification has been done before, e.g., using FMEA on UML models for improving the interaction between design and dependability analysis [8], comparing system sequence diagrams with textual use cases in an experiment, for evaluating what is better for identifying hazards related to a system [9], or, closest to our work, the use of UML diagrams for safety analysis of a medical robot [10]. In the latter work, FMEA is used together with sequence diagrams and errors are modelled. However, in comparison to our work the three approaches do not extend the UML diagrams with an own notation for supporting FMEA specifically. To our knowledge they do also not attempt to improve the FMEA process with focus on interactions and failure propagation. Finally, they do not evaluate the optimal combination of interactive failure visualization and a structured use of a worksheet.

3   Method

The purpose of the case study was to evaluate how FSD could be used together with FMEA. In particular, we wanted to gain experiences on the industrial use of FSD and the interaction between the two techniques.

3.1   Research Questions

For the case study design we developed three research questions with sub-questions to guide our observations in the meetings to obtain qualitative data on the usage of FSD together with FMEA.

1. Can FSD support FMEA?
   a.   Is it possible to use FSD along with FMEA?
   b.   Is it easy to use FSD in combination with FMEA?
   c.   Can FSD improve discussions among participants?
   d.   Can FSD increase understanding of the system?
2. How should the two techniques be used together?
   a.   What are the pros and cons of the ways of combining the techniques?
   b.   What is the optimal way to combine the techniques?
3. Can FSD cover the weaknesses of FMEA?
   a.   Can FSD show multiple failures?
   b.   Can FSD help relating failures and their effects to interactions?
   c.   Integration of safety assessments and model-based system engineering?

3.2   Choice of Research Method

Case study as a method was discussed with the Air Navigation Service Provider (ANSP) organization according to their needs for safety analysis of system changes. A research method that would let them conduct the safety analysis as required, but at the same time could allow for research taking place within their organization, was seen as beneficial to both parties. Therefore, case study was selected for observing the use of the two techniques together in a real setting. In the following sub-sections the case study design is described.

3.3   The ANSP Case

We followed a European ANSPs assessing the safety of introducing the Flight Management Transfer Protocol (FMTP) [11], [12]. A procedure based on [3] was used for deciding the scope of the change, whether a safety assessment was required and which technique to use. The ANSP decided to use FMEA and to structure the safety assessment through FMEA meetings. An earlier safety assessment of the coordination function between air traffic control units was used to establish the required safety level and possible hazards.

Meetings were organized, taking place in a meeting room with the needed facilities, e.g., a big table, a video projector and a white board. An FMEA team was established, with a facilitator, a secretary, three systems engineers and an air traffic control officer. Several of the participants were familiar with UML, but only one of them had previous experience with sequence diagrams.

In advance all participants received a document describing the FMTP system and the overall system, relevant safety documentation and a procedure for conducting the FMEA. The latter consisted of a worksheet with the columns component number, component, failure mode, causal factor, immediate effect, system effect, current controls and recommended action. Furthermore, it included a list of typical failure modes for components and software as described in [5].

3.4   Procedure for Conducting the Case Study

During the case study we observed three strategies of using the two techniques together in the meetings. Below the activities taking place during each strategy is described and referred to as sessions:

1. First session (day one – five hours' meeting)
   a.   Introduction of case study, purpose, techniques and basic usage
   b.   Explaining a simplified notation without mitigation
   c.   Conducting the FMEA
   d.   Applying the FSD to the FMEA result
   e.   Summarizing the FSD and FMEA session
2. Second session (day two and three – six and two and a half hours' meetings)
   a.   Summary of the first session
   b.   Explaining the full notation with example similar to Fig. 2
   c.   Conducting the FMEA together with FSD
   d.   Summarizing the FSD and FMEA session
3. Third session (day four – three hours' meeting)
   a.   Repeating the full notation
   b.   Conducting the FSD
   c.   Summarizing the results with FMEA
   d.   Summary of all sessions

3.5   Data Collection during the Sessions

In the first two sessions, the first author acted as an observer. The participants were encouraged to use FSD and FMEA as seen beneficial to their task. Whenever experiencing difficulties, they were told to discuss among themselves and identify a natural solution. If they were not able to find a solution, they could ask the observer for advice. For the third session, the first author supported the facilitator and drew the FSDs as a participating observer, before taking a passive role with the FMEA.

For collecting relevant data, we decided to focus on three types of data:

1. Verbal – which questions were asked, e.g., to us or between themselves, discussions and general comments regarding the technique.
2. Interactions – how was the interaction with FSD, e.g., drawing, pointing, referring to, looking at while talking or thinking.
3. Notes – which parts of the notation were or weren't used, and which parts of the notation were used wrongly or correctly.

For the data types, all relevant observations from the sessions were written down. The sessions were also video-taped for extracting more information relevant to our data types. Pictures were taken of the FSD diagrams for each component, which we used together with our notes to reconstruct how the notation was used. The video recorder only captured the participant standing next to the white board and it was not possible to reconstruct the interaction of participants pointing to the drawing by analysing the video recordings.

In the last session the first author did not take notes as he facilitated the meeting and relied solely on the video recordings for the data collection. When summarizing the FMEA worksheet, we did not video record the worksheet and the participants. The video camera was directed towards the white board, only recording the use of FSD to support the summary. However, we reconstructed the discussions by using the audio part of the recording.

3.6   Data Collection through Interviews

The first author interviewed the participants after the sessions as follows:

1. Explaining the purpose and procedure for the interview
2. Asking for their own comments
3. 11 questions based on Technology Acceptance Model (TAM) [13]
4. Asking for comments on a summary of our analysis

For the interviews it was only possible to conduct two face to face meetings. Of the remaining three participants we were able to interview two of them through email, with the same structure for the interview. The answers were returned and analysed along with the notes from the two other interviews. The last participant, a system engineer, was not able to respond due to time constraints.

In the interview they gave their general opinion on the usage of FSD to support FMEA, before answering the TAM questions regarding perceived usefulness, perceived ease of use and intention of use. In the end of the interview they discussed the summary of the case study and either agreed or disagreed with our findings.

4   Using FSD for Supporting FMEA

In this section we describe how the techniques were used in each session.

4.1   First Session

The participants started the regular FMEA process and discussed some components for clarification. FSD was used after finishing the FMEA analysis of the first component. There was a discussion on how to use the FSD, where the participants concluded to use it for supplementing FMEA. A natural start for them was to draw up all components identified in the FMEA worksheet, but they discussed this and also asked us as observers. Another issue discussed and questioned was to use one or more FSD diagram per failure mode. As they progressed some modifications were done, e.g., that power supply was not included as it seemed hard fit it to the FSD as a specific component. The participants agreed that a good start would be to draw the normal sequence of messages in the FSD, before analysing the failure, its causes, related effects and mitigations.

While drawing the normal sequence there were several discussions on the functions of the components involved. There were a number of clarifications, e.g., the role of a monitoring system and what kind of functionality that was allocated to this component. These clarifications led to statements such as "we are better in thinking around graphical notation" and "FSD gives us an overview of the system". At the same time they commented on only using one FSD diagram per failure mode, or else "the FSD would become too complex".

The participants used wrong notation on some occasions, e.g., not including message text above the arrows or using the lifeline for symbolizing an external actor. Furthermore, the only FSD specific notation used was the failure markings.

Several participants engaged in diagram drawing. In the beginning the task was left to one of the system engineers, but several times the facilitator and another system engineer participated in the drawing. All participants used the drawings when discussing, either by pointing to components or referring to them by name. Several of the participants went up to the white board when explaining details about the system.

4.2   Second Session

This session started with summarizing the advantages of using FSD for bringing clarity of components and how they interrelate, and giving a good overview of the system. The participants also discussed further use of FSD and it was decided that FSD should support FMEA in a more iterative manner. Furthermore, they discussed using FSD for identifying failure modes and causal factors, but concluded FMEA better suited for this. They used FSD for investigating the immediate and system effects, along with the current controls.

The participants used FSD from the beginning of the session and shortly discussed which messages to look at before using FSD to draw a normal sequence of messages in the system. They also marked the failure mode in the FSD, but used the FMEA worksheet to discuss the causal factors. Immediate effects and system effects together with the current control were usually discussed by use of FSD, with recommended actions identified from these discussions. This continued throughout the session, where FSD and FMEA were used iteratively on the components.

Support for Discussion. Inclusion of both inbound and outbound messages in the FSD drawings was also discussed by the participants. Most of the discussions were on understanding the system and components, along with interactions, not on usage of FSD. Nevertheless, the facilitator found it hard to draw some of the messages, as different levels of the OSI model [14] were discussed with respect to corrupted data and detection of such data. In the end diagrams were drawn and notes were used to state at which level the messages were drawn. Sometimes they used an FSD as starting point for discussion on failures, but only marked the failure of a component in FSD and then summarizing it in the worksheet. They also commented that they did not see the need to draw diagrams of failures of the external system. However, they used FSD to draw and discuss how such failures would affect the system under analysis.

Use of Notation. The participants were able to use the notation for drawing situations of corrupted data going into the system, and wrote assumption as notes of the data going unnoticed through the system. Often they used the numbering from FMEA for failure modes and current control and also wrote names above the messages correctly. Still, for component failure they often only drew the initial failure marking and then used the FSD more for discussions than drawing the complete sequence of messages. Once they also left the FSD drawings and drew a sketch for explaining how the messages could be switched by the system. Moreover, the note notations were seldom used to comment their drawings. For current control green arrows were used instead of the combining green circles and black arrows. They repeatedly used a component symbol for representing an external system as opposed to the actor symbol suggested. Once they used the actor symbol, but did not include the name. The participants also suggested using a red cross over a message to indicate that it did not reach the receiver as intended, as a new notation. Later, when looking at specific part of the system, they did not draw all the components, but only those interacting with the specific component. In the beginning they used wrong notation for corrupted data, i.e., black arrows instead of red, but it was used correctly later.

Combining the Techniques. In this session they combined FSD and FMEA in an interesting way. They often drew failure modes, but went back to the FMEA worksheet for discussing causal factors and immediate effects. FSD was still used in these discussions, either for looking at and referring to parts in the FSD or for letting the facilitator point out things in the drawings. All participants pointed to FSD for identifying components and messages in discussions, and for reasoning about messages at different levels in the OSI model. They also used FSD more systematically to show how corrupted data went unnoticed through the system and explaining intermittent loss of messages or handshake functionality. Once a recommended action was found by use of FSD, but usually the FMEA worksheet was used for this. Sometimes system engineers corrected the facilitator in drawing current control wrongly, but they also corrected each other's representations of message flow in the system. Although FSD was not used for drawing failure of power supply, they used it to get an overview of which components that would be affected by such a failure. Some participants also used FSD as reminder for further discussions, when the secretary needed time to update the FMEA worksheet. In some circumstances they also asked each other for oral explanations, and used the FSD to follow the explanation given.

4.3   Third Session

Before the FMEA meeting started, small icons of the FSD notation was prepared by the first author on the sides of the white board. The participants and first author agreed to only use FSD for facilitating the meeting, but let the secretary note the discussions in the FMEA worksheet (not visible to the participants). After finishing the analysis with FSD, the worksheet was shown for further refinement. In this session we also analysed the software of some components, compared to the other sessions where the analysis was more concerned with components at a system level.

Although the first author drew the FSD with the defined notation it was not always straightforward. He found some problems drawing software components, as the decomposition feature of UML sequence diagrams [2] was not used. The diagrams became too complex, as software components were added to the lifelines with the specialized FSD notation. Often all the information would not fit on the white board. Nevertheless, the relevant FSD notation was used and a new alt operator [2] notation was introduced, which worked well for representing system effects of failure modes. The participants seemed to understand this operator as they referred to it as different scenarios of system effects. The participants also corrected the FSD, e.g., when the notation was used incorrectly or messages were drawn to the wrong components.

The session was facilitated by drawing the FSD and then asking for comments. Drawing the FSD in front of everyone allowed for corrections of everyone's understanding. Many corrections were also made by walking through the drawings, pointing to the flow of messages and asking the participants to explain accordingly. This was evident as the FSD was changed gradually, as discussions revealed new aspects both with respect to system effects of failures and functionality in the system. When the FMEA worksheet was brought up in the last part of the session, some corrections also had to be made here. The facilitator used FSD to point out these corrections to the secretary.

There were few discussions or questions on how to use the FSD, perhaps because the first author drew the diagrams and facilitated the meeting. Nevertheless, when he suggested drawing a recommended action the participants agreed that it was out of scope, but it was further discussed and noted in the FMEA worksheet. In the end everybody discussed facilitating with FSD and summarizing the results with FMEA worksheet. The participants had used the FSD repeatedly to understand the system and ensure a common understanding, but missed the structure of the FMEA worksheet and preferred to use it for brainstorming failure modes first and then using FSD. It was argued that with FSD only the focus became more on how the system works and the interaction of the components than on failure modes and causal factors.

5   Results

In this section we present the results from analysing the data from the previous section. We present the results for each research question from section 3.1.

5.1   Can FSD Support FMEA?

Verbal. We noted no direct questions related to whether FSD was able to support FMEA. Mainly there were discussions and general comments regarding the support. In the first and last session, the participants clearly stated that FSD gave an overview of the system and allowed for better reasoning due to use of graphical notation. Additionally, FSD ensured common understanding among the participants. This shows that using FSD supports FMEA. The participants were not being able to use FSD for representing failure of power supply. From this we conclude that the support is not possible for analysing all aspects of a system and is limited to the notation of sequence diagrams. This is further supported by the representation of corruption of messages at different layers in the OSI model.

Interactions. Although the main use of the FSD was to draw diagrams, the participants also used them actively in discussions, both in explaining to each other and for checking their understanding, by pointing at or referring to names of components or messages and the related failure notations in the drawings. Often they used the FSD to make all participants join the discussion. The FSD supported the FMEA by giving the participants a common overview of both system artefacts and the relevant failures aspects, which was used for discussions and understanding.
Notes. From the data collected we saw that the notation was improved gradually during the sessions. Although the participants did not use much time for learning the notation in advance, they applied it quite easily. From this we conclude that FSD is a light-weight technique that can easily be used to support FMEA. The entire notation was not used, but the notation that was used was helpful and adequate in supporting the FMEA.

5.2   How Should the Two Techniques Be Used Together?

Verbal. How FSD and FMEA can be used together was commented on several times in the three sessions. Firstly, there was a discussion about in which order the techniques should be applied, resulting in three strategies of using the techniques together: sequentially, with either technique being used before the other, or in parallel. The benefit from using the techniques in sequence, done in the first and second sessions, seemed lower than parallel use. The FMEA worksheet structure was missed when using the techniques sequentially compared to when using them in parallel. Secondly, it was discussed that the FMEA allowed for more specific brainstorming on the failure modes, which was neglected when only using FSD. From this we conclude that it is best to use the techniques in parallel. It allows for better brainstorming and a more structured approach through FMEA, while FSD offers the overview of components and details about their interactions, along with relevant failure effects.

Interactions. FSD was used interactively for explaining and exploring how the system works and for ensuring a common understanding among the participants. We could see from the increased common understanding of the participants that there was a benefit from first drawing the normal sequence of messages with FSD, then using the FMEA for brainstorming on the failure modes and causal factors, before going back to the FSD to discuss and explore the effects of the failures. Whereas completing the FMEA worksheet first, and then using the FSD for drawing the results gave a good verification, the understanding of the system was not as good among the participants. Conversely, when using the FSD first and then summarizing with the FMEA worksheet, understanding was better, but there was a lack of structure and brainstorming. We conclude that using the two techniques in parallel gave the best results and the optimal use of the two techniques together.

Notes. Only parts of the notation were used and the notation that was used was not always used correctly during the first two sessions. For the last session more of the notation was used, as the FMEA worksheet was used after the FSD and not in parallel. However, for the parallel use the notation that was particularly useful was *failure, failure effect, component, event message* and *current control*. We conclude that the FMEA worksheet covered the need for the three types of notes and the recommended action.

5.3   Can FSD Cover the Weakness of FMEA?

Verbal. The previously described common understanding between the participants could be compared to the use of adequate system documentation as input to the FMEA without support from FSD. It is a general weakness of techniques that do not allow for interactively exploring a system while assessing it. The use of FSD generated discussions on how the system worked, especially how the components interact with respect to failures. Some of the discussions would not have taken place only using FMEA and system documentation. FMEA's weakness is that it does not allow for assessing multiple failures. The discussion suggests that FSD would become too complex for showing multiple failures in one diagram. Although multiple failures were not modelled with FSD, the discussions revealed that FSD gave a good overview and understanding of the system. Through the graphical notation and overview obtained it supports the participants in keeping other identified failures in mind.

Interactions. Much time was spent on investigating the interaction between components. In the first session FMEA was used before FSD. When the participants started using FSD they did not only draw the diagrams, but used the FSD for pointing, referring and explaining the interaction of components and how failure effects propagated through the system. Although FMEA had already been used, the interactive use of FSD, exploring and explaining to each other, increased the participants' understanding of the system failures and interaction between components in particular.

Notes. While our observations indicate that FSD is not suitable for modelling multiple failures, we find the use of the alt operator promising for showing multiple system effects. The effects of a failure propagating through the system could be connected to other failures identified in the system. Nevertheless, we conclude that FSD is limited in covering this weakness of FMEA.

5.4   Analysis of the Interview

The interviews mainly showed that the FSD increased the understanding among the participants of how the system worked, especially through the visual notation and allowing for an interactive use. They preferred to use FSD and FMEA in parallel, not in sequence, but saw the benefit of using FSD first to ensure a common understanding of the system. They stressed that FMEA should be used to give the structure of the analysis. Some of the participants also stated that more time was spent, but that they felt more sure about the analysis being thorough.

From the answers to our questions we observed that the participants perceived the technique as useful. It indicated that FSD was easy to use, but that more time would be needed for learning the notation, and remembering it. All participants would use the technique again, but some made it contingent on using it in a group and if they believed that it would help making all participants understand the system under assessment. Most of the participants agreed with our findings from the case study, but some of them mentioned not always paying attention to use the notation correctly.

5.5   Threats to Validity and Reliability

There are several threats to validity of case studies [15] and in the following we discuss construct validity, external validity, internal validity and reliability.

A threat to construct validity is whether we identified the correct operational measures for the concepts being studied. To handle this threat we have focussed on using common, well-understood vocabularies that are common in the security, safety and modelling areas, and we have used the interviews to let the participants comment on our summary of the case study.

Threats to external validity are concerned with whether a study's findings can be generalized. As is common for a single case study, external validity is limited for our study, since we studied a specific system in a specific organization with only one project. However, there may be some generalizability because we used FSD together with a commonly used technique on a change in natural environments that will have to be implemented in all ATM systems of the European ANSPs.

In this work internal validity can be threatened when concluding on the data collected. To address this threat we have used video recording for analysing the data, allowing thorough data analysis. Nevertheless, the threat could have been further reduced if including more researchers in the analysis of the data, but was not possible due to the wish of the ANSP to be anonymous.

Reliability is concerned with whether the data collection can be repeated with the same data obtained. For this we have addressed our procedure for conducting the case study. As the ANSP organization preferred anonymity, it was not possible to include examples of the data collected. They did not wish the organization's procedures and documentation related to their systems to be published or referenced. However, most of the procedures are based on standards and guidelines which are commonly used by ANSPs in Europe.

6   Discussion

Previous sections show that the participants were able to use FSD with little prior training. In the first session they were enthusiastic about using the FSD. Several were involved in drawing and explaining by use of FSD. We observed that the mutual understanding of the different components and their role in the total system increased when using the FSD. Furthermore, when developing the FSD in parallel with FMEA, we also saw their mutual understanding of the system increase. In the third session we witnessed the same, but it also became evident that not using the FMEA worksheet gave a disadvantage due to the lack of structure with respect to brainstorming for failure modes and causal factors. Although some information was recorded in the worksheet, the participants felt that it was important to have a brainstorming session, ensuring the complete set of failure modes and causal factors being assessed.

6.1   Sequence Diagrams and Failure Notation

One could argue that performing FMEA on a sequence diagram (SD) without the failure notation could give the same effect. From our observations however it is clear that the interaction between the participants when drawing the diagrams and including failure notation has an own benefit, particularly evident when modelling how the effects of a failure propagate through the system. The notation forces the participants to identify how the interacting components react to failures. Also the related notation for mitigations of the failures and their effects is valuable, as it makes the participants consider the different components for best possible failure mitigation. Although the notation was not used correctly in the beginning, it was clear that it improved and that the participants needed to gain experience. Their understanding of the notation also became clear as they corrected each other during the study. We conclude that FSD was easy to use for the participants. Using existing SDs as an input to FSD and extend them with the failure notation, would give a further benefit with respect to time and effort. The ANSP organization does model some of their systems with UML, but not with SD at the time. However, SD is utilized in ATM [16], and our work of integrating it with safety should be of particular interest. Other safety domains can also benefit of using our approach, especially those familiar with SD and FMEA.

6.2   The System Assessed and Decomposition

Only parts of the notation were used by the participants, but we do not conclude that there is no need for the full notation. The system analysed was only a small part of a system, and the analysis was only about a minor change of this system. Therefore, not all the parts of the notation fitted. If the analysis would be on a system under development we believe that, e.g., the use of recommended action would increase and current control decrease accordingly.

When using the notation we observed challenges caused by increased complexity when assessing software components with the FSD and recognize the necessity of reducing such complexity. SD offers this through decomposition and we see the need for incorporating decomposition into FSD when used for detailed assessment of software components. In this case the participants felt that such a detailed level was not necessary, since no major software changes were needed for introducing FMTP. Specialized versions of FMEA exist for assessing software, and FSD should be capable of supporting these if the decomposition feature is adopted.

6.3   Tool Support

While using FSD we also noted general comments about tool support. The participants perceived FSD as helpful, but pointed out that a tool would make it possible to integrate FMEA and FSD further. A tool could give FSD the needed structure from the FMEA worksheet and allow for collecting all the relevant information directly in the FSD. Although this was not within the scope of our case study, we believe it shows their interest for FSD and possible future use.

7   Conclusion and Further Work

In this paper we have presented the new technique FSD with the results of using it to support FMEA. This was done by a case study in an ANSP organization, where the introduction of FMTP was assessed with respect to safety. FSD, when used together with FMEA, allowed for an interactive failure-oriented approach, ensuring a mutual understanding among the participants on how the system would work and would not work during failures. It allowed for looking at failure propagation through the system, with particular focus on components and their interactions.

We have shown that it is possible to use FSD for supporting FMEA and outlined an optimal usage of the techniques together. FSD is not able to cover all weaknesses of FMEA, especially not the assessment of multiple failures. FSD addresses components and their interactions in particular, which we conclude is an improvement of the FMEA technique and the overall safety assessment.

The optimal use of FSD and FMEA is to draw SDs first, then use FMEA to do a structured brainstorming for failure modes and causal factors, before drawing the effects of the failures along with mitigations. Depending on the completeness of the FSD, it should be kept for documentation purposes and have clear relations to the FMEA worksheet. During our case study, the participants in some cases used the numbering of, e.g., failure modes and system effects from of the FMEA worksheet in the FSD. If done consistently, it is an adequate way of keeping the link between the FSD and FMEA and for documenting the joint results.

Even though not emphasized by the participants, the discussions showed that FSD supports visualization of error propagation very well. One goal of FMEA is to relate an identified failure's immediate effect with the system effect, in order to analyse whether the failure can lead to system hazards. By drawing this error propagation with failure effect messages in FSD, it allows for a very sound and structured way of following a failure through the system. In the interviews the participants emphasized that by using FSD they had higher belief of correctness and completeness of the identified effects of failures, than compared to only using FMEA.

The case study gives valuable industrial experience. It shows practical use of a new technique that may not only be used for drawing diagrams, but can facilitate discussions, explore and correlate the understanding among the participants. This is valuable input to our understanding of several practical aspects on the use of these techniques. However, the FSD was not evaluated for its effectiveness to identify failures, related effects and mitigations. Therefore, experiments on comparing it to other techniques would be valuable, such as [6].

Further work will explore the decomposition feature of SD and how it can be incorporated into FSD to support FMEA of software components. We will also investigate how FSD can support FMEA in analysing multiple failures, as the overview of components and their interactions should be suitable for this. Finally, we will conduct further evaluations by applying our approach to a system under development, to further investigate the techniques for mitigation identification.

Acknowledgement. We would like to thank Peter Karpati and Guttorm Sindre for sharing their observations and viewpoints. Furthermore, we thank Vikash Katta for sharing his ideas and material on MUSD. Finally, the Norwegian Research Council is thanked for financing our research.

References

1. SESAR Joint Undertaking, http://www.sesarju.eu/about
2. Unified Modeling Language, http://www.uml.org/
3. Eurocontrol: Air Navigation System Safety Assessment Methodology. Ed. 2.1 (2006)
4. Eurocontrol Safety Assessment Methodology Task Force: Functional Hazard Assessment – Guidance Material B1. Ed. 2.0 (2004)
5. Ericson, C.A.: Hazard Analysis Techniques for System Safety. John Wiley & Sons Inc., New Jersey (2005)
6. Katta, V., Karpati, P., Opdahl, A.L., Raspotnig, C., Sindre, G.: Comparing Two Techniques for Intrusion Visualization. In: van Bommel, P., Hoppenbrouwers, S., Overbeek, S., Proper, E., Barjis, J. (eds.) PoEM 2010. LNBIP, vol. 68, pp. 1–15. Springer, Heidelberg (2010)
7. Avizienis, A., Laprie, J., Randell, B.: Fundamental Concepts of Dependability. Research Report No 1145, LAAS-CNRS (2001)
8. David, P., Idasiak, V., Kratz, F.: Towards a better interaction between design and dependability analysis: FMEA derived from UML/SysML models. In: Proc. ESREL 2008 and 17th SRA-Europe Annual Conference, Valencia (2008)
9. Stålhane, T., Sindre, G., du Bousquet, L.: Comparing Safety Analysis Based on Sequence Diagrams and Textual Use Cases. In: Pernici, B. (ed.) CAiSE 2010. LNCS, vol. 6051, pp. 165–179. Springer, Heidelberg (2010)
10. Guiochet, J., Vilchis, A.: Safety analysis of a medical robot for tele-echography. In: Proc. of the 2nd IARP IEEE/RAS Joint Workshop on Technical Challenge for Dependable Robots in Human Environments, Toulouse, pp. 217–227 (2002)
11. Eurocontrol: EUROCONTROL Specification of Interoperability and Preformance Requirements for the Flight Message Transfer Protocol (FMTP). EUROCONTROL-SPEC-0100 (2007)
12. Commission of the European Communities: Regulation 633/2007 Laying down requirements for the application of a flight message transfer protocol used for the purpose of notification, coordination and transfer of flights between air traffic control units (2007)
13. Davis, F.D.: Perceived Usefulness, Perceived Ease of Use, and User Acceptance of Information Technology. MIS Quarterly 13, 319–340 (1989)
14. Stallings, W.: Data and computer communications. Prentice Hall, New Jersey (2000)
15. Yin, R.K.: Case Study Research. SAGE, California (2009)
16. Eurocontrol: EUROCONTROL Specification For On-Line Data Interchange (2007)

Aligning Mal-activity Diagrams and Security Risk Management for Security Requirements Definitions

Mohammad Jabed Morshed Chowdhury[1, 2], Raimundas Matulevičius[1], Guttorm Sindre[2], and Peter Karpati[2]

[1] University of Tartu, Estonia
[2] Norwegian University of Science and Technology, Norway,
jabedmorshed@gmail.com, rma@ut.ee,
{guttors,kpeter}@idi.ntnu.no

Abstract. [**Context and motivation**] Security engineering is one of the important concerns during system development. It should be addressed throughout the whole system development process. There are several languages for security modelling that help dealing with security risk management at the requirements stage. [**Question/problem**] In this paper, we are focusing on Mal-activity diagrams that are used from requirement engineering to system design stage. More specifically we investigate how this language supports information systems security risks management (ISSRM). [**Principal ideas/results**] The outcome of this work is an alignment table between the Mal-activity diagrams language constructs to the ISSRM domain model concepts. [**Contribution**] This result may help developers understand how to model security risks at the system requirement and design stages. Also, it paves the way for interoperability between the modelling languages that are analysed using the same conceptual framework, thus facilitating transformation between these modelling approaches.

Keywords: Mal-activity diagrams, Information system security risk management, Requirement engineering, Risk management.

1 Introduction

Nowadays, business critical functions in various organisations depend on information systems (IS). Thus, the significance of security technologies in IS is widely accepted and receiving increased attention. But the security is not free; it requires investment. The return on security investment (ROSI) has become a major concern [5] in many organisations. This involves a risk management process to justify investment for security measures. To support systematic security risk management, security should be addressed and realised at all the stages of IS development.

Different modelling approaches (e.g., [3] [4]) have been proposed to cope with security in different development stages. In this work we focus on Mal-activity diagrams [6] to define security requirements. Mal-activity diagrams, henceforth, abbreviated MAD, are proposed as an extension of UML activity diagrams. Their major objective is to describe procedural logic, business process, and workflow. MAD

B. Regnell and D. Damian (Eds.): REFSQ 2012, LNCS 7195, pp. 132–139, 2012.
© Springer-Verlag Berlin Heidelberg 2012

extend activity diagrams with harmful behaviour of security attackers. A basic way to build a MAD is to draw a normal process first, then add unwanted behaviour by extra concepts, such as *Mal-activity, Mal-swimlane* and *Mal-decision*. In [6] MAD were applied to model 46 social engineering scenarios. However, they still lack clear and structured application guidance. In this paper, based on the running example, we align MAD to the domain model of the information systems security risk management (ISSRM) [2] [5]. This yields a grounded and fine-grained reasoning for how MAD can be used to understand system security risks. The analysis is illustrated through a running example gradually establishing guidelines for the application of MAD.

The structure of this paper is as follows: Section 2 introduces the ISSRM domain model, which is the basis for analysing MAD. Section 3 illustrates how MAD could be applied for security risk management and how Mal-activity constructs are aligned to the concepts of the ISSRM domain model. Section 4 presents the lessons learnt.

2   The ISSRM Domain Model

A domain model (Fig. 1) for IS security risk management (ISSRM) [2] [5] is influenced by and derived from different security risk management standards and methods, security-related standards, security-oriented frameworks (see [2] and [5] for concrete details). We have selected ISSRM to analyse MAD because it has already been successfully applied to analyse other security-modelling languages (see [3] and [4]). In addition, this domain model defines security risk management concepts at three interrelated levels, which help developers identify specific IS security risk management constructs of the analysed language.

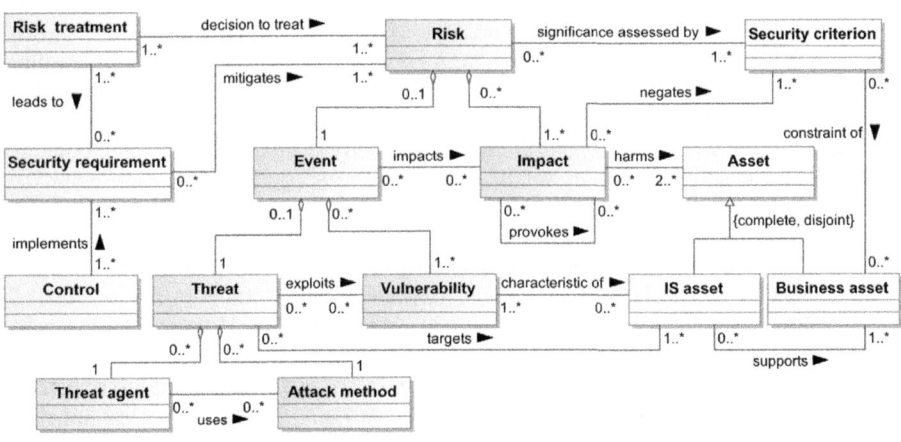

Fig. 1. The ISSRM Domain Model (adapted from [2] [5])

Asset-related concepts (i.e., *business and IS assets, IS assets, and security criterion*) explain the organisation's values that need to be protected. The needed protection level is defined as the security needs, typically in terms of confidentiality, availability and integrity. *Risk-related concepts* (i.e., *risk, impact, event, vulnerability, threat, attack method*, and *threat agent*) define the risk itself and its components. Risk is a combination of threat with one or more vulnerabilities, which leads to a negative impact, harming some assets. An impact shows the negative consequence of a risk on an asset if the threat is accomplished. A vulnerability is a weakness or flaw of one or more IS assets. An attack method is a standard means by which a threat agent executes a threat. *Risk treatment-related concepts* (i.e., *risk treatment* decision, *security requirement* and *control*) describe how to treat the identified risks. A risk treatment leads to security requirements mitigating the risk, implemented as security controls.

3   Alignment of MAD to ISSRM

Our research goal is to understand how MAD help model assets, security risks, and countermeasures during IS development. We approached this goal through three steps. Firstly, we developed a meta-model for Mal-activity diagrams in [1]. The second step was to understand how MAD could be applied to manage security risk and how their constructs correspond to the concepts of the ISSRM domain model. We approach this goal through a running example from *online-banking* discussed in Section 3.1. Finally, we have recorded the observations and discuss them in Section 3.2.

3.1   Running Example

The running example describes a correspondence between a bank officer and customer, and how a hacker could potentially harm such a correspondence. We model it using MAD following the steps of the ISSRM process [2] [5].

The ISSRM process consists of six steps. The <u>first step</u> is *content and asset identification.* Fig. 2 shows a *Bank officer's* request to the bank *Customer* to update the home address using the *Online banking system.* Hence the major business process starts by *email request to update home address* sent by the bank officer and continues to activities executed by *Customer,* e.g., *Open email, Agree to update home address,* etc. Each business activity requires support from the *Online banking system;* for example, after the customer opens the email (see activity *Open email*), email content is displayed (see activity *Display email content*). The <u>second</u> ISSRM step is *security objective determination.* In our example these are integrity of the home address updating process and confidentiality of the login name and password.

The <u>third</u> ISSRM step is risk analysis and assessment. Fig. 3 introduces a *Hacker* who sends an email with malware to the *Customer.* If the customer opens the email the malware is installed in the *Online banking system.* Using this *Malware,* the *Hacker* is capable to receive customer's *login name and password.*

In the <u>fourth</u> step the *risk treatment decision* – in our case, a decision to reduce risk – is made. The <u>fifth</u> step is *security requirements definition.* In Fig. 4 we introduce activities, such as *Enable email filtering, Check for malware,* and *Enable traffic scanner,* which potentially reduce the effect of the mal-activities. Finally, the <u>sixth</u> step of ISSRM is security *control selection and implementation.*

3.2   MAD and the ISSRM Domain Model

Our observations are summarised in Table 1.

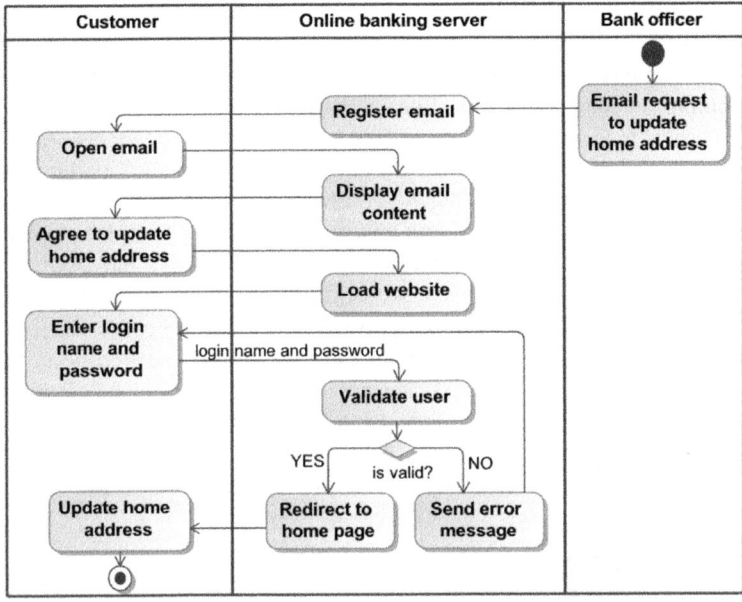

Fig. 2. Content and Asset Identification

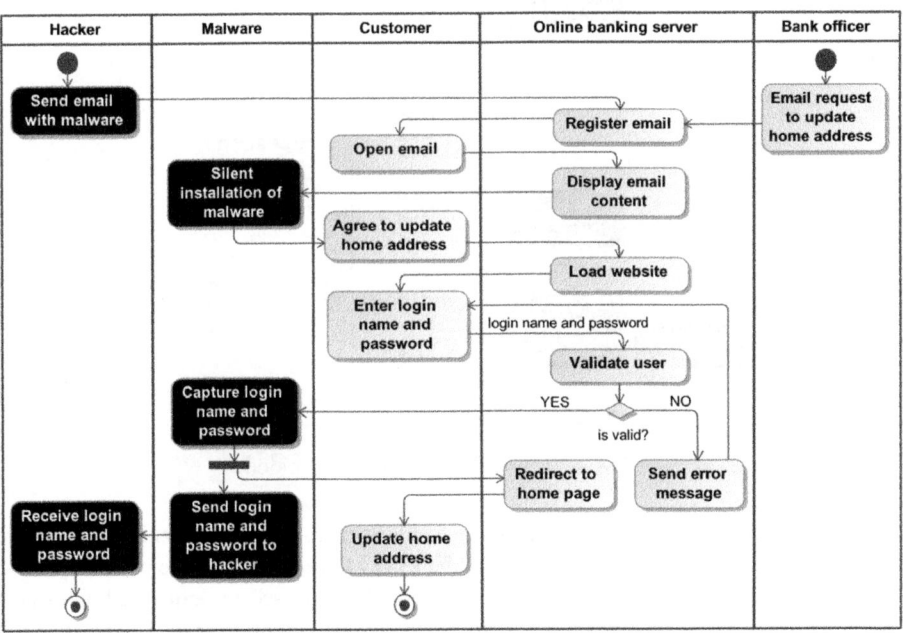

Fig. 3. Risk Analysis

Asset-related Concepts. The ISSRM *asset* represents something of value for the organisation. The *business asset* is defined as the information, process, or skill that is essential for the business. Activity diagrams are used to show the (business) workflow by combining together constructs, like: Activity, Decision and ControlFlow. We map these constructs to the ISSRM *business asset*. In addition we recognise that data (e.g., *Login name and password*) could be important to business participants. Thus, implicitly we can identify such data as an ISSRM *business* asset, too. The ISSRM *IS asset* is an IS component that supports a *business asset*. The Swimlane construct (e.g., *Online banking system*) holds the constructs (i.e., like Activity and Decision) that are needed to support execution of business workflows. Thus we align all these constructs (i.e., Swimlane, Activity, Decision and ControlFlow) to the IS assets. So, we consider Activity, Decision, ControlFlow and Swimlane as *IS asset*. We find no construct that would help representing the ISSRM *security criterion*. However the diagram gives an implicit understanding (see Table 1) of such criteria regarding the business assets.

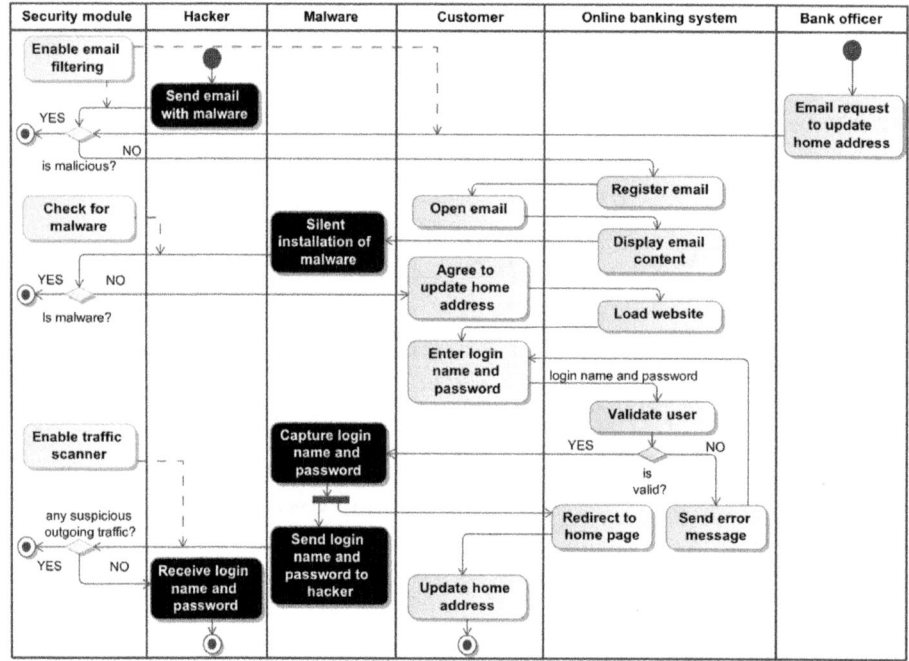

Fig. 4. Security Requirements Definition

Risk-related Concepts. An ISSRM *threat agent* is characterised by expertise, available means and motivation to harm the IS, and the ISSRM *attack method* are means by which a threat agent carries a threat. In MAD, Mal-swimlane is used to define malicious actor (e.g., *Hacker*) that will harm the system by malicious activities (e.g., *Send email with malware*), i.e., the Mal-activity constructs that are combined using Mal-decision and ControlFlow constructs. We align Mal-swimlane to the ISSRM *threat agent* and process defined by combining Mal-activity constructs, to the ISSRM *attack method*. In addition we observe that in MAD the malicious actor could use some means (e.g., *Malware*), which are defined as Mal-swimlane. Thus we align the Mal-swimlane construct to the concept of ISSRM *attack method*, too. Although we are able implicitly to define the vulnerabilities of the modelled system (see Table 1), we have not found any Mal-activity construct to represent the ISSRM *vulnerabilities*.

Table 1. Alignment Between MAD and ISSRM Domain Model

ISSRM domain model		Mal-activity diagram	Example
Asset	Asset	–	–
	Business asset	- Process described using Activity, Decision and ControlFlow constructs. - Objects used to perform activities (implicit)	- *Email request to update home address, Open email, Agree to update home address, Enter login name and password,* and *Update home address;* - *Login name and password.*
	IS asset	- Swimlane; - Activity, Decision (connected using ControlFlow constructs)	- *Online banking system;* - *Validate user, Register email, Display email, Load website, Validate user, Is valid?, Redirect ...,* and *Send error message.*
	Security criterion	–	*Integrity of the message sending process; Confidentiality of login name and password.*
Risk	Risk	–	–
	Impact	Mal-activities	*Silent installation of malware, Capture/Send login name and password*
	Event	–	–
	Vulnerability	–	*No email scanning, No installation controls, No controls for outgoing traffic.*
	Threat	Combination of constructs that represent a Threat agent and Attack method	*Hacker Sends an email with malware* and *Receives login name and password.*
	Threat agent	Mal-Swimlane	*Hacker*
	Attack method	- Process described using Mal-activities, Mal-decision, and ControlFlow - Mal-Swimlane	- *Send an email with malware* and *Receive login name and password;* - *Malware.*
Risk treat-ment	Risk treatm.	–	*Risk reduction.*
	Security requirement	MitigationActivity, MitigationLink	*Enable email filtering, Check for malware, Enable traffic scanner.*
	Control	Swimlane	*Security module*

The ISSRM *impact* is a negative consequence of a risk that harms two or more assets (at least one *business* and one *IS asset*). In MAD we can express the ISSRM *impact* using Mal-activity constructs that belong to the Mal-swimlane, characterised as the ISSRM *attack method*. For example, in Fig. 3 Mal-activity *Silent installation of malware* shows how the *Online banking system* (an ISSRM *IS asset*) is harmed by illegal installation of malware; Mal-activity *Capture login name and password* illustrates how this risk harms the *business asset*, i.e., the login name and password; finally Mal-activity *Send login name and password to hacker* specifies negation of the ISSRM *security criterion*, i.e., the *Confidentiality of login name and password*.

Risk Treatment-related Concepts. In MAD the MitigationActivity construct is understood as a countermeasure (i.e., ISSRM *security requirement*). The Swimlane (e.g., *Security module* in Fig. 4) holding the MitigationActivity constructs implements the countermeasures. Thus, we align such a Swimlane to the ISSRM *controls*.

4   Lessons Learnt

This paper has shown how the ISSRM domain model could guide application of MAD. Our analysis has a certain level of subjectivity to interpret the language constructs regarding the ISSRM concepts. To mitigate this threat other examples could be analyzed by other people (e.g., practitioners, if they are willing to use MAD).

Our study results in the alignment of the Mal-activity constructs to the ISSRM domain model. This has shown several limitations of MAD to address security risk:

- *MAD do not provide guidelines on how to use its constructs.* For example, Activity addresses both the ISSRM *business asset* and *IS asset*; Mal-activity represents both the ISSRM *impact* and *attack method*; and others.
- *MAD are unable to specify some ISSRM concepts*, like *security criterion*, *vulnerability*, *event*, and *risk*. Although *risk* and *event* constructs could be expressed using other constructs, constructs for *security criterion* and *vulnerability* should be introduced. Anyway, the ISSRM process helps developers understand (not represent) these concepts, at least implicitly.

MAD is not the only language assessed for the IS security risk management. The ISSRM domain model has been used to evaluated Secure Tropos [4], misuse cases [3], and KAOS extensions to security [5]. We envision that after analyzing a number of security languages it will be possible to facilitate model transformation and interoperability between different security languages that are analysed using the ISSRM domain model. This would allow representing IS using different perspectives and ensuring IS sustainability through different development stages.

Acknowledgement. This research is partly funded by an ETF grant (contract number ETF8704, Estonian Science Foundation).

References

1. Chowdhury, M.J.M.: Modeling Security Risks at the System Design Stage: Alignment of Mal-activity Diagrams and SecureUML to the ISSRM Domain Model. Master Theses (2011), http://nordsecmob.tkk.fi/thesis.html
2. Dubois, E., Heymans, P., Mayer, N., Matulevičius, R.: A Systematic Approach to Define the Domain of Information System Security Risk Management. In: Nurcan, S., Salinesi, C., Souveyet, C., Ralyté, J. (eds.) International Perspectives on Information Systems Engineering, pp. 289–306. Springer, Heidelberg (2010)
3. Matulevičius, R., Mayer, N., Heymans, P.: Alignment of Misuse cases with Security Risk Management. In: 3rd International Conference on Availability, Reliability and Security, pp. 1397–1404. IEEE Computer Society, Washington (2008)

4. Matulevičius, R., Mayer, N., Mouratidis, H., Dubois, E., Heymans, P., Genon, N.: Adapting Secure Tropos for Security Risk Management in the Early Phases of Information Systems Development. In: Bellahsène, Z., Léonard, M. (eds.) CAiSE 2008. LNCS, vol. 5074, pp. 541–555. Springer, Heidelberg (2008)
5. Mayer, N.: Model Based Management of Information System Security Risk. Doctoral Thesis, University of Namur (2009)
6. Sindre, G.: Mal-Activity Diagrams for Capturing Attacks on Business Processes. In: Sawyer, P., Paech, B., Heymans, P. (eds.) REFSQ 2007. LNCS, vol. 4542, pp. 355–366. Springer, Heidelberg (2007)

Towards a More Semantically Transparent
*i** Visual Syntax

Nicolas Genon[1], Patrice Caire[1], Hubert Toussaint[1],
Patrick Heymans[1,2], and Daniel Moody[3]

[1] PReCISE Research Centre, University of Namur, Belgium
[2] INRIA Lille-Nord Europe, Université Lille 1 – LIFL – CNRS, France
[3] Ozemantics Pty Ltd., Sydney, Australia
{nge,pca,hto,phe}@info.fundp.ac.be,
daniel@ozemantics.com.au

Abstract. **[Context and motivation]** *i** is one of the most popular modelling
languages in Requirements Engineering. *i** models are meant to support communication between technical and non-technical stakeholders about the goals of the
future system. Recent research has established that the effectiveness of model-
mediated communication heavily depends on the visual syntax of the modelling
language. A number of flaws in the visual syntax of *i** have been uncovered
and possible improvements have been suggested. **[Question/problem]** Producing effective visual notations is a complex task that requires taking into account
various interacting quality criteria. In this paper, we focus on one of those criteria: *Semantic Transparency*, that is, the ability of notation symbols to suggest
their meaning. **[Principal ideas/results]** Complementarily to previous research,
we take an empirical approach. We give a preview of a series of experiments
designed to identify a new symbol set for *i** and to evaluate its semantic transparency. **[Contribution]** The reported work is an important milestone on the path
towards cognitively effective requirements modelling notations. Although it does
not solve all the problems in the *i** notation, it illustrates the usefulness of an empirical approach to visual syntax definition. This approach can later be transposed
to other quality criteria and other notations.

Keywords: *i**, Goal-oriented modelling, Empirical evaluation, Physics of
Notation, Semantic Transparency.

1 Introduction

i* [1] is one of the most popular modelling languages for Requirements Engineering
(RE). It provides conceptual and visual means to express, and reason on, the functional
and non-functional goals of a system. Its visual syntax is meant to facilitate communication between technical and non-technical stakeholders. However, this assumption
has been challenged recently. Moody *et al.* [2,3] have evaluated the visual syntax of
i* against the Physics of Notations [4] (PoN). PoN is a theory comprised of nine principles, namely Semiotic Clarity, Perceptual Discriminability, Semantic Transparency,
Complexity Management, Cognitive Integration, Visual Expressiveness, Dual Coding,
Graphic Economy and Cognitive Fit. A major advantage of those principles is that they

B. Regnell and D. Damian (Eds.): REFSQ 2012, LNCS 7195, pp. 140–146, 2012.

are evidence-based: they do not rely on common sense and experience but on theory and empirical evidence from a wide range of fields, including linguistics, cartography, cognitive psychology. . .

Following these principles is meant to lead to more *cognitively effective* notations, i.e. notations which diagrams can be understood quickly, easily and accurately. In [2,3], a number of suggestions were made in order to improve the cognitive effectiveness of *i**. Although those were made on the basis of the evidence-based principles of PoN, an open question remained: how and to which extent the principles coming from other disciplines transpose to software engineering, and more particularly to RE.

Moody *et al.*'s analysis uncovered a number of flaws in the visual syntax of *i** and suggested various improvements. One of them was to improve the *Semantic Transparency* of *i**. Semantic Transparency refers to the ability of the symbols of a notation to suggest their meaning. Semantically transparent symbols can be seen as the visual equivalent of onomatopoeia. For example, a stick figure is more semantically transparent than an abstract shape (e.g., a circle) to represent the concept of person. According to the PoN, Semantic Transparency has a major influence on the cognitive effectiveness of a notation.

In [2,3], Moody *et al.* proposed a set of supposedly more semantically transparent symbols for *i**. Our work aims at evaluating and complementing their proposal with experimental studies. We defined a series of controlled experiments to identify a "super" symbol set for *i** and to assess its semantic transparency. The main difference with previous research lies in the way new symbols were obtained: the authors of the present work did not design a new symbol set by themselves, based on some theory. On the contrary, an experiment was set up where participants were asked to draw what they thought would be the most appropriate symbols given the *i** concepts and their definitions.

We present the plan of this experiment series in Section 2. Then, we describe the three experiments of that series that were already performed: the "production of drawings" experiment (Section 3), the "population stereotype" experiment (Section 4), and the "population prototype" experiment (Section 5). We share the preliminary results obtained for each experiment. Section 6 wraps up the paper and gives an overview of future work.

2 Experiment Plan

This series of controlled experiments consists in identifying a "super" symbol set for *i** and assessing its semantic transparency. By "super symbol set", we mean the symbols that are judged the most semantically transparent by *i** users. The eligible symbols are taken from 4 sources: the original *i** symbol set [1], the symbols proposed in [3], and 2 sets based on the outcome of the present experiments. In this work, we do not evaluate the semantic transparency of the symbol sets *in context*, i.e, by exposing participants to diagrams and letting them perform RE tasks based on these diagrams. Instead, we focus on the symbols on their own. Thereby, we avoid the biases that occur when dealing with diagrams (e.g., bias due to the relative positioning of symbols; bias due to the number of symbols on the diagram; bias due to the complexity of the diagram; shift of attention introduced by the colour and size of some symbols on the diagram, etc.).

Experiment 1 is concerned with the *production of drawings*. The goal of this experiment is to obtain drawings hand-sketched by participants to represent each *i** concept. We used a sign production technique that relies on the following assumption: "[experiment] subjects, when properly instructed, can actually produce signs for referent concepts and will do so in frequencies proportional to stereotype strength" [5]. The *population stereotype* refers to the sign(s) that is/are the most frequently produced by participants to denote the referent concept. The outcome of the experiment are symbols designed by *i** users for *i** users, contrary to the symbols proposed in [2,3]. Indeed, the latter may suffer from a strong bias of the authors being RE experts, which could result in symbols that are ineffective for novices or non-technical users.

Experiment 2 focused on identifying the stereotypical drawings out of the results of Experiment 1. All the stereotypes resulting from Experiment 2 would constitute our first new set of hand-sketched symbols for *i**. However, the population stereotype is not sufficient by itself because it does not take into account the level of approximation of the idea depicted by the drawing wrt. the referent *i** concept. Actually, the drawing that is the *most frequently* produced to denote a concept, is not necessarily expressing the idea that is the *closest approximation* to that concept. Conversely, the most "evocative" drawing is usually designed by only a small part of the participants, and then not identified by population stereotype. In other words, while population stereotype can be seen as the best *median* drawing, creativity and originality is captured through the *population prototype*.

Population prototype is the purpose of Experiment 3. This experiment looks for the drawing that *best* represents the corresponding *i** concept. We rely on the personal opinion of participants to elect the drawing that is the most semantically transparent for a given referent concept. The outcome of Experiment 3 would be the second new set of hand-sketched symbols for *i**.

Instead of addressing all the *i** concepts, we limited the scope of this work to 13 concepts: actor, agent, role, position, actor boundary, goal, softgoal, task, resource, belief, means-end link, decomposition link and dependency link. The rationale for this choice is to focus on the subset of the *i** language that appears to be most used in practice.

3   Experiment 1: Production of Drawings

The **question** we addressed in the experiment is the following: "What kinds of drawings can novices produce when presented with a set of concepts and their definitions?"

Experiment Design. The participants were composed of 104 students (53 females and 51 males) in 1st year Bachelor in Economics and Management from the University of Namur. These students had no previous knowledge of *i** or modelling in general, which is a profile we expect to find in many real-life RE settings, for stakeholders like users, subject matter experts, and managers. The participants were not remunerated for their contribution.

Each participant was provided with a 14-page booklet, a pencil and an eraser. The first page presented a form to collect participants' demographic data. The remaining 13 pages were respectively dedicated to the 13 *i** concepts. A 2-column table was added at the top of each page. The first column provided the name of the *i** concept in French and English. The second column contained the French definition of the concept[1].

A (3" x 3") frame where participants were asked to sketch their drawing was printed in the middle of the page. The sketching instructions were repeated on each page and placed above the frame. A 5-point scale and the corresponding instructions were added at the bottom of the page. The 5 values of the scale were "easy", "fairly easy", "neither easy nor difficult", "fairly difficult" and "difficult".

We deliberately decided not to randomise the presentation order of the concepts because the definitions of part of the *i** concepts rely on the definitions of other concepts, e.g. Agent, Role and Position refer to Actor; Softgoal refers to Goal.

The 104 students were brought together in an auditorium. The average time for completion of this experiment was around 45 minutes. For each *i** concept, participants were asked *(a)* to sketch what they estimate to be the best drawing to represent the name and the definition of this concept. There was no time limit but they were asked to sketch as quickly as possible. The intent was to capture their intuition. We drew their attention on the fact that we would focus on the idea(s) expressed by the drawing, not the quality of the sketching. *(b)* Each time a drawing was produced, the participant had to evaluate the difficulty of the task on the 5-point scale. Participants were also told to respond one page at time and not to go back in the booklet.

Results. We eventually retrieved 1352 drawings (blank and null drawings included[2]). One of the main observations is that participants had much more difficulty sketching drawings for concepts denoting relationships than for the concepts denoting objects or persons. The reasons to this observation still have to be investigated. We also observed that the produced drawings often do not rely on both the name *and* the definition of the concept. Moreover, some participants depicted concepts not through a single symbol but through several symbols interacting in a scene (e.g., the concept of Task can be represented by a stick figure performing some action on an object).

4   Experiment 2: Population Stereotype

The **question** we addressed in this experiment is the following: "Among the presented drawings, what is the stereotypical representation for the selected concepts?" The population stereotype is the best *median* drawing, that is the representation that is most frequently recognised and selected by people to depict the concept.

Experiment Design. We applied a judges' ranking method [6]. Concept per concept, three of the authors categorised the drawings obtained from Experiment 1 based on the similarity of ideas that they expressed. Hence, 13 times (because we considered 13 *i** concepts), each author had to split the 104 drawings into piles. All the drawings from a pile depicted the same idea(s) and thus form a category. The three judges were instructed to define as many categories as needed relying on their personal opinion.

The categorisation process was inevitably prone to a certain degree of interpretation and subjectivity. However, it was required for the judges to follow instructions and to

---

[1] The French version was used to avoid bias regarding the English skills of the participants.

[2] These range from 5 to 15% of the drawings, depending on the concept.

perform the work independently. Afterwards, the judges compared their respective categories and agreed on a common set of categories. In this operation, several categories from different judges were merged into one common category. Finally, for each concept, the judges selected, from the category that contained the largest number of drawings, the drawing that best expressed the ideas of the category.

Results. The outcome of this experiment is the set of 13 stereotypical drawings (one per concept) presented in Figure 1. It is noteworthy that, except for relationship concepts, there is no abstract shape in the population stereotypes.

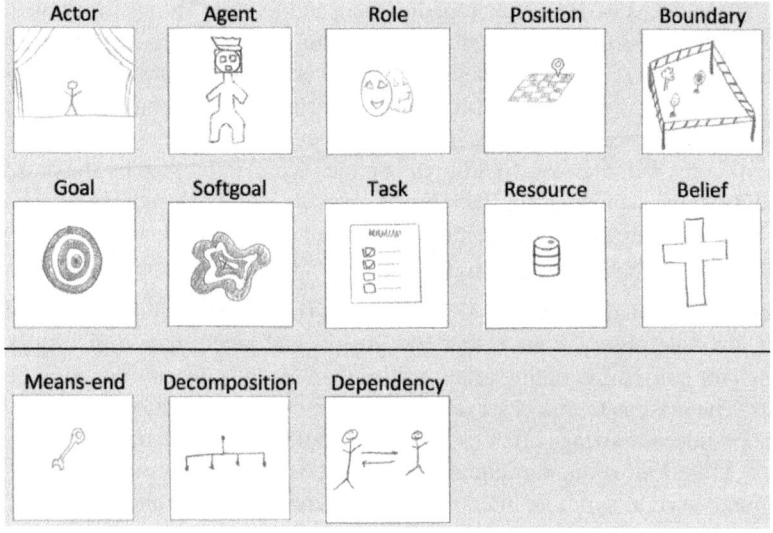

Fig. 1. The population stereotypes for the *i** concepts

5   Experiment 3: Population Prototype

The **question** we addressed in this experiment is the following: "Among the presented drawings, what is the prototypical representation for selected concepts?"

Experiment Design. We conducted this experiment on a different sample of population (no overlap) but the participants had the same profile, i.e. they had neither knowledge of *i** nor modelling in general. We opened the experiment to students in 1st year Bachelor in Computer Science or Economics and Management. We welcomed 30 participants (1 female, 29 males). They were not remunerated for their participation. Instructions were to choose one best drawing per concept. As for the drawing production experiment, they were provided with the name and the definition of the concept. The eligible set of drawings was composed of 160 drawings: the 13 stereotypes along with one representative of each category of the 13 *i** concepts. It was a deliberate decision not to expose the participants to all 1352 drawings. This would have been counter-productive: taking them too much time and leading to bias caused by tiredness.

An online questionnaire was set up. The participants were asked to enter their demographic data on the first page and then they navigated through 13 pages, one per *i** concept. Each page displayed the French name and the definition of the concept at the top of the page. The middle of the page was dedicated to instructions for selecting (using radio buttons) the best drawing among the matrix of representatives. The difficulty of the selection task was evaluated on a visual analogue scale (VAS) at the bottom of the page. The order the concepts appearing in the questionnaire as well as the position of the drawings in each matrix were randomised for each participant.

As we built an online questionnaire, we booked a pool hosting 30 computers. To be as compliant as possible with the students' schedules, we ran the experiment from 10.30 AM to 6.00 PM. The 30 students came at their best convenience. The experiment was not constrained by time limit and the average duration was between 5 to 15 minutes.

Results. We have only preliminary results and observations to report. The population prototype obtained for each concept is shown in Figure 2. There was most of the time one indisputable leader – low level of vote dispersal – except for the concept of Dependency Link where we had an *ex-aequo*.

We also noticed that four prototypical drawings matched the stereotype of the concepts: Actor, Goal, Task and Decomposition Link. These drawings can be assumed to have a significant level of semantic transparency: they depict the idea that is the most frequently used by participants and that evokes the referent *i** concept most clearly.

Regarding the difficulty to select the best drawing (measured on the VAS), the value ranged from 30% to 60%. As discussed in the results of Experiment 1, drawings depicting concrete objects or persons seem to be preferred. Except for relationship concepts, there is no abstract shape in the population prototypes.

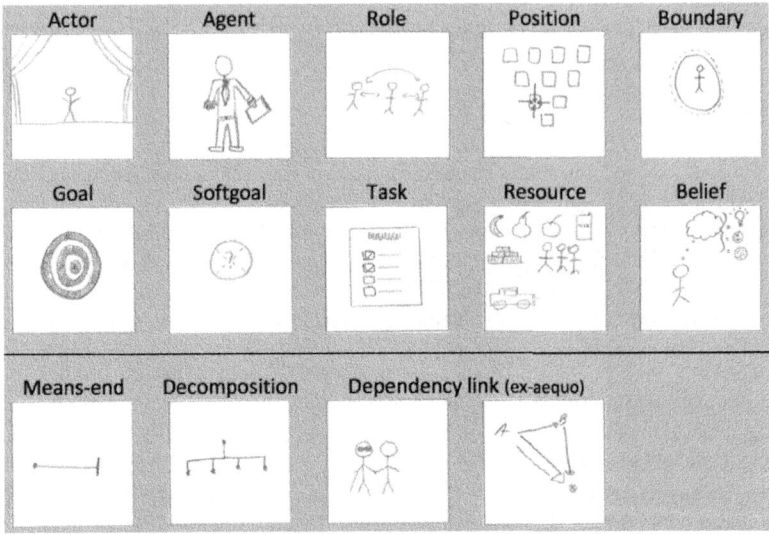

Fig. 2. The population prototypes for the *i** concepts

We observed an adequacy between the nature of the concepts denoting relationships and the nature of their representations: these concepts are depicted with "links".

6 Conclusion and Future Work

In this paper, we gave a preview of a series of empirical studies that aim at improving the semantic transparency of the i^* symbols. So far, we have performed 3 experiments: the first one is concerned with the empirical production of drawings for the i^* concepts by inexperienced subjects. Based on the drawings from Experiment 1, Experiment 2 looked for population stereotypes, i.e., drawings that are *the most frequently* produced to denote a referent concept. Experiment 3 aimed at identifying population prototypes, i.e., drawings depicting the idea that is *the closest approximation* to the semantics of a referent concept. At this stage, we have empirically obtained two new i^* symbols sets: one set is composed of the stereotypical drawings; the second set gathers the best drawings selected in Experiment 3. We also have promising preliminary results that allow us to envision the next steps of our work. We plan to confront our two new symbol sets with two other sets of i^* symbols: the original i^* symbols [1] and the symbols proposed in [3]. The final objective is twofold: to empirically evaluate which of the four symbol sets is the more semantically transparent, and to propose a new *super i**, that could be a combination of all 4 symbol sets.

From a broader perspective, the reported work is an important milestone on the path towards cognitively effective notations in RE and software engineering. Although it does not solve all the problems in the i^* notation [7], it illustrates the usefulness of an empirical approach to visual syntax definition. This approach can later be transposed to other quality criteria and other notations.

Acknowledgement. This work was supported by the Interuniversity Attraction Poles Programme - Belgian State - Belgian Science Policy (MoVES) and the BNB.

References

1. Yu, E.: Towards Modeling and Reasoning Support for Early-Phase Requirements Engineering. In: Proc. of RE 1997, pp. 226–235 (1997)
2. Moody, D.L., Heymans, P., Matulevičius, R.: Improving the Effectiveness of Visual Representations in Requirements Engineering: An Evaluation of i^* Visual Syntax (Best Paper Award). In: Proc. of RE 2009, pp. 171–180 (2009)
3. Moody, D.L., Heymans, P., Matulevičius, R.: Visual syntax does matter: improving the cognitive effectiveness of the i^* visual notation. Requirements Engineering 15(2), 141–175 (2010)
4. Moody, D.L.: The "Physics" of Notations: Towards a Scientific Basis for Constructing Visual Notations in Software Engineering. TSE 35, 756–779 (2009)
5. Howell, W.C., Fuchs, A.H.: Population Stereotype in Code Design. Organizational Behavior and Human Performance 3, 310–339 (1968)
6. Jones, S.: Stereotypy in Pictograms of Abstract Concepts. Ergonomics 26, 605–611 (1983)
7. Mussbacher, G., Amyot, D., Heymans, P.: Eight Deadly Sins of GRL. In: Proc. of the 5th International i^* Workshop, Trento, Italy (August 2011)

Providing Software Product Line Knowledge to Requirements Engineers – A Template for Elicitation Instructions

Sebastian Adam

Fraunhofer IESE, Fraunhofer Platz 1, 67663 Kaiserslautern
sebastian.adam@iese.fraunhofer.de

Abstract. **[Context & Motivation]** Developing new software systems based on a software product line (SPL) in so-called application engineering (AE) projects is still a time-consuming and expensive task. Especially when a large number of customer-specific requirements exists, there is still no systematic support for efficiently aligning these non-anticipated requirements with SPL characteristics early on. **[Question/problem]** In order to improve this process significantly, sound knowledge about an SPL must be available when guiding the requirements elicitation during AE. Thus, an appropriate reflection of SPL characteristics in process-supporting artifacts is indispensable for actually supporting a requirements engineer in this task. **[Principal ideas/results]** In this paper, a validated template for elicitation instructions that aims at providing a requirements engineer with knowledge about an underlying SPL in an appropriate manner is presented. This template consists of predefined text blocks and algorithms that explain how SPL-relevant product and process knowledge can be systematically reflected into capability-aware elicitation instructions. **[Contribution]** By using such elicitation instructions, requirements engineers are enabled to elicit requirements in an AE project more effectively.

1   Motivation

As a key concept for streamlining software development, software product lines (SPL) [2] have proven to be a promising strategy, especially when time to market is a crucial success factor. Nevertheless, developing new systems based on an SPL (which is denoted as application engineering (AE) in the community) is still a time-consuming task [3], and the benefits of using an SPL approach are often less than expected [4].

One important reason for the low efficiency in AE is the non-systematic mapping of customer-specific requirements [6], even though it has been recognized that the success of AE mainly depends on how requirements are treated. This is especially a problem in SPLs, in which a significant number of requirements cannot be anticipated during domain engineering (DE) by means of explicitly predefined variants only, what is, for instance, often the case in information systems (IS).

On the one hand, current approaches rather foster the direct reuse of predefined SPL requirements than the effective alignment of a customer's actual needs with the

B. Regnell and D. Damian (Eds.): REFSQ 2012, LNCS 7195, pp. 147–164, 2012.

available SPL capabilities [8] [9]. However, especially IS development that is merely based on picking reusable requirements, which then imply a predefined system behavior, is not feasible, because such systems also have to reflect a large number of individual requirements in order to allow the customer to stand out from the competition. Therefore, many costly corrections are typically needed during AE until a delivered system fulfills its expectations. On the other hand, eliciting customer requirements without considering SPL characteristics early on is also not an appropriate option. Particularly since selecting an SPL implies a certain set of constraints, it becomes apparent that not all customer requirements can be realized as initially stated. Rather, trade-offs between ideal requirements and rapid development benefits must be made. However, making this trade-off is challenging, because information about the realizability of requirements is (beyond predefined variability models) neither formalized nor available in the early requirements phase. Requirements elicitation therefore becomes an error-prone task, and it relies on experts to predict the impact of requirements that can only be realized with additional development [6]. Unfortunately, guidance on how to proactively elicit and negotiate actual customer requirements and align them with SPL capabilities is not supported systematically yet [6] [8]. Hence, it is still hard to elicit requirements during AE, especially when the number of requirements that can be explicitly anticipated and described by means of variability or decision models is limited.

A requirements engineering (RE) approach for AE (called AERE) that precisely guides the elicitation based on the characteristics of a given SPL in a more flexible and rather constraint-based than enumerative manner is therefore needed. However, as making requirements engineers aware of SPL characteristics is not easy (and typically limited to anticipated variants only), the *scientific problem* to be addressed therefore deals with the question of how requirements engineers can be enabled to use sound SPL product and process knowledge for appropriately guiding the elicitation (i.e., how can they made aware of important SPL capabilities, constraints and needs). This includes two research questions:

1. How can SPL product and process knowledge be economically extracted and incorporated into the AERE process when a complete, explicit anticipation of customer requirements is neither economic nor possible?
2. How can this knowledge be represented to an AE requirements engineer to guide their elicitation without the need to adhere to predefined variants only?

While we have already discussed our ideas on how to cope with the first issue (see [10] [24]), this paper focuses on the second[1]. In the next section, related work is discussed. In section 3, we then introduce a template for elicitation instructions including the underlying research approach. An evaluation of this template is then shown in section 4, while section 5 summaries the whole paper.

[1] The work presented in this paper was performed in the context of the Software-Cluster project EMERGENT (www.software-cluster.org). It was partially funded by the German Federal Ministry of Education and Research (BMBF) under grant no. "01IC10S01". The authors assume responsibility for the content.

2   Related Work

While much effort has been spent on how to build up SPLs during the so-called domain engineering phase (DE), actual reuse during AE has not received sufficient attention yet [4] [11] [12]. This holds especially true for RE activities: While there are many publications about product line scoping (e.g., [13]) or RE in DE (see [1] for an overview), only few exist that focus on AE [12].

In this regard, many proposed AE approaches share the ideas of Deelstra et al. [3] and distinguish an initial configuration phase and a phase of tuning iterations. The purpose of the latter is to modify and extend the initial configuration until all customer requirements are sufficiently met. Thus, additional development is typically required also [3][6], as it is unusual that all requirements can be fulfilled by existing assets only.

Within AERE, one can therefore distinguish the instantiation of variable requirements that were created during DE, and the elicitation of customer-specific requirements from scratch [14]. Even if both activities are important, most approaches such as from Sinnema et al. [15] only focus on the instantiation step. For this purpose, AE requirements engineers are only provided with feature catalogues, variability models, or decision models that have to be processed during elicitation. Indeed, these approaches work very efficiently, but they are applicable only in highly predictable and stable domains, as they rely on the restrictive assumption that all requirements can be explicitly prescribed during the DE phase (which is otherwise neither economic nor feasible due to the size and complexity of modern SPLs [3]). Thus, even for requirements that differ only slightly from the foreseen variants, these approaches are not applicable anymore [9], which results in manual, typically not guided, and thus costly extensions. Guelfi et al. [9][11] therefore propose a constraint-based rather than enumerative approach that allows deriving products that are not explicitly foreseen but close enough to the SPL. However, their approach only addresses the actual instantiation, but does not support the requirements elicitation in a systematic manner.

For eliciting new requirements that have not been covered during DE, only some initial work exists [12]. So far, mostly the tasks of communicating the variability [17], selecting variants, specifying system requirements (i.e., selected variants), and supporting trade-off decisions have been proposed as being important in this context [18]. For this purpose, Bühne et al. [19] describe a scenario-based approach and Rabiser et al. [12], too, introduce an approach for more systematic AERE. However, one remaining problem is the fact that requirements are still identified in a solution-driven (bottom-up) way instead of in a problem-driven way [8], as the aim is rather to obtain a large degree of direct requirements reuse than to satisfy actual needs with available assets. Hence, when high individuality is required in order to satisfy a customer, guidance on how to elicit such needs and reconcile them with reuse capabilities more flexibly is not supported systematically yet. In particular, unaligned approaches such as from Djebbi et al. [8] or those from "traditional top-down" elicitation make a sufficient fit almost impossible without costly rework.

Beyond AERE, RE for COTS-based development does not seem to be sufficient either, as it just deals with the selection [20] and adaptation [21] of COTS components. Furthermore, existing COTS-RE approaches do not give any guidance on how requirements are to be elicited and negotiated in order to fit existing assets.

Tailoring AERE processes based on existing SPL capabilities and constraints is probably the only means to solve the introduced problem. The work of Doerr et al. [22], for instance, aimed at improving RE processes, is maybe one of the few existing approaches that explicitly reflects the specific needs and constraints of a development organization in an RE process. However, this approach lacks both a systematic identification of important product and process knowledge, and an appropriate reflection of this knowledge in process-supporting artifacts. Furthermore, the specific context of SPL organizations is not considered. Also more recent work dealing with the identification of (information) needs such as [23], does not offer guidance on how to derive important issues in this regard either. So far, the problem mentioned in the motivation cannot be solved satisfactorily yet with current approaches.

3   Research Approach

The general idea for defining a template for elicitation instructions as mentioned before has been based on our practical experience in industry, where we discovered (however, outside SPLs) that precise instructions are able to support systematic elicitation even for non-experts. In a consulting project some years ago, for instance, our requirements engineering team at Fraunhofer IESE enabled people with low RE experience to perform rather good elicitation merely by following precise instructions. However, when we then performed a literature analysis, we found out that similar work has not been proposed yet. Rather, most approaches found still "lack sufficiently precise and prescriptive instructions" [16].

A first step towards our template for elicitation instructions was the clarification of important SPL concepts and their interplay with AERE processes. For this purpose, we iteratively developed a comprehensive conceptual AE model based on literature reviews and several discussions with SPL experts (parts of this model are published in [10]). The elements of this model (e.g., assumptions, existing realizations, etc.) were then used to derive hypothetic requirements regarding the content that the elicitation instructions should provide to AE requirements engineers. As we assume our model to be complete, we also assume the derived hypothetic requirements to be rather complete. However, based on our own elicitation experience, we additionally defined a couple of hypothetic requirements regarding the general nature of elicitation instructions that could not already be expressed in our model.

In a third step, we then performed a survey with eight experienced requirements engineers in order to elicit their requirements on elicitation instructions for AERE. What all involved engineers had in common was that they had an academic background but also much experience in performing RE in industry. Besides one internationally renowned professor, two heads of a leading German requirements engineering group participated in the study. In general, five participants had elicited requirements in more than 12 projects already, so, it can be assumed that they were aware of the most important success factors and pitfalls there.

The survey was done by means of a questionnaire with open and closed questions. The open questions were used to gain new insights about content and structure suitable for elicitation instructions. The closed questions (using the scale "totally disagree, ..., totally agree") were additionally used to get confirmation for our hypothetic requirements, and for eliciting the general acceptance of the intended instructions. In this regard, we considered a hypothetic requirement as confirmed if the median in the answers was "rather agree" or "totally agree" and the minimum in the answers not lower than "neither agree nor disagree".

Based on the confirmed requirements (22 of 33 hypothetic requirements could be confirmed), we then developed the template for elicitation instructions. A central step during this task was the definition of text blocks (called "phrases") to be used for providing the required information. For choosing appropriate formulations for these text blocks, as well as for determining rules regarding their incorporation in a meaningful order, we then recapitulated, discussed, and formalized our own way of how we have successfully performed requirements elicitation in many projects so far.

In one of the last steps, we then checked by means of traceability links whether our template addressed all requirements. Furthermore, we developed a tool for automatically generating concrete elicitation instructions based on our template. The purpose of this tool development was twofold: first, to demonstrate the preciseness of our template via its ability to be implemented in software, and, second, to avoid the tedious work when defining corresponding instructions manually.

In order to finally validate the benefits and applicability of the template, we prepared a two-step evaluation approach that includes an expert validation and a controlled experiment. During the former step, which is described at the end of this paper, we let eight requirements engineering experts use and review an exemplary instruction according to our template to validate whether it is basically applicable and useful. During the latter step, which is still in progress, requirements engineering students are going to use another exemplary instruction for eliciting requirements in a realistic role play. The goal of this second study is to objectively evaluate the elicitation performance in comparison to state-of-the-art instructions. Furthermore, subjective assessment of the material will also be gathered.

4   A Template for Elicitation Instructions

Our basic idea for representing SPL knowledge is to provide precise and prescriptive AERE instructions (i.e., elicitation instruction) that define a meaningful sequence of elicitation steps based on a given SPL (see Figure 1). If AE requirements engineers have such instructions, they are expected to perform the elicitation better, even if not all customer requirements have been explicitly defined during DE. This is especially important for SPLs in which not all requirements have been documented.

To realize this notion, AERE instructions have to describe regarding which issues requirements have to be elicited and which constraints must be considered. Hence, detection, negotiation, and correction of unrealizable, missing, or superfluous requirements can be done much more proactively and thus faster during AE projects leading to a more efficient AE in general. The main benefit of this approach in contrast to the decision model or feature diagram questionnaires traditionally applied in AE is that instead of purely asking which features a system should have (solution-oriented requirements), the really necessary requirements can be systematically derived based on the given business problems (problem-oriented requirements). Thus, requirements that are already part of the SPL and those which are not can be handled in an integrated manner. Despite this, the approach always enables a requirements engineer to be aware of all the basic SPL capabilities and limitations when a certain issue is discussed. Thus, (s)he is always able to immediately start negotiations about requirements that might lead to unexpected project delay. For this purpose, however, a constraint-based rather than enumerative description of the SPL is applied in order to cope with the challenge that an explicit variability expression is often limited.

Of course, we are aware that each elicitation instruction is basically rigid, and that it may be complicated to keep it in mind during real customer conversations. However, we do not expect that our AERE instructions are straightly used, but that they are used as an abstract process or even just as a mnemonic to inform requirements engineers about the content to elicit and the constraints that exist. Whether this works has been checked during an evaluation described in chapter 4. In this section, a template for such AERE elicitation instructions (called elicitation instructions below) and the research that has led to it is introduced.

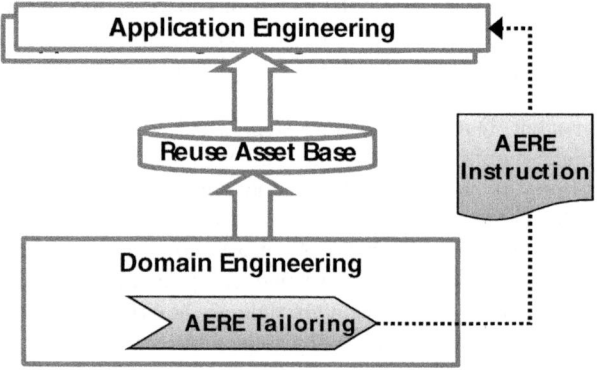

Fig. 1. Usage of tailored AERE instructions during AE

4.1   Requirements on Elicitation Instructions

Basically, six (75%) of the RE experts we involved in the requirements elicitation mentioned that a precise elicitation instruction would be of high or even very high value to support their elicitation activities in AERE. Especially some sort of clear, stepwise, procedural guidance that allows achieving a high degree of completeness in a constructive manner was demanded by almost all of the interviewed engineers in the open questions section. In this regard, the interviewed persons also mentioned that each statement in the instruction must be easy to understand and allow a requirements engineer to deviate if necessary. This means that an instruction should only guide and support a requirements engineer but not force him to do something that does not make sense in a concrete situation. Nevertheless, the instructions should be precise enough that a requirements engineer does not get lost when performing elicitation.

Besides this open feedback, the hypothetic requirements shown in Table 1 were confirmed by the survey participants based on their answers to the closed questions.

Table 1. Requirements on Elicitation Instructions

	An elicitation instruction should...
R.N.2.	clearly mention a sequence of steps to be carried out (clear how-to)
R.N.3.	explain how to proceed with the elicited requirements (e.g., visualizing, describing, classifying, ...)
R.N.4.	be specific, i.e., customized for a certain development context or SPL
R.S.1.	make clear in which order elicitation steps should be performed best
R.S.2.	be modularized and allow taking breaks between sessions
R.S.4.	provide good indications for knowing when finished with elicitation
R.C.1.	mention the issues that are relevant for discussion
R.C.2.	make clear until which point in time certain issues have to be discussed
R.C.3.	name the typical stakeholders needed in a certain step
R.C.4.	inform about the details to be elicited with regard to a certain issue
R.C.6.	make clear about which issues a discussion is unnecessary (e.g., because no one in the subsequent development process will care about them)
R.C.7.	inform about which requirements are implemented by default anyway (e.g., common requirements / features)
R.C.8.	inform about whether requirements concerning a certain issue are restricted by architectural constraints
R.C.9.	make clear which properties a requirement must fulfill in order to be implementable
R.C.10.	inform about capabilities that already exist
R.C.12.	inform about conceptual dependencies between issues

4.2   Basic Structure

The overall purpose of elicitation instructions is to guide requirements engineers through a requirements elicitation process. Thus, the general structure of elicitation processes must be appropriately covered in the elicitation instruction template.

Basically, a requirements elicitation process consists of phases in which several (requirements) activities are performed. Phases are logical timespans reaching a milestone at which a certain result is achieved. Thus, the activities within a phase are needed to elaborate the outcome at the phase's milestone.

In Figure 2, our basic template for elicitation instructions according to a requirements elicitation process structure is depicted. For each phase, respectively requirements milestone, within a process, the elicitation instruction should provide a corresponding milestone section. The purpose of a milestone section is to collect concrete instructions for all activities that are needed to elaborate the requirements that must exist before the corresponding requirements milestone can be reached (addresses R.C.2 and R.S.4). If, for instance, a phase "business analysis" is part of a requirements process, the corresponding milestone section has to guide all activities that are needed to elaborate the business-relevant issues such as business goals, business objects, business rules, business processes, etc.

Each milestone section is therefore further subdivided into issue sections, which provide instructions for the elicitation of all requirements concerning one specific issue (e.g., for business process, business objects, ,…). In the context of our work, an issue is a conceptual class of elements that are either part of system or a part of the system's usage environment. Thus, a requirements activity according to our model always deals with the elicitation of requirements regarding one specific class of elements.

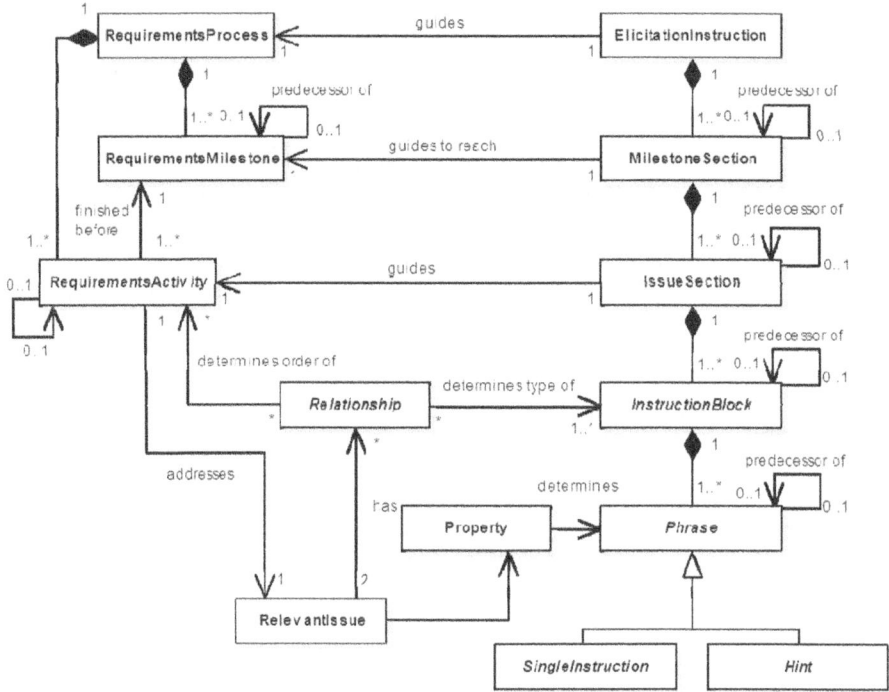

Fig. 2. Basic structure of elicitation instructions and its interplay with a requirements process

Within each issue section, concrete guidance on how to elicit and analyze the requirements concerning a specific issue is then given (addresses R.N.2). For this purpose, an issue section (see Figure 3 for an example) contains precise phrases (i.e., single instructions and hints), which are organized into so-called instruction blocks (addresses R.S.2). While the phrases comprise concrete statements for the requirements engineer on what to do or what to consider, the instruction blocks group these phrases in order to align different sub-activities such as asking, describing, classifying, clarifying, etc. more logically. Both instruction blocks and phrases therefore always depend on the actual issues of interest, respectively their properties and relationships (addresses R.N.4).

4.3   Single Instructions and Hints

The phrases, i.e., the single instructions and hints, are the core of each elicitation instruction as they form the elements that provide a requirements engineer with actual knowledge. While the single instructions support the requirements elicitation through the predefined description of actions that are typically needed, the hints contain information that the requirements engineers should be aware of. This is especially needed to avoid the elicitation of non-fitting, superfluous, or missing requirements and, thus, to accelerate the alignment of customer requirements with SPL characteristics.

So far, we have identified 14 phrases (eight single instructions and six hints). Below, we briefly explain each of these. The underlined words in the examples are the words that are variable within the phrase's text block. However, besides the shown examples, other text block variants also exist to cover more specific situations.

Identifying Instruction. The purpose of this instruction is to find out what a customer basically wants or needs without defining his / her requirements in detail. The instruction therefore provides templates for "which"-questions based on the issue for which requirements are to be elicited (addresses R.C.1). In this context, the instruction makes use of an issue's relationships (addresses R.C.12). Example: "Ask the stakeholder the following question: Which <u>User Groups</u> are <u>performing</u> this <u>Use Case</u>?"

Collecting Instruction. The purpose of this instruction is to collect all identified requirements in an enumerative manner (e.g., bullet list) in order to handle the mass of gathered information (again without specifying details). The notion to focus only on enumeration reflects our strategy that details for each requirement should not be defined before a quite stable set of requirements has been achieved. Example: "Collect the identified <u>User Groups</u> in a corresponding list and add a link back to the related <u>Use Case</u>."

Describing Instruction. While identifying and collecting instructions just focus on gathering keywords of requirements without defining any details, the purpose of describing instructions is exactly to elicit and record this information (addresses R.N.3. and R.C.4). Describing instructions should therefore help a requirements engineer to motivate the stakeholders to provide detailed information about a requirement according to the attributes of the issue the requirement is concerned with. Example: "Ask the stakeholders the following question: Could you please describe this <u>User Group</u> especially with regard to <u>average age, experience, ...</u>"

Classifying Instruction. The purpose of this instruction is to support the classification of requirements into more specific groups (addresses R.N.3). The rationale for this instruction is based on the observation that requirements concerning different issues are sometimes identified and collected in an integrated way, but need to be separated before they can be described in detail. Example: "Discuss with the stakeholders if this <u>User Group</u> is a <u>Primary User Group</u> or <u>Secondary User Group</u> and categorize it accordingly."

Visualizing Instruction. In elicitation sessions, requirements are often visualized, because visualization helps to clarify details or relationships much better than just spoken words. The visualizing instruction therefore aims at motivating a requirements engineer to use graphical representations during elicitation sessions (addresses R.N.3). Example: "Draw an <u>Exchange Diagram</u> to clarify the interplay between all <u>User Groups</u>."

Decomposing Instruction. The purpose of this instruction is to prompt a requirements engineer to decompose hierarchical structures in order to elaborate the included requirements (addresses R.N.3). The rationale for decomposing instructions is based on the fact that requirements are sometimes too coarse-grained to provide sufficient information for development. Example: "Decompose the hierarchy of this User Group until no further decomposition is possible. Collect the identified User Groups in a corresponding list and add a link to the parent User Group."

Selecting Instruction. The purpose of the selection instruction is to foster the reuse of requirements already defined during DE wherever possible. This instruction prompts a requirements engineer to consider the SPL specification, and to motivate the stakeholders to choose predefined requirements instead of letting them state these from scratch (addresses R.C.10). Example: "Motivate the stakeholders to select a best fitting Use Case from the SPL specification and map it accordingly. If the required Use Case is not covered sufficiently in the SPL specification, describe this Use Case especially with regard to name, precondition, flow of events, ... from scratch."

Involving Instruction. The purpose of this instruction is to invite the stakeholders who are needed for a certain elicitation step (addresses R.C.3). This instruction is needed in order to assure that the right stakeholder group is available when requirements that concern a certain issue are discussed. Example: "Invite and involve a (group of) Business Area Managers to an elicitation session in order to discuss requirements concerning User Groups."

Influence hint. The purpose of this hint is to inform about influence relationships that exist between different issues, and that may also apply to corresponding requirements (addresses R.C.12). Example: "Important hint: Consider especially the Business Area when determining the User Groups."

Commonality Hint. The purpose of the commonality hint is to inform about requirements that are implemented by default anyway in order to proactively avoid unnecessary elicitations (addresses R.C.7). Example: "Important hint: Be aware that a set of Use Cases is already implemented by default and need not to be elicited again. Consider the list of these Use Cases in the SPL specification and break discussions immediately as soon as stakeholders start asking for the collection of these common requirements. Additional requirements are of course allowed."

Assumption Hint. The assumption hint is probably the most important hint for reflecting SPL characteristics and constraints in an elicitation instruction without the need to specify all possible requirements in an explicit manner upfront. Assumption hints describe the assumptions the product line architecture makes about a certain issue with respect to the flexibility the architecture has intentionally been designed for (addresses R.C.9). The purpose of this hint is therefore the description of constraints a requirement must meet in order to be assessable as being realizable by a requirements engineer without expert involvement. Example: "Important hint: Be aware that there are constraints defined for Business Document requirements. Hence, the Business Documents stakeholders may ask for are restricted as follows: pages<10, words<10000. If the stakeholders require something that contravenes these constraints, inform them about possible (significant) extra costs and that an expert check must be done before you can accept this requirement."

Selection Hint. The purpose of the selection hint is also to support SPL alignment. However, in contrast to assumption hints, selection hints directly aim at considering predefined requirements in the SPL specification and are therefore to be used together with selection instructions (addresses R.C.10). Example: "Consider the set of existing Adapters in the SPL specification."

Flexibility Hint. The purpose of the flexibility hint is to inform about possible extra costs when stakeholders require specific extensions or modifications even though reuse candidates already exist. Example: "If the stakeholders require specific Adapters that are not covered in the SPL yet, inform them about high extra costs even if the mentioned assumptions are kept."

Documentation Hint. There are issues that are actually relevant for development, and those that are only implicitly relevant for the elicitation of the former. The purpose of documentation hints is to inform the requirements engineer for which requirements it is not worthwhile spending effort for the description of corresponding details (addresses R.C.6). Example: "Important hint: It is not necessary to elicit or describe details about Business Processes."

4.4   Implemented Elicitation Strategy

It is evident that the milestone sections, the issue sections, as well as the phrases within each issue section must be ordered in a meaningful way in order to provide actual support. Besides a basic structure and several text blocks, our template for elicitation instructions therefore also comprises a set of rules to make that happen. These rules constitute an overall strategy that is implemented in the template.

The milestone sections basically define clear points until which certain requirements types (i.e., issues) have to be discussed. The idea behind this approach is that requirements concerning different issues are typically needed at different points in time during subsequent development. For instance, the requirements concerning the technical environment in which a system should be integrated may be needed very early, while requirements concerning concrete functionality may be sufficient at a later point in time. Therefore, the order of the milestone sections must be the same as the order of the requirements milestones within the requirements (elicitation) process.

Within each milestone section, the issue section of the issues belonging to the corresponding milestone must also be ordered in a meaningful way in order to avoid redundancies. To define this order, the conceptual relationships between the issues must be considered. Basically, issues can have an "Influence", "Require", "Contain" and "Specialize" relationship (according to [5], [7]). When defining a logical order of requirements activities and corresponding issue sections, it is evident that requirements cannot be elicited in a random order. Therefore, the order of issue sections must be defined based on these relationships. In our template, we have defined several rules addressing this fact:

1.   Discuss all issues in a random order that do not have any relationship to another issue.

2.   Discuss all issues in a random order that are not required by, not contained in, not influenced by, and not a specialization of another issue. If there is none,

discuss at least those issues in a random order that are influenced by an issue already discussed, but that have no further relationships.

3.   Discuss all those issues that are required by, contained in, influenced by, or a specialization of an issue already discussed, and that are neither required by, contained in, influenced by, nor a specialization of an issue that has not been discussed yet. If there is more than one, discuss them in the following order: 1) issues that specialize an already discussed one, 2) issues that are contained in an already discussed one, 3) issues that are required by an already discussed one, 4) issues that are influenced by an already discussed one. If there is more than one in each sub-order, discuss them in the order in which the specialized / containing / requiring / influencing issue has appeared. Adapt the order continuously and repeat this procedure until all issues related to a certain milestone have been discussed.

---

6. Elicitation Section for System Function

Definition: An atomic reaction (i.e., state change or response) of the system under development that is triggered by an external stimulus, e.g., an environmental change, or an explicit request of a user or an external system.

Invite and involve a (group of) process participantss to an elicitation session in order to discuss requirements concerning System Functions.

Important hint: Be aware that a set of System Functions is already implemented by default and need not to be elicited again. Consider the list of these System Functions in the SPL specification and break discussions immediately as soon as stakeholders start asking for the collection of these common requirements. Additional requirements are of course allowed.

For each System Activity:

Ask the stakeholders the following question: Which System Functions are realizing this System Activity (*)?

Collect the identified System Functions in a corresponding list (if not yet done) and add a link to the related System Activity.

For each System Use Case:

Ask the stakeholders the following question: Which System Functions are invoked by this System Use Case (*)?

Collect the identified System Functions in a corresponding list (if not yet done) and add a link to the related System Use Case.

Ask the stakeholders the following question: Which (additional) System Functions are required?

Collect the identified System Functions in a corresponding list (if not yet done).

Consider the set of predefined System Functions in the SPL specification.

For each System Function identified so far:

Motivate the stakeholders to select a best fitting System Function from the SPL specification and map it accordingly. If the required System Function is not covered sufficiently in the SPL specification, describe this System Function especially with regard to logic from scratch.

Important hint: If the stakeholders require specific System Functions that are not covered in the SPL yet, inform them about high extra costs (even if the given constraints are hold).

Fig. 3. Example of issue section "System Function"

When developing elicitation instructions based on these rules, it can be constructively assured that all requirements are available before the elicitation of related requirements starts. This is a key concept in our approach, as it is based on the assumption that stakeholders can name requirements concerning a certain issue better when they consider the context of this issue by means of its conceptual relationships.

Within an issue section, our template therefore also proposes to elicit all requirements concerning a certain issue by considering its relationships to other issue. Thus, each issue section should first contain phrases that aim at identifying and collecting requirements, while the definition of requirements details should then take place afterwards; i.e., when all requirements have been identified by processing the issue's relationships. At the beginning of each issue section, one or more instruction blocks should therefore be implemented, where each instruction block reflects one (contained in or required by) relationship that the issue of interest has to another issue. For instance, a system function that is required by system activities and by system use cases would have two instruction blocks reflecting these relationships (see Figure 3).

The selection and instantiation of concrete phrases within an issue section is then based on the properties of the issue to be discussed, respectively on the properties of its related issues. The most important properties in this regard are the status of an issue and the degree of freedom provided by the underlying SPL. While the former expresses whether and how many instances an issue may have (normal = n, singleton = 1, abstract = 0), the latter expresses whether requirements concerning an issue are already predefined in the SPL, respectively restricted by the SPL architecture or strategy. In Figure 3, for instance, the degree of freedom states that a couple of system functions are already covered in the SPL specification, but that additional system functions may be specified also. Hence, corresponding hints and single instructions that inform a requirements engineer about this fact are included in the issue section.

5 Evaluation

To evaluate our template, we prepared a two-step approach comprising an expert validation and a controlled experiment. While the purpose of the first validation step, which is described below, was just to assess the practical applicability and usefulness of the elicitation instructions in general, its concrete benefits with regard to elicitation effectiveness are still to be evaluated in the second study that will be subject of a future publication.

Taking into account the individual background, a similar subject sample as during the requirements analysis was chosen for the expert validation (including the renowned professor). The overall goal of this first study was to assess our template with regard to its practical applicability and basic usefulness from the viewpoint of requirements engineering experts in the context of fictive interviews. In these fictive interviews, we let the experts use an exemplary elicitation instruction that was defined based on our template before. However, as we were only interested in an assessment of the instruction itself, the requirements stated by the interviewees were not considered here and often just brainstormed, non-controlled ideas.

5.1 Results

For the purpose of measuring the quality of the elicitation instruction, we used a questionnaire similar to the one for the requirements elicitation described above, including a set of open questions and closed (agreement) questions. In Table 2, the assessments ranging from "very small" to "very high" received by the eight experts are listed, where MIN is the minimum, MED the medium, MAX the maximum, and Q_1 the 25%-quartile respectively Q_2 the 75%-quartile in the expert ratings.

Table 2. Expert assessment

Assessment Criterion	Statistics
Overall helpfulness in a SPL-based project	MIN = very small, Q_1 = medium, **MED = high,** Q_2 = very high , MAX = very high
Readability / understandability	MIN = low, Q_1 = high, **MED = high,** Q_2 = very high , MAX = very high
Usability / applicability	MIN = very low, Q_1 = medium, **MED = high,** Q_2 = very high, MAX = very high
Conformance with experts' personal elicitation style	MIN = very low, Q_1 = low, **MED = high,** Q_2 = very high, MAX = very high
Improvement of elicitation effectiveness (quality)	MIN = very low, Q_1 = medium, **MED = medium,** Q_2 = high, MAX = very high
Improvement of elicitation efficiency	MIN = very low, Q_1 = very low, **MED = medium,** Q_2 = high, MAX = high
Improvement in comparison to state of the art material	MIN = very low, Q_1 = medium, **MED = high,** Q_2 = very high, MAX = very high
Benefits for average requirements engineers	MIN = very low, Q_1 = medium, **MED = high,** Q_2 = very high, MAX = very high

The overall usefulness of the elicitation instruction according to our template was assessed as "high" or even "very high" by most involved experts. In particular, all participants stated that the detailed and consistent nature of the elicitation instruction as well as the provision of precise hints and clear instructions could support their work, even if they were experienced experts. Most RE experts also found the elicitation instruction easy to read and easy to use. Furthermore, five of the eight participants would use such instructions at least as an abstract process to follow during a project, as for most of them the elicitation instruction is compliant to their personal style of elicitation. Thus, it is expected that elicitation instructions following our template can be actually used in industry.

Regarding elicitation quality and efficiency, most of the experts expected a "medium" improvement in their own work when using instructions according to our template. In direct comparison to known (state-of-the-art) material in AE requirements elicitation, these improvements were even assessed as "high" in average. Thus, even if not every requirement engineer will benefit to the same degree from using instructions according to our template, there seems to be a real target audience. In particular, the RE experts expected that at least less or average-experienced requirements engineers could highly benefit from using such elicitation instructions (what is to be evaluated in our second study).

However, with regard to the fulfillment of the requirements on the requirements elicitation instructions (see section 4.1), only the following requirements were considered as fulfilled in the expert ratings. In this regard, we considered a requirement fulfillment as confirmed if the median in the answers was "rather agree" or "totally agree" and the 25%-quartile in the answers not lower than "neither agree nor disagree".

- R.S.1. The elicitation instruction should make clear in which order elicitation steps should be performed best
- R.C.1. The elicitation instruction should mention the issues that are relevant for discussion
- R.C.3. The elicitation instruction should name the typical stakeholders needed in a certain step
- R.C.4. The elicitation instruction should inform about the details to be elicited with regard to a certain issue

The main reason for the low confirmation of the other requirements is the fact that the corresponding information in the exemplary elicitation instructions was not sufficiently highlighted and that a concrete application context was missing in order to assess the fulfillment of the requirements more thoroughly. This was also mentioned in the open part of the questionnaire, in which the involved RE experts made a few (minor) suggestions on what should be improved.

First of all, more rationales and background information about the elicitation instruction itself were required. In particular, this should include an explanation on how the instructions are to be used (e.g., regarding the order of steps, etc.) and what exactly they aim at. Second, the reasons behind each mentioned SPL constraint should be reflected in the instructions too in order to be aware why something works or does not. Third, links to notations and specific elicitation techniques should be included in order to provide a requirements engineer with access to more information on how to use them. Forth, more information should be provided regarding the purpose and content of the milestone sections in order to understand why the listed issues are to be discussed in its given order. Fifth, additional information on how to combine different steps into an elicitation workshop is required, including a coarse estimation of the time required for each step. Sixth, examples should be incorporated in order to show what the results of each step should look like. As a general feedback, we therefore claim that it is critical that the elicitation instruction itself is explained exhaustively to requirements engineers before they will use them in real projects.

5.2   Threats to Validity and Outlook on Controlled Experiment

The insights gathered by the expert validation confirmed the basic suitability of our template and also enabled us to improve it according to the feedback comments.

However, there are a few threats to validity that need to be discussed and also considered during the preparation of the controlled experiment.

Construction Validity. An important threat to construction validity was the fact that only one exemplary elicitation instruction based on our template was used for validation (mono-operation bias). Thus, there was neither a second elicitation instruction based on our template, nor a control group using an elicitation instruction based on another template. Another threat with regard to construction validity is the usage of only a questionnaire to measure data (mono-method bias). In particular, only subjective impressions and no objective data (e.g., regarding effectiveness) were collected. In order to avoid these threats in the controlled experiment, we will therefore setup two groups here; one using an elicitation instruction based on our template, and another group using a similar elicitation instruction according to best practice. Furthermore, both subjective data (based on questionnaires) and objective data (based on measurable observations) will be collected.

Conclusion Validity. Regarding conclusion validity the low statistical power due to the small sample size of only eight participants is an important threat to validity. In order to avoid this threat in the controlled experiment, we will involve approximately 30 participants here.

Internal Validity. The internal validity of the expert validation is mainly affected by the participant selection and the low degree of control during the study itself. Regarding the former, the experts were not randomly selected from a larger population, but only personally known experts were asked to participate. Regarding the latter, the study was done offline by each expert why we did not have any control how the fictive interviews were done. In particular, there is a risk that the elicitation instructions were rather reviewed than actually used. In the controlled experiment, we will therefore select the participants randomly from a set of unknown RE students, and perform their interviews in a controlled and comparable environment.

External Validity. As we involved real requirements engineers, the external validity is basically high. However, as elicitation instructions or methods in general do typically not address experienced experts, but rather less or only average-experienced requirements engineers, it would be interesting to gather also feedback from such people. In the controlled experiment, we will therefore give the same questionnaire to the participating students.

6   Conclusion and Future Work

AE based on an SPL is still a time-consuming task in practice. One important reason is the misfit between customer requirements and a given SPL, especially when a high degree of customizability is required. In order to resolve this misfit, AE requirements engineers must be enabled to use sound knowledge about a given SPL to better guide the elicitation of customer requirements.

As a first step towards this aim, this paper has introduced a template for elicitation instructions. Even if this template can basically be used in non-SPL environments also, its intended purpose is to appropriately provide requirements engineers with all the important information they need for performing more effective elicitation in AE projects. A first validation with RE expert has confirmed that the template is basically suitable for this purpose, even if some minor issues still have to be improved.

However, as a concrete elicitation instruction always depends on a specific development context, each elicitation instruction must be defined individually for an SPL organization. Thus, the template introduced here is just one part of a larger research program. As mentioned in the introduction, the question, "How can knowledge about an SPL be economically extracted and incorporated into the AERE process?" cannot be answered by the template only, of course. For this purpose, we are developing a tailoring approach that systematically guides a method engineer in in incorporating SPL knowledge into elicitation instructions (see [24] for a first version of this approach). The work described in this paper presents valuable input for this aim, as it clarifies how the extracted knowledge shall be represented appropriately.

References

1. Alves, V., Niu, N., Alves, C., Valenca, G.: Requirements engineering for software product lines. A systematic literature review. In: Information and Software. Elsevier (2010)
2. Clements, P., Northrop, L.: Software Product Lines: Patterns and Practice. Addison Wesley (2001)
3. Deelstra, S., Sinnema, M., Bosch, J.: Product derivation in software product families: a case study. The Journal of Systems and Software 74 (2005)
4. Rabiser, R., Grünbacher, P., Dhungana, D.: Supporting Product Derivation by Adapting and Augmenting Variability Models. In: SPLC. IEEE (2007)
5. Vicente-Chicote, C., Moros, B., Toval, A.: REMM-Studio: an Integrated Model-Driven Environment for Requirements Specification, Validation and Formatting. Journal of Object Technology, ETH Zurich 6(9) (2007)
6. O'Leary, P., Rabiser, R., Richardson, I., Thiel, S.: Important Issues and Key Activities in Product Derivation: Experiences from Independent Research Projects. In: SPLC (2009)
7. Goknil, A., Kurtev, I., van den Berg, K.: A Metamodeling Approach for Reasoning about Requirements. In: Schieferdecker, I., Hartman, A. (eds.) ECMDA-FA 2008. LNCS, vol. 5095, pp. 310–325. Springer, Heidelberg (2008)
8. Djebbi, O., Salinesi, C.: RED-PL, a Method for Deriving Product Requirements from a Product Line Requirements Model. In: Krogstie, J., Opdahl, A.L., Sindre, G. (eds.) CAiSE 2007 and WES 2007. LNCS, vol. 4495, pp. 279–293. Springer, Heidelberg (2007)
9. Guelfi, N., Perrouin, G.: A Flexible Requirements Analysis Approach for Software Product Lines. In: Sawyer, P., Heymans, P. (eds.) REFSQ 2007. LNCS, vol. 4542, pp. 78–92. Springer, Heidelberg (2007)
10. Adam, S.: Towards Faster Application Engineering through Better Informed Elicitation – A Research Preview. In: REEW@RefSQ 2011, Essen (2011)
11. Perrouin, G., Klein, J., Guelfi, N., Jezequel, J.: Reconciling Automation and Flexibility in Product Derivation. In: Software Product Line Conference. IEEE (2008)
12. Rabiser, R., Dhungana, D.: Integrated Support for Product Configuration and Requirements Engineering in Product Derivation. In: SEAA. IEEE (2007)
13. Schmid, K.: Planning Software Reuse - A Disciplined Scoping Approach for Software Product Lines. PhD Theses in Experimental Software Engineering 12. Fraunhofer (2003)
14. Eriksson, M., Börstler, J., Borg, K.: Managing requirements specifications for product lines – An approach and industry case study. Journal of Systems and Software (2009)

15. Sinnema, M., Deelstra, S., Hoekstra, P.: The COVAMOF Derivation Process. In: Morisio, M. (ed.) ICSR 2006. LNCS, vol. 4039, pp. 101–114. Springer, Heidelberg (2006)
16. Cheng, B., Atlee, J.: Research Directions in Requirements Engineering. In: Proceedings of Future of Software Engineering (FOSE). IEEE Computer Society (2007)
17. Halmans, G., Pohl, K.: Communicating the variability of a software-product family to customers. In: Software and System Modeling 2003/2. Springer, Heidelberg (2003)
18. Pohl, K.: Requirements Engineering – Grundlagen, Prinzipien, Techniken. dpunkt (2007)
19. Bühne, S., Halmans, G., Lauenroth, K., Pohl, K.: Scenario-Based Application Requirements Engineering. In: Software Product Lines. Springer, Heidelberg (2006)
20. Alves, C.: COTS-Based Requirements Engineering. In: Cechich, A., Piattini, M., Vallecillo, A. (eds.) Component-Based Software Quality. LNCS, vol. 2693, pp. 21–39. Springer, Heidelberg (2003)
21. Alves, C., Franch, X., Carvallo, J.P., Finkelstein, A.: Using Goals and Quality Models to Support the Matching Analysis During COTS Selection. In: Franch, X., Port, D. (eds.) ICCBSS 2005. LNCS, vol. 3412, pp. 146–156. Springer, Heidelberg (2005)
22. Doerr, J., Paech, B., Koehler, M.: Requirements Engineering Process Improvement Based on an Information Model. In: Requirements Engineering Conference. IEEE (2004)
23. Sommerville, I., Lock, R., Storer, T., Dobson, J.: Deriving Information Requirements from Responsibility Models. In: van Eck, P., Gordijn, J., Wieringa, R. (eds.) CAiSE 2009. LNCS, vol. 5565, pp. 515–529. Springer, Heidelberg (2009)
24. Adam, S., Doerr, J., Ehresmann, M., Wenzel, P.: Incorporating SPL Knowledge into a Requirements Process for Information Systems. In: PLREQ @ REfSQ 2010. Essen (2010)

Supporting Learning Organisations in Writing Better Requirements Documents Based on Heuristic Critiques

Eric Knauss and Kurt Schneider

Software Engineering Group, Leibniz Universität Hannover, Germany
{eric.knauss,kurt.schneider}@inf.uni-hannover.de

Abstract. Context & motivation: Despite significant advances in requirements engineering (RE) research and practice, software developing organisations still struggle to create requirements documentation in sufficient quality and in a repeatable way. **Question/problem:** The notion of good-enough quality is domain and project specific. Software developing organisations need concepts that i) allow adopting a suitable set of RE methods for their domain and projects and ii) allow improving these methods continuously. **Principal ideas/results:** Automatic analysis of requirements documentation can support a process of organisational learning. Such approaches help improve requirements documents, but can also start a discussion about its desired quality. **Contribution:** We present a learning model based on heuristic critiques. The paper shows how this concept can support learning on both the organisational and individual levels.

Keywords: heuristic critiques, requirements documentation, learning software organisations, experience management.

1 Introduction

Requirements Engineering is a key success factor for software projects. A number of approaches exist to support assessing the quality of software requirements automatically [1–4]. If such approaches identify problems in requirements documents, these documents can be improved in a most efficient way. Still, there remains an important question: What is good requirements quality?

Existing approaches focus on removing ambiguity [4, 5]. But ambiguity is not always bad [6]. Removing ambiguous wording might lead to false precision. False precision is always bad. The notion of *good requirements documentation* is often specific to an organisation or even a project. Automatic checks of requirements documents are even more valuable if they support writing requirements in the specific structure. Therefore, automatic checks of requirements documents need to be adjustable. In this paper we investigate if adjustable automated requirements checkers (= experience based requirements tools) can support organisational learning.

Research Question: Can experience based requirements tools support organisational learning?

Contribution. In this paper we describe a *learning model* based on adjustable automatic checks of requirements documents. We show how organisational and individual learning is supported and that requirements engineers can adjust such checkers to their needs, thus encoding their experiences.

B. Regnell and D. Damian (Eds.): REFSQ 2012, LNCS 7195, pp. 165–171, 2012.

2   Related Work

Requirements are often specified using natural language, if only as an intermediate solution before formal modelling. As natural language is inherently ambiguous [7], several approaches have been proposed to automatically analyse natural language requirements in order to support requirements engineers in creating good requirements specifications [1–4]. Typically, such approaches define a specific quality model first. Then indicators are defined for the quality aspects that can be automatically evaluated, as in the ARM tool by Wilson et al. [1]. Often these indicators are based on simple mechanisms, e.g. keyword lists. Newer approaches leverage sophisticated analysis of natural language, e.g. the search for *under specification* in the QuARS tool [8]. Kof, Lee et al. work on extracting semantics from natural language texts [2, 3] by focusing on the semi automatic extraction of an ontology from a requirements document. Their goal is to identify ambiguities in requirements specifications. Gleich and Kof present a tool that is able to detect a comprehensive set of ambiguities in natural language requirements [4].

Often, the discussion of tools that automatically analyse requirements documentation is limited to the discussion of their recall and precision [5]. In this paper, we use a broader model for requirements analysis tools that allows us to describe their usefulness for supporting continuous improvement and organisational learning in requirements engineering activities. We feel supported in this goal by Gervasi's discussion on why ambiguity is not always bad [6]. He argues that people are able to articulate missing knowledge in ways that are then identified as ambiguities. Removing these ambiguities can only be beneficial, if the underlaying uncertainty is removed.

3   Experience Based Tools and Learning

In this paper, we continue previous work on learning (c.f. [9]). Here, we focus on experience based requirements tools: tools that automatically check requirements, give constructive feedback (i.e. an experience), and can be extended with new experience from its users. For further discussion, we introduce the concept of *heuristic critiques*:

Definition 1: *Heuristic Critique* — Computer based feedback to an activity or work product (e.g. requirements documentation) based on experience. A heuristic critique consists of
  – a *heuristic rule* that can be evaluated by a computer,
  – a notion of the critique's *criticality* (e.g. info, warning, error),
  – a *meaningful and constructive message*.

A heuristic critique represents a single automatic requirements check. Furthermore, it supports organizational learning, when integrated in requirements engineering tools [9]: A heuristic critique is a suitable representation of an experience (defined as (i) an observation, associated with (ii) an emotion and (iii) a conclusion or hypothesis [10]).

Example. A developer *observes* that requirements are misunderstood, because they do not specify who is responsible for an action. The developer is annoyed (*emotion*), and *concludes* that passive voice should be avoided. Based on this experience, a heuristic critique can be created: If a *heuristic rule* detects passive voice, it could give a warning (i.e. medium *criticality*), and ask the user to use active voice and state responsibility *constructive message*.

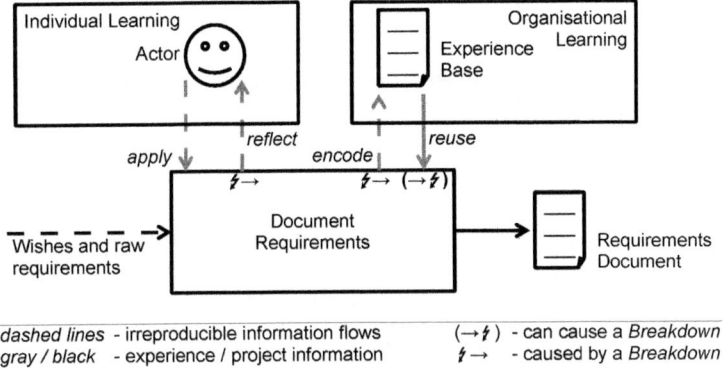

dashed lines - irreproducible information flows   (→ϟ) - can cause a *Breakdown*
gray / black - experience / project information   ϟ→   - caused by a *Breakdown*

Fig. 1. Learning model: *Heuristic Critiques* stimulate information flows by causing *breakdowns*

We call this concept a *heuristic* critique to emphasize the fact that neither 100% recall nor precision is required. It is more important that these heuristic critiques can be adopted to a specific domain or project environment. By this, it becomes easier to encode new experiences. This is important to support learning. Figure 1 shows two areas of learning, supported by heuristic feedback. Learning occurs on individual and organizational levels during the activity of writing requirements.

Individual Learning: Reflect and Apply. If a heuristic critique fires its warning, the requirements engineer is interrupted in his task. This enables him to *reflect* about the current activity and status, a breakdown occurs. Thus, heuristic critiques facilitate learning through reflection. The requirements engineer might already know how to write good requirements in general. Nevertheless, passive sentences may slip into a specification during periods of intense writing. Reminders and warnings help to *apply* and repeat the knowledge. Thus, they support internalizing abstract knowledge into skills and help writing good requirements.

Organizational Learning: Reuse and Encode. Heuristic critiques allow codifying experiences in a useful way. They support *reuse* of experience, because they enable computers to find situations matching the observation that led to the original experience. Based on the emotion reported, a more or less disruptive message points to potential improvements. Heuristic warnings are not always correct, e.g. an actor could be specified even in a passive sentence. Furthermore, they are not always applicable. If a condition is stated in requirements documentation, use of passive voice is unproblematic. If such a situation is observed during a breakdown, the requirements engineer can refine the heuristic warning and specify that it should not be applied to conditions. Thus, experience is added to the organizations knowledge base. As a by-product, the growing body of codified experience adopts a manageable granularity for an organisation's knowledge base. These advantages have a price: *encoding* experiences as heuristic critiques is more difficult than just writing them down as plain text. In the scope of this paper, we want to concentrate on encoding of new experience.

4   Study: Encoding of New Experience

In this section, we evaluate whether typical requirements engineers are able to encode experiences as heuristic critiques. For the evaluation we need an examplary implementation of an experience based tool. We chose the Heuristic Requirements Assistant (HeRA) [11], a smart use case editor. In HeRA, heuristic critiques can be directly changed by its user during runtime. All users can change the message of the critique or parameters (e.g. keyword lists). In addition, heuristic rules (encoded in Javascript) can be adjusted. All use cases written in HeRA can be accessed from these scripts.

HeRA has been widely used by students in projects at the end of their Bachelors or during their Masters. We consider this group to be representative for our evaluation: (tomorrow's) young professionals with good background knowledge (software engineering, requirements engineering), but limited experience. In our evaluation, we want to investigate whether a representative selection from this target group is able to solve defined tasks under laboratory conditions. We were able to recruit seven volunteers., two of them still in their Bachelors (3rd and 5th year / regular: 3 years).

If a heuristic critique is encoded, it needs to be stored and managed. These rather technical aspects (c.f. [10]) are beyond the scope of this paper. Thus, our research question can be detailed as follows:

Specific Research Question. Can our subjects change existing or create new heuristic critiques? In this evaluation we focus on the heuristic rules, because we consider them most difficult when encoding experiences as heuristic critiques. We approach this question based on the goal question metric paradigm [12]. Accordingly, we have to define beforehand, when we would accept the results to be positive (see Baseline Hypothesis in Table 1).

Evaluation Approach. Our subjects were asked to solve a number of tasks (c.f. Table 1) under supervision within 45 minutes. First, the subjects should show if they were able to understand an intermediate and a complex heuristic rule (Task 1.a). Then, the subjects should change an existing heuristic rule (Task 1.b) and create new rules; a simple, an intermediate, and a complex rule (Task 2). All subjects had a language description with the most important language constructs for the heuristic rules at hand. In addition, they had the data model of use cases in HeRA.

The first part should show our subjects how heuristic rules work. The heuristic rules in this part served as examples for the other tasks. This part was considered part of the instrumentation and not used in the evaluation. The subjects were asked to log their time for completing tasks.

Discussion of Validity. We give a short discussion of the validity of our study to support correct interpretation of our results.

Internal Validity. The most important internal aspect concerns learning effects. It is much more difficult and takes longer to solve a task of a new type. It can be expected that subjects will learn and solve even more difficult subsequent tasks of the same type better and faster. Our evaluation design reflects this aspect by using Task 1.a only for instrumentation. The experiment was conducted in the late afternoon. Many participants

Table 1. Overview of the tasks

Task	Description	Baseline Hypothesis
Task 1.a.1	Describe the goal of a heuristic rule (correct answer: triggers warning, if use case title has more characters than description).	n/a
Task 1.a.2	Describe the goal of a heuristic rule (correct answer: triggers warning, if condition part of an use case extension is empty).	n/a
Task 1.b	Change rule from Task 1.a.2 to trigger a warning if the reference to the extended step is empty.	> 75% correct < 10 minutes time
Task 2.1	Create a heuristic rule that triggers a warning ... if the title of a use case is empty.	> 75% correct < 15 minutes time
Task 2.2	... if the main success scenario has less than three or more than 9 steps.	> 75% correct < 15 minutes time
Task 2.3	... if two use cases have the same title.	> 50% correct < 15 minutes time

*Answers with small errors are counted as 0.5.

had a class before and might have been tired. Task sheet and language description had minor errors. Luckily, these errors could be accounted for during analysis.

Construct Validity. The main construct aspect concerns our baseline hypothesis. Is it valid to conclude from 75% (50%) correct answers under exam conditions that users are able to create correct simple (complex) heuristic rules? Are 10 minutes for changing and 15 minutes for creating heuristic rules short enough to allow users doing this during their workday? Because of the strict evaluation of the answers, we consider such results to be good compared to exams in programming language classes. Analysts could integrate these tasks in their daily work, given they take less than 15 minutes. As opposed to our experiment, analysts would be supported by error messages from a compiler and could directly observe the effects of their rules in HeRA.

Conclusion Validity. Because of the low statistical power, small or medium derivations in the result could be expected in case of replication of the experiment. The specific time of the experiment in the late afternoon after another class could have affected the performance of the subjects negatively in comparison to a replication.

External Validity. For an analyst in industry it might be hard to bring herself to work on heuristic critiques on top of their main tasks. As opposed to our subjects, the analyst has to switch her cognitive context from the current task to the programming of a heuristic rule. We expect the effort for this to be lowest, while the analyst is concerned with quality assurance of requirements documentation.

Results. Figure 2 shows the results of our study. The figure shows the minimal, average, and maximal time it took our subjects to solve the tasks (black). In addition the percentage of correct answers is shown in gray. The working time for Task 1.a.2 is considerably lower then for Task 1.a.1, probably due to learning effects. It took the subjects only 1–2 minutes to change a heuristic rule (a rule they had already understood

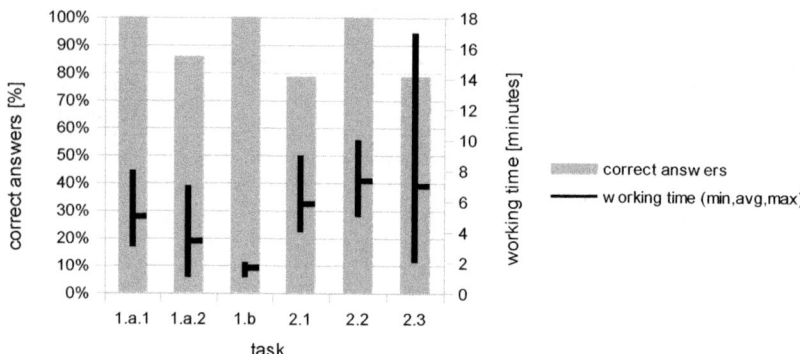

Fig. 2. Results of the experiment. The working time for each task is depicted in black, the percentage of correct answers is shown in gray.

when solving task 1.a.2). The rising difficulty of Tasks 2.1 – 2.3 shows in the maximal working time. The average time goes down from Task 2.2 to Task 2.3. At this time our students were well trained and could easily cope with the complexity. All in all we received 89% correct answers: 100% of the changes at existing heuristic rules were correct and 86% of the newly created heuristic rules. Small changes lasted less than 2 minutes. A new heuristic rule could be created in less than 7 minutes. We expect that these values will even improve if the programming is not performed with pen and paper but with suitable tool support. Thus, this study indicates that users of experience based requirements tools are able to encode new experiences or to adjust existing ones.

5 Discussion and Outlook

Automatic requirements checking has been reported to be beneficial. Yet, automatic requirements checkers are not widely accepted in industry, especially by tool vendors. We argue that existing approaches are either too generic or specific to a too narrow application domain for being widely used. In this paper, we propose to regard automatic requirements checkers as experience based requirements tools. We presented a learning model that helps to tackle effects that follow from the notion of experience based requirements tools. In short, there is more to these tools than just improving requirements documentation. In Section 4 we presented evidence that requirements engineers are able to add new experience to these tools. From a knowledge management perspective, this is an encouraging result. Computational rules that allow to check given documentation allow to formalise knowledge of an organisation in a most useful way. Individuals are confronted with these *heuristic critiques* and are invited to discuss them, based on examples they encounter in their daily work. Our evaluation results suggest that analysts are able to write useful critiques with reasonable effort: Our subjects encoded heuristic critiques that we identified to be useful in less than 7 minutes. Even without special tool support (e.g. wizards, compiler) they did this at a surprisingly low error rate. We conclude that analysts with a computer science background are perfectly capable to express their experience as heuristic critiques. Based on these results, tools are imaginable that help organisations build an experience base of heuristic critiques specialised on their domain. Our work leads to a number of questions that demand future research. Based on the learning model in Figure 1, we only investigated the *encoding* of new experience. There is still need to gather prove that automated requirements checkers improve requirements documentation. The impact of heuristic critiques on *individual learning* and on the *reuse* of experience should be further investigated.

References

1. Wilson, W.M., Rosenberg, L.H., Hyatt, L.E.: Automated analysis of requirement specifications. In: Proceedings of the 19th International Conference on Software Engineering (ICSE 1997), pp. 161–171. ACM, New York (1997)
2. Kof, L.: Text Analysis for Requirements Engineering. PhD thesis, Technische Universität München, München (2005)
3. Lee, S.W., Muthurajan, D., Gandhi, R.A., Yavagal, D.S., Ahn, G.J.: Building Decision Support Problem Domain Ontology from Natural Language Requirements for Software Assurance. International Journal of Software Engineering and Knowledge Engineering 16(6), 851–884 (2006)
4. Gleich, B., Creighton, O., Kof, L.: Ambiguity Detection: Towards a Tool Explaining Ambiguity Sources. In: Wieringa, R., Persson, A. (eds.) REFSQ 2010. LNCS, vol. 6182, pp. 218–232. Springer, Heidelberg (2010)
5. Kiyavitskaya, N., Zeni, N., Mich, L., Berry, D.M.: Requirements for tools for ambiguity identification and measurement in natural language requirements specifications. Requirements Engineering Journal 13(3), 207–239 (2008)
6. Gervasi, V., Zowghi, D.: On the Role of Ambiguity in RE. In: Wieringa, R., Persson, A. (eds.) REFSQ 2010. LNCS, vol. 6182, pp. 248–254. Springer, Heidelberg (2010)
7. Berry, D., Kamsties, E.: 2. Ambiguity in Requirements Specification. In: Perspectives on Requirements Engineering, pp. 7–44. Kluwer (2004)
8. Fabbrini, F., Fusani, M., Gnesi, S., Lami, G.: An Automatic Quality Evaluation for Natural Language Requirements. In: Proceedings of the Seventh International Workshop on RE: Foundation for Software Quality (REFSQ 2001), Interlaken, Switzerland, pp. 150–164 (2001)
9. Knauss, E., Schneider, K., Stapel, K.: Learning to Write Better Requirements through Heuristic Critiques. In: Proceedings of the 17th IEEE Requirementes Engineering Conference (RE 2009), pp. 387–388. IEEE Computer Society, Atlanta (2009)
10. Schneider, K.: Experience and Knowledge Management in Software Engineering. Springer, Heidelberg (2009)
11. Knauss, E., Lübke, D., Meyer, S.: Feedback-Driven Requirements Engineering: The Heuristic Requirements Assistant. In: Proceedings of the 31st International Conference on Software Engineering (ICSE 2009), Vancouver, Canada, pp. 587–590 (May 2009)
12. van Solingen, R., Berghout, E.: The Goal/Question/Metric Method: A Practical Guide for Quality Improvement of Software Development. McGraw-Hill Publishing Company (1999)

Managing Implicit Requirements
Using Semantic Case-Based Reasoning
Research Preview

Olawande Daramola[1], Thomas Moser[2], Guttorm Sindre[1], and Stefan Biffl[2]

[1] Department of Computer and Information Science
Norwegian University of Science and Technology, Trondheim, Norway
{wande,guttors}@idi.ntnu.no
[2] Christian Doppler Laboratory for Software Engineering
Integration for Flexible Automation Systems
Vienna University of Technology, Austria
{thomas.moser,stefan.biffl}@tuwien.ac.at

Abstract. [**Context and motivation**] Implicit requirements (ImRs) are defined as requirements of a system which are not explicitly expressed during requirements elicitation, often because they are considered so basic that developers should already know them. Many products have been rejected or users made unhappy because implicit requirements were not sufficiently addressed. [**Question/Problem**] Requirement management tools have not addressed the issue of managing ImRs, also despite the challenges of managing ImRs that exist in practice the issue has not received sufficient attention in the literature. [**Principal Idea/results**] This planned research will investigate how automated support can be provided for managing ImRs within an organizational context, which is currently lacking in practice. This work proposed an approach that is based on semantic case-based reasoning for managing ImRs. [**Contribution**] We present the concept of a tool which enables managing of ImRs through the analogy-based requirements reuse of previously known ImRs. This ensures the discovery, structured documentation, proper prioritization, and evolution of ImRs, which improves the overall success of software development processes.

Keywords: implicit requirements, requirement reuse, case-based reasoning, analogy-based reuse, semantic analysis.

1 Introduction and Motivation

Implicit requirements (ImRs) are hidden or assumed requirements that a system is expected to fulfill even though not explicitly elicited during requirements gathering. According to [1, 2] the quality of software is dependent on the measure of its conformance to both explicit and implicit requirements. Hence good quality cannot be guaranteed if only explicit requirements are satisfied while implicit requirements are omitted [2-4]. So far, issues of ImRs have not received as much attention in requirement management related discussions compared to explicit requirements, but yet it

B. Regnell and D. Damian (Eds.): REFSQ 2012, LNCS 7195, pp. 172–178, 2012.

remains a problem in practice [3-6]. ImRs are handled by requirements engineers using their own initiative and personal experience so as to ensure that delivered products satisfy implicit customer expectations [7-9]. In cases of omission of important ImRs from the requirements specification (RS), the Software Architect (SA) must be able to identify them and ensure that they are well addressed during the design phase. Often, this is done without any corresponding modification to the RS, which creates an information gap between the RS and the design specification.

According to Glinz [10], it may not be necessary to specify ImRs when there is an implicit shared understanding among all stakeholders about a quality requirement, but when this is not the case, failures to make ImRs explicit could lead to serious problems. Examples of instances when identifying and specifying ImRs becomes crucial include: when software products are developed in a new domain by a software development organization, or when products have been subcontracted to external organizations that belong to different cultural or operational contexts through outsourcing or offshoring [11]. In these cases, lack of adequate approach to effectively manage ImRs could lead to poor quality of the software products or failure of projects as a whole.

Generally, managing ImRs presents a number of challenges: **I**- *there are instances when ImRs are not well known by developers* – e.g. developing a product in a new domain; **II** - *ImRs can lead to budget overrun if not well managed and properly prioritized*; **III** - *ImRs evolve over time* – this could be due to increasing sophistication of users or new technologies; **IV** - *some ImRs concerns (on issues like scalability, security, usability) carry certain risks, and have costly and far reaching effects on the software architecture, if not discovered and addressed early enough* [1, 6, 9].

Although the issues **I-IV** can be partly addressed through good requirements elicitation procedures or inclusive software development paradigms such as agile approaches, there are many practical situations in which these alternatives are not the preferred choice. Regardless, within an organizational context, there exists significant merit in providing tool support for managing ImRs. The existence of such tool support would ensure that 1) previously documented ImRs can be reused in a systematic way and leveraged for improved requirements engineering (RE) in new projects; 2) hidden ImRs can be discovered, particularly those that have been overlooked during requirements elicitation – avoiding extra cost; and 3) ImRs are addressed based on established organizational standards, in terms of the required scope and level of priority.

Existing requirements management tool such as DOORS, Requisite PRO, CaliberRM [12] have failed to directly address these issues. Also, requirement analysis techniques like the KANO model [13, 14] can only assist to classify already known (elicited) requirements into basic needs (implicit), performance needs (explicit), and excitements (delighters) categories, and thus helps with requirements prioritization, it cannot ensure the discovery of non-elicited ImRs. This scenario motivates the need for "systematic tool support" to be used for managing ImRs. Typically, we envision a recommender system tool that will suggest probable ImRs to users based on documentation of requirements from previous projects that tend to be implicit. We define "systematic tool support" as a framework which can be integrated into an organization's RE procedures with the potential to improve the efficiency of the RE process, and ultimately the entire software development task.

This paper presents an approach that enables systematic tool support for managing ImRs using semantic case-based reasoning (CBR). The remainder of this paper is organized as follows. Section 2 presents related work. Section 3 gives an overview of our approach including an example. Section 4 discusses the potential merits of the approach and concludes.

2   Related Work

Reports on tool-based support for the management of ImRs are scarce in the literature despite the reality of challenges that exists in practice. Prominent requirement management tools such as DOORS, Requisite Pro or CaliberRM [12] lack specific provisions for managing ImRs. KANO analysis [13, 14] is a requirement analysis activity which enables the classification of elicited requirements into implicit, explicit, and exciters categories in order to correctly prioritize requirements. Requirements reuse, which is the core basis of our approach, is one of more interesting topics of RE discourse in recent years. A few of the more recent works include practical approaches to requirements reuse in product families [15]. It is an experience report of requirement reuse in a case study of On-Board systems. The study aims at discovering how requirements reuse can be integrated into DOORS. However, the focus is not to provide systematic support for RE within a framework as proposed in this work.

A model for requirements reuse based of the forecast of user needs using factual knowledge of users was proposed by Perednikas [16]. However the reuse model did not distinguish between the specific types of requirements to be reused. Singer *et al.* [6] report on the application of rules derivation for the elicitation of ImRs in IT ecosystems. The emphasis was the discovery of new ImRs by using agents to monitor deviations from predefined rules in the IT infrastructure, as users interact with the IT ecosystem. It is then expected that data mining can be applied on the observed deviations to uncover new implicit requirements that will ensure effective evolution of services provided by the IT ecosystem. In summary, the novelty of our proposal stems from the provision of systematic tool support for managing ImRs within an organizational context, which has not be adequately addressed in other published research.

3   Semantic CBR for Implicit Requirements

This section describes the proposed approach. First, a model for the reuse of implicit requirements in introduced, and then an application example from the e-Banking domain is described. Furthermore a conceptual overview of the approach is given, and the two major components, semantic matching for requirements similarity and analogy-based reasoning for fine-grained cross domain reuse, are described in more details.

3.1   Model for Implicit Requirement Reuse

In order to manage ImRs, a reuse-based implicit requirements model (RM) is essential in order to facilitate the reuse of ImRs across projects whenever substantial similarity can be established between a new requirement and older requirements. An RM is a formal representation of requirements that creates a basis for the reuse of implicit requirements associated with existing requirements in order to discover the implicit concerns of new requirements. Our RM is influenced by Maiden [17], where it was stated that in order to realistically reuse software specifications by analogy, three types of knowledge about reusable artifacts must be provided: 1) *domain knowledge* – concepts that describe the real world domain that the artifact can be associated with; 2) *solution knowledge* – concepts that are described in the reusable specification; 3) *goal knowledge* – concepts that describe the purpose of the reusable artifact. These three dimensions have been considered in the formulation of the RM. Hence the RM is a seven tuple denoted as $RM = < D, S, G, R_{id}, RQ_i, M_{id}, M_i>$ where D is a description of the domain of the software project; S is a description of the solution approach adopted by software project; G is a description of goals of the system under development; R_{id} is the unique id of a requirement; RQ_i is the requirement statement represented by R_{id}; M_{id} is the unique id of the implicit requirements associated with R_{id}; and M_i is the description of implicit aspects associated with the requirement RQ_i denoted as R_{id}.

3.2   E-Banking Application Example

Consider the example of an e-Banking application, whose goal is to facilitate dependable on-line transactions by the bank's customers with the following sample requirements:

- **A1:** *The system shall allow transfer of funds from a customer's account to a valid payee account.*
- **A2:** *The system shall allow transfer of funds between two separate accounts owned by the same person in the bank.*

Two categories of implicit requirements exist here which are: 1) domain ImRs - which are general for systems in the e-banking domain, e.g. expectations for a secure financial transaction on the web such as user access control, authentication or privacy; 2) ImRs directly associated with the each of A1 and A2 – which relate to issues of data validation and conformity with established banking rules. Both categories of ImRs must be well addressed to produce a good e-Banking system. Some ImRs are stated below:

- **A1-IR1:** *The system shall ensure that account balance after fund transfer to payee does not fall below set minimum limit by the bank for such accounts.*
- **A1-IR2:** *The system shall ensure that amount transferred to payee is stated in one of the acceptable currencies and transaction done at prevailing exchange rate set by the bank.*
- **A2-IR1:** *The system shall ensure that accounts listed for own fund transfer belong to the same owner and balance in drawn account must not fall below the minimum limit set by the bank for such accounts.*

3.3   Approach Overview

An overview of our planned solution approach is presented next. It is a concise description of the systematic workflow for managing ImRs using our approach. Typically, a description of the approach is defined as follows:

1. The user inputs requirements document captured in boilerplate format [18].
2. The requirement document (req. doc) is parsed by the prototype tool.
3. The tool identifies viable domains for analogy-based requirements reuse.
4. The user selects a domain for reuse out of candidates presented by the tool.
5. For each requirements statement in the req. doc, search requirements reposi-tory for similar requirements in the domain for reuse using semantic match-ing. If candidates found then tool ranks the retrieved candidates based on computed similarity score.
6. The tool generates new requirements specification report.

Semantic-Matching for Requirements Similarity - The objective of semantic matching (SM) – which originates from the field of lexical semantics - is to improve syntactic matches by exploring the semantic relatedness of terms using a concept hierarchy or ontology. Usually, graph representations of entities to be compared are extracted and then SM done either at the element level or at the structural level [19]. Generally, element level matchers compare information contained in elements of two graphs and return the semantic relation that exist between them (*equivalence, part-of, kind-of, disjoint* etc.), while structure level matchers often aggregates the results of several element level matchers and also compare the structural properties of the two graphs to determine the overall similarity coefficient (between 0 and 1) of the two graphs. In performing SM for requirements similarity, we favor the use of general knowledge bases or upper level ontologies such as WordNet, ResearchCyc, DBpedia as concept hierarchy. The proposed framework also supports using an existing do-main ontology as concept hierarchy where such an ontology already exists or can be developed. The selected concept hierarchy then provides basis for computing the semantic relatedness of two requirements. We believe that the right basis to associate similar ImRs with two separate requirements is, if they are contextually equivalent to some degree, and not necessarily their structural similarity. Hence, element level SM is preferred, such that we are able to compare the semantic-relatedness of concepts of the two graphs at the atomic level using a knowledge base and ultimately obtain a cumulative score that represents the contextual similarity between two requirements.

Analogy-Based Reasoning for Fine-Grained Cross-Domain Reuse - While CBR is mostly associated with reuse within the same domain, analogy-based reasoning (ABR) facilitates reuse across different domains. However, cross domain reuse for ImRs is only realistic when fine-grained. ABR for cross domain ImRs reuse is facili-tated in our approach through the specification of the domain, solution, and goal knowledge of the software project in RM. The requirements repository is also indexed along these dimensions. However, according to Maiden [17] goal knowledge is too generic to provide adequate basis for analogy-based reuse, but could be very comple-mentary to domain and solution knowledge. Hence, a weighted semantic similarity metric for determining the most appropriate base analogy model for cross domain reuse is preferred. Weights should be assigned to domain, solution and goal know-ledge respectively, in the order of their perceived importance to influencing the choice of a good base analogy for reuse.

4   Discussion and Conclusion

The proposed approach has the potential to address management of implicit requirements. The ability to discover unknown and un-elicited requirements will mitigate many risks that can adversely affect system architecture design and project cost.

We are aware that this is early stage work where not all issues of the proposed approach have been addressed, however we plan to implement a prototype based on the concepts canvassed in this paper. The idea is to build an Eclipse plug-in tool that can be integrated with other Eclipse based requirements management tools such as Papyrus or other emerging open source requirements management tools. Another promising aspect of this proposal is that there exists a lot of openly available tool support in particular in the areas of semantic analysis, NLP and conceptual graphs to facilitate implementation.

In conclusion, we have presented a conceptual framework for managing ImRs. This is a direct response to problems in the practice of many organizations which have not been addressed by existing requirements management tools. Hence, the provision of systematic tool support for managing ImRs will be useful for RE practitioners. We see many more opportunities for research in this area, particularly in facilitating more elaborate but realistic analogy-based reuse in RE. Also the issues of interdependencies among ImRs and their effect on impact analysis will be interesting to study. Additionally, an investment in developing an upper level ontology of reusable software artifacts in several domains can provide a more realistic basis for analogy-based reuse, and selection of reusable artifacts through semantic clustering and other semantic based methods.

Acknowledgments. This work has been supported by the Norwegian Research Council through the ReqSec project, Norway and by the Christian Doppler Forschungsgesellschaft and the BMWFJ, Austria.

References

1. ISO/IEC 9126: Software Engineering – Product Quality- Part 1: Quality Model. Int'l Organization for Standard (2001)
2. Ahamed, R.: An Integrated and Comprehensive Approach to Software Quality. International Journal of Engineering Science and Technology 2(2), 59–66 (2010)
3. Leffingwell, D., Widrig, D.: Managing Software Requirements: A Unified Ap-proach. Addison-Wesley Longman Publishing Co., Boston (2000) ISBN: 0-201-61593-2
4. Drysdale, D.: High-Quality Software Engineering: Lessons from Six-Nines World. David Drysdale (2007)
5. Grehag, Å.: Requirements Management in a Life-Cycle Perspective - A Position Paper. In: Proceedings of the 7th International Workshop on REFSQ 2001, Interlaken, Switzerland, pp. 183–188 (2001)
6. Singer, L., Brill, O., Meyer, S., Schneider, K.: Utilizing Rule Deviations in IT Ecosystems for Implicit Requirements Elicitation. In: Proceedings of the Second International Workshop on Managing Requirements Knowledge (MaRK), pp. 22–26 (2009)
7. Jha, R.: Gathering Implicit Requirements (10-06-2009), http://alturl.com/ocyb5

8. Parameswaran, A.: Capturing Implicit Requirements (02-08-2011),
   `http://alturl.com/emeej`
9. Douglass, D.: Understanding Implicit Requirements of Software Architecture (06-08-2009),
   `http://alturl.com/wauae`
10. Glinz, M.: A Risk-based Value-oriented Approach to Quality Requirements. IEEE Software, 34–41 (2008)
11. Deshpande, S., Richardson, I.: Management at the Outsourcing Destination - Global Software Development in India. In: Int'l Conf. on Global Software Engineering, pp. 217–225. IEEE Press (2009)
12. Larsson, A., Steen, O.: Tool Support for Requirements Management Quality from a User Perspective. In: Proceedings of IRIS29, Helsingör, Denmark (2008)
13. Kano, N., Nobuhiku, S., Fumio, T., Shinichi, T.: Attractive Quality and Must-be Quality. Journal of the Japanese Society for Quality Control 14(2), 39–48 (1984)
14. Xu, Q.L., Jiao, R.J., Yang, X., Helander, M.G., Khalid, H.M., Anders, O.: Customer Requirement Analysis Based on an Analytical Kano Model. In: Industrial Engineering and Engineering Management, pp. 1287–1291. IEEE Press (2007)
15. Monzon, A.: A Practical Approach to Requirements Reuse in Product Families of On-Board Systems. In: International Requirements Engineering, pp. 223–228. IEEE Press (2008)
16. Perednikas, E.: Requirements Reuse Based on Forecast of User Needs. In: Proceedings of the 20th EURO Mini Conference on Continuous Optimization and Knowledge-Based Technologies, Neringa, Lithuania, pp. 450–455 (2008)
17. Maiden, N.: Analogy as a Paradigm for Specification Reuse. Software Engineering Journal 6, 3–15 (1991)
18. Hull, E., Jackson, K., Dick, J.: Requirements Engineering. Springer, Heidelberg (2004)
19. Giunchiglia, F., Shvaiko, P.: Semantic Matching. The Knowledge Engineering Review 18, 265–280 (2003)

Trace Queries for Safety Requirements in High Assurance Systems

Jane Cleland-Huang[1], Mats Heimdahl[2], Jane Huffman Hayes[3],
Robyn Lutz[4], and Patrick Maeder[5]

[1] DePaul University, Chicago, IL 60422, USA
jhuang@cs.depaul.edu
[2] University of Minneapolis, Minneapolis, MN, USA
heimd002@umn.edu
[3] Kentucky State University, Lexington, KY, USA
hayes@cs.uky.edu
[4] Iowa State University, Ames, IA, USA, and Jet Propulsion Laboratory/Caltech
rlutz@iastate.edu
[5] Johannes Kepler University, Linz, Austria
patrick.maeder@jku.at

Abstract. [**Context and motivation**] Safety critical software systems pervade almost every facet of our lives. We rely on them for safe air and automative travel, healthcare diagnosis and treatment, power generation and distribution, factory robotics, and advanced assistance systems for special-needs consumers. [**Question/Problem**] Delivering demonstrably safe systems is difficult, so certification and regulatory agencies routinely require full life-cycle traceability to assist in evaluating them. In practice, however, the traceability links provided by software producers are often incomplete, inaccurate, and ineffective for demonstrating software safety. Also, there has been insufficient integration of formal method artifacts into such traceability. [**Principal ideas/results**] To address these weaknesses we propose a family of reusable traceability queries that serve as a blueprint for traceability in safety critical systems. In particular we present queries that consider formal artifacts, designed to help demonstrate that: 1) identified hazards are addressed in the safety-related requirements, and 2) the safety-related requirements are realized in the implemented system. We model these traceability queries using the Visual Trace Modeling Language, which has been shown to be more intuitive than the defacto SQL standard. [**Contribution**] Practitioners building safety critical systems can use these trace queries to make their traceability efforts more complete, accurate and effective. This, in turn, can assist in building safer software systems and in demonstrating their adequate handling of hazards.

Keywords: safety critical software, fault trees, traceability, visual trace queries, formal methods.

B. Regnell and D. Damian (Eds.): REFSQ 2012, LNCS 7195, pp. 179–193, 2012.
© Springer-Verlag Berlin Heidelberg 2012

1   Introduction

Requirements traceability, defined as the "ability to follow the life of a requirement in both a backward and forward direction" [6] is a critical element of any
rigorous software development process. For example, the U.S. Food and Drug
Administration (FDA) states that traceability analysis must be used to verify
that the software design implements the specified software requirements, that
all aspects of the design are traceable to software requirements, and that all
code is linked to established specifications and test procedures [5]. Similarly,
the Federal Aviation Administration (FAA) has established DO-178B [4] as the
accepted means of certifying all new aviation software, and this standard specifies that at each stage of development "software developers must be able to
demonstrate traceability of designs against requirements." Software Process Improvement standards that are being adopted by many organizations, such as
CMMI, require similar traceability practices.

Traceability is broadly recognized as an important factor in building high-
assurance software systems. Much of this software is safety critical, meaning
that there could be devastating harm if the software fails to operate correctly.
Safety-critical software systems permeate our society and are entrusted with the
lives of everyday people on a daily basis. For example, a commuter on a train
depends on the switching software, an airline passenger depends on the air traffic
control software, and a patient in a hospital depends on the e-pharmacy software.

However, there is almost universal failure across both industry and government projects to implement successful traceability, even in safety-critical systems
that require it. This has been found to be due in large part to the difficulty of constructing useful traceability queries using existing tools [18]. Traceability links
may be generated at a high level, may be too generic, may be incomplete, may
be inaccurate [21], and/or may not be deemed appropriate as evidence of software safety. Changes to artifacts, and hence to their traceability, often require
an inordinate amount of traceability effort on the part of analysts attempting to
obtain certification of even a small change to an already certified system.

The failure of traceability is of special concern in safety-critical systems where
the tracking of hazards to their resolutions is mandated by certification authorities. In such systems, the traceability from hazards to software safety requirements to implemented and verified design solutions forms an essential piece of
the evidence chain used to show that the resulting system is safe [1, 11, 17].
The full potential of traceability as a value-enhancing activity has not yet been
realized in safety-critical systems.

To address these shortcomings, we consider the work of two stakeholder types
as a safety-critical system is built, certified or modified: *developer* and *software
safety engineer*. The developer prepares traditional development artifacts such as
system requirements, software requirements, design (perhaps as UML diagrams),
code, and test cases. Traceability matrices are generated for these artifacts (such
as from system to software requirements, from code to test cases, etc.). The
software safety engineer focuses on how software can contribute to a systems
safety or can compromise it by putting the system into an unsafe state, and

is interested in tracing the relationship between fault tree analysis results and software requirements and verification artifacts. These safety-related items also require associated traceability support.

To focus on the traceability needs of these stakeholders, this paper extends our prior work. It identifies and describes a set of twelve safety-related traceability goals that address essential traceability questions needed to demonstrate that a software intensive system meets its safety requirements. These queries cover basic life-cycle activities such as tracing from requirements to test cases, as well as more complex activities such as integrating hazard analysis and formal models and their results into the traceability environment. The trace queries are presented using the Visual Trace Modeling Language (VTML), which has been demonstrated in our prior work to be more intuitive for users to understand than the defacto standard of SQL [18]. The traceability queries are designed to deliver value-enhanced traceability in support of the producers of safety-critical software systems.

In other areas of software engineering and requirements engineering, reusable solutions, often in the form of patterns, are used to increase productivity and improve quality by capturing and applying domain knowledge to repeated problems. Traceability is no exception. Certain questions must be answered about a software system in order to achieve certification, such as "have all hazards been addressed in the requirements?" The software traceability techniques presented here help answer these questions. Like design patterns, the traceability queries are constructed to be reusable both as the system evolves and, more generally, across different systems. If modeled in advance, the traceability queries provide strategic guidance to software developers as they plan their traceability infrastructure and associated process. Reusing proven and familiar traceability queries can ease the effort of the initial certification process and provide the necessary infrastructure for supporting change, as well as helping to demonstrate safety following that change.

The remainder of paper is laid out as follows. Section 2 discusses the challenges of delivering effective traceability in a safety critical project, and introduces the concept of the Traceability Information Model (TIM). Section 3 introduces a pacemaker example, which is used to illustrate our approach. Section 4 briefly describes the VTML. Section 5 introduces and models the safety-related traceability queries, and illustrates their usefulness for the pacemaker example. Section 6 describes related work, and finally, section 7 summarizes our contribution and discusses future work.

2   Traceability in a Safety Critical Environment

Traceability decisions in a project should be documented in and driven by a traceability information model (TIM) or traceability meta-model, as depicted in Figure 1 [2, 19]. A TIM is often represented as a UML class diagram and is composed of two basic types of entities: traceable artifact types represented as classes, and the permitted trace types between the artifact types represented as associations. Traceable artifact types serve as the abstractions supporting the traceability perspective of a project.

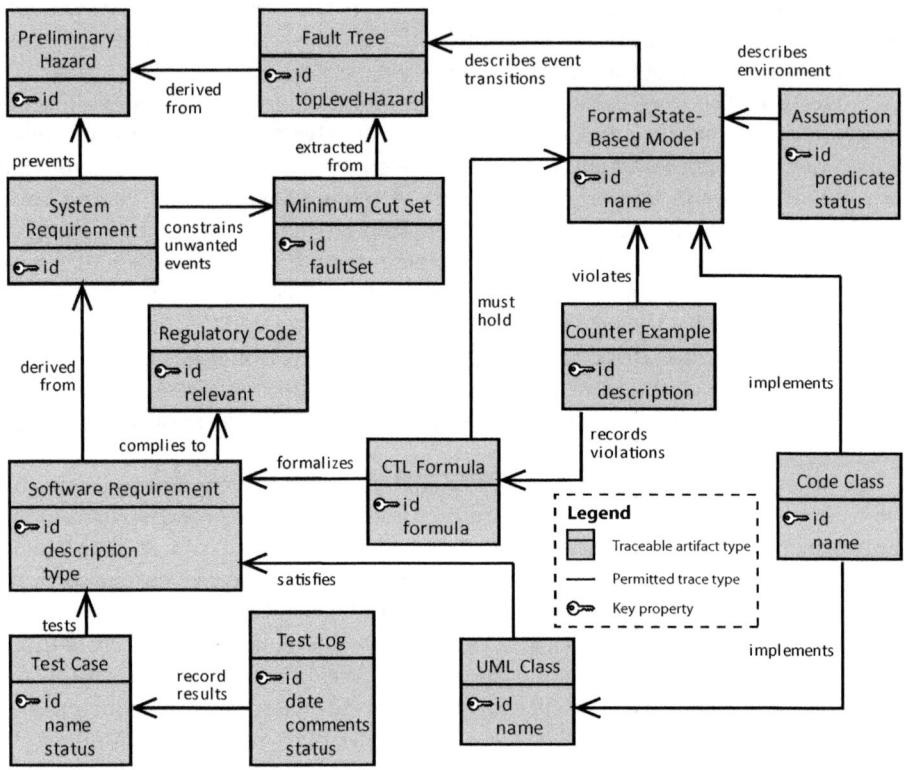

Fig. 1. A Traceability Information Model for a Safety Critical System

Figure 1 depicts the core traceable components of a safety critical system. The typical software development artifacts are seen along the left side of the diagram: system requirements are allocated to software requirements which are allocated to design elements documented as UML classes which are implemented by code. Test cases are used to test the software requirements with results being logged. Meanwhile, the safety critical nature of the software system requires additional artifacts which must also be traced, shown mainly on the right hand side of the diagram. The Preliminary Hazard artifact documents hazards that could lead to system failure. Such hazards are examined in more detail in a fault tree which looks at events that could lead to the hazards. The possible states and transitions for a system are documented in a formal state-based model. Certain assumptions about the environment are also captured. Formal analysis of the system may detect counter examples that show that a state can be entered which violates safety properties, formalized in this TIM using Computation Tree Logic (CTL). System Requirements are specified to prevent hazards from occuring by preventing the unwanted events documented in the Minimum Cut Sets. The Software Requirements may also have to comply with Regulatory Codes. Note that because this paper does not address the safety case, we have chosen not to include it in this TIM. Similarly, since we focus on product requirements, we have not shown process requirements in this TIM.

Each traceable artifact type may also possess one or more properties, which are used later in the process to specify traceability queries. For example, the "Software Requirement" artifact type includes 'id', 'description,' and 'type.' Property values can be included in trace query results, while properties or multiplicities can be used to define constraints that filter out unwanted artifacts. Filters can also be created based on trace types associated with each of the traceability paths.

Investing the effort to define a TIM is worthwhile because the TIM makes it simpler to generate and execute traceability queries. Furthermore, the TIM can be mapped to physical artifacts, and therefore a TIM and its associated trace queries can be reused across different products simply by re-establishing mappings in the new project [18]. In this paper, we present a basic TIM and define a set of reusable trace queries that are specific to the safety-critical domain.

3   Illustrative Example

We introduce a simplified pacemaker to illustrate the traceability infrastructure and to contextualize the proposed trace queries. A pacemaker [3] is an embedded medical device that monitors the heartbeat (HB) and regulates the heart when it is not beating at a normal rate. A pacemaker is safety critical because certain failures can harm the patient's health or contribute to loss of life [3, 13].

3.1   Fault Tree

One of the initial tasks in building a safety-critical software system is a preliminary hazard analysis (PHA) [12] to identify a set of potential high-level hazards, representing undesirable states of the system. System-level hazard analysis is used to help decide which hazards can be avoided (e.g., by changing the operational environment) and which hazards must be handled by the system. The PHA informs both the system safety requirements and the derived software safety requirements that constrain the design of the system. Each of the hazards in the PHA is typically explored by constructing an associated fault tree (FT) [23, 24]. A fault tree refines an initial hazard into a series of lower level intermediate or basic events, which, if they occur, would contribute toward the occurrence of the hazard. The FT uses boolean logic to depict the causal events leading to the root node. Figure 2 shows an excerpt from a fault tree constructed to investigate the ways in which the pacemaker could fail to provide treatment to the patient when needed [15].

As depicted, the hazard under analysis is *Failure to pace when patient needs it*. Two identified intermediate faults are *Failure to identify heartbeat correctly* and *Failure to generate a required pulse*. The first of these has three contributing faults, namely sensing, calculation, and reporting failures, any one of which can

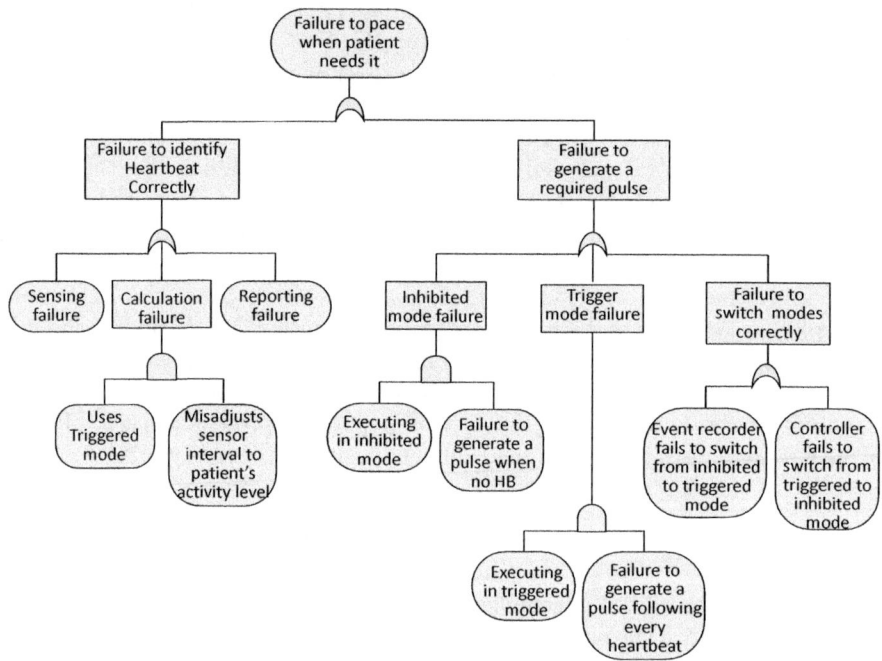

Fig. 2. A Fault Tree

cause the pacemaker to fail to pace correctly. The second intermediate fault has sub-faults related to inhibited mode failures, trigger mode failures, and transitioning from one mode to another. For purposes of this example, we are particularly interested in the inhibited mode failure which can occur when the pacemaker is in inhibited mode and there is a failure to generate a pulse when no heartbeat is detected. We are also interested in the calculation failure that occurs when triggered mode is used and the pacemaker fails to adjust the sensor interval to the patient's activity level.

A cut set in a fault tree is defined as a set of basic events (leaf nodes) whose simultaneous occurrence would cause the top event in the fault tree to occur [12]. A cut set is said to be minimum if it cannot be reduced without losing its status as a cut set. An example of a minimum cut set for the pacemaker is "failing to generate a pulse when no heartbeat is detected" while "in inhibited mode." If both of these leaf nodes occur at the same time, the pacemaker will fail to pace when needed, a hazard to the patient. Almost every fault-tree modeling tool has the capability to return the set of minimum cut sets that can be used to identify common cause failures across multiple fault trees, i.e., events that occur in the minimum cut sets of multiple fault trees. In addition, some tools can return common cause events.

Table 1. A Subset of Requirements for the PaceMaker System

REQ101	**Inhibited Mode**: While in inhibited mode, if no heart beat is detected by the pacemaker's sensor during a programmable sensing interval, the pacemaker shall generate a pulse.
REQ102	**Triggered Mode**: While in triggered mode, the pacemaker shall regulate the heartbeat by generating a pulse following every heartbeat.
REQ103	**Track Heartbeat Rate**: While in inhibited mode, the EventRecorder shall track the heartbeat rate.
REQ104	**Transition to Triggered Mode**: While in inhibited mode, if the heartbeat rate exceeds a threshold, the EventRecorder shall command a switch to triggered mode.
REQ105	**Transition to Inhibited Mode**: While in Triggered mode, if the number of heartbeats exceeds 24 in a 6000 msec recording interval, the Controller shall command a switch to Inhibited mode.
REQ106	**Activity Sensor**: The pacemaker shall monitor the activity level of the patient.
REQ107	**Activity Response**: The pacemaker shall adjust the duration of the sensing interval to match the patient's current activity level.

3.2   Safety-Related Software Requirements

The basic functionality of the pacemaker involves two different operation modes: inhibited and triggered [14]. In inhibited mode, the pacemaker generates a pulse only if the heart fails to generate its own pulse, while in triggered mode, the pacemaker generates a pulse following each heartbeat. Some pacemakers, such as the one illustrated here, also have the ability to monitor the activity level of a patient in order to adjust the sensing interval accordingly. These requirements are more formally depicted in Table 1. Note that these requirements may be found as a subset of the System or Safety Requirements from the TIM shown in Figure 1.

3.3   Safety Analysis

Once failure causes are well understood and the software requirements to address these (called *software safety requirements*) are specified and validated, developers construct the design to satisfy the requirements and produce code to implement the design. Certain properties must be satisfied by the pacemaker design and implementation in order to assure patient safety. Moreover, these properties must be shown to be satisfied in order for the company producing the pacemaker to gain approval to market and sell their devices. An example of such a safety-related property is requirement REQ101 related to pulse generation. An examination of the fault tree in Figure 2 shows that this property is the inverse of the minimum cut set containing the two leaf nodes "Fails to generate a pulse" and "Is in inhibited mode."

Many of the safety engineer's tasks thus involve assurance that traceability exists between the safety requirements and the intermediate and final products. Some of the assurances the safety engineer is responsible for providing involve relatively straightforward queries such as "Are all initially identified hazards covered by a fault tree?" Other assurances involve more complicated traceability

queries such as "Do all minimum cut sets have an associated mitigating requirement?" or "Are all common cause failures in the set of fault trees addressed by
one or more design mechanisms?" In previous work we presented a set of eleven
standard trace query patterns needed for the assurance of requirements for an
e-health software system that did not have explicit safety requirements [18]. In
this paper we extend those queries to include trace queries needed to handle the
assurance of software safety requirements.

For each trace query, we describe how the query is represented using our Visual Trace Modeling Language (VTML), and discuss the results returned by
an example of the traceability query for the pacemaker. Each of these queries
addresses a common question that must be repeatedly posed by either a safety
engineer or a developer in the safety-critical domain, for which current techniques generally require significant manual effort to answer. Representation of
the queries in VTML enables the associated queries to be used and reused across
the artifacts in the TIM. If a query returns bad news, the safety engineer can
place this item on a watch list. New queries then can be periodically run behind
the scenes. If new fault trees are identified or existing fault trees are updated
in response to evolution in requirements, design, or operational experience [17],
the safety engineer can perform a delta trace to determine if added or modified
hazards are adequately covered.

4   Visual Trace Modeling Language (VTML)

We illustrate the trace queries in this paper using VTML. VTML assumes the
presence of an underlying TIM and then represents queries as a set of filters
applied to a structural subset of that model. A VTML query is composed of a
connected subset of the artifacts and trace types defined in the TIM as well as
a set of associated filter conditions. These filters are used to eliminate unwanted
artifacts or to define the data to be returned by the trace query.

Figure 3 depicts the basic elements of a VTML query. The initial query scope
specifies the subset of artifacts for which the trace is to be executed, where scope
could be as small as a single artifact, or as broad as the entire set of artifacts of
that type. VTML depicts this scope visually using the *start* symbol. The three
compartments of the class notation are used respectively to depict the name of
the class, properties used in filter conditions or to specify return results, and
functions used to compose and extract aggregate data from the class. Return
values are annotated with a bar chart symbol, while properties used to filter
results are annotated with a filter symbol and also depict a valid filter expression.
As shown in this example, filters can be applied at both the class and the trace
matrix level. The example in Figure 3 can be read as follows assuming source
artifacts are *use cases* and target artifacts are *test cases*: "For the selected use
cases, return the description of all use cases which trace to more than two failed
test cases. Aggregate the results according to some function f, and display the
description and the aggregated value." A more complete description of VTML
including its metamodel and an extensive set of queries is provided in our prior
work [18].

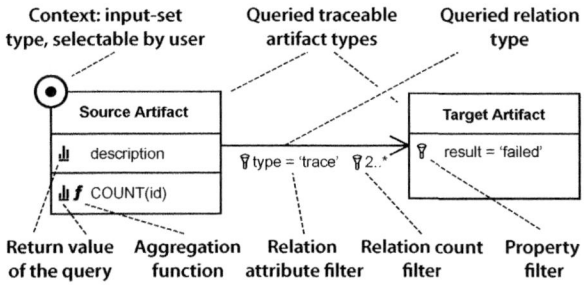

Fig. 3. Features of a visual traceability query

5   Safety-Related Trace Queries

Traceability provides support for specific software engineering goals, as depicted in Table 2. These goals are derived from a number of sources including Leveson's set of basic software system safety tasks [12], our own experiences working with safety-critical systems [7,16], an analysis of several documents prepared as submissions for approval of medical devices, and a study of related literature, handbooks, and guides [9].

For each of these traceability goals, there are several different supportive traceability queries that can be used by the safety analyst. For example, if we are interested in Traceability Goals #2 (safety-related requirements covered by design) and #6 (safety-related requirements have been tested), we might focus on tracing *requirements* to *code*. Queries of interest might include (a) "return a list of all requirements and the associated classes in which they are implemented", and (b) "count the number of requirements without implemented classes." These queries reveal something about the coverage of requirements in the implementation. Similarly, (c) "return a list of all requirements without associated implemented classes" or (d) "count the number of requirements without implemented classes" both reveal information about lack of coverage. We could also execute transitive trace queries such as (e) "return a list of all requirements with classes that have failed test cases in the past week," or we could incorporate customized functions into the trace queries as (f) "return a list of requirements with classes that exhibit cyclomatic complexity values in the top 5 percentile."

As it is not feasible for us to illustrate each type of query for each of the twelve proposed trace queries, we illustrate our approach with trace queries for three of the goals that are particularly relevant to the safety-domain, and which are quite different from queries found in non-safety critical domains. All of these queries assume the underlying presence of the TIM depicted in Figure 1.

5.1   Requirement Coverage of all Common Cause Failures

In support of traceability goal # 1, it is important to show that all minimum cut sets derived from the modeled fault trees are covered by requirements. Showing

Table 2. Safety-Related Traceability Goals

1.	Demonstrate that all common cause failures in the set of fault trees are covered by requirements.
2.	Demonstrate that all safety-related requirements are satisfied in the design.
3.	Determine which regulatory codes are covered by requirements.
4.	Demonstrate that all safety-related design elements are fully realized in the code.
5.	Identify parts of the code which represent standard safety mechanisms including architectural or design mechanisms such as safety interlocks, heartbeat or fault-data redundancy, to prevent a specific hazard from occurring.
6.	Demonstrate coverage of safety-related requirements by test cases.
7.	Demonstrate that safety-related test cases have passed.
8.	Demonstrate that properties specifying safety-related requirements to be model checked have been model checked.
9.	Demonstrate that all counter-examples produced by the formal model checker for any of the safety-related requirements have been reviewed by a safety engineer.
10.	Determine the potential impact of changing a requirement on its associated downstream, safety-related TIM artifacts.
11.	Determine which requirements might be impacted by failure of a safety-related test case.
12.	Determine which formal models might be impacted by a change to an environmental assumption.

that each minimum cut set is associated with one or more mitigating requirements can provide a safety engineer with the information he or she needs to assess whether the hazard is fully mitigated. We present an example of one supporting trace query in Figure 4. This query returns a list of minimum cut sets and their associated requirements for one or more fault trees. As the VTML assumes a default cardinality of *1..**, the query only returns the minimum cut sets which have related system and software requirements. A similar query in which a cardinality filter of *0* is placed on the link between *Minimum Cut Set* and *System Requirement* would list only the minimum cut sets without system level requirements coverage.

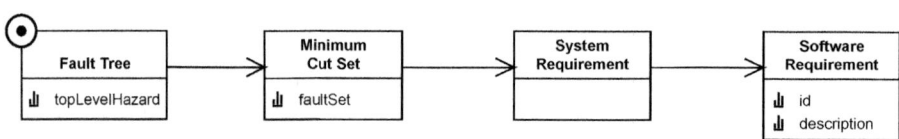

Fig. 4. Trace Query: Retrieve requirements providing coverage for minimum cut sets derived from one or more fault trees

Applying the trace in Figure 4 to the pacemaker example produces a trace matrix that includes the entries depicted in Table 3. These traces not only demonstrate that the minimum cut sets are associated with software requirements, but provide the safety engineer with information needed to assess how well they mitigate the common cause failures.

5.2   Integrating Formal Method Results

There is an increasing trend in safety-critical software development toward more formally verifying the correctness of the design through model checking [14].

Table 3. A Subset of Results Returned by the Minimum Cut Set Coverage Query

Fault Tree	Minimum Cut Set	System Requirement	Software Requirement
Failure to pace when patient needs it	(i)executing in inhibited mode,(ii)failure to generate a pulse when no HB	Monitor battery power to ensure pulse can be given.	Log failure event internally for diagnosis; Send wireless phone warning to health provider upon recurrence.
Failure to pace when patient needs it	(i)uses triggered model, (ii)adjusts sensor interval to patient's activity level	Activity sensors are monitored at all times for correct function.	If the respiration sensor (indicating activity level) fails, the pacemaker shall use Inhibited mode

However in current practice, the model checking results are often disconnected from other software artifacts and are therefore often not used in the traceability scheme. In this section we propose a trace queriy for integrating model checking results into the TIM in support of Trace Goal #8. The query depicted in Figure 5 utilizes the formal model components of the TIM. First, it identifies any counter examples produced by the model checker. If any are identified, it returns a list of the associated CTL formulas and related requirements.

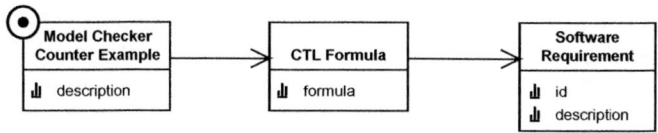

Fig. 5. List all CTL formulas and related requirements for any counter examples produced by the model checker

To illustrate this query, consider the pacemaker requirement REQ101 which states that "While in inhibited mode, if no heart beat is detected by the pacemaker's sensor during a programmable sensing interval, the pacemaker shall generate a pulse." An associated CTL could be defined as follows [14]:

$$AG((sensed = 0 \ \wedge \ timerSenseTimeUp = 1 \ \wedge \ inhibitedMode = 1))$$
$$\implies EF(pulseGen = 1 \ \wedge \ inhibitedMode = 1))$$

This and similar CTL properties are checked by the model, and results are stored in a model checking repository. Assuming no counterexamples are produced, the query in Figure 5 returns an empty list, adding some degree of confidence that given the as-modeled behavior of the system, this requirement is always satisfied.

Figure 6 depicts two additional kinds of supporting trace queries for counting artifacts and for identifying missing elements. The first shows how a trace query can be used to return a simple count of counter examples produced by the most recent model checking run, while the second one returns a list of mitigating requirements without associated CTL formulas. Both of these trace queries and their results can be used by a safety engineer to help manage safety requirements throughout the software development effort.

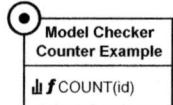

(a) Query 3a: Return a count of counter examples produced by the most recent model checking run

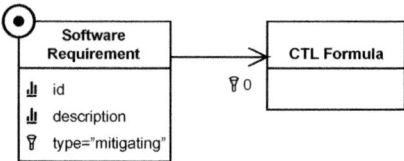

(b) Query 3b: Return a list of mitigating requirements without associated CTL formulas

Fig. 6. Supporting Traces for Integrating Results from the Model Checker

5.3   Assumptions

In our final example we present a trace query that supports Goal #12. Each formal model typically has a set of assumptions associated with it. These assumptions are often in the form of predicates such as "A patient's heartbeat is always (can be assumed to be) in the range x to y." or "the sensor that checks the patient's respiration rate never (can be assumed to never) fails." Sometimes during use of the system, or due to changes in the environment, these assumptions are found to be, or become, incorrect. The properties verified on that model were based on those assumptions, so we can no longer be confident in safety arguments based on the model. In the trace query depicted in Figure 7, we therefore retrieve a list of all CTL properties and associated requirements that are impacted by a change in one or more assumptions.

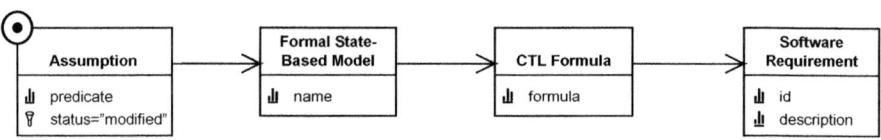

Fig. 7. Trace Query:List all requirements impacted by a change in an environmental assumption and the formal models that must be re-checked

5.4   Prototype

One of the major benefits of VTML is that trace queries are defined over the TIM, and do not reference project-specific data structures. However, the queries must be transformed into a query format that can be applied to the physical data sources. All of the trace queries described in this paper are fully executable in our prototype tool. Our prototype transforms the features of a visual traceability query step by step into an executable SQL query. It first uses an XSLT script that translates queries into XMI format, and then transforms them into executable SQL statements [18]. Defining and writing trace queries using VTML applied over a standard TIM, makes the queries fully portable across projects. It means that an organization adopting our appproach could create both a reusable TIM and a reusable set of safety-related trace queries which address all of the traceability goals defined in Table 2. This portability is achieved by mapping the conceptual elements of the TIM, including the artifact types and their properties, to physical fields in the underlying database.

6   Related Work

Most discussion of traceability in the development of safety-critical systems is in the form of standards and guidebooks that mandate the tracking of hazards and their mitigations through the software life cycle but do not describe query techniques to help achieve this. However, safety cases [11], dependability cases [1], and assurance cases all use traceability to construct structured arguments to justify goals by tracing and managing the links from evidence to those goals. Recommended practice is to maintain the case while constructing the system so that every step of development preserves the established chain of evidence. Although there is a large body of work in the more general area of traceability, to the best of our knowledge, there is little or no research that investigates techniques for using traceability to support a broad spectrum of safety-related queries in the way described in this paper. Extending the work described here to support assemblage and maintenance of safety case evidence is a natural and planned extension.

Peraldi-Frati and Albinet proposed a model for traceability in safety-critical systems [20]. Their work focused on requirements, design, and test cases, and showed how to establish *satisfies* relationships from design to requirements, and *verifies* relationships between test cases and requirements. Their proposed infrastructure incorporates formal models that demonstrate the satisfaction of a specific requirement. Katta and Stalhane define a conceptual model of traceability for safety systems [10]. Their approach creates a traceability graph (similar to a TIM) depicting a wide variety of artifacts and their associated traceability links. For example, they include hazards, system level requirements, software requirements, architectural components, and common cause failures. However, neither of these approaches incorporates results from fault tree analysis nor integrates formal methods into the traceability infrastructure. Furthermore, in general, any publications we found on tracing safety-critical requirements focus upon describing the actual artifacts to be traced, and fail to highlight the tracing benefits achieved through a useful and effective set of traceability queries.

Hill and Tilley propose a traceability approach for supporting the assurance and recertification of safety-critical legacy systems [8]. However, they primarily describe traces between requirements, process improvement standards, and a risk taxonomy and do not discuss any specific types of software artifacts beyond requirements. Finally, other researchers such as Sanchez et al. have explored the role of traceability in safety-critical, model-driven environments [22]. Their approach is designed to demonstrate that hazards translate into requirements, and that architectural decisions designed to satisfy those requirements are successfully transformed into the final code.

7   Conclusions

The traceability goals and queries described in this paper support a number of critical safety engineering tasks. First, they can be used during the development process to ensure that safety is being built into the system, and second, they can be used to generate traceability matrices needed by certification and approval bodies such as the FDA. Combining the various types of coverage queries produces relatively sophisticated and clearly useful trace matrices. It also identifies problem areas such as safety-related requirements without passed test cases, or safety-related requirements potentially impacted by changed values of environmental variables which provide significant support towards building a demonstrably safe software system.

The primary contribution of this paper is the presentation of a query-driven approach to tracing requirements in safety-critical software systems. At the start of a project, safety engineers and developers can strategically plan the TIM, map it to specific database tables or other data structures, and carefully define the safety-related trace queries that are to be accessible throughout the project. This kind of approach enables engineers to build traceability into the software development life-cycle, so that traceability links can be used not only for documentation purposes during the certification process, but for actually improving developers' understanding of safety-related issues throughout the software development life-cycle.

Acknowledgments. This work was supported by NSF grants CCF-0916275 with funds from the American Recovery and Reinvestment Act of 2009, CCF-1143830, CCF-1143734, CCF-0810924 and CCF-0811140. This research is also funded in part by the Austrian Science Fund (FWF): M1268-N23.

References

1. Jackson, D., Thomas, M., Millet, L.I.: Software for Dependable Systems: Sufficient Evidence? National Research Council (2007)
2. Dömges, R., Pohl, K.: Adapting Tracability Environments to Project-Specific Needs. Communications of the ACM 41(12), 54–62 (1998) ISSN 0001-0782
3. Ellenbogen, K.A., Wood, M.A.: Cardiac Pacing and ICDs. Blackwell Publishing (2005)
4. Federal Aviation Authority (FAA). DO-178B: Software Considerations in Airborne Systems and Equipment Certification, faa's advisory circular ac20-115b edition

5. Food and Drug Administration. Guidance for the Content of Premarket Submissions for Software Contained in Medical Devices (2005)
6. Gotel, O., Finkelstein, C.: An analysis of the requirements traceability problem. In: Proceedings of the First International Conference on Requirements Engineering, pp. 94–101 (April 1994)
7. Heimdahl, M.P.E.: Safety and software intensive systems: Challenges old and new. In: FOSE, pp. 137–152 (2007)
8. Hill, J., Tilley, S.: Creating safety requirements traceability for assuring and recertifying legacy safety-critical systems. In: 18th IEEE International Requirements Engineering Conference (RE), September 27-October 1, pp. 297–302 (2010)
9. Joint Software System Safety Committee. Software System Safety Handbook Technical and Manegerial Team Approach, edition (1999)
10. Katta, V., Stalhane, T.: A conceptual model of traceability for safety systems. In: CSDM - Poster Presentation (2010)
11. Kelly, T.P., McDermid, J.A.: A Systematic Approach to Safety Case Maintenance. In: Felici, M., Kanoun, K., Pasquini, A. (eds.) SAFECOMP 1999. LNCS, vol. 1698, pp. 13–26. Springer, Heidelberg (1999)
12. Leveson, N.G.: Safeware, System Safety and Computers. Addison Wesley (1995)
13. Littlewood, B., Strigini, L.: Validation of ultrahigh dependability for software-based systems. Commun. ACM 36(11), 69–80 (1993)
14. Liu, J., Basu, S., Lutz, R.: Generating variation point obligations for compositional model checking of software product lines. Journal of Automated Software Engineering 18(1), 39–76 (2011)
15. Liu, J., Dehlinger, J., Sun, H., Lutz, R.R.: State-based modeling to support the evolution and maintenance of safety-critical software product lines. In: ECBS, pp. 596–608 (2007)
16. Lutz, R.R.: Software engineering for safety: a roadmap. In: ICSE - Future of SE Track, pp. 213–226 (2000)
17. Lutz, R.R., Mikulski, I.C.: Requirements discovery during the testing of safety-critical software. In: ICSE, pp. 578–585 (2003)
18. Mäder, P., Cleland-Huang, J.: A Visual Traceability Modeling Language. In: Petriu, D.C., Rouquette, N., Haugen, Ø. (eds.) MODELS 2010, Part I. LNCS, vol. 6394, pp. 226–240. Springer, Heidelberg (2010)
19. Mäder, P., Gotel, O., Philippow, I.: Getting Back to Basics: Promoting the Use of a Traceability Information Model in Practice. In: 5th Workshop on Traceability in Emerging Forms of Software Engineering (TEFSE 2009). In Conjunction with ICSE 2009, Vancouver, Canada (May 2009)
20. Peraldi-Frati, M.-A., Albinet, A.: Requirement traceability in safety critical systems. In: Proceedings of the 1st Workshop on Critical Automotive Applications: Robustness & Safety, CARS 2010, pp. 11–14. ACM, New York (2010)
21. Ramesh, B., Jarke, M.: Toward reference models for requirements traceability. IEEE Trans. Softw. Eng. 27, 58–93 (2001)
22. Sánchez, P., Alonso, D., Rosique, F., Álvarez, B., Pastor, J.A.: Introducing safety requirements traceability support in model-driven development of robotic applications. IEEE Trans. Computers 60(8), 1059–1071 (2011)
23. Storey, N.R.: Safety Critical Computer Systems. Addison-Wesley Longman Publishing Co., Inc., Boston (1996)
24. Sullivan, K.J., Dugan, J.B., Coppit, D.: The galileo fault tree analysis tool. In: FTCS, pp. 232–235 (1999)

Which Traceability Visualization Is Suitable in This Context? A Comparative Study

Yang Li and Walid Maalej

Technische Universität München
Munich, Germany
{liya,maalejw}@cs.tum.edu

Abstract. Traceability supports users in describing and tracking the relationships between software artifacts. Techniques such as traceability matrices and graphs visualize these relationships and help users to access and understand them. Researchers agree that different visualization techniques add valuable information in different contexts. However, there is an ambiguity which visualization is suitable for which context. To clarify this we conducted a comparative study of common visualization techniques, including an experiment and interviews with 24 participants.

We found that traceability matrices and graphs are most preferred in management tasks, while hyperlinks are preferred in implementation and testing tasks. Traceability lists seem to be the least attractive technique for most participants. Graphs are preferred to navigate linked artifacts, while matrices are appropriate for overview. Hyperlinks are regarded to fit for fine-grained information. Participants stressed the importance of visualizing semantics of artifacts and links. Our finding also indicates that users are not always able to choose the most suitable visualization.

Keywords: Traceability, Visualization, Context, Empirical Experiment.

1 Introduction

Over the last years, research has shown how traceability supports various software engineering tasks such as design, implementation, testing, and management tasks [1,6]. Traceability links provide valuable information such as related artifacts and the nature of the relationship. These links enable following the evolution of an artifact, in particular of a requirement from its origin to its deployment [10].

As the number of links and the complexity of their usage increased, researchers suggested various techniques for traceability visualization. The objective is to help users to understand the "cloud of links" and efficiently access underlying information [7, 12]. However, visualization might introduce new overhead, be too trivial, or too complex for the task at hand. For example, checking the implementation status of a release based on hyperlinks between requirements and code might be a repetitive tedious task. Therefore, how to visualize traceability links strongly depends on the usage context.

B. Regnell and D. Damian (Eds.): REFSQ 2012, LNCS 7195, pp. 194–210, 2012.

Various authors have discussed the problem of traceability visualization. Marcus et al. [24] found that a traceability management tool should contain different views – each may best fit specific tasks. Similarly, Winkler [32] deduced from a survey that future traceability visualization should focus more on users and tasks. Gotel et al. [10] analyzed requirements traceability problems and found that added value of traceability depends on the user, the task, and the project characteristics. There is a common agreement that appropriate traceability visualization should consider "the trade-off between the *effort* needed to capture complex information and the *value* of this information for the development situation" [21, 27]. This paper is a part of a larger research that examines this trade-off for recommending the suitable visualization in a particular context.

The paper reports on a comparative study, which includes a literature review, an experiment, and interviews with 24 participants. The paper's contribution is threefold. First, it summarizes the literature on traceability visualization in a meta-model, which describes the relationship between traceability information, visualization techniques, and task contexts. Second, it provides empirical evidence on the suitability of four common visualization techniques (matrix, graph, list, and hyperlink) for particular contexts. Third, it gives tool vendors and researchers insights into how to integrate and fine-tune visualization techniques in requirements engineering processes and tools.

Section 2 reviews the literature introducing the studied concepts. Section 3 presents the design of our study including the research questions and methods. Section 4 and 5 report on the quantitative and qualitative results of the study, respectively. We discuss our findings in section 6. Section 7 discusses the limitations of the study, while Section 8 concludes the paper.

2   Foundation

Traceability visualization involves three main concepts: the traceability information (what to visualize), the visualization technique (how to visualize), and the task context (when to visualize). Traceability information is the set of intrinsic properties of links and the related artifacts to be traced. Visualization techniques depict the traceability information e.g. in graphs, lists, or images. A task context describes a particular situation where a user interacts with certain artifacts and traceability information to achieve a goal. Fig. 2 illustrates these concepts and their associations:

- Visualization helps understanding traceability information. This association is also called *understandability* [9].
- Traceability information is valuable for accomplishing a task in a particular context. This association is also called *information value* [8].
- A visualization technique is suitable for a particular task context. We call this *suitability*.

The trade-off between the information value and the understandability of the visualization represents the visualization suitability from a different perspective.

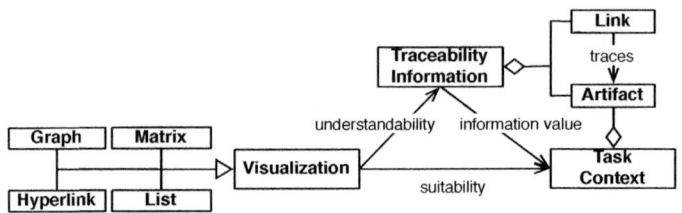

Fig. 1. Traceability Visualization Meta-Model

2.1 Traceability Information: What to Visualize

A traceability link connects a source artifact with a target artifact, which are
created and updated during the software life cycle. Traceability information to
be visualized includes information about the *artifacts* and *links*. Concerning the
artifacts authors suggested visualizing the type, metadata, granularity, as well
as other artifacts attributes:

Artifact types such as requirements, class diagrams, and source code are
created by various stakeholders in different tasks to describe different aspects of
a system or a project [27]. Traceability links might trace artifacts from the same
types or from different types.

Artifact metadata provides information about the artifact state and its
evolution. Artifact metadata can include the creation time, the update time, and
the version of an artifact [24]. Metadata might include additional information
such as the main author or the collaborators.

Granularity represents the level of information details included in the artifact and pointed by the link. Coarse-grained information can result in the loss
of useful detail, while fine-grained representations can create trivial knowledge
whose benefits do not warrant its creation cost [27].

Artifact attributes describe certain semantic properties of an artifact, such
as the status of an action item or the priority of a requirement [33]. These
attributes typically depend on the artifact type.

In addition to the artifacts linked, the link itself presents other information,
which needs to be visualized:

Link type describes how the artifacts are related to each other and implies
how the relationship should be used in different contexts [30]. Ramesh et al. [27]
classified traceability links into four basic types: satisfaction, dependency, rationale, and evolution. In their classification, high-level artifact such as goals or
constraints can be satisfied by lower-level artifacts. Dependencies exist between
lower-level artifacts. A lower-level artifact evolves to another artifact through
some actions, whose rationale is captured in the higher-level artifact.

Link metadata contains the link creation time, the update time [24], or the
link version providing information on the link state and evolution. The author
of the link and other related information can also be included in the metadata.

Link strength measures how much an artifact affects others, or how important is a link to a project or a task. The strength of a link highlights the most useful information to a user. However, Ramesh et al. found that users are often unable to precisely identify the strength of a link [27].

Confidence denotes the degree of belief on the correctness of the results returned by an automated or semi-automated link recovery scheme [2, 3]. It provides a reference to users when presenting the recovered links.

2.2 Visualization Technique: How to Visualize

We focus on four visualization techniques[1]: matrices, graphs, lists, and hyperlinks as illustrated in Fig. 2. These are widely referenced in the literature and used in many tools. Other techniques are introduced in [3, 24, 25, 28].

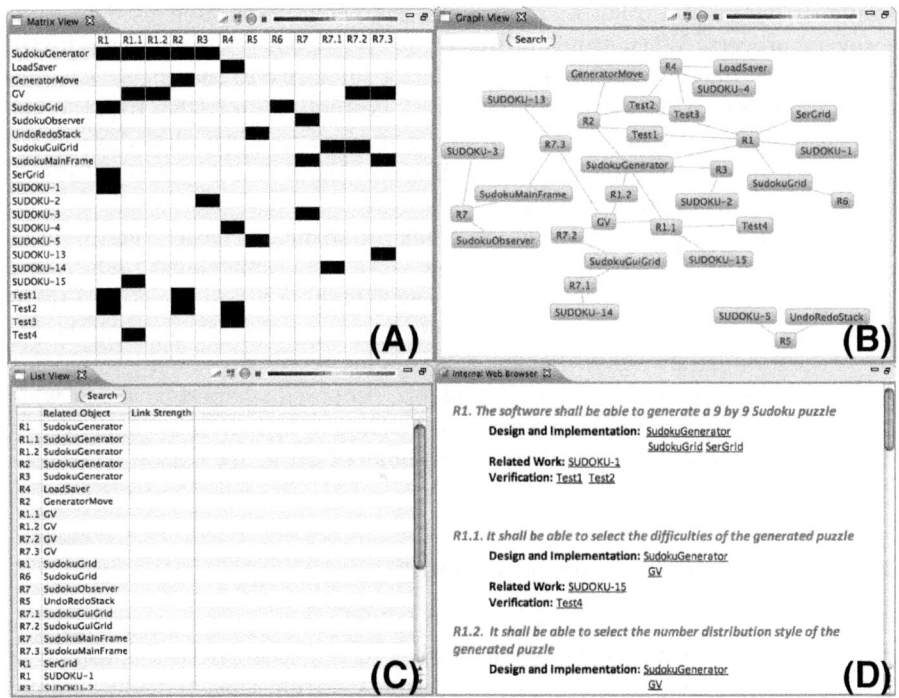

Fig. 2. Common Visualizations: Matrix (A), Graph (B), List (C), and Hyperlink (D)

Matrix or a requirements traceability matrix (RTM) maps requirements to other artifacts through a two dimensional representation. Typically, the columns

---

[1] In the following the term visualization means visualization technique.

represent requirements while the rows represent other artifacts. A matrix element $a_{i,j}$ being marked (e.g. black) means that the requirement of column j and the artifact of row i are linked. Example implementations include DocTrace and VisMatrix. DocTrace automatically creates RTMs, which show the traceability and coverage of requirements throughout the set of documents [29]. VisMatrix focuses on link recovery [7]. It creates a representation of RTMs showing not only where candidate links exist, but also the strength of those links.

Graphs allow visualization of multidimensional relationships between requirements and other artifacts by representing artifacts as nodes and relationships between them as edges. Two nodes are connected if a traceability link exists between the corresponding artifacts. Traceline and ChainGraphs implement this visualization technique. Traceline is a DOORS extension, which provides graph-based visualizations for requirements traceability [14]. ChainGraph visualizes shared metadata between requirements in a graph [12].

Lists represent each traceability link (along with the information of source, target artifacts, and other attributes) in one entry. It is often used in a link recovery process. When candidate links are rendered, they are generally displayed as a sequential list, ranked in order of similarity to the query. The most likely links appear at the top of the list. The tools Poirot [18], RETRO [11], and ADAMS [4, 5] represent dynamically generated candidate links as a list. A confidence score that indicates the likelihood of the link is displayed. Users can choose to accept or reject candidate links.

Hyperlinks enable users while browsing an artifact to easily "jump" to another linked artifact (possibly in a different tool). Hyperlinks connect related concepts, keywords, or phrases in a natural way. Kaindl et al. proposed RETH [16], a tool that uses hypertext to provide links among requirements and the representation of artifacts in a domain model. This representation allows users to make relationships explicit. Maletic et al. [22] proposed a hypertext model which supports complex linking structures and versioning of individual links for link recovery. In DOORS, out- and incoming links of an artifact are visualized as bidirectional hyperlinks.

2.3   Task Context: When to Visualize

A particular task at hand decides when and why to represent traceability information [10] and influences how and what to represent. A task is usually an assigned piece of work to be finished within a certain time [17]. To complete a task, a set of information and events is involved, which can be observed or interpreted [19, 20]. We call this set a *task context*. It consists of *artifacts* used during the task (e.g. the requirements read or the code edited) as well as the *interaction* of the user with the tools and the artifacts (e.g. read, edit, navigate).

Table 1 depicts the contexts of common tasks, how users interact with artifacts in these task contexts and which traceability links are involved.

Table 1. Task Contexts Examples

Task	Traceability Usage	Linked Artifacts
Management	Monitor progress of implementation and testing [32] Plan open issues [6, 26]	Work items, requirements, test cases, and source code
Design	Identify components and objects which satisfies a requirement [15] Propagate changes during redesign [6]	Models and requirements
Implementation	Comprehend a program in order to fix a bug or implement a new feature [1]	Source code, requirements, and models
Testing	Check if requirements have been implemented correctly [15]	Test cases and requirements

3   Research Design

We first introduce the research questions that drive our research, and then present the method followed and the setup used to collect the research data.

3.1   Research Questions

The main goal of our research is to answer two main research questions:

RQ1. Which visualization is suitable in a particular task context?

We study the suitability from four perspectives. First, the *perceived suitability*, is the user's assessment of the direct relationship between a particular visualization and a particular context. Second, the *information comprehension ratio* describes the trade-off between the understandability of traceability visualization and its underlying information value for a context. To measure this we define: $f = \frac{informationValue}{difficulty}$. The higher f is, the easier is it to capture valuable information for the task through the visualization. Therefore, a larger information comprehension ratio also means a better suitability of that visualization. Third, we assume that a suitable visualization helps accomplishing a task in less time. Thus we examine the *time needed* for a task using different visualizations. Finally, we study the *preferences* of users, i.e. which visualization a user would use for a particular task context.

RQ2. What traceability information should be visualized?

In a particular task context, certain traceability information (e.g. particular attributes of the related artifacts) can be crucial. This information needs to be represented. Further, we study how to visualize various types of information so that users are able to easily access and understand it.

3.2   Research Method

We study the usage of the introduced traceability visualization techniques for the management, design, implementation, and testing tasks. The study consists of three phases as shown in Fig. 3: a preparation phase, an experiment phase, and an interview phase. In the *preparation phase* we introduce the concept of traceability, the purpose of the experiment, the dummy project, and how to use the four traceability visualization techniques. We randomly divide the participants into two groups: a control group and an experimental group. In the experimental group a participant is required to finish each task using an assigned traceability visualization. The mapping of the tasks and the visualization is randomly generated. In the control group participants are required to finish each task by using their favorite traceability visualization (the one a participant thinks it is suitable).

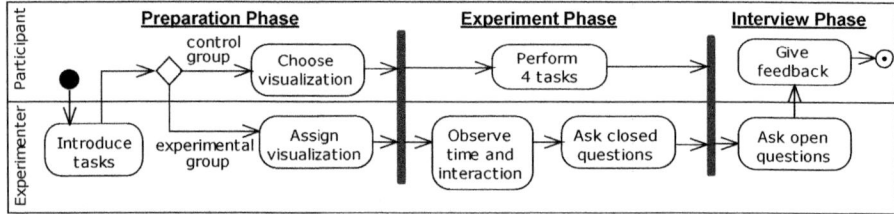

Fig. 3. Experiment Process

In the *experiment phase* each participant is required to finish four tasks that represent different contexts. A participant starts with the management task. The implementation task, design task, and testing task are then ordered randomly. The management task is ordered first since participants who gain project knowledge from other tasks can perform this task without using traceability visualization. The other tasks are independent from each other and are related to three different parts of the project. After each task is completed, the participants are presented with the following statements

1. This visualization is easy to understand.
2. The underlying information is valuable for this task.
3. This visualization is suitable in this context.

Participants rate their agreement with these statements by selecting one option on the following Likert scales: ① strongly disagree, ② disagree, ③ undecided, ④ agree, and ⑤ strongly agree. During this phase we also measure the time needed to accomplish each task. After completion of tasks, we ask each participant the following open questions in the *interview phase*:

1. Would you use any of these visualizations during your real work? Why?
2. Do you think that a particular visualization is more suitable for a particular context?
3. Do you have any other comments or suggestions?

Overall, the whole process lasted approximately one hour for each participant.

3.3   Research Setup

We recruited 24 participants for the experiment. Eight were industry engineers with more than two years of professional experience. Eight were researchers who work on software engineering research topics. Eight were master level students with basic software engineering knowledge and programming skills. 16 participants were randomly assigned to the experimental group and eight participants to the control group.

For the experiment, we used the java open source project "Sudoku". The project includes 11 requirements, 17 class diagrams of each class and each package, 11 source code files in 3 packages, 11 test cases for UI testing, and 15 open work items managed in the JIRA issue tracking system. In total, 34 traceability links exist between requirements and class diagrams, requirements and source code, requirements and work items, and requirements and test cases.

In the management task a participant reviews the current project status, and then prioritizes and plans all open issues. In the implementation task a participant fixes a bug in Sudoku. In the design task a participant redesigns a package by refactoring a large class. Finally, in the testing task a participant tests whether a given requirement is implemented correctly.

To reduce the tool and usability biases, we implemented four Eclipse views in the same look-and-feel as illustrated in Fig. 2. The matrix view displays the traceability matrix of the "Sudoku" project. The columns represent requirements; the rows represent work items, test cases, code, and models. The graph view is zoomable and shows the relationships between all artifact types. Each line in the list view contains information of the source artifact and the target artifact of a traceability link. Finally, the hyperlink view displays hyperlinks in the requirements document. Related artifacts are hyperlinked with a short text description and get opened, if the hyperlink is clicked. Additional features such as showing link strength and link types were available in the different views in the same way. All views present the same traceability information.

4   Quantitative Results

We summarize the quantitative results in Fig. 4. Part A shows the assessments of all participants for the understandability, information value, and perceived suitability. The column "Count agree & str. agree" denotes the number of participants who agreed or strongly agreed with the given statement, and the proportion to the total number of ratings for the visualization in the respective

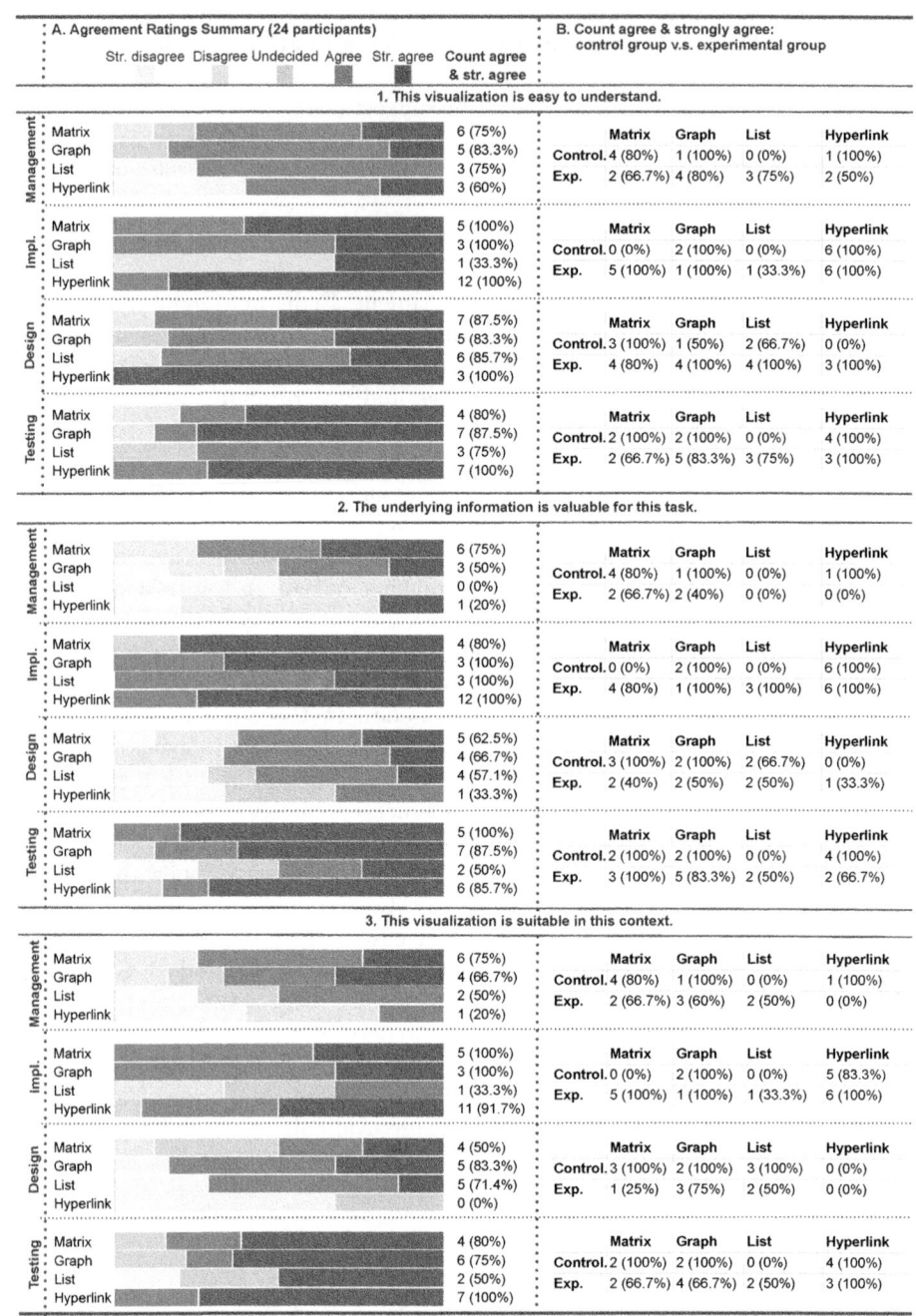

Fig. 4. Agreement Ratings and Comparison of Control Group v.s. Experimental Group (str. disagree = strongly disagree; str. agree = strongly agree; impl. = implementation; exp. = experimental)

task. For instance, for the understandability assessment, 6 out of 8 participants (i.e. $6/8 = 75\%$) chose agree or strongly agree for the matrix visualization in the management task. Part B compares the ratings between the control group (self-chosen visualizations) and the experimental group (assigned visualization) for each task.

Overall, participants rated all visualization techniques as easy to *understand* in the different contexts. Concerning means there were almost no significant differences between the four visualizations ($p > 0.05$). In particular, participants similarly rated the understandability of the matrix and graph visualizations in the different contexts. Visualizations were rated as less understandable in the management task. One reason is that none of the visualization can be immediately used without additional interpretation of the information in this context. Another reason might be that participants get more used to the visualization in the course of the experiment after performing the management task. In the testing task, hyperlinks were significantly more understandable than lists ($p < 0.02$).

The results on the *information value* are more differentiated. The visualizations seem to satisfy more information need during the implementation and testing tasks than during the management and design tasks (where more valuable and accessible information were needed). Graphs ranked best to visualize valuable information in the design task, while matrix ranked best for the management task. In this management context, matrix and graph visualization depicted significantly more valuable information than the list visualization ($p < 0.03$).

Concerning the *perceived suitability*, the matrix and graph visualization ranked significantly better than the hyperlink visualization for the management task ($p < 0.02$). For the design task, the graph visualization was significantly more suitable than the hyperlink visualization ($p < 0.02$). For the implementation and testing tasks, the matrix, graph, and hyperlink were similarly ranked.

Comparing the ranks of understandability, information value, and perceived suitability between the control group (self-chosen visualization) and the experimental group (assigned visualization), we found that participants gave much higher ranks for their self-chosen visualization. The exceptional case was in the design task, in which two out of eight participants were undecided about the chosen graph visualization's understandability and disagreed with the list's understandability. But they both agree that the chosen visualization represented valuable information and is suitable for this task context.

Fig. 5 illustrates the *information comprehension ratio* $f = \frac{informationValue}{difficulty}$ for the studied tasks. To measure *difficulty* in the same Likert scale, we assume $difficulty = 6 - understandability$. If a participant finds e.g. the visualization very easy to understand ($understandability = 5$), the $difficulty = 6 - understandability = 1$. $f \in [1/5, 5]$, the higher f is, the easier is it to capture valuable information through the visualization. As shown in Fig. 5, the management and design tasks require more valuable information to be easily understood. For the management task, the matrix and graph can better help the participants to retrieve valuable information with less effort. The matrix visualization has significantly higher information comprehension ratio than the list visualization ($p < 0.01$). The hyperlink visualization has relatively high information comprehension ratio except for the management task. The hyperlink visualization has significantly greater results than the list visualization for both implementation and testing tasks ($p < 0.04$). The matrix and graph visualization have also significantly greater information comprehension ratio than the list visualization for the testing task ($p < 0.03$).

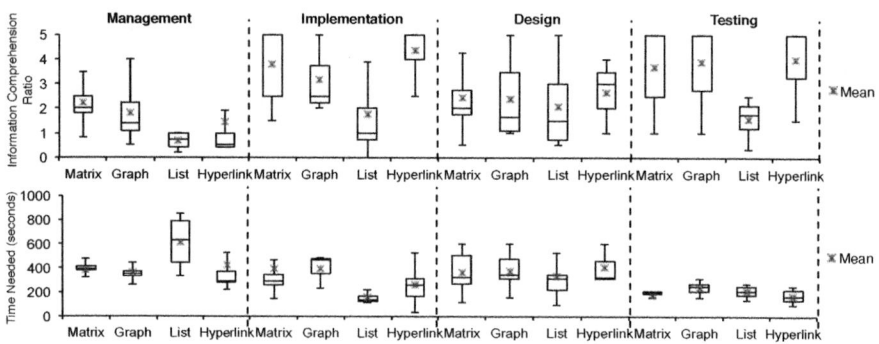

Fig. 5. Information Comprehension Ratios and Times Needed to Accomplish Tasks

When analyzing the *time needed* (see Fig. 5), we only found two significant results ($p < 0.05$). In the implementation tasks, participants who used hyperlinks needed significantly longer time than those who used lists ($p < 0.04$). In the testing task, participants who used graphs took significantly longer time than those who used matrices ($p < 0.05$). We believe the reason behind this is that the time needed of each task highly depends on the knowledge and skills of each participant. On average participants needed more time for each task when the visualization is assigned.

In Fig. 6, the result of the *self-choices* implies that for the management task, participants clearly preferred the matrix visualization to others. For the implementation task, participants preferred the hyperlink visualization. For the design task, matrix, graph and list were similarly selected. The list visualization was the least attractive to all participants.

	Matrix	Graph	List	Hyperlink
Management	5	1	0	1
Implementation	0	2	0	6
Design	3	2	3	0
Testing	2	2	0	4

Fig. 6. Self-choices of Visualization

5   Qualitative Results

We summarize the qualitative results from the interviews and the observations.

5.1   Which Visualization Is Suitable in a Particular Task Context?

Matrices represent a structured overview of the relationships between artifacts. Each requirement is explicitly associated with related artifacts through a matrix element. 13 participants would use the matrix during their work, claiming that "it represents a quick overview of all artifacts and links" and "is easy to navigate". A traceability matrix represents "valuable information in contexts such as reporting or planning". Our results suggest that matrices can be used in particular tasks when an abstract structured view of a project is needed.

Graphs are "vivid and intuitive to represent and explore relationships". 16 participants would use graphs during their work, claiming that graphs "give a first impression on what and how all artifacts are linked". Similar to matrices, graphs also represent an overview of artifacts and links, but in a rather "informal" and "explorative" way. Graphs are suitable for management and design tasks with relatively high information comprehension ratio, since "transitive relationships are also obvious" to help locating influenced artifacts.

Lists are simple but can be tailored to meet specific information needs. The list visualization is relatively plain compared to other techniques. Consequently, its information comprehension ratio is generally lower. However, it has advantages for focusing on a small amount of traceability links. One participant said "it is just like a checklist, very clear to me". Lists are suitable for performing bulk operations on the listed links e.g. which tests need to be conducted for this release. Three participants claimed "it is easy to manipulate lists in order to find the desired information step by step". A list can be easily filtered or sorted to satisfy a user's information need. For example in the design and testing task, participants filtered the requirements-related class diagrams and test cases.

Hyperlinks fit for fine-grained information needs. They guide users to access the related artifacts easily. Participants found that "the hyperlink visualization provides more detailed information". Therefore, the information comprehension ratio is higher except for the management task, where overview information is more desired. Hyperlinks are suitable for implementation tasks or for acceptance testing, because customers can easily trigger the proper test cases while browsing the requirements document. 15 participants liked hyperlinks, while three participants were "not at all" interested in the hyperlink visualization, because they "have no time to read". They "want to see things directly".

5.2   What Information Should Be Visualized and How?

We found that artifacts of various types need to be easily distinguished. One participant suggested "it would be nice, if different types of artifact are marked with different colors to provide more visual evidence for identifying artifact types".

Certain metadata or artifact attributes can be crucial to the task accomplishment. For instance, the priority and status of each work item influence how the next release is planed. One participant mentioned, "I would like to see directly in the traceability tool which linked bug is fixed and which is still open".

In the experiment, participants could enable showing the type of each link. They found this is helpful to their tasks. They suggested "a more specific link semantics can be even more useful". In the experiment we used the basic link types introduced in Section 2.1. More specialized link types can be defined depending on the project.

Users were also able to visualize link strengths by using a strength bar and a color map. The former is an icon similar to the battery strength display in a mobile phone. The latter uses different colors to denote the strength of a link according to a defined color map. Participants agreed that the link strength help them to find the most closely related links quickly. About half of them preferred the strength bar and the other half the color map. Most participants stressed the importance of *transparently* defining and showing *how and why* this strength is established since this impacts their reasoning.

Concerning visualization features, two participants claimed "graphs should automatically layout the linked artifacts on a circle around my chosen artifact". We found the acceptance of graphs strongly depend on the layout. Participants desired to have suitable layouts that "properly" reflect the artifacts and relationships "in a desired level of abstraction". For example, they should be able to choose a hierarchical layout to represent linked artifacts in a top-down direction depicting levels of abstraction. Users should also be able to apply radial layout to place artifacts on concentric circles depending on their relationship distance from a given artifact.

Hyperlinks should be combined with other visualizations. Hyperlinked information is organized in interlinked fragments and accessed non-linearly [23]. Therefore, we observed that users easily became disoriented while navigating hyperlinked information. A combination of hyperlinks and other visualizations can guide users to the hyperlinked information based on the understanding of other visualizations.

During the interview, participants asked "what if the project size increases and a lot of artifacts are involved?". For real-world projects, traceability matrices become very large and unreadable [32]. Graph-based visualizations often do not scale well to large data sets because their presentation tends to result in a complex structure that is hardly manageable or understandable [12]. Special features such as fisheye or filtering can deal with scalability issues [12,13].

Overall, we found that users should be able to interactively select and customize their visualizations, as also suggested in [31]. For instance, a participant suggested that related artifacts should get highlighted in a matrix if a user chooses a requirement. In a traceability graph, users can reorganize artifacts and their links to satisfy special needs. Interaction and customization are necessary for searching or recovering links. Features such as filtering help reducing a user's cognitive effort and concentrate on a subset of link information.

6 Discussion

Not surprising to us, the quantitative and qualitative results suggest that matrices and graphs are particularly suitable for management tasks, while hyperlinks for both implementation and testing tasks. However, there are three surprising findings, which we discuss in the following.

Visualization Suitability Is Ambiguous. Whether a visualization is suitable for a particular task context does not seem to be a simple yes/no question. Even if the results include clear trends (e.g. a traceability matrix is suitable in the context of a management task), the data still involves high variations and many "yes, but". We think that the task type itself is not the only influencing factor for selecting the suitable visualization. The concrete information need (what a user needs to know in order to accomplish the task at hand), the experience of the user with the visualization and with the artifacts involved, as well as the whole interaction sequence using the visualization can considerably influence whether a visualization is suitable for the current task. Therefore, our definition of task context, exclusively focusing on the task type, is too simple for a precise answer of the main research question of this paper. We argue that a context should include both a short and a long-term interaction history. While the long-term interaction history reveals the experience of the user with the visualization and the artifacts at hand, the short-term history reveals the concrete information need and the type of the task being performed [19, 20].

Lists Were under-estimated by Participants. Lists were the least selected visualization by the control group (only 3 out of 32 selections) and low ranked in the perceived suitability for all task contexts. We expected lists to be ranked higher, as they clearly represent information and provide a guidance to perform bulk operations (i.e. check lists). In addition, using lists does not require an artifact switch to navigate to the target information, as it is the case for hyperlinks. Indeed, participants who used hyperlinks took significantly longer time to finish their implementation tasks than those who used lists. We have two hypothetical explanations for lists' low attractiveness. First, our experiment settings and the implementation of the list visualization might have negatively influenced the participants' assessments. Second, user might not always be able to assess what is the best visualization to use at first glance. The second hypothesis is discussed in the next paragraph.

Users Are Not Always Able to Choose the Most Suitable Visualization. There is a difference between perceived suitability and "real" suitability. We found that participants in the control group were not always able to choose suitable visualizations for their tasks. For instance, one participant chose hyperlinks for the management task, which he then considered to be less suitable. Other participants assessed the visualizations to be highly suitable. But they ranked the understandability and the information value lower, or required more time to finish the task than others who used different visualizations. We think that in particular cases, context-aware visualizations could help users access the traceability information needed more efficiently [17] and possibly learn to use a different visualization. Such tools can provide an entry point to access traceability information. A concrete visualization is then shown based on the current context. The tool can learn from (a) users' interaction with the visualization and artifacts during their work and (b) empirical studies on the visualization suitability such as ours. For example, when a user performs a refactoring task, such tool can recommend using list visualization, which might be less attractive at first glance but can effectively present filtered information of impacted artifacts.

7   Limitations

During this study we made several simplifications, which might affect the internal and external validity of the results. Concerning the internal validity, the order of performing the tasks might influence a participant's understanding about the dummy project. To mitigate this threat we designed the tasks to be independent from each other. Moreover, the usability of the tools used in such experiment might influence participant choices. To mitigate this threat, we implemented all visualizations in the same look-and-feel instead of using different existing tools. We also explained the functionality of the tools in details during the preparation phase. Finally, we carefully selected the dummy project to be realistic enough but expose task that can be managed in the experiment setting. Soduku is an open source game, with 65 artifacts from different types. This gives us confidence that the studied variables are measured in realistic environments. However, the dummy project still remains relatively small when compared to other industrial projects. Our research questions were designed to be independent from scalability issues. Some qualitative findings give insight on how to deal with these issues.

Concerning the external validity, our results are based on the observation of 24 participants. Given the high effort required to conduct each experiments (e.g. compared to surveys), a larger number was not possible in the frame of this project. This might influence the statistical power of the results, but not the overall results and observed trends. Similar results from other studies also give confidence about validity of our results. Nevertheless, we plan to formulate our findings as hypotheses and check them in other rather quantitative studies. Finally, all participants had similar prior software engineering knowledge. None of them knew the dummy project. While this is an ideal setting for a comparative study to minimize external influencing factors, we are unable to generalize the results to a random user. Indeed we think that the user itself is an important part of the context to decide about the suitable visualization. We plan to conduct future long-term studies where we continuously observe the users to deduce their experience and preferences and quantify them as a part of the decision.

8   Conclusion

Which traceability visualization is suitable for which context? To answer this question we proposed a meta-model, which specifies the traceability information (what to visualize), the visualization technique (how to visualize), and the task context (when to visualize). Suitability is a relationship between visualization techniques and task contexts. It can also be seen as a composite relationship of understandability and information value. Based on the meta-model, we designed an empirical study to compare four common visualization techniques in different task contexts, check whether users are able to select the most suitable visualization for a particular context, and gather additional feedback on the why and the how. The result indicates that the four visualization techniques are generally easy to understand. Matrices give structured overviews and seem to suit best for management tasks, while hyperlinks depict fine-grained relationships and suit for implementation and testing tasks. The result also shows that users are not always able to decide which visualization is suitable.

Acknowledgement. We would like to thank all the participants of our empirical study. This work is partly supported by the German Research Foundation (DFG).

References

1. Antoniol, G., Canfora, G., Casazza, G., De Lucia, A., Merlo, E.: Recovering traceability links between code and documentation. IEEE Transactions on Software Engineering (2002)
2. Cleland-Huang, J., Habrat, R.: Visual Support In Automated Tracing. In: Second International Workshop on Requirements Engineering Visualization (2007)
3. Cleland-Huang, J., Settimi, R., Duan, C., Zou, X.: Utilizing Supporting Evidence to Improve Dynamic Requirements Traceability. In: Proceedings of RE 2005 (2005)
4. De Lucia, A., Fasano, F., Oliveto, R., Tortora, G.: ADAMS Re-Trace: A Traceability Recovery Tool. In: Ninth European Conference on Software Maintenance and Reengineering (2005)
5. De Lucia, A., Fasano, F., Oliveto, R., Tortora, G.: Can information retrieval techniques effectively support traceability link recovery? In: 14th IEEE International Conference on Program Comprehension, ICPC 2006 (2006)
6. Dömges, R., Pohl, K.: Adapting traceability environments to project-specific needs. Commun. ACM (1998)
7. Duan, C., Cleland-Huang, J.: Visualization and Analysis in Automated Trace Retrieval. In: Proceedings of First International Workshop on Requirements Engineering Visualization (2006)
8. Fekete, J.-D., van Wijk, J.J., Stasko, J.T., North, C.: The Value of Information Visualization. In: Kerren, A., Stasko, J.T., Fekete, J.-D., North, C. (eds.) Information Visualization. LNCS, vol. 4950, pp. 1–18. Springer, Heidelberg (2008)
9. Gotel, O.C., Marchese, F.T., Morris, S.J.: On Requirements Visualization. In: Second International Workshop on Requirements Engineering Visualization (2007)
10. Gotel, O.C.Z., Finkelstein, A.C.W.: An analysis of the requirements traceability problem, pp. 94–101 (1994)
11. Hayes, J., Dekhtyar, A., Sundaram, S.: Advancing candidate link generation for requirements tracing: the study of methods. IEEE Transactions on Software Engineering 32 (2006)

12. Heim, P., Lohmann, S., Lauenroth, K., Ziegler, J.: Graph-based Visualization of Requirements Relationships. In: Requirements Engineering Visualization (2008)
13. Herman, I., Melançon, G., Marshall, M.S.: Graph visualization and navigation in information visualization: A survey (2000)
14. Integrate. Traceline for doors, http://www.integrate.biz/traceline/
15. Egyed, A., Grünbacher, P.: Supporting software understanding with automated requirements traceability. International Journal of Software Engineering and Knowledge Engineering (2005)
16. Kaindl, H.: The missing link in requirements engineering (1993)
17. Kersten, M., Murphy, G.C.: Using task context to improve programmer productivity. In: SIGSOFT 2006/FSE-14. ACM (2006)
18. Lin, J., Lin, C.C., Huang, J., Settimi, R., Amaya, J., Bedford, G., Berenbach, B., Khadra, O., Duan, C., Zou, X.: Poirot: A distributed tool supporting enterprise-wide automated traceability. In: RE 2006 (2006)
19. Maalej, W.: Task-first or context-first? Tool integration revisited. In: Proceedings of the 24th ACM/IEEE Int. Conference on Automated Software Engineering. IEEE Computer Society (May 2009)
20. Maalej, W., Sahm, A.: Assisting engineers in switching artifacts by using task semantic and interaction history. In: RSSE 2010 (2010)
21. Mader, P., Gotel, O., Philippow, I.: Getting back to basics: Promoting the use of a traceability information model in practice. In: Traceability in Emerging Forms of Software Engineering, TEFSE 2009 (2009)
22. Maletic, J.I., Munson, E.V., Marcus, A., Nguyen, T.N.: Using a hypertext model for traceability link conformance analysis. In: Traceability in Emerging Forms of Software Engineering (2003)
23. Marchionini, G.: Finding facts vs. browsing knowledge in hypertext systems. Computer 21(1), 70–79 (1988)
24. Marcus, A., Xie, X., Poshyvanyk, D.: When and how to visualize traceability links? In: Traceability in Emerging Forms of Software Engineering, TEFSE 2005 (2005)
25. Merten, T., Juppner, D., Delater, A.: Improved representation of traceability links in requirements engineering knowledge using sunburst and netmap visualizations. In: Proceedings of Fourth International Workshop on Managing Requirements Knowledge, MARK (2011)
26. Ramesh, B., Edwards, M.: Issues in the development of a requirements traceability model. In: Proceedings of IEEE International Symposium on Requirements Engineering (1993)
27. Ramesh, B., Jarke, M.: Toward reference models for requirements traceability. IEEE Transactions on Software Engineering (2001)
28. Ratanotayanon, S., Sim, S.E., Raycraft, D.J.: Cross-artifact traceability using lightweight links. In: Traceability in Emerging Forms of Software Engineering, TEFSE 2009 (2009)
29. Robinsons. Doctrace, http://www.robinsons.co.uk/doctrace.html
30. Spanoudakis, G., Zisman, A.: Software traceability: A roadmap. In: Handbook of Software Engineering and Knowledge Engineering (2004)
31. Spence, R.: Information Visualization: Design for Interaction, 2nd edn. Prentice Hall (2007)
32. Winkler, S.: On Usability in Requirements Trace Visualizations. In: Requirements Engineering Visualization (2008)
33. Winkler, S., Pilgrim, J.: A survey of traceability in requirements engineering and model-driven development. Softw. Syst. Model. 9 (2010)

The Case for Dumb Requirements Engineering Tools

Daniel Berry[1], Ricardo Gacitua[2], Pete Sawyer[2,4], and Sri Fatimah Tjong[3]

[1] Cheriton School of Computer Science
University of Waterloo, Canada
dberry@uwaterloo.ca

[2] School of Computing and Communications
Lancaster University, UK
r.gacitua@acm.org, p.sawyer@lancs.ac.uk

[3] University of Nottingham Malaysia Campus, Malaysia
nien34@gmail.com

[4] INRIA Paris — Rocquencourt
78153 Le Chesnay, France

Abstract. **[Context and Motivation]** This paper notes the advanced state of the natural language (NL) processing art and considers four broad categories of tools for processing NL requirements documents. These tools are used in a variety of scenarios. The strength of a tool for a NL processing task is measured by its recall and precision. **[Question/Problem]** In some scenarios, for some tasks, any tool with less than 100% recall is not helpful and the user may be better off doing the task entirely manually. **[Principal Ideas/Results]** The paper suggests that perhaps a dumb tool doing an identifiable part of such a task may be better than an intelligent tool trying but failing in unidentifiable ways to do the entire task. **[Contribution]** Perhaps a new direction is needed in research for RE tools.

1 Introduction

Most requirements are still written in natural language (NL)[1]. Practitioners are understandably reluctant to adopt something more formal, and NL allows all the actors on a project to communicate. NL requirements are therefore not going away anytime soon. Consequently, there has been a steady interest in developing tools to help analysts deal with NL and to mitigate the shortcomings of NL as a medium for precise, concise, and unambiguous requirements description. Many of these tools draw on established research in NL processing (NLP) and information retrieval (IR). For simplicity, we refer to techniques originating from either field as NLP techniques.

Research in NLP has achieved excellent results, including the creation of the search engine. As impressive as these results are, this article argues that RE has characteristics that impose particular requirements on NLP-based tools applied to it. These requirements mean that particular care is needed when assessing how well any such tool works and whether the tool is appropriate to the RE task to which it is being applied.

2 Categories of NL RE Tools

Most tools for processing NL requirements fall into one of four broad categories:

B. Regnell and D. Damian (Eds.): REFSQ 2012, LNCS 7195, pp. 211–217, 2012.

a. tools to find defects and deviations from good practice in NL requirements documents; examples include ARM [2] and QuARS [3], each of which detects a range of bad practices such as the use of weak phrases, and tools focused on the detection of ambiguous requirement statements such as SREE [4] and the nocuous ambiguity finder of Chantree *et al.* [5],

b. tools to generate models from NL descriptions; examples include Scenario [6], which generates sequence diagrams from use case descriptions, and Dowser, which generates a class diagram from a NL Software Requirements Specification [7],

c. tools to infer trace links between NL descriptions of requirements or between requirements and other artifacts of the development process; examples include Poirot [8] and RETRO [9].

d. tools to identify the key abstractions from NL documents to, for example, help an analyst gain understanding of an unfamiliar domain; examples include AbstFinder [10] and RAI [11].

With the exception of some tools of category (a), in which part of the task may include checking for formatting and syntactic conventions, each of the RE tasks supported by the tools fundamentally and ultimately requires an understanding of the analysed documents' contents. However, the automatic understanding of NL texts is still way beyond current computational capabilities and only a very limited form of semantic-level processing is currently possible [12]. As a consequence, most RE applications of NLP use relatively mature techniques for identifying lexical or syntactic properties, and use these to *infer* semantic properties.

For example, in a tracing tool, of category (c), lexical similarity between two utterances in two artefacts leads to proposed links between the pairs of utterances and the pairs of artefacts. If the lexical similarity was between terms with no domain relevance, then the human user would reject the proposal. Regardless, lexical similarity will fail to find all relevant links. Consequently, a human analyst always has to validate the results of any application of the tool, and NL requirements engineering tools are nearly always designed for interactive use.

In interactively using any tool, e.g., a tracing tool, that attempts to simulate understanding with lexical or syntactic properties, the user–analyst will have to be aware that the output is likely to include false positives and will not include some true positives. What action the analyst takes will depend on the cost of failing to have the correct output, i.e., the links that allow determining the impact of a proposed change, balanced against the cost of finding the true positives manually and eliminating false positives manually. The first of these manual tasks is usually both harder and more critical for the tool's purpose.

3   Scenarios of Tool Use and Their Implications

Why does this balancing act matter? It is important to understand the limitations of NLP-based tools for RE, because although good but imperfect performance is often helpful to the analyst, in certain circumstances it is of no help to the analyst at all. It may even make his or her job harder. Consider the two following scenarios.

The first scenario is that an analyst is responsible for formulating the requirements for a system without high-dependability (HD) requirements, i.e. it is *not* safety, security- or mission-critical. Although undesirable, occasional failures can be tolerated. While a complete analysis of all documents would be nice, it would be too costly to carry one out. If an automated tool is available to do the analysis and it does a good enough job, with "good enough" defined differently in each situation, then such a tool will be useful. For example, tracing tools of category (c) are a response to the fact that although the benefits of tracing are known, the manual documenting of traces is a tedious burden, so it often does not get done. Thus, faced with a need to do change impact analysis at some later date, an analyst will probably consider the *post-hoc* automatic inference of some of the trace relationships to be much better than the manual alternative. This judgement will be valid if the alternative is that all traces have to be found manually, and the following conditions hold:

- a tool will find $n\%$ of the genuine trace relationships;
- n is sufficiently large that there is only a small risk that the missing $100 - n\%$ of genuine trace relationships contains any that would significantly affect the analyst's assessment of the impact of the proposed change,
- the cost of manually detecting and eliminating the false positive trace relationships is less than that of manually finding the true positive trace relationships.

The number n is known as the tool's *recall*, which is the proportion of all possible correct results that are returned. High recall means few false negatives. The number of false positives is measured by *precision*, which is the proportion of the results returned by the tool that are correct. High precision means few false positives. Recall and precision are the metrics most commonly used to quantify the performance of NLP techniques. For most NLP tools, it is hard to achieve each of high recall and high precision, and it is even harder to achieve both high recall and high precision. A NLP tool for RE should be tuned to favour recall over precision because errors of commission are generally easier to correct than errors of omission. Thus, for the tracing tool example, it is easier to check every inferred trace relationship to filter out the spurious links than it is to find the missing correct trace relationships to add the missing links.

Now contrast the first scenario with one in which the analyst is responsible for formulating the requirements for a system *with* HD requirements. A complete analysis of all documents is essential in order to find all the defects, abstractions, traces or modeling elements and relationships that are present or implicit in the documents. Normally, a human analyst would be doing the entire analysis manually with the help of only his or her thinking. The human analyst has the uniquely human ability to extract semantics from text and to cope with complicating factors such as context, poor spelling, poor grammar, and implicit information that are beyond the capabilities of NLP techniques. Thus, with appropriate knowledge, training, and experience, the analyst has the potential to achieve 100% recall and 100% precision.

In practice, of course, a human suffers fatigue, and his or her attention wavers, resulting in slips, lapses, and mistakes [13]. In short, humans are fallible [14]. Unfortunately, the development of a HD system usually requires copious documentation, making fatigue and distraction likely enough that tool support has an obvious attraction. Consider how this situation relates to the four categories of tools:

a. *tools to find defects and deviations from good practice in NL requirements documents*: No tool of this type is capable of detecting all possible requirements defects. For example, detecting requirements that specify the wrong behaviour is beyond the capabilities of any algorithm, let alone NLP technique. Consequently, even if a tool successfully detects 100% of the types of defects it is designed to detect, it can still guarantee to find only a subset of all the document's defects. Thus, the human analyst will still need to read the complete requirements document to find the tougher defects [4]. On the other hand, if the set of defects that the tool finds with 100% recall is easily described, then the human can focus his or her search on defects outside the tool's 100%-recall domain [4].

b. *tools to generate models from NL descriptions*: Most modeling notations add a degree of formality that is absent from NL. Thus, while there may be a correct requirements model that represents the *intent* of a NL requirements specification, such a model can almost never be automatically derived from what is actually written. The imprecision and incompleteness in the NL description that conspire to make this inability so, are sometimes usefully revealed as a side effect of the failed model generation [7]. While such a tool cannot be relied upon to generate a useable model, the tool is probably useful for exposing defects in the NL descriptions prior to their being used as input to a human's model generation.

In contrast to tools of categories (a) and (b) the quality of the output of tools of categories (c) and (d) have a direct effect on the quality of the system under development.

c. *tools to infer trace links between NL descriptions of requirements or between requirements and other artifacts of the development process*: For a HD system, the tasks that depend upon tracing are themselves critical. For example, it is critical to find all of a security requirement's dependencies to ensure that a proposed change cannot introduce a security vulnerability. To avoid manual tracing, 100% recall is required of a tracing tool. Unfortunately, the fundamental limitations of NLP means that 100% recall is impossible, short of returning every possible link, which leads to complete manual tracing. Thus, automatic tracers are not well suited to HD systems.

d. *tools to identify the key abstractions from NL documents*: The set of abstractions for a system are the bones of the system's universe of discourse. For a HD system, the set of abstractions needs to be complete to avoid overlooking anything that is relevant. Again, the fundamental limitations of NLP means that 100% recall is impossible, short of returning every possible abstraction, which leads to complete manual finding [10]. Thus, automatic abstraction finders are not well suited to HD systems.

In short, some categories of tools offer no advantage for HD systems, for which *completeness* as well as correctness of a tool's output is essential. Worse, naive use of such a tool may

a. worsen the analyst's workload by forcing the analyst to spend time looking at the output of the tool's incomplete analysis in addition to doing the manual analysis that he or she has to do anyway or

b. introduce risks for the necessary manual analysis by lulling the analyst with unjustified confidence in the tool's output.

Thus, for any NLP-based RE tool, a thinking requirements analyst must carefully consider how used the tool is in enhancing his or her ability to do the required analysis of a NL document. If the tool cannot really save him or her work by doing 100% of analysis and in any case, he or she has to manually analyse the whole document, it might be best to forgo the tool and do what is necessary to do the whole analysis very well manually; doing what is necessary might include getting a good night's sleep the night before!

Nevertheless, humans make mistakes when doing any task no matter how simple, and will certainly make mistakes in tasks such as tracing [14]. Thus, while a human potentially has 100% recall, he or she, in fact, does not. Perhaps a tool, even with less than 100% recall, should be used to help find mistakes that the human has made. The risks of naive tool use mentioned in the previous paragraph suggest that the optimal time to use a tool with less than 100% recall during the development of a HD system is *after* the humans doing the task manually have done their best and are satisfied that more effort will not improve their recall. Anything that the tool finds

a. that the humans did not find or
b. that prompts the humans to find something they did not find before

is a bonus achieved at relatively low cost. This recommendation is consistent with the observation of Dekhtyar *et al.* [14] that when humans are asked to vet traces proposed by an automatic tracer, a tool of category (c), they tended to decrease both the recall and precision of the traces.

In the case in which a tool cannot do an analysis with 100% recall, but there is an algorithmically *identifiable* part of the analysis that can be handled with 100% recall by a tool, then it might be useful to let the tool do what it can, so that the analyst can focus thinking on only the rest of the analysis, which of course is equally algorithmically identifiable. For example, SREE, Tjong's ambiguity finding tool, of category (a), finds only those potential ambiguities that are identifiable with 100% recall by design, by a lexical scannner. It leaves all other ambiguities to be found manually. For example, SREE finds all potential instances of the "only" ambiguity by finding each sentence with the word "only". Ambiguities that require parsing of NL sentences, correct part-of-speech identification, seeing context, or understanding semantics are left to the analyst to find manually. SREE has 100% recall for the ambiguities in its clearly specified domain and less than 100% precision for these ambiguities since it finds, e.g., all instances of "only", not just the ambiguous ones. The analyst can quickly eliminate the false positives in SREE's output and then focus on the amgiguities that are outside SREE's clearly specified domain [4].

4 Future Research Agenda

The analysis of the previous section suggests a research agenda to discover and build new kinds of NL RE tools. For each RE task to which NLP tools are being applied, e.g., abstraction identification, ambiguity identification, and tracing, try to find an *algorithmically identifiable* partition of the task into

a. a *clerical* part that can be done by a dumb tool with 100% recall and not too much imprecision and
b. a *thinking-required* part that must be left to a human analyst to do manually.

With such a partition, the analyst can use the dumb tool to do the clerical part and then can focus on doing the thinking-required part very well manually without the distraction of having also to do the clerical part manually. Indeed, the fourth author's experiences in the trenches of RE is

a. that often the information obtained from what would be the clerical part is nearly empty or is not very helpful and
b. that no matter what, she must carefully do what would be the thinking-required part to expose highly contextual ambiguities, obscure tacit assumptions, and deeply buried inconsistencies.

It would be nice to be able to do this careful thinking with fewer distractions.

Finding this partition for any task will require research to think of a different way to decompose the task. It will require a thorough understanding of the task and of what is algorithmically possible. It will likely require ingenuity in finding perhaps multiple, orthogonal lexical proxies for the semantics of the task, whose combined capture of false positives is significantly reduced from that of any one lexical proxy.

For any task, the partitioning will take into account

– the burden to the human analyst of the imprecision of the clerical part and
– the difficulty to the human analyst of the thinking-required part.

Obtaining this information will require research like that done by Dekhtyar *et al.* [14] for tracing tools to determine what is really difficult for humans and how well humans perform parts of the task with and without automation. Addressing the issue of how to separate the clerical and thinking-required parts of a task is of course one of many research questions that challenge the developers of NLP-based tools for RE. The challenge of ensuring industrial adoption of the tools remains. However, separating the clerical and thinking-required parts is, we believe, a critical step in promoting industrial adoption, since the separation will lead to a better understanding of what such tools can realistically deliver to their users.

5   Conclusion

What is the nature of a tool that can do an analysis with 100% recall? It is one whose task is 100% computable. If a tool that uses some advanced NLP technique to do a less than perfect job on an analysis that requires semantic understanding is called artificially intelligent, then a tool that is using algorithmic techniques to do a perfect job on an analysis that requires only computable processing must be called really[1] dumb. Thus, ARM and QuARS, also of category (a), try to be intelligent, and SREE resigns itself to being dumb. The argument of this paper can be summarised as that sometimes it might

---

[1] "really" in opposition to "artificially" and not "really" as a synonym for "very".

be better (1) to apply a dumb tool to an algorithmically determinable subpart of an analysis, thus freeing up the human analyst to focus his or her thinking on the equally algorithmically determinable rest of the analysis than (2) to apply a so-called intelligent tool to the whole analysis with less than 100% recall and with no way to know what part of the analysis still needs to be done.

Acknowledgments.   Berry's work was supported by NSERC grant NSERC-RGPIN227055-00 and by an NSERC–Scotia Bank Industrial Research Chair NSERC-IRCPJ365473-05. Gacitua's and Sawyer's work was supported by EPSRC grant EP/F069227/1.

References

1. Mich, L., Franch, M., Inverardi, P.N.: Market research for requirements analysis using linguistic tools. Requirements Engineering Journal 9, 40–56 (2004)
2. Wilson, W.M., Rosenberg, L.H., Hyatt, L.E.: Automated analysis of requirement specifications. In: Proc. 19th Int. Conf. on Software Engineering (ICSE), pp. 161–171 (1997)
3. Bucchiarone, A., Gnesi, S., Pierini, P.: Quality analysis of NL requirements: An industrial case study. In: Proc. 13th IEEE Int. Requirements Engineering Conf. (RE), pp. 390–394 (2005)
4. Tjong, S.F.: Avoiding Ambiguities in Requirements Specifications. PhD thesis, University of Nottingham, Maylasia Campus (2008)
5. Chantree, F., Nuseibeh, B., de Roeck, A., Willis, A.: Identifying nocuous ambiguities in natural language requirements. In: Proc. 14th IEEE Int. Requirements Engineering Conf. (RE), pp. 56–65 (2006)
6. Kof, L.: Scenarios: Identifying missing objects and actions by means of computational linguistics. In: Proc. 15th IEEE Int. Requirements Engineering Conf. (RE), pp. 121–130 (2007)
7. Popescu, D., Rugaber, S., Medvidovic, N., Berry, D.M.: Reducing ambiguities in requirements specifications via automatically created object-oriented models. In: Paech, B., Martell, C. (eds.) Innovations for Requirement Analysis: From Stakeholders' Needs to Formal Designs, pp. 103–124 (2008)
8. Cleland-Huang, J., Berenbach, B., Clark, S., Settimi, R., Romanova, E.: Best practices for automated traceability. IEEE Computer 40, 27–35 (2007)
9. Hayes, J.H., Dekhtyar, A., Sundaram, S.K.: Advancing candidate link generation for requirements tracing: The study of methods. IEEE Transactions on Software Engineering 32, 4–19 (2006)
10. Goldin, L., Berry, D.M.: AbstFinder: A prototype abstraction finder for natural language text for use in requirements elicitation. Automated Software Engineering 4, 375–412 (1997)
11. Gacitua, R., Sawyer, P., Gervasi, V.: On the effectiveness of abstraction identification in requirements engineering. In: Proc. 18th IEEE Int. Requirements Engineering Conf. (RE), pp. 5–14 (2010)
12. Ryan, K.: The role of natural language in requirements engineering. In: Proc. IEEE Int. Symp. on Requirements Engineering (RE), pp. 240–242 (1993)
13. Viller, S., Bowers, J., Rodden, T.: Human factors in requirements engineering: A survey of human sciences literature relevant to the improvement of dependable systems development processes. Interacting with Computers 11, 665–698 (1999)
14. Dekhtyar, A., Dekhtyar, O., Holden, J., Hayes, J., Cuddeback, D., Kong, W.K.: On human analyst performance in assisted requirements tracing: Statistical analysis. In: Proc. 19th IEEE Int. Requirements Engineering Conf. (RE), pp. 111–120 (2011)

Automatic Analysis
of Multimodal Requirements:
A Research Preview

Elia Bruni[1], Alessio Ferrari[2], Norbert Seyff[3], and Gabriele Tolomei[2]

[1] University of Trento, CIMeC, Trento, Italy
`elia.bruni@unitn.it`
[2] ISTI-CNR, Pisa, Italy
{`alessio.ferrari,gabriele.tolomei`}`@isti.cnr.it`
[3] University of Zurich, RERG, Zurich, Switzerland
`seyff@ifi.uzh.ch`

Abstract. **[Context and motivation]** Traditionally, requirements are documented using natural language text. However, there exist several approaches that promote the use of rich media requirements descriptions. Apart from text-based descriptions these multimodal requirements can be enriched by images, audio, or even video. **[Question/Problem]** The transcription and automated analysis of multimodal information is an important open question, which has not been sufficiently addressed by the Requirement Engineering (RE) community so far. Therefore, in this research preview paper we sketch how we plan to tackle research challenges related to the field of multimodal requirements analysis. We are in particular focusing on the automation of the analysis process. **[Principal idea/results]** In our recent research we have started to gather and manually analyze multimodal requirements. Furthermore, we have worked on concepts which initially allow the analysis of multimodal information. The purpose of the planned research is to combine and extend our recent work and to come up with an approach supporting the automatic analysis of multimodal requirements. **[Contribution]** In this paper we give a preview on the planned work. We present our research goal, discuss research challenges and depict an early conceptual solution.

Keywords: Requirements analysis, multimodal requirement descriptions, similarity-based clustering, distributional semantics.

1 Introduction

Rich media requirements descriptions are used in several RE approaches to capture relevant information and to improve the needs gathering process [16,4,1,13]. These multimodal needs are often captured in early requirements elicitation steps. In later stages the captured text, audio and video information is analyzed and often transcribed into well-defined (text-based) requirements. Depending on the actual process and the project at hand, this task might be time consuming and costly.

B. Regnell and D. Damian (Eds.): REFSQ 2012, LNCS 7195, pp. 218–224, 2012.

Researchers have started to deal with the issue of multimodal information representation [11]. There are several attempts in computer vision to combine the visual and textual information in a common space. Taking inspiration from methods originally used in text processing, algorithms for search and retrieval have been built [18,5]. Enriching the images with text-based information allows a better description of images, and consequently enforces the semantic manipulation of the graphical data. Very recently, the Natural Language Processing (NLP) community has turned its attention to multimodality. However, the task is reversed: instead of using text to better describe the content of images, the images are exploited to improve word meaning [2].

The aim of our planned research is to take advantage from these results and to apply and extend these novel methods for requirements engineering. In particular, we aim to support the automatic analysis of multimodal requirements. We envision that future requirements engineering approaches support the use of various media types to describe requirements. This key information enables analysts to understand needs. However, we foresee that it is not the analyst who has to analyze these multimodal needs in the first place.

In Section 2 we discuss relevant work in the field. Section 3 presents our research goal and discusses research challenges and ideas on a conceptual solution. Finally, in Section 4 we discuss the benefits and limitations of the planned research and conclude the paper.

2   Background

Several research groups have been working on the automatic analysis of natural language requirements [10,7], e.g., by leveraging statistical approaches borrowed from the information retrieval and data mining domains. The majority of recent research aims at classifying system requirements on the basis of their pairwise similarity in order to ease their analysis [14]. Requirements are classified by domain-related topic using iterative classification algorithms, e.g., to discriminate among different categories of non-functional requirements, as proposed by Casamayor *et al.* [3]. The aim of this recent research is to partition a large set of requirements into more manageable subsets. Furthermore, contributions are concerned with the usage of typical information retrieval distance metrics to establish the similarity among two requirements. For example, Haynes *et al.* present an approach that exploits a clustering algorithm to identify common high-level customer needs expressed in natural language [8].

The ISTI-CNR and the University of Trento have a thorough experience in the discussed field. Their research on applying data mining technologies to the Web and novel algorithms to cluster information is considered to be a cornerstone of the planned research [12]. These technologies have been recently applied also to natural language requirements [6]. Furthermore, Bruni *et al.* [2] have introduced a distributional semantic model combining text- and image-based features, as a first step to enrich traditional semantic models with perceptual information. Their research has been driven by the endeavor of better satisfy psychological models discussing how we humans acquire and use semantic knowledge. This work highlights that we cannot only rely on linguistic context, but also on our rich perceptual experience.

The University of Zurich has started to intensively use multimodal requirements descriptions to support end-users in documenting needs and feedback. The iRequire approach enables end-users to document needs with the help of pictures, audio and text descriptions [16,17]. An end-user first takes a picture of a relevant environmental aspect (e.g., a picture of a bus stop). Furthermore, the end-user documents a need using text or audio recording (e.g., "*I would like to have the time shown on my mobile when the next one is coming*"). In a last step the end-user enters a rational and gives a short task description (e.g., "*I am waiting for the 25er. I would like to know if there is enough time left to buy a snack?*"). An analyst so far analyzes the gathered end-user needs manually. Early evaluations have shown that in most of the cases the gathered information allows humans to understand needs and to transcribe them into well-defined requirements [16]. However, this approach suffers from scalability issues if we consider a large number of end-user needs.

3   Automatic Analysis of Multimodal Requirements

The goal of our research is to investigate the automatic analysis of multimodal requirements. We plan to provide analysis methods and tools which support analysts in handling a large number of multimodal requirements. In the context of our research we define multimodal requirements as following: "*Multimodal requirements use different media types to represent information that needs to be combined to fully describe a particular requirement or need*". In other words, the information to fully understand a particular requirement is scattered and can be found in different sources. In our research we are not just focusing on cases where one requirement is described using only one media type. Our focus lies on requirements represented by information spread over multiple modalities instead. In the following, we identify three key research challenges (RC) and discuss how we plan to address them.

RC-1: Semantic Representation of Multimodal Requirements. Currently, multimodal requirements are manually identified and need to be understood by domain experts [16]. Our aim is to turn this activity from manual into automatic. A first cornerstone is identifying a common and integrated model for representing such multimodal needs which can be either composed of text, images, speech, video, or a combination of those. Therefore, several feature spaces might be chosen in order to capture different aspects of multimodal needs. In a first step, we intend to focus our attention on the text- and image-based channels, that only very recently have been managed to cohabit into the same feature space [2]. While tailoring the results of these novel studies to our context, we are able to define two vector models, i.e., a text-based distributional vector and an image-based distributional vector. Thereby, the idea is to represent each need as a vector with two sequential components. The textual component is a vector of fixed length representing the textual content, according to the text-based distributional model. The graphical component is another vector of fixed length representing the graphical content, according to the image-based distributional model. A particular advantage of this approach is that the text- and image-based models are independently constructed from different sources. As a first output of this research, we plan to be able to feed a model with text- and image-based needs to allow further processing.

RC-2: Similarity-Based Clustering of Multimodal Requirements. Requirements analysis includes the identification of needs that, though documented in different forms by the end-users, express similar or even the same actual need. To automate this, our strategy is based on the common-sense belief that there is a tendency for things to look more similar the more related they are [15]. We plan to explore several multimodal similarity functions that take care of multiple feature spaces (text- and image-based). Those functions will be used for discovering groups of similar needs. The actual needs could be thus extracted by analyzing the groups generated as the output of the algorithm. As the needs and resulting groups are not known *a priori*, we suggest to adopt an unsupervised technique, i.e., a clustering algorithm, to partition the needs into distinct groups. This can be done by applying a specific multimodal similarity function and would result in a group found to be related to a specific need. In addition, we foresee an environment in which we have to deal with a massive number of needs, therefore the clustering algorithm adopted to discover similar needs shall be designed to provide high efficiency for both static and dynamic load. We foresee that needs can be clustered off-line when we start collecting first needs. In this initial phase, an algorithm that is efficient on static data is desirable. In particular, we expect promising results from the Head-Tail Component (HTC) algorithm, which, in a recent work of one of the authors, has been proven to be effective for discovering groups of queries stored in Web Search Engine logs [12]. We expect to provide stable clusters of similar needs. To cope with a continuous stream of incoming new needs, these needs will be dynamically associated with the relevant cluster and new clusters will appear. This will allow us to automatically generate requirements topics (i.e., themes). Furthermore, we expect that clustering also supports requirements prioritization as the number of similar needs might indicate their importance.

RC-3: Improving Gathering and Analysis Processes. Within our research we plan to tackle both the automatic analysis of multimodal requirements itself and its consequences. We foresee that, by better understanding automatic requirements analysis with the help of first prototype approaches, we will learn more about the gathering process. For example, we might discover a general inclination towards needs composed of text and images, instead of speech. Or we might detect a correlation between the medium used for documentation and a particular group of needs (e.g., some types of need might be more naturally expressed through images, while others are easier to represent through text). All this information can be exploited to gradually improve the effectiveness of the analysis. Furthermore, this information might support us in better aligning the gathering process and analysis. We might be able to tailor the requirements gathering process and come up with new strategies to cluster together particular groups of needs. Moreover, gathering and analyzing contextual information (e.g., date, time, place) in addition to needs is another option for enhancement. Identifying correlations between gathered information might allow further process improvements. For example, if an end-user sends a need from a particular position where he already sent needs before or within a certain timeframe: this might indicate that the new need also belongs to the group of previously discussed ones. We plan a step-by-step validation of these hypotheses. This research challenge also highlights the we expect a process, which will gradually become mature in order to not only provide high quantity, but also to provide high quality requirements.

Figure 1 illustrates the envisioned conceptual solution and highlights key research issues discussed in the previous paragraphs: the gathering process (*RC-3*), the data representation issue (*RC-1*), the choices of a multimodal similarity function and similarity-based clustering algorithm (*RC-2*). Apart from work on the conceptual solution we have started a literature review. Next steps include the refinement of the conceptual solution (e.g., selection of adequate algorithms). We then plan to tailor these algorithms and to provide a tool prototype allowing the automatic analysis of needs. This prototype will be used to automatically analyze end-user needs gathered with iRequire. The evaluation results will support us in identifying issues regarding end-user needs gathering and analysis.

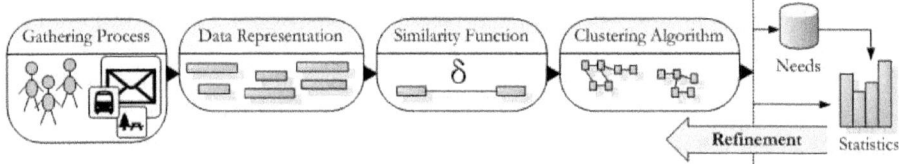

Fig. 1. Analysis of multimodal requirements: an early conceptual solution

4   Discussion and Conclusions

An important question for us is: *to what degree is automatic analysis of multimodal requirements possible?* The envisioned approach will be able to automatically group incoming needs by identifying similarity. We foresee that this will also allow establishing automated prioritization mechanisms. However, the approach will not be able to identify missing information (requirements completeness). Furthermore, we do not see the possibility to automatically detect conflicting requirements. At some point the human analyst will be needed to continue the requirements analysis. Therefore, the presentation of the automatic analysis results is a relevant issue for future work. So far we consider the discussion of research challenges and an early conceptual solution to be the first contributions of our research.

Automatic analysis of requirements might not be the only option to deal with a high number of multimodal requirements. We also consider crowd-sourcing as an option to achieve this goal [9]. However, crowd-sourcing might not ensure an independent analysis process.

Ideally, our solution will be able to analyze any kind of multimodal requirements. However, it will be necessary to tailor the method to a particular requirements gathering approach following a predefined structure for documenting multimodal requirements. We will focus on one particular gathering process and plan to support the iRequire approach [16,17]. Approaches such as iRequire can be used to gather a high number of needs requiring analysis. The discussed automated analysis mechanisms might be used within particular projects where end-users are asked to gather needs on a predefined subject (e.g., commuting). On a larger scale we also envision to analyze any end-user needs that are sent to certain receivers. With the help of automated analysis we would be able to identify needs, e.g., on novel systems, which end-user would require and which do not exist so far.

Acknowledgements. This work was partially supported by the EU-FP7-215483 (S-Cube) project, and by the PAR-FAS-2007-2013 (TRACE-IT) project.

References

1. Brill, O., Schneider, K., Knauss, E.: Videos vs. Use Cases: Can Videos Capture More Requirements under Time Pressure? In: Wieringa, R., Persson, A. (eds.) REFSQ 2010. LNCS, vol. 6182, pp. 30–44. Springer, Heidelberg (2010)
2. Bruni, E., Tran, G.B., Baroni, M.: Distributional semantics from text and images. In: Proc. of the EMNLP GEMS Workshop, Edinburgh (2011)
3. Casamayor, A., Godoy, D., Campo, M.: Identification of non-functional requirements in textual specifications: A semi-supervised learning approach. IST 52, 436–445 (2010)
4. Creighton, O., Ott, M., Bruegge, B.: Software cinema-video-based requirements engineering. In: Proc. of RE 2006, pp. 106–115. IEEE CS, Washington, DC (2006)
5. Datta, R., Joshi, D., Li, J., Wang, J.Z.: Image retrieval: Ideas, influences, and trends of the new age. ACM Comput. Surv. 40(2) (2008)
6. Ferrari, A., Tolomei, G., Gnesi, S.: A clustering-based approach for discovering flaws in requirements specifications. In: Proc. of SAC 2012 (to appear, 2012)
7. Gervasi, V., Zowghi, D.: Reasoning about inconsistencies in natural language requirements. ACM TSEM 14, 277–330 (2005)
8. Hayes, J.H., Antoniol, G., Guéhéneuc, Y.G.: Prereqir: Recovering pre-requirements via cluster analysis. In: Proc. of WCRE 2008, pp. 165–174. IEEE CS, Washington, DC (2008)
9. Huberman, B.A., Romero, D.M., Wu, F.: Crowdsourcing, attention and productivity. Journal of Information Science 35(6), 758–765 (2009)
10. Kof, L., Penzenstadler, B.: From Requirements to Models: Feedback Generation as a Result of Formalization. In: Mouratidis, H., Rolland, C. (eds.) CAiSE 2011. LNCS, vol. 6741, pp. 93–107. Springer, Heidelberg (2011)
11. Louwerse, M.: Symbol interdependency in symbolic and embodied cognition. Topics in Cognitive Science 3, 273–302 (2011)

12. Lucchese, C., Orlando, S., Perego, R., Silvestri, F., Tolomei, G.: Identifying task-based sessions in search engine query logs. In: Proc. of WSDM 2011, pp. 277–286. ACM, New York (2011)
13. Maiden, N., Seyff, N., Grunbacher, P., Otojare, O., Mitteregger, K.: Making mobile requirements engineering tools usable and useful. In: Proc. of RE 2006, pp. 26–35. IEEE CS, Washington, DC (2006)
14. Palmer, J., Liang, Y.: Indexing and clustering of software requirements specifications. IDT 18, 283–299 (1992)
15. Patwardhan, S., Pedersen, T.: Using WordNet-based Context Vectors to Estimate the Semantic Relatedness of Concepts. In: Proc. of the EACL 2006 Workshop, Trento, Italy, pp. 1–8 (April 2006)
16. Seyff, N., Graf, F., Maiden, N.: Using mobile re tools to give end-users their own voice. In: Proc. of RE 2010, pp. 37–46. IEEE CS, Los Alamitos (2010)
17. Seyff, N., Ollmann, G., Bortenschlager, M.: irequire: Gathering end-user requirements for new apps. In: Proc. of RE 2011, pp. 347–348. IEEE CS, Los Alamitos (2011)
18. Sivic, J., Zisserman, A.: Video Google: A text retrieval approach to object matching in videos. In: Proc. of ICCV 2003, pp. 1470–1477. IEEE CS, Washington, DC (2003)

10 Myths of Software Quality

Elke Hochmüller

Carinthia University of Applied Sciences, Klagenfurt, Austria
E.Hochmueller@cuas.at

Abstract. **[Context and motivation]** Quality is one of the most critical success factors of software products. **[Question / problem]** Nevertheless, during software development processes software quality is still not given the proper attention and relevance it deserves. **[Principal ideas / results]** This paper outlines ten common myths about software quality prevailing in practice. **[Contribution]** The discussion of these myths unveils challenges which need further attention in requirements engineering (RE) research and practice.

Keywords: non-functional requirements, software processes, RE challenges.

1 Introduction

More than forty years ago, the computing industry became aware of being right in the middle of a software crisis. Deficiencies in software product quality (e.g. lack in *reliable* software which *efficiently* works on real machines [8]) as well as in software process quality were the most prominent symptoms. What has changed over the years since that time? Structured analysis and design methods, structured programming languages and new process models emerged. Paradigm changes occurred; now, object-orientation dominates the technology. Software development is being guided by standards and supported by tools. These and further achievements contributed to the fact that software development is today broadly recognized as an engineering discipline.

Most of these advances in software engineering (SE) had their positive effects on software process quality, but projects still run into troubles or even fail spectacularly because of unacceptable software products due to insufficient product quality. Software quality as a rather general, wide-ranging term can easily be underestimated or even neglected regarding its importance in comparison to functionality requirements which can be dealt with more easily. As a consequence, software quality is often regarded as a mere byproduct which can be accounted for only when resources (time, money) remain. Often, it is noticed too late that product quality requirements would have called for highest attention being paid for from the very beginning of the project.

Software product quality is surrounded by many myths. Some of them have been known for many years and are still prevailing in practice. This paper lists ten myths which the author collected during the last twenty years of her experience in RE research and practice. Based on a discussion of these myths, open issues which are still a challenge to RE research and practice are outlined.

B. Regnell and D. Damian (Eds.): REFSQ 2012, LNCS 7195, pp. 225–231, 2012.
© Springer-Verlag Berlin Heidelberg 2012

2   Myths by Category

The ten software quality myths presented here particularly concern product-related quality requirements (also known as non-functional or extra-functional requirements [3]). These myths can be broadly classified into three categories:

1. *Myths about the relevance of software quality.*
2. *Myths about software quality as an inconvenience.*
3. *Myths about the notion of software quality.*

In each of the following three sections, the myths of each category will be individually dissected. Some of the myths to be discussed in detail are closely related. For the purpose of referring easily to and between particular myths throughout the three sections, the individual myths are stated in an absolute, numerical order. Nevertheless, this order does not necessarily reflect any particular ranking of the myths.

2.1   Myths about the Relevance of Software Quality

The myths within this category have one thing in common: they all tend to underestimate the importance of product quality requirements.

Myth #1: Quality Is No First Class Requirement. For sure, software product quality without any functionality is nonsense because without any functional requirements no product would exist at all. But, is this a sound base to state that quality requirements are not as important as functional ones? Functionality without quality can be useless, too. The fact that functional requirements are easier to handle (by applying use cases, scenarios, ...) does not relieve us from adequately considering quality requirements.

In cases when quality requirements regarding e.g. usability, security, or performance are neglected or not properly treated from the very beginning of a development process, they tend to turn up again rather late during acceptance test or even during operation. But, in contrast to incorrect or missing functions which can be easily corrected or added to systems which are structured in a modular way, quality cannot just be added to an existing system a-posteriori [3].

As the degree of compliance with quality requirements usually will be crucial for the success of a software product, quality requirements are very well first class requirements and call for useful methods to be able to treat them properly.

Myth #2: Quality Is Not my Business. People partaking in a software development process usually concentrate on their role-specific activities. Management deals with planning, budgeting, organizing and controlling the development process. Customers/users express their immediate needs which primarily will include the most prominent functionality required. Software developers focus on designing and implementing the software product which delivers the required functionality.

The role of a quality engineer - as emerged during recent years - traces back to the demand to assure process quality and to verify the correctness of intermediate products like analysis and design documents. However, the activities of persons fulfilling this role in practice often are confined to post-code quality assurance only.

Hence, it seems that the quality of the final software product is a topic which is left to the requirements engineers to assure that this kind of requirements is properly tackled within the software development process. Nevertheless, quality requirements concern everyone: customers/users who need them, requirements analysts who acquire them, managers who need them for planning and budgeting, and developers who are in charge for their compliance. This is valid for phase-oriented software processes. See myth #4 for a discussion on product quality in agile processes.

Myth #3: Quality Is a Direct Result of a Good Process. Is it true that a high-quality software development process is sufficient to guarantee high-quality products? Certainly, a well-defined software process is just one prerequisite for aiming at a software product which can be delivered as scheduled, within estimated costs and in accordance to the specified requirements. But, what can we expect regarding the (unstated portion of) quality of a product developed during a "good" process using good SE practices? In order to reflect this question we have to distinguish between two types of product quality requirements, developer-driven and customer-driven ones.

Developer-driven quality requirements are those which should be of interest to the software developers themselves during the development or maintenance processes. Relevant quality criteria will be e.g. understandability, testability, and modifiability.

Customer-driven quality requirements are those which are of interest to customers/users only. Such requirements depend on the context and will arise from domain-specific situations or user needs, e.g. security, performance, usability.

While developer-driven quality requirements tend to be considered in the first place during a "good" development process, customer-driven quality requirements need to be explicitly addressed. Only if properly identified and precisely stated (in order to be verifiable), chances are high that these requirements will be fulfilled satisfactorily during a well-defined software development process.

However, research and practice are still challenged not only to propose useful quality-related practices dealing with customer-driven quality requirements but also to strive for their inherent integration into software development processes (cf. [3], [7]).

Myth #4: Quality Will Unfold Sooner or Later Anyway. This myth coincides with agile processes which welcome late or even changing requirements. Allowing for adding, changing, or deleting functionality in a straightforward and timely manner is certainly beneficial to functional requirements which may emerge over time.

However, certain kinds of quality requirements (like security, interoperability, performance, maintainability, availability, reliability, portability, usability) will substantially influence decisions on the overall architecture of a system [1]. Therefore and in light of the discussion on myth #1, they have to be identified (elicited, negotiated, and prioritized) at a very early stage of the development process respectively during the very first iterations in agile processes in order to avoid misdirected investments due to wrong architectural decisions (cf. myths #5 and #6).

As these requirements tend not to be readily available in the users' minds, they have to be "invented" [9] and explicitly addressed using e.g. templates or checklists [3]. Furthermore, the shift of responsibilities in agile projects from developers towards the customers raises the issue of reasoning about the role of an agile requirements engineer acting as a customer companion. [4]

2.2   Myths about Software Quality as an Inconvenience

The following myths criticize software quality as an unnecessary evil. Here, software quality is regarded as primary reason for project delays and cost overruns.

Myth #5: Quality Delays. One prevailing opinion in practice is that too much emphasis on quality will cause an unnecessary project delay. This myth concerns project-related and process-related quality in a similar manner. The involvement of users (in user-interface design, requirements validation and verification), the analysis of architectural needs, and the utilization of sound software engineering methods and techniques are just some examples for practices which will be thrown over-board in projects when potential delays are on the horizon.

The core of the problem lies in the decision (often made implicitly) that deadline compliance is regarded to be more important than quality. The challenge for RE practice is to identify and consider the most influencing and crucial requirements (i.e. Orr's "great" requirements [9]) in time in order to avoid even bigger delays because of unnecessary rework at later stages of development due to rushing through a process and ignoring product-determining quality requirements (cf. myth #4).

Myth #6: Quality Costs. This myth is closely related to myth #5. Putting more effort on quality will certainly increase costs. But, what if the extra effort in quality saved resulted in a product unacceptable by the customers/users or in a product which will not be easy to maintain? Savings in the short-term often mean losses in the long-run.

As already mentioned (cf. myths #1, #4, and #5), requirements influencing the project's progress and determining early decisions on the architecture and the system's external behaviour have to be taken into account in due time. This ensures to unveil problems (e.g. open issues to be solved, conflicting requirements) early enough to react accordingly in order to avoid misinvestments or even failed products (based on architectural decisions due to neglected quality or incorrect implicit assumptions on quality requirements), to be able to deliver a more realistic cost estimation, and to even enable a proper risk analysis.

2.3   Myths about the Notion of Software Quality

This last group of myths deals with problems regarding the definition, notion, and common understanding of product-related quality requirements as already recognized in literature (cf. [2], [3], [10], [11]).

Myth #7: Quality Is Universally and Well Understood. When talking about quality, people tend to think that there is a common understanding of quality. However, quality is a non-singular domain. Let us consider experts from different application domains like banking, patient monitoring, power station control – each one would not dare to think that (s)he can work with equal competence in another domain.

Quality has many different dimensions and facets. Similar to the many different areas of expertise existing in accordance with various application domains, nowadays there are already dedicated experts competent in particular quality dimensions, like usability engineers, security experts, and so on. Therefore, the multifaceted structure of quality requirements and their potential trade-offs have to be taken into account in accordance with the context of every single project at hand.

Myth #8: Quality Is Sufficiently Defined by Standards. There are many international, national, and industrial standards available in software engineering, like standards for high-quality processes (e.g. CMM(I), SPICE), standards for product quality requirements (e.g. ISO 9126 [6]), standards for intermediate quality products like software requirements specifications (cf. [5]), and standards for modelling techniques and languages (e.g. UML). But, does this mean that quality is sufficiently defined by standards? "Sufficiently defined" for what purpose exactly?

Each of these standards consists of a framework of notions and rules which have to be obeyed when instantiating it in terms of a product (also a development process can be regarded as a product instantiating a process standard). It is this instantiation which usually causes the problem. Especially in case of product quality requirements, standards and other classification schemes can only serve as a rough and general guideline for eliciting quality requirements which apply for the specific project at hand. The actual kinds of quality requirements relevant for a project will depend on the context and have to be derived from the domain and the customers'/users' needs.

Hence, a thorough investigation in how to close the gap between "objective" quality requirements (as stated by standards and classification schemes) and "subjective" quality requirements (relevant for a software project at hand) is needed (cf. [10]).

Myth #9: Quality Is Easy to Implement. If stated in a complete and precise manner, quality requirements are straightforward to accomplish. This might be true for rather small projects without any quality-related trade-offs and contradictions. However, quality requirements are not easy to elicit (cf. myth #10), conflicting requirements have to be identified, negotiated, prioritized, and properly represented, too [10]. Moreover, design conflicts between functional and quality requirements may occur [3]. In contrast to testing compliance of functional requirements, testing the degree of quality accomplishment is still a challenge in practice and might often require the system to be already available as a whole or even exceed the system boundary in being a matter of interaction with the environment (e.g. usability testing).

Myth #10: Quality Is Fuzzy. In contrast to myth #9, this myth recognizes that quality is not easy to cope with. However, the main reason for the problem at hand is attributed to customers and users who can not properly state their quality-related needs or even do not know what they want.

Usually, clients and users know very well what they want, but they may not be able to express their quality-related needs in a definite manner or may have implicit expectations in form of tacit knowledge. Moreover, they might not be aware about the importance of some quality requirements in the context of their needs, too.

Hence, quality is not fuzzy per se, we just have to get rid of vague quality requirements statements and aim at sufficiently "definite" quality requirements. RE research came up with various proposals for dealing with quality requirements (cf. [2], [3], [7], [11]). Nevertheless, it is still an issue of applying adequate elicitation practices to unveil and nail down the project-determining quality requirements of a software product.

3   The Myths at a Glance

The described myths may lead to common consequences like late projects, products which are difficult to maintain, increased costs of development and maintenance, and unsatisfied users because of inadequate product quality.

Table 1 gives a myth-wise summary of related symptoms and problems which are likely consequences when a myth manifests. The table also refers to challenges the RE community is faced with when fighting the respective myth. Multiple occurrences of single entries are due to the fact that some myths are interrelated. Most challenges address RE researchers as well as practitioners in a likewise manner; cases with a higher research potential are indicated with (R).

Table 1. Symptoms/problems & RE challenges per myth (QR - quality requirements)

#	*Quality Myths*	*Symptoms/Problems*	*RE Challenges*
1	Quality is no first class requirement.	- QR are dealt with too late, if at all - maintenance problems	- useful methods dealing with QR (R) - early QR elicitation
2	Quality is not my business.	- activities focus on functional requirements	- QR methods & management (R) - integrating QR into dev. processes
3	Quality is a direct result of a good process.	- esp. high degree of neglecting customer-oriented quality	- QR analysis & verification (metrics) - integrating QR into dev. processes
4	Quality will unfold sooner or later anyway.	- wrong architectural decisions - maintenance problems	- early identification of product-determining QR
5	Quality delays.	- time pressure outweighs quality - unnecessary rework afterwards	- early identification of product-determining QR
6	Quality costs.	- poor cost estimation - unsatisfied users	- early identification of product-determining QR
7	Quality is universally and well understood.	- oversimplification - scalability problems & trade-offs	- analysis of domain-specific QR (R)
8	Quality is sufficiently defined by standards.	- problems in instantiating standards	- transition from objective (standard) to subjective (actual) QR
9	Quality is easy to implement.	- presence of multifaceted QR - trade-offs and contradictions - scalability problems	- QR elicitation and negotiation - conflict detection & resolution - QR metrics and compliance tests
10	Quality is fuzzy.	- implicit expectations - unclear/vague req. statements - relevance of QR underestimated	- QR elicitation practices (R) - refinement of QR statements - QR metrics and compliance tests

4   Conclusion

Despite increased research in quality requirements, only methods dealing with functional requirements were acknowledged and successfully adopted by industry so far. Nevertheless, based on the above discussion, our community should strive to continually refute the myths mentioned above whenever their symptoms appear in practice.

Software product quality has to be accounted for properly. Therefore, quality-related methods and tasks have to be explicitly integrated into software development processes. It is not only a matter of requirements engineering research to continue investigating in useful practices to deal with software quality requirements but rather a challenge to bridge the gap between research and practice in order to apply, experience and assess the results of related requirements engineering research.

References

1. Albin, S.T.: The Art of Software Architecture: Design Methods and Techniques. Wiley, Indianapolis (2003)
2. Glinz, M.: On Non-Functional Requirements. In: 15th IEEE International Requirements Engineering Conference (RE 2007), Delhi, pp. 21–26. IEEE (2007)
3. Hochmüller, E.: Towards the Proper Integration of Extra-Functional Requirements. The Australian Journal of Information Systems 6(2), 98–117 (1999)
4. Hochmüller, E.: The Requirements Engineer as a Liaison Officer in Agile Software Development. In: 1st Agile Requirements Engineering Workshop, Lancaster. ACM (2011)
5. IEEE: IEEE Recommended Practice for Software Requirements Specifications. IEEE Std. 830-1993 (1993)
6. ISO/IEC: Software Engineering – Product Quality. Part 1: Quality Model. ISO/IEC 9126-1 (2001)
7. Jung, H.T., Lee, G.H.: A Systematic Software Development Process for Non-Functional Requirements. In: International Conference on Information and Communication Technology Convergence (ICTC 2010), Jeju Island, pp. 431–436 (2010)
8. Naur, P., Randell, B. (eds.): Software engineering. Report of a conference sponsored by the NATO Science Committee, Garmisch (1968)
9. Orr, K.: Agile Requirements: Opportunity or Oxymoron? IEEE Software 21(3), 71–73 (2004)
10. Paech, B., Kerkow, D.: Non-Functional Requirements Engineering – Quality is Essential. In: REFSQ 2004 - 10th Anniversary Booklet, Riga, pp. 27–40 (2004)
11. Ullah, S., Iqbal, M., Khan, A.M.: A Survey on Issues in Non-Functional Requirements Elicitation. In: International Conference on Computer Networks and Information Technology (ICCNIT), Abbottabad, pp. 333–340. IEEE (2011)

Empirical Analysis of the Impact
of Requirements Engineering on Software Quality

Łukasz Radliński

University of Szczecin, Institute of Information Technology in Management
ul. Mickiewicza 64, 71-101 Szczecin, Poland
lukasz@radlinski.edu.pl

Abstract. [**Context & motivation**] The process of requirements engineering affects software quality. However, stronger empirical evaluation of this impact is required. [**Question/problem**] This paper aims to answer the following questions: (1) which factors related to requirements engineering affect software quality, (2) what is the nature of these relationships, and (3) how are soft quality features related to each other? [**Principal ideas/results**] To answer these questions we performed a quantitative and visual analysis using the extended ISBSG dataset. Obtained results cover a discussion on identified and unconfirmed relationships. [**Contribution**] The main contribution is an investigation of the relationships between factors of requirements engineering and software quality. Provided results can be used in further research and to guide industrial decision makers. The main limitation in generalizing the results is related to the high number of missing values in the dataset.

Keywords: empirical analysis, process factors, requirements engineering, software quality.

1   Introduction

Requirements engineering (RE) is a major area that influences software quality [6]. Significant effort has been spent on developing various techniques of RE [15]. A variety of empirical analyses have been performed to provide evidence for RE methods, techniques, activities and tools [3, 4, 5, 7]. However, discussions at various forums on RE, including previous REFSQ conferences [1], indicate the need for yet increased empirical support in RE.

Empirical analyses of software quality are typically focused on aspects such as defectiveness or reliability [10, 14]. An earlier study [17] performed on the same dataset identified a set of factors influencing the number of defects, defect rate and achievement of zero defects. That study involved analysis of potential influences of various project-level factors. The current paper extends the previous work and focuses on soft (subjective) aspects software quality, usually more important for end-users, which describe a degree of user satisfaction in various areas (listed later in Section 2). Furthermore, it is focused on investigating detailed influences of RE factors. Thus, it

B. Regnell and D. Damian (Eds.): REFSQ 2012, LNCS 7195, pp. 232–238, 2012.

contributes to the area of empirical research at the intersection of RE and software quality. This paper attempts to answer the following three research questions:

- **RQ1:** Which factors related to RE affect software quality?
- **RQ2:** What is the nature of these relationships?
- **RQ3:** How are soft quality features related to each other?

To answer these questions we performed an analysis using ISBSG dataset of software projects. This dataset has been widely used by research community, mainly in studies on development cost and effort [13]. In contrast with other publicly available datasets, its extended version contains data on soft aspects of software quality, not just the number of defects. Performed analysis involved usage of various quantitative and visual techniques (explained briefly in Section 2).

This paper is organized as follows: Section 2 explains the research approach followed in this study and the dataset used in analyses. Section 3 provides the details on obtained results with their discussion. Section 4 considers the threats to validity of the results. Section 5 draws the conclusions and discusses plans for future work.

2   Research Approach

The ISBSG dataset [8] contains data on 5024 software projects of various types. In the extended edition of this dataset these projects are described by 205 variables. In this study we used a subset of this dataset with the focus to investigate the impact of factors related to RE on quality features.

We used seven features (indicators) of software quality as dependent variables: *meet stated objectives* (MSO), *meet business requirements* (MBR), *quality of functionality* (QF), *quality of documentation* (QD), *ease of use* (EU), *speed of defining solution* (SDS), and *speed of providing solution* (SPS). All these variables are expressed on a ranked scale from 1 to 4, except MBR – from 2 to 4. These values reflect the degree of satisfying seven aspects of quality according to the stakeholders.

As in the previous study [17], the research procedure involved the following steps:

1. Data preparation – cleaning the data; pre-selection of variables potentially influencing soft aspects of software quality; creation of dummy Boolean variables from multiple-response variables; excluding projects with data quality not assessed as 'A' or 'B', as suggested in [9]. Almost all independent variables are Boolean, except *training given* and four project objectives that are ranked, and *functional size*, *summary work effort* and proportions of effort that are numeric.
2. Basic data analysis – analysis of basic statistics, histograms and frequency tables. Based on them, and following the guidelines in [2, 12], we decided to use non-parametric techniques in the main analysis.
3. Detailed analysis of correlations and associations – using the following techniques:
   - For all variables: Spearman' rank correlation coefficient (ρ);
   - For ranked variables: Kruskal-Wallis (H), phi coefficient (ϕ), contingency coefficient (C), Cramer's V, and uncertainty coefficient (u);
   - For Boolean variables: Mann-Whitney (U), phi coefficient (ϕ), contingency coefficient (C), and uncertainty coefficient (u);

- Visual techniques: frequency plots, box-plots, scatter-plots, and categorized histograms.
4. Interpretation of results – analysis of identified and unconfirmed relationships in the context of effectiveness of RE practices.

3   Results

Tables 1 and 2 summarize the relationships between independent variables and seven aspects of software quality (defined as dependent variables in Section 2). The majority of independent variables are related to requirements engineering. However, we also include more general variables describing a development process as a whole. Thus, it is possible to compare the impact of requirements engineering factors on software quality with the impact of general process factors.

Due to space constraints we are unable to provide detailed numeric values of statistical tests. Hence, if the value of the test was significant at $p<0.1$ we put a symbol of this test in corresponding cell. An underlined symbol denotes at least medium level of strength of relationship (an equivalent of value >0.4 for Pearson correlation coefficient). Full results of these analyses are available online [16].

The following factors appear to be in relationship with all quality features: *Lower CASE (with code gen), Metrics program, Training given*. For these factors almost all calculated statistics indicate a relationship with all quality features. However, an analysis of pure values of statistics may be misleading. For example, the high impact of *Lower CASE (with code gen)* has been calculated on highly unbalanced data – only four projects involving usage of such tools and 80 without them.

MSO and MBR have the fewest influential factors identified. In addition, very few of these factors strictly refer to specification documents and techniques. On the other hand, SDS and SPS have the most influential to RE factors.

Surprisingly, factors such as *Dev. tech.: Prototyping, Plan docs: Quality plan, Spec. docs: Requirements spec., Spec. docs: Use case model*, and *Spec. docs: User interface prototype* were usually not confirmed to be related with quality features such as MSO, MBR, QF and EU, i.e., features important for customers and end users. Additionally, no statistically significant correlation was found for *Functional size* and *Summary work effort* with any quality feature.

Table 1. Overview of relationships between independent and dependent variables (part)

Variable	MSO	MBR	QF	QD	EU	SDS	SPS
CASE Tool Used		ρUφC	ρUφC		φC	φCu	φC
Used Methodology	ρUφCu		ρφC			ρU	ρUφC
Upper CASE Used	U					ρ	
Lower CASE (with code gen)	ρUφCu	ρUφCu	ρUφCu	ρUφCu	ρUφCu	ρUφCu	ρUφCu
Project user involvement	ρUφCu		ρ	ρ		ρ	
Portability requirements			φCu		φC	φCu	
Metrics Program	ρUu	ρUφCu	ρUφCu	ρUφCu	ρUφCu	φCu	ρu
User satisfaction survey	ρUφCu		ρφC		ρUφC	ρUφC	ρUφC
Training given	ρHφCV	ρHφCVu	ρHφCVu	ρHφCVu	ρHφCVu	φCV	ρH
Process improvement pgm						ρUφCu	ρUφCu

Table 2. Overview of relationships between independent and dependent variables (cont.)

Variable	MSO	MBR	QF	QD	EU	SDS	SPS
Project objective: all functionality		ρHφCVu			H	φCVu	ρu
Project objective: min. defects			H	H		ρHu	ρHu
Project objective: min. cost		φCVu		ρ		ρHφCVu	ρ
Project objective: shortest time			u	H			
Dev. tech.: Business area modeling			ρUφCu	ρUφCu	ρUφCu	ρUφCu	ρUφCu
Dev. tech.: Data modelling		ρ	φCu	ρUφC	φC		
Dev. tech.: Event modelling	ρUφCu		φC			ρU	
Dev. tech.: Multifunct. teams				ρφC			
Dev. tech.: OO analysis			φCu	ρφC	ρφCu	φCu	φCu
Dev. tech.: OO design	ρUφC		φCu	φC	φC	φCu	
Dev. tech.: OO			φCu		φC	φCu	φC
Dev. tech.: Process modelling			φC		φC	φCu	ρ
Dev. tech.: Prototyping	ρ						
Dev. tech.: Timeboxing	ρ	ρ	ρ				
Dev. tech.: Waterfall				ρφC		ρU	ρU
Plan docs: Budget		ρφCu	ρφCu	ρUφC	ρφC	φCu	ρφC
Plan docs: Business case		ρφC				φCu	φC
Plan docs: Feasibility study						ρUφC	ρ
Plan docs: Project schedule			φCu	ρUφCu	ρUφC		φC
Plan docs: Proposal/tender	φCu		ρφCu	ρUφCu		ρ	
Plan docs: Quality plan						ρUφCu	ρUφCu
Plan docs: Resource plan				ρU			
Plan docs: Risk analysis						ρUφCu	ρUφCu
Plan docs: Software dev. plan				ρUφCu		φC	
Spec. docs: None			ρφC				ρ
Spec. docs: Functional spec.	φCu		φCu	ρφCu		ρUφCu	ρUφCu
Spec. docs: Graph. look & feel						ρUφCu	ρU
Spec. docs: Log. data ER model		ρ	ρu	ρUφCu	ρU	ρUφCu	ρUφCu
Spec. docs: Requirements spec.						ρUφC	ρUφC
Spec. docs: System concept doc.				ρUφCu	φC	ρUφCu	ρUφCu
Spec. docs: Use case model						ρUφC	ρ
Spec. docs: User interface prototype		φC	ρ				
Spec. docs: Ext. syst. interface spec.							ρ
Spec. docs: User manual				ρφC	ρU	ρUφCu	ρU
Spec. docs: Data flow model			φCu	ρUφCu		ρUφCu	ρUφCu
Spec. tech. Activity diagram			ρφCu	ρφCu	ρ		
Spec. tech. JAD		ρφCu	ρ	ρ	ρUφCu	ρUφCu	ρφCu
Spec. tech. Timeboxing							ρ
Proportion of effort on plan				ρ			
Proportion of effort on spec.				ρ			
Activity planning			φC			ρUφCu	ρUφC
Activity specification	φC					ρU	

Analysis of these relationships also involved using various types of graphs. The aim of this additional analysis was to investigate if the relationships identified using statistical tests are meaningful, in particular from a causal perspective. As illustrated in Fig. 1, developing a document of requirements specification increases the SDS, developing a risk analysis during project planning increases SDS, user involvement in a project increases MSO, and with increase of proportion of effort on specification the quality of documentation is expected to be higher. These graphs visualize the strength of such relationships and indicate the uncertainty of expected outcomes. For example, while with the increase of proportion of effort on specification we should expect an increase of QD, there are projects with over 25% of effort spent on specification and deliver poor documentation, and there are projects with just 2% of effort spent on specification and deliver exceptional documentation. To our surprise, proportion of effort on planning and specification was found to be in relationship only with QD; relationships with all other quality features were not statistically significant.

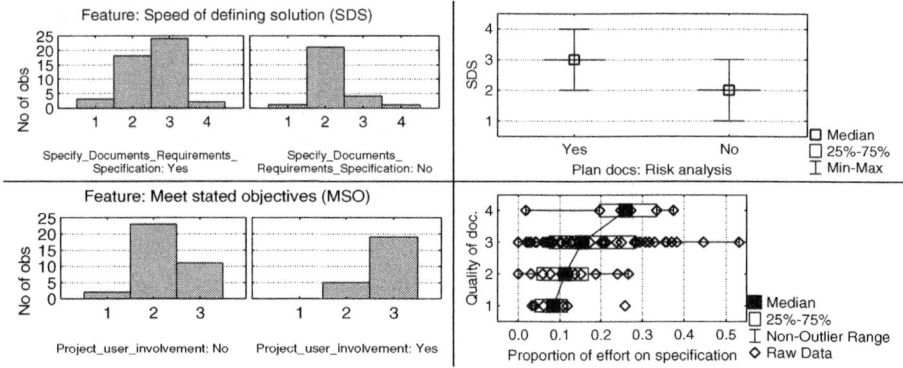

Fig. 1. Examples of visualized relationships between RE factors and software quality features

To answer RQ3, we investigated the relationships among quality features using Spearman's ρ and Kruskal-Wallis' H. Table 3 provides the values of ρ, significant at $p<0.05$. The analysis of H in large part confirms these results. According to these results no quality feature appears to be contradictory to another one. The results do not confirm any negative correlations even for factors typically perceived as being in trade-off, for example between project quality and speed of delivery [11].

Table 3. Values of Spearman's ρ between quality features

Feature	MSO	MBR	QF	QD	EU	SDS	SPS
MSO	–	0.45	0.58	0.19	0.29		
MBR	0.45	–	0.44	0.31	0.39	0.21	0.23
QF	0.58	0.44	–	0.33	0.33	0.22	0.30
QD	0.19	0.31	0.33	–	0.23		
EU	0.29	0.39	0.33	0.23	–		0.34
SDS		0.21	0.22			–	0.59
SPS		0.23	0.30		0.34	0.59	–

4   Threats to Validity

Results obtained in this study are subject to the following threats to validity:

- High number of missing data reduces the ability to generalize the results – most analyses have been performed on about 50-70 cases (projects); the fewest cases were available for *Metrics program* (13-19, depending on particular quality feature investigated); rarely more than 100 cases were available.

- The need to use nonparametric statistical tests with fewer assumptions but which are usually less explanatory/discriminative.
- Unbalanced data provide very few cases for some combinations of states and may bias the values of statistical tests.
- The study covered a variety of RE factors, but there are other RE factors not investigated here because the dataset does not contain them.
- Investigated quality features are subjective and no detailed information is available on the process of gathering of them and their source.
- We used various values of p in different statistical tests – although a value '0.05' is the most frequent in the literature, in some less popular tests we also used a value '0.1' since the aim was to identify a wide range factors that *might* be related to software quality.
- Performed analyses involved using "classical" statistics and not other techniques, which will be considered in future work.

5   Conclusions and Future Work

This study involved the analysis of RE factors that influence soft software quality features. Obtained preliminary results lead to the following conclusions that answer initially stated research questions:

- RQ1: There is a variety of RE factors, listed in Tables 1 and 2, which are in statistically significant relationships with selected soft quality features.
- RQ2: The majority of RE factors positively influence soft quality features. However, there are factors that decrease software quality features related to speed, e.g., *used methodology*, *project objective: min. costs*, and usage of various specification documents decrease SDS and SPS.
- RQ3: The majority of quality features are positively correlated with each other (Table 3). No negative correlations between quality features have been identified.

Results obtained in this study may be valuable both for researchers and practitioners in analysis of effectiveness of RE, building analytical and predictive models, and guiding and supporting decision makers.

In future we plan to extend this analysis by using other techniques from statistics and artificial intelligence, including cluster analysis, decision trees, rule induction techniques, neural networks, rough sets, and Bayesian networks. We also plan to investigate the relationships between RE factors and other factors like development effort and productivity, and factors reflecting other phases of software development.

Acknowledgments. I am indebted to Professor Norman Fenton from Queen Mary, University of London for funding the ISBSG dataset. This work has been supported by research funds from the Ministry of Science and Higher Education in Poland as a research grant no. N N111 291738 for years 2010-2012.

References

1. Berry, D., Franch, X.: REFSQ 2010. LNCS, vol. 6182. Springer, Heidelberg (2010)
2. Cann, A.: Maths from Scratch for Biologists. Wiley (2003)
3. Cheng, B.H.C., Atlee, J.M.: Research Directions in Requirements Engineering. In: Future of Software Engineering, pp. 285–303. IEEE Computer Society, Washington, DC (2007)
4. Damian, D., Chisan, J.: An Empirical Study of the Complex Relationships between Requirements Engineering Processes and Other Processes that Lead to Payoffs in Productivity, Quality, and Risk Management. IEEE Trans. Softw. Eng. 32, 433–453 (2006)
5. Ferrari, R., Madhavji, N.H.: Software architecting without requirements knowledge and experience: What are the repercussions? J. Syst. Softw. 81, 1470–1490 (2008)
6. Finkelstein, A.: Requirements engineering: a review and research agenda. In: Proceedings of the 1994 First Asia-Pacific Software Engineering Conference, pp. 10–19 (1994)
7. Hall, T., Beecham, S., Rainer, A.: Requirements problems in twelve software companies: an empirical analysis. IEE Proc. – Softw. 149, 153–160 (2002)
8. ISBSG: Repository Data Release 11. International Software Benchmarking Standards Group (2009), http://www.isbsg.org
9. ISBSG: ISBSG Comparative Estimating Tool V4.0 – User Guide. International Software Benchmarking Standards Group (2005), http://www.isbsg.org
10. Jones, C.: Applied Software Measurement: Global Analysis of Productivity and Quality, 3rd edn. McGraw-Hill, New York (2008)
11. Kerzner, H.: Project management. Van Nostrand Reinhold, New York (1992)
12. Maxwell, K.D.: Applied Statistics for Software Managers. Prentice Hall PTR, Upper Saddle River (2002)
13. Mendes, E., Lokan, C.: Replicating studies on cross- vs single-company effort models using the ISBSG Database. Emp. Softw. Eng. 13, 3–37 (2008)
14. Musa, J.D.: Software Reliability Engineering: More Reliable Software Faster and Cheaper, 2nd edn. Authorhouse, Boston (2004)
15. Pohl, K.: Requirements Engineering - Fundamentals, Principles, and Techniques. Springer, Heidelberg (2010)
16. Radliński, Ł.: Empirical Analysis of the Impact of Requirements Engineering on Software Quality – Raw Results, http://lukrad.univ.szczecin.pl/refsq2012/
17. Radliński, Ł.: Factors of Software Quality – Analysis of Extended ISBSG Dataset. Found. Comput. Dec. Stud. 36, 293–313 (2011)

A Systematic Literature Review on Service Description Methods

Abelneh Y. Teka, Nelly Condori-Fernandez, and Brahmananda Sapkota

University of Twente,
Enschede, The Netherlands
a.y.teka@student.utwente.nl,
{n.condorifernandez,b.sapkota}@utwente.nl

Abstract. **[Context and Motivation]** As a result of recent trends in enhancing Service Oriented Requirement Engineering activities, a number of service description methods have been proposed for describing services. The availability of different service description methods can give developers a range of options to choose from so that they can have an appropriate description method that fits best their services. **[Question/problem]** But there is neither holistic information on service description methods nor a clear understanding of the strengths and weaknesses of each service description method. The aim of this paper is to identify problems of service descriptions that have been researched so far, and the techniques or methods available to tackle these problems. **[Principle ideas/results]** Thus, to gather this relevant information available in the literature, a systematic review was conducted. A total of 191 articles were examined, of which 24 articles focus on service description related concepts. The results show that, despite the recent efforts in describing the nonfunctional requirements of services through approaches like semantic annotations and policy attachments, there is still a lot to do in enhancing the description of quality aspects of services. Furthermore, this study reveals that a negligible effort is given to the description of consumer oriented services. **[Contribution]** This paper identifies and analyzes the current service description methods that exist in the literature and explains the pros and cons inherent to these methods.

Keywords: systematic review, service description, service specification, functional, non-functional requirements.

1   Introduction

A successful Requirements Engineering (RE) process involves understanding the needs of customers, and other stakeholders; understanding the contexts in which the to-be-developed software will be used; modeling, analyzing, negotiating, and documenting the stakeholders' requirements; validating that the documented requirements match the negotiated requirements; and managing requirements evolution [1]. Service Oriented Requirements Engineering (SORE) shares with these activities, but some of them are conducted in a different way. The most remarkable

B. Regnell and D. Damian (Eds.): REFSQ 2012, LNCS 7195, pp. 239–255, 2012.
© Springer-Verlag Berlin Heidelberg 2012

difference is that service and workflow discovery has a very significant role in SORE as part of the requirement elicitation and analysis activities [8],[39]. SORE focuses on determining requirements of systems which are going to be developed in a service-oriented manner [2].

Although RE is a key part in software development process; there is still a lack of well-established and widely accepted RE methods even in the commonly used system development approaches like Object Oriented approaches [3]. The same is true in the newly Service Oriented Computing (SOC) paradigm, where one of the consequences, associated with this lack of appropriate RE techniques, is the absence of accurate service descriptions[1], which will affect other SOC activities like service discovery and service composition [5], [6].

This lack in accurate service description is manifested by the presence of gaps between the specifications of requirements of a system and the service oriented description of the system. The gap is due to the difference in focuses of the two systems, i.e. Requirement engineering is primarily concerned with goals and requirements while service descriptions are mainly about technical operations and bindings [37].

Thus currently, researchers are enthusiastically producing new techniques in order to cover this gap. And the development of new approaches for describing services is not a problem by itself; in fact, it gives an opportunity for practitioners to have a range of choices to use in specific situations. The real problem is the lack of holistic information on available methods and techniques along with their respective strengths and weakness. Though scarce studies that allow gaining this holistic view of existing methods have been carried out [13], [10], a comprehensive analysis covering different aspects of the available service description methods is still missing.

This paper aims to analyze the current service description methods that exist in the literature, by identifying pros and cons of these methods. To do this, a Systematic Literature Review (SLR) is performed based on the guidelines suggested by Kitchenham et al. [11]. We decided to conduct a SLR instead of a Mapping Study because our research goes beyond of identifying the quantity and type of research and results available within a research area [40].

The remaining parts of this paper are organized as follow: Section 2 introduces the main issue of our review, service description, from a SORE viewpoint. Section 3 focuses on the methodology used in conducting the research. Section 4 presents the results of this review. Finally, section 5 concludes the paper.

2   Background: Service Description

Requirement engineering in SOC plays a vital role in identifying and specifying service requirements that have been defined through service level agreements (SLAs) [12]. SORE focuses on identification, specification and analysis of requirements. But the specification of SLAs need different approaches in requirement engineering as there are a number of activities in SORE that are not available in the traditional RE

---

[1] A Service description comprises a service specification and, if available, some service additional Information. A service specification is usually defined by the service developer and may include both functional and non-functional information [39].

activities. Examples of such activities include the requirements elicitation from service description and service discovery processes.

Utilization of a service based application involves a number of entities playing different roles. Among these entities, service providers, service repositories and service consumers are the key stakeholders that SORE is focusing on. Service providers publish their service descriptions on Service repositories and service consumers use these descriptions for discovering and binding to services in order to utilize them [2]. This means, service consumers need information about services available at repositories so that they can discover and ultimately utilize it. Thus, it is important to have an expressive service description that enables service consumers to decide which services are best suited for satisfying their requirements.

Currently services are described by service description languages like Web Service Description Language (WSDL), but service orientation itself needs its own requirement engineering activities, since a service described in terms of operations and bindings may not be enough to specify the desired goals and domain assumptions of stakeholders [41].

This does not mean available service description methods are all unable to specify requirements as they are supposed to do so. In fact there are considerable number of emerging approaches ([7], [16], [17], [27]) targeted at closing the gap between technical service description techniques and the common RE specifications.

3   Review Methodology

The major steps taken to conduct this literature study are taken from the guidelines proposed by Kitchenham et. al [11], which are discussed in the following subsections:

3.1   Defining the Research Questions

As we mentioned in the Section 1, this paper focuses on existing service description methods, associated problems and possible approaches to tackle these problems. In particular, we aim at answering the following research questions:

RQ1. What are the existing service description methods reported in literature?
RQ2. What are the problems faced during service description process as reported in the literature?
RQ3. What are the strengths and weaknesses of these service description methods?

3.2   Search and Selection Process

The principal source used while searching relevant papers was Scopus (www.scopus.com). As Scopus provides access to well-known bibliographic-databases like IEEE Explore, SpringerLinks, ACM digital library etc. at the same place, it was fruitful using it as a search engine for the search process.

In the search process, the identification of our search string was carried out in an iterative way. We started with a number of combinations of search terms like: "Service Description" AND "Requirement specification", "Service Specification"

AND "requirement specification", "service oriented architecture" AND "requirement engineering". As thousands of articles were retrieved, we restricted these preliminary search results by limiting the subject area to computer science and discarding papers published earlier than 2002[2]. Doing so helped us to discard irrelevant articles much easily from other areas (e.g. economics). The list of search terms was adapted several times and the search was re-run with the new terms. (See Table 1).

Table 1. Search hits from Scopus

Search Term	Number of first hits	Restriction to computer science subject area	Restriction to publication date year 2002 and above	Restriction to conference papers and articles
"service oriented architecture" AND "requirement engineering"	572	432	408	366
"Service Description" AND "Requirement specification",	38	29	29	28
"Service Specification" AND "Requirement specification"	3,518	1,514	1,187	1112

After an iterative refinement, the search string used was the following: ((("service oriented architecture") OR SOA) AND ((("service description" OR "service specification") AND ("requirement specification"))).

A total of 191 articles were retrieved from this search string. From these articles, a further refinement was carried out. 11 studies were identified by reading their abstract; 3 studies were identified by reading the introduction part; and 8 studies were identified by reading whole article. At this phase the authors observe that the approaches discussed in [29] and [31] are similar and merged to one approach making the relevant service description methods count to be 21 articles.

While we were reviewing these 21 articles, 3 more ([10], [15], [31]) were identified as relevant for our study. These articles were incorporated in the relevant list, thereby ending up in 24 articles selected for the study presented in this paper.

3.3   Study Quality Assessment and Data Collection

For studying the quality assessment, a qualitative assessing was carried out within the selection process. We consider an article as relevant for our review whether it reports "enough" information to answer our main research questions. In addition, although the 70% of the articles were refereed, the criteria by number of citation was not also considered in order to do a filter of our 24 articles, since a good number of the articles were published in the last year (2010).

---

[2] It is starting time of Service Oriented Architecture.

Each of the 24 papers selected was analyzed, by identifying 1) the problem to be solved by the service description method proposed, 2) the technique(s)/language used to tackle the problem, 3) their strengths and weaknesses, and 4) the approach employed to evaluate or validate the respective description method.

4   Review Results

4.1   RQ1: Service Description Methods

The literature study reveals that there has been a significant effort in improving requirement engineering practices for SOA. For instance, as shown in Figure 1, from the 24 service description methods, 19 of them are published in and after 2007.

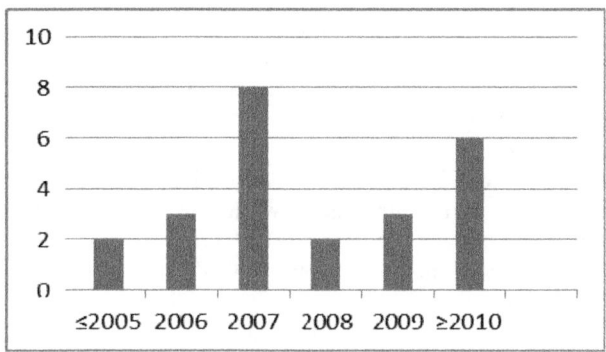

Fig. 1. Frequency of newly emerged description methods by year

As the service description methods found are diverse and this broad variety makes it difficult to classify them based on certain criteria, we consider to use three dimensions with the purpose of facilitating the analysis of each one of the 24 service description methods. Figure 2 shows these three dimensions: Representation (syntactic, semantic), Content (Functional requirements, Non-functional requirements, additional information), and Perspective (business, operational and technical). Table 4 (See Appendix) shows an overview of these 24 methods according to these three dimensions.

Syntax Based vs. Semantic Based Methods. Syntax based service descriptions are the most commonly employed description methods up to date. These methods hide what is going on inside the service and expose the necessary input and output values of the service interfaces. Syntax based service description employs techniques based on languages like WSDL to expose the interface of the service and other service description mechanisms like Web Service Level Agreement (WSLA).

The syntax based description methods that use WSDL as service description language at least as their base in describing services are [16], [20], [24], [28].

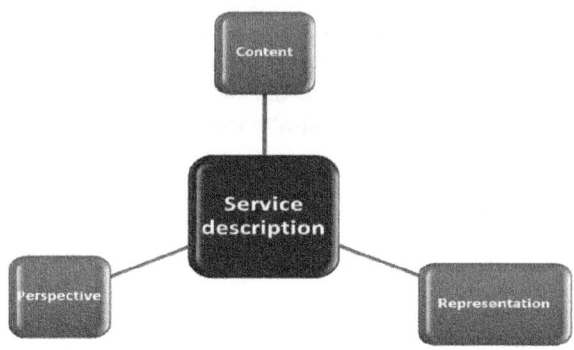

Fig. 2. Dimensions used to analyze service description methods

Semantic based service descriptions are emerging approaches that describe service based on various forms of meanings like ontology annotation and Context information based methods [10].Semantic based descriptions can be an extension of services described in WSDL [20], but can also be entirely dependent on ontology for describing services [14].

The extension of WSDL approaches adds additional semantic description to WSDL components by using annotations while the pure semantic approaches use modifications of Web Ontology Language (OWL) for specifying the functionalities of a service and the associated inputs and outputs. OWL is not the only language used in semantic service descriptions. Its predecessor DARPA Agent Markup Language (DAML) can be used for describing services as a process not as a one shoot activity while retaining the semantic meanings [32].

Functional vs. Non Functional Requirements Description Methods. The functional requirements of services can be described in terms of syntax based, behavior description based and semantic description based approaches [10]. Though most service description techniques are intended for describing the functional requirements of services [5], [16], [28], [29], [35] ; there are a considerable number of approached that aim in giving emphasis to the non-functional requirements too[18], [21].

The presence of the non-functional requirements like quality, cost, legal issues, etc. will definitely add more options for customers to choose the right service for their requirements. Some of these methods are helpful in describing even frequently changing Quality of Services (QoSs) that helps service users in selecting services that matches their requirements [21]. Contrary to this distinction between functional and non-functional requirements descriptions, there are also more promising approaches which consider both the functional and non-functional requirements [20], [30].

Business Process - Technology Mapping approaches. SOC is targeted for developing enterprise applications based on autonomous services [16]. Previous trends in developing such applications were technology oriented. Under such approach, services are usually defined in terms of technical functionalities. These approaches describe services based on the various operations defined at their interfaces to be invoked at different port types [4], [16], [36].

The most important thing to consider here is that applications are usually developed to achieve some kind of business goal. Such business goals are generally realized/represented in terms of some business processes expressed in business processes modeling languages like be BPEL or BPMN. In SOA approach, these business processes are realized by service based applications which are represented in terms of technical service development process so that the service based application can assist in achieving the business goals. Business Process - Technology Mapping approaches help in a better alignment of business processes to services based applications. From the 24 service description methods found in the study [7], [16], [17], [27] were targeted at a better alignment of business – technology mappings.

Using a unified service description language is one of the approaches discovered for such enhanced alignment [7]. This approach proposes model-based description of services from business operational and technical perspectives. Another candidate approach discovered to handle such an issue is formulating business specifications to include SOA application specification [17]. Such approaches are designed to improve the poor role played by the current service description methods in business-software mapping mechanisms.

Model Based Service Description Approaches. Requirements engineers in SOA usually use model driven approaches to specify the requirements of the services. Among the 24 service description methods found in the review, [7], [24], [25], [30], [26] use various model based approaches to describe services. There are modeling approaches like SMMA (Single Model Multiple Analysis) that can help even in generating codes from the models alone [15]. PSML-S (Process Specification and Modeling Language) is a typical language used for implementing SMMA approach. An alternative language that can be used in specifying services is BPEL4WS which is mainly used in defining the flow and coordination between service components [29].

There are also formal model based techniques for describing services though they still need more time to mature enough to be applicable in service oriented applications [15]. But efforts to improve the applicability of these formal methods are already taking place. ForSel (Formal Service description language) is a typical example of such efforts. ForSel describes services by describing the necessary functionalities in terms of finite or infinite reactions [5]. Using calculus of communication systems (CCS) to model behavior of services is also another approach discovered for describing services [33].

Service Descriptions for Adaptable Services. In today's competitive business environment, business goals and requirements tend to change regularly. Consequently, applications that support in realization of these requirements need to be updated regularly. And for effective dynamic realizations of business processes, dynamic composition of services is essential.

Moreover, for dynamic service composition, presence of dynamic service description techniques is important. From the 21 service description methods found in the review [9], [14], [23], [28] target at providing descriptions for such dynamic and adaptable services.

An interesting approach dynamic service description approach found during the study is the adaptation of situation awareness in service specification. In support of this, a new extension of OWL-S, named as SAW-OWL-S, was developed to enable services to realize their business context [9]. Related to these, a new approach named Extended Web Service Agreement was proposed to enable renegotiations of SLAs that can help in modifying QoSs while the service is being provided [28]. This approach uses a new element named modifiable service level objective that can be modified at run time.

Along with the growth in popularity of SOA, service based applications is being used not only in large business process contexts but also in small scale businesses and even in our day to day personal activities. Developing services for such processes is usually cumbersome as the developer may not have even a concrete clue on the customer requirements. Such kind of problems can be tackled by letting consumers to specify and publish their requirements and then developers can design services based on clients' requirements [29].

We also found methods for describing services based on mathematical/formal specifications. For instance, in order to describe services developed for reactive systems, a method named Formal Service description is proposed in [5]. This approach specifies services as a composition of precondition, triggering event and the system reaction. Furthermore, an additional method named Formal specification of data aspects of Web services [35] was proposed for ensuring that customers' requirements are still satisfied during change of services implementations by service providers.

4.2   RQ2: Problem Faced in Describing Services

The second step taken in reviewing the selected 24 papers was to find what type of problem is the proposed methods are aiming to solve. We found that majority of the papers focus on problems related to lack of describing semantic meaning and the Quality of Service (QoS) properties of services.

We also observe that there is a wide gap in services realized from business process perspective and from the software engineering perspective. There are also problems associated with services described in terms of producer centric approaches. Table 2 shows the major problems discovered in the literature study.

Table 2. Problems addressed by the 24 service description methods

Problem	References
Lack of Semantic in syntactic Descriptions and failure in describing QoS.	[4], [9], [14], [18-26]
Gap between business oriented and IT oriented Service Realizations.	[7], [16], [17], [27]
Lack of dynamic adaptability and situation awareness	[9], [14], [23], [28]
Producer only centric approaches	[29], [31]
Imprecise Requirements Specification	[5]
Lack of Behavior Description	[32], [33]

Lack of QoS Descriptions. It has been noted that even though message oriented description techniques, like WSDL [14], are most popular ones; they have their own limitations. WSDL describes services in terms of various operations defined at interfaces. These descriptions are published on the publicly accessible service registries. Users will discover such services by matching the inputs and outputs of operations at these interfaces [4]. Such approaches in service descriptions employ syntactic matching in service discovery. A typical problem associated with this is the keywords used in service description may fail in describing all the relevant services as keywords can have different synonyms [10]. It is possible to use wildcards during service discovery to alleviate such situation but doing so is not the best solution as it will result in many irrelevant service for the service consumer.

As nonfunctional requirements are also integral parts of services, QoS should also need to be described just like the functional requirements [4]. Unfortunately, the syntax based service description techniques like WSDL fail in realizing this crucial part of a service description.

Gap between Business Service and IT Service. Services are designed to automate a certain business process. So they can be realized from two perspectives: business services and technical services. Business services are concerned with the end to end delivery and an outcome of the process while most of the current service description methods fail in describing the details of these processes as they specify services in terms of a mere input and output operations [7]. This introduces difficulties in aligning business-software realizations [17]. If such details are not realized in the service implementations, there is no guarantee that the developed services will fully realize the business requirements.

Lack of Adaptability and Situation Awareness. Consumers will start utilizing services once they agreed with the providers and establish a Service Level Agreements (SLAs). Sometimes, after starting to use the agreed services, the service users' requirements may change, which may lead to the change in SLAs altogether. These changes are in fact a highly probable situation to arise in today's dynamic business environment.

Additionally, changes can be requested not only by the service consumers but also by the service providers. Unfortunately, the current service description methods are not capable of handling changes in service level agreements once it is set in to operation [28].

Service composition is also one of the vital activities in SOA as it can provide new functionality by composing existing services. But unfortunately, services described based on syntactic approach fails in composing services dynamically, i.e., service composition needs human involvement [14]. In addition, there is also a considerable lack of support in incorporating context and situation awareness of the service environment during service description. Such lack in situation description will result in less flexible service design [9].

Lack of Consumer Oriented Service Description. As SOC is used for more and more applications, applications for personal uses are being developed based on services. Even end-users with no technical background are creating their own web applications [8]. Such users may not know the exact requirements of their applications. In addition, service based applications for individuals face problems associated with the broad variety of customer needs. Developing services that can satisfy such varying needs is difficult, if not impossible, for service developers [29].

4.3   RQ3: Strengths and Weakness of Current Service Description Methods

Each group of service description approaches shown in Table 3 and Table 4 (See Appendix) has their own strengths and weakness. In this section, we present the strong and weak points of these methods. At this point, we would like to remind that some methods are designed to tackle the limitation of another method. This can result in a situation where one method's limitation is some other method's good feature.

Syntax Based Approaches. Syntactic service description methods are the most frequently used service description methods to date [32]. These methods describe a service by explaining the values that are entering and leaving the services without specifying the details of the internal structure of the services. These methods separate the interface of their services from the actual bindings necessary to access services [16]. This will enhance the modularity of the services as they are no longer tied to one implementation. Furthermore, as these methods expose the public interfaces only, developers can use any implementation technique as long as it can provide the desired operations at the interfaces [4].

The huge problem associated with describing services in terms of their syntactic signature is the complete lack in describing QoS [14]. As nonfunctional requirements are the integral parts of any service, the inability of syntax based description methods to describe these crucial parts of services is a severe drawback that forces developers to seek for other approaches for describing services [4].

The inability to describe QoS is not the only problem faced by developers using syntactic description methods. As there is no semantic representation of services in these approaches, they can also result in a low precision service discovery results [21]. In addition, the lack in semantic meaning of inputs and outputs makes it impossible for a complete automation of finding and invoking required services [14].

Semantic Based Approaches. Semantic description of services has a wide range of advantages as they can provide meaning to service descriptions. A semantic rich description can describe not only the functional requirements but also the nonfunctional requirements of services too [20]. Such availability of semantic meaning to services will enable users to select the right service for their business process when they are faced with vague syntax based descriptions [23].

Though semantic based approaches are successful especially in mitigating major weakness of syntax based service description methods, they also come with their own limitation. Their first limitation is associated with the complexity of ontological concepts and relation between them. It is usually cumbersome to use these complex concepts by both service providers and consumers to avoid semantic heterogeneity [10]. Context aware service development is also one of the emerging approaches in service based applications industry. But let alone the syntax based approaches, ontology based description techniques like OWL-S also lack appropriate mechanisms in formal expression of context and situations [9].

Functional Requirement Based Description. The functional requirements descriptions of services are crucial in ensuring users that the services they are going to utilize will satisfy their demands. Web service repositories like UDDI usually store information about the functionality of services [10]. As these functionalities are the primary concerns of the majority service users, service description techniques based on these approaches are preferred by users with their primary concern, which is the automation of the main business process.

The limitations of theses functional requirement descriptions are mainly related with their lack in describing the quality and dynamic aspects of the services [19], [20]. These limitations are directly related to the limitations of syntax based approaches as the functional requirement description methods use the syntax based approaches in describing services.

Model Based Descriptions. Most of the SORE activities employ one or more types of model –driven approaches. One of the benefits of using such models is that once there is a well-established set of core models it will be relatively easier to analyze and maintain custom built models based on these core service models. Furthermore, it is possible to use these models for automatic code generation [8]. Modeling of services in using formal methods like Calculus of Communicating Systems (CCS) will also enable for description of the behavior of services that were not available in syntax based approaches [33]. The prominent limitation of describing services by using models is the complexity involved in the formal specification of services. To avoid such problems, service providers should have adequate knowledge on modeling languages like CCS and automata.

Finally, we also reviewed the efforts aimed in validating or evaluating the existing service description methods. The observed result was not encouraging since 10 out of 24 description methods use simple examples only for showing their validity, and 8 out of the remaining 14 papers do not specify any validation or evaluation approach at all. This clearly indicates the need for more research to evaluate more rigorously in real-life settings. The complete list of service description methods identified in this study can be referred in Appendix (See Table 3).

4.4   Limitations of This Review

The main limitations of this review are bias in the selection of relevant articles and a data extraction bias. Our search string was limited only to computer science subject area due to "service" term is used by other disciplines (e.g. medicine, economics, social sciences, engineering). Besides, it was also necessary to limit year of publication to 2002 to increase the precision search. However, these both limitations could be affecting our recall search.

Another limitation is related to the accuracy of data extraction; several articles lacked sufficient information regarding the dimensions considered for describing services. For example, some articles do not precisely state the type of content described, whether it is functional or nonfunctional (e.g. [6]) description or they do not precisely state the type of representation, whether it is semantic and syntactic (e.g. [29]) description. There is, therefore, a possibility that the extraction process may have resulted in some inaccuracy in the data.

Moreover, with respect to the synthesis of our findings, we recognize that it could have been carried out in a more systematic way, if we had used some of the tools for synthetizing qualitative studies (e.g. EPPI-reviewer 4[3]). However at the moment of conducting the present review we did not have a software license available to use the tool.

5   Conclusions and Future Work

Service descriptions are one of the major activities included in SORE as it is a crucial prerequisite to service discovery process. This paper presents problems faced in describing services, 24 service description methods discovered from literature study and the strengths and weakness of these service description methods. The result of the study was presented according to the major categories of service description methods currently employed or proposed to be employed.

Though WSDL is the most widely used service description language, it comes with its own limitation: It fails in describing nonfunctional requirements of services which are of course crucial parts of services [4]. Such and related problems along with the possible solutions are discussed in Section 4.

The study shows that there is a considerable limitation in describing QoS – nonfunctional requirements of services despite the presence of some efforts in describing these quality attributes. A possible approach observed to handle this lack of support for describing QoS in service description is to integrate syntactic based descriptions like WSDL and ontology based descriptions like OWL-S. As WSDL descriptions are quite extensible, adding OWL annotations can be fruitful in describing both the functional and QoS aspects of services.

Considering the recent trends in developing service oriented applications targeted mainly for personal use, the authors observe a negligible amount of effort in handling requirement specifications of these user-centric applications. There is also a significant difference in business process specification and how the current service implementation technologies realize and describe these business processes.

On the other hand, from this SLR, we think that a list of possible combinations of service description methods could have resulted to yield much better description approach, thereby increasing the expressiveness of the specification document. In fact we have observed such possibilities. For instance Syntax based service descriptions work nicely only if specification documents are available to explain the details of the capabilities of the service as well as the conditions necessary for using the service [22]. But if such specification document is not available, verbose service description methods ([19]) come in to play. Syntax based and semantic based service description methods can be combined to provide rich service description approaches [20]. But this and other possibilities of combining two or more description methods will be part of our future work.

In addition, we will be also focused on investigating further approaches aimed at enhancing the current efforts in describing QoS. As the quality attributes are crucial in specifying service capabilities, more study on service descriptions focusing on QoS will be quite relevant.

---

[3] http://eppi.ioe.ac.uk/cms/

We also plan to integrate this study with existing service description and service discovery mechanisms to create a holistic view of the basic activities in SORE.

Acknowledgments. This work was supported in part by the EU Marie Curie Fellowship Grant 50911302 PIEF-2010. Authors would like also to thank the anonymous reviewers, and colleagues Klaas Sikel and Zortnitza Bakalova for their valuable comments for improvement.

References

1. Cheng, B., Atlee, J.M.: Research Directions in Requirements Engineering. Requirements Engineering, 285–303 (2007)
2. Galster, M., Bucherer, E.: Towards Requirements Engineering in a Service-Oriented Environment–Extending the SOA Interaction Triangle. In: Proceedings of the International Conference on Computational Intelligence for Modelling Control & Automation, pp. 1099–1104 (2008)
3. Davis, A.M., Hickey, A.M.: A New Paradigmfor Planning and Evaluating Requirements Engineering Research (2004)
4. Papazoglou, M.: Web Services: Principles and Technology, 1st edn. Prentice Hall (2007)
5. Hartmann, J., Rittmann, S., Wild, D., Scholz, P.: Formal incremental requirements specification of service-oriented automotive software systems. In: Proceedings of the Second IEEE International Symposium on Service-Oriented System Engineering, pp. 130–133 (2006)
6. Edmond, D., Hofstede, A.H.M., O'sullivan, J.: Service Description: A survey of the general nature of services, University of Queensland, vol. 12, pp. 117–133
7. Cardoso, J., Barros, A., May, N., Kylau, U.: Towards a unified service description language for the internet of services: Requirements and first developments. In: Proceedings of the IEEE 7th International Conference on Services Computing, pp. 602–609 (2010)
8. Tsai, W.T., Jin, Z., Wang, P., Wu, B.: Requirement Engineering in Service-Oriented System Engineering. In: Proceedings of the IEEE International Conference on e-Business Engineering, pp. 661–668 (2007)
9. Yau, S.S., Liu, J.: Incorporating situation awareness in service specifications. In: Proceedings of the Ninth IEEE International Symposium on Object-Oriented Real-Time Distributed Computing, pp. 287–294 (2006)
10. D'Mello, D.A., Ananthanarayana, V.S.: A review of dynamic web service description and discovery techniques. In: Proceedings of the 1st International Conference on Integrated Intelligent Computing, pp. 246–251 (2010)
11. Kitchenham, B.: Procedures for Performing Systematic Reviews, Technical Report, TR/SE-0401, Keele University (2004)
12. Lichtenstein, S., Nguyen, L., Hunter, A.: Issues in IT service-oriented requirements engineering, http://www.deakin.edu.au/dro/view/DU:30005308 (accessed: June 01, 2011)
13. Gu, Q., Lago, P.: Service Identification Methods: A Systematic Literature Review. In: Di Nitto, E., Yahyapour, R. (eds.) ServiceWave 2010. LNCS, vol. 6481, pp. 37–50. Springer, Heidelberg (2010)
14. Martin, D., Paolucci, M., McIlraith, S.A., Burstein, M., McDermott, D., McGuinness, D.L., Parsia, B., Payne, T.R., Sabou, M., Solanki, M., Srinivasan, N., Sycara, K.: Bringing Semantics to Web Services: The OWL-S Approach. In: Cardoso, J., Sheth, A.P. (eds.) SWSWPC 2004. LNCS, vol. 3387, pp. 26–42. Springer, Heidelberg (2005)

15. Tsai, W.T., Chen, Y., Fan, C.: PESOI: Process Embedded Service-Oriented Architecture *
16. Rychlý, M., Weiss, P.: Modeling of service oriented architecture from business process to service realisation. In: Proceedings of the 3rd International Conference on Evaluation of Novel Approaches to Software Engineering, pp. 140–146 (2008)
17. Shishkov, B., Dietz, J.L.G., van Sinderen, M.: Closing the Business-Application GAP in SOA challenges and solution directions. In: Proceeding of 2nd International Conference on Software and Data Technologies, vol. SE, pp. 333–336 (2007)
18. Slimane, A.A.A., Pinheiro, M.K., Souveyet, C.: Goal reasoning for quality elicitation in the ISOA approach. In: Proceedings of the 3rd International Conference on Research Challenges in Information Science, pp. 39–48 (2009)
19. Stefanovic, M., Matijević, M., Erić, M., Simic, V.: Method of design and specification of web services based on quality system documentation. Information Systems Frontiers 11(1), 75–86 (2009)
20. Qiu, Q., Xiong, Q.: An Ontology for Semantic Web Services. In: Perrott, R., Chapman, B.M., Subhlok, J., de Mello, R.F., Yang, L.T. (eds.) HPCC 2007. LNCS, vol. 4782, pp. 776–784. Springer, Heidelberg (2007)
21. Kritikos, K., Plexousakis, D.: Requirements for QoS-based Web service description and discovery. IEEE Transactions on Services Computing 2(4), 320–337 (2009)
22. Pfeffer, H., Linner, D., Jacob, C., Radusch, I., Steglich, S.: Towards light-weight semantic descriptions for decentralized service-oriented systems. In: International Conference on Semantic Computing, pp. 295–303 (2007)
23. Sirin, E., Hendler, J., Parsia, B.: Semi-automatic Composition of Web Services using Semantic Descriptions. In: Web Services: Modeling, Architecture and Infrastructure Workshop 2003, pp. 17–24 (2002)
24. Bocciarelli, P., D'Ambrogio, A.: A model-driven method for describing and predicting the reliability of composite services. Software & Systems Modeling 10(2), 265–280 (2010)
25. Di Marco, A., Sabetta, A.: Model-based dynamic QoS-driven service composition. In: ACM International Conference Proceeding Series (2010)
26. Fornasier, P., Webber, J., Gorton, I.: Soya: A Programming Model and Runtime Environment for Component Composition Using SSDL. In: Schmidt, H.W., Crnković, I., Heineman, G.T., Stafford, J.A. (eds.) CBSE 2007. LNCS, vol. 4608, pp. 227–241. Springer, Heidelberg (2007)
27. Rolland, C., Kirsch-Pinheiro, M., Souveyet, C.: An intentional approach to service engineering. IEEE Transactions on Services Computing 3(4), 292–305 (2010)
28. Di Modica, G., Regalbuto, V., Tomarchio, O., Vita, L.: Enabling re-negotiations of SLA by extending the WS-Agreement specification. In: Proceedings of the IEEE International Conference on Services Computing, pp. 248–251 (2007)
29. Tsai, W.T., Bingnan, X., Paul, R., Qian, H., Yinong, C.: Global software enterprise: A new software constructing architecture. In: CEC/EEE 2006 Joint Conferences (2006)
30. Narendra, N.C., Ponnalagu, K.: Variation-Oriented Requirements Analysis (VORA). In: Proceedings of the IEEE Congress on Services, SERVICES 2007, pp. 159–166 (2007)
31. Tsai, W.T., Xiao, B., Paul, R.A., Chen, Y.: Consumer-centric service-oriented architecture: A new approach. In: Proceedings of the Fourth IEEE Workshop on Software Technology for Future Embedded and Ubiquitous Systems, and the Second International Workshop on Collaborative Computing, Integration, and Assur, pp. 175–180 (2006)
32. Klein, M., König-Ries, B., Obreiter, P.: Stepwise Refinable Service Descriptions: Adapting DAML-S to Staged Service Trading. In: Orlowska, M.E., Weerawarana, S., Papazoglou, M.P., Yang, J. (eds.) ICSOC 2003. LNCS, vol. 2910, pp. 178–193. Springer, Heidelberg (2003)

33. Yun, B., Yan, J., Liu, M.: Behavior-Based Web Services Matchmaking. In: Proceedings of the 2008 IFIP International Conference on Network and Parallel Computing, pp. 483–487 (2008)
34. Zelkowitz, M.V., Wallace, D.: Experimental validation in software engineering. Information and Software Technology 39(11), 735–743 (1997)
35. Saleh, I., Kulczycki, G., Blake, M.B.: Formal specification and verification of data-centric service composition. In: Proceedings of the IEEE 8th International Conference on Web Services, pp. 131–138 (2010)
36. Bocciarelli, P., D'Ambrogio, A.: A model-driven method for describing and predicting the reliability of composite services. Software and Systems Modeling 10(2), 265–280 (2011)
37. Verlaine, B., Dubois, Y., Jureta, I.J., Faulkner, S.: Towards automated alignment of Web Services to requirements. In: 2010 First International Workshop on the Web and Requirements Engineering (WeRE), pp. 5–12 (2010)
38. Hummer, W., Leitner, P., Dustdar, S.: SEPL-a domain-specific language and execution environment for protocols of stateful Web services (2011)
39. Papazoglou, M.P., Pohl, K., Parkin, M., Metzger, A.: Service Research Challenges and Solutions for the Future Internet - S-Cube - Towards Engineering, Managing and Adapting Service-Based Systems. LNCS, vol. 6500. Springer, Heidelberg (2010)
40. Petersen, K., Feldt, R., Shahid, M., Mattsson, M.: Systematic Mapping Studies in Software Engineering. In: 12th International Conference on Evaluation and Assessment in Software Engineering (EASE), Department of Informatics, University of Bari, Italy (June 2008)
41. Verlaine, B., Jureta, I.J., Faulkner, S.: Towards conceptual foundations of requirements engineering for services. In: 2011 Fifth International Conference on Research Challenges in Information Science (RCIS), pp. 1–11 (2011)

Appendix

Table 3. An overview of existing service description methods

Ref.	Method name	Technique/Language used	Validation/evaluative approach
M1 [18]	Intentional Service, for Quality of Service	Text based, no specific language employed	Quality model
M2 [7]	Modeling business and technical services	USDL	Testing
M3 [28]	Extended WS agreement	WSLA	Not Specified
M4 [19]	Specifications based on quality system documentation	Documentation based	Questionnaire
M5 [5]	Formal service description	ForSeL Calculus	Case study on progress
M6 [16]	Modeling of business process to service diagrams	WSDL like operation specification	Example
M7 [17]	SOA driven specification	SOA-driven business-software mapping	Not Specified
M8 [29]	Consumer Oriented SOA	Tools like PSML-S and BPEL	Example
M9 [30]	Variation Oriented requirement analysis	VORA tractability model	Example
M10 [27]	Intentional approach for service description	Intentional Service Modeling	Example
M11 [38]	Service protocol	SEPL	Testing
M12 [24]	Model base approach for describing QOS	Q-WSDL	Example
M13 [33]	Behavior based service description	Formal description based on CCS	Example
M14 [25]	Model-based dynamic QoS-driven service composition	SMART	Not specified
M15 [26]	SOYA	SSDL	Not specified
M16 [20]	Semantic annotation for WSDL	Annotation of WSDL components	Example
M17 [9]	Situation aware service based systems	SAW-OWL-S (Extension of OWL-S)	Example
M18 [4]	WS-Policy attachment	WS Policy and WS agreement	Example
M19 [35]	Formal Specification of data aspects of web services	Formal representation of contracts	Formal verification: Symbolic reasoning
M20 [21]	Ontology for QoS	OWL – Q	Not Specified
M21 [14]	Semantic for Web services	OWL-S	Example

Table 3. (*continued*)

Ref.	Method name	Technique/Language used	Validation/evaluative approach
M22 [22]	Semantics for Service Descriptions	Distributed semantic trees.	Not Specified
M23 [23]	Semi-automatic semantic descriptions for web services	DAML	Prototype Evaluation
M24 [32]	Refining service Descriptions	DAML-S (DAML for services)	Not Specified

Table 4. Service description Methods

	Content			Representation			Perspective		
Method	Fu	NonF	Other	Verb	Synt	Sema	Buss	Oper	Tech
M1		X		X			X		
M2	X	X			X		X	X	X
M3	X								
M4	X	X		X			X		
M5	X				X	X			
M6	X				X		X		
M7	X						X		
M8	X		X				X		
M9	X	X							
M10	X						X		
M11	X								
M12		X							
M13	X								
M14		X							
M15	X					X			X
M16	X	X				X			
M17		X	X						
M18		X							
M19	X								
M20	X	X				X			
M21		X			X				
M22	X					X			
M23	X		X			X			
M24	X				X				

Legend:

Fu: Functional Requirements

NonF: Non Functional Requirements

Other: Additional information

Verb: Verbose

Synt: Syntactic

Sema: Semantic

Buss: Bussiness

Oper: Operational

Tech: Technical

A Pattern-Based Method
for Identifying and Analyzing Laws[*]

Kristian Beckers[1], Stephan Faßbender[1],
Jan-Christoph Küster[2], and Holger Schmidt[1]

[1] paluno - The Ruhr Institute for Software Technology – University of Duisburg-Essen
firstname.lastname@paluno.uni-due.de
[2] Australian National University, Canberra, Australia
Jan-Christoph.Kuester@anu.edu.au

Abstract. Nowadays many legislators decided to enact different laws, which all enforce legal and natural persons to deal more carefully with IT systems. Hence, there is a need for techniques to identify and analyze laws which are relevant for an IT system. But identifying relevant *compliance* regulations for an IT system and aligning it to be *compliant* is a challenging task. This paper presents a novel *method for identifying and analyzing laws*. The method makes use of different kinds of *law analysis patterns* that allow legal experts and software and system developers to understand and elicit relevant laws for the given development problem. Our approach also helps to detect dependent laws. We illustrate our method using an online-banking cloud scenario.

Keywords: law, compliance, requirements engineering.

1 Introduction

Identifying relevant *compliance* regulations for a software system and aligning it to be *compliant* is a challenging task. The construction of software systems that meet compliance regulations, such as laws, is considered to be difficult, because it is a cross-disciplinary task in laws and software and systems engineering [1]. Otto and Antón [2] conclude in their survey about research on laws in requirements engineering that there is a need for techniques to identify and analyze laws, and to derive requirements from laws.

We present a *pattern-based method for identifying and analyzing laws*. We introduce *law analysis patterns* that allow legal experts and software developers to understand and elicit laws that are relevant for a given development problem.

In this paper, we consider compliance in the field of *cloud computing systems* (or short *clouds*) as an example domain, because using clouds to store and manage critical data and to support sensitive IT processes harbors several problems with respect to compliance. We illustrate our approach using the example of a bank offering an online-banking service for their customers. Customer data such as account number, balance,

---

[*] This research was partially supported by the EU project Network of Excellence on Engineering Secure Future Internet Software Services and Systems (NESSoS, ICT-2009.1.4 Trustworthy ICT, Grant No. 256980).

B. Regnell and D. Damian (Eds.): REFSQ 2012, LNCS 7195, pp. 256–262, 2012.

and transaction history are stored in the cloud, and transactions like credit transfer are processed in the cloud. The bank authorizes the software department to design and build the cloud-specific software according to the interface and platform specification of the cloud provider.For simplicity's sake, we focus in our running example on relevant compliance regulations for privacy. In 1995, the European Union (EU) adopted the *Directive 95/46/EC* on the processing of personal data that represents the minimum privacy standards that have to be included in every national law. Germany implements the European Privacy Directive in the *Federal Data Protection Act (BDSG)*.

The rest of the paper is organized as follows: We present patterns to deal with laws in requirements engineering in Sect. 2. Then, in Sect. 3, we discuss related work. In Sect. 4, we give a summary and directions for future research.

2   Pattern-Based Law Analysis

Commonly, laws are not adequately considered during requirements engineering. Therefore, they are not covered in the subsequent system development phases. One fundamental reason for this is that the involved engineers are typically not cross-disciplinary experts in law and software and systems engineering. Hence, we present in this section a pattern-based approach to systematically consider laws in the requirements engineering process. For our method we chose the German law as the binding law.

2.1   Structure of Laws, Sections and Dictates of Justice

The German law is a *statute law* in the tradition of the Roman jurisdiction. Statute laws are specified by the legislator and written down in legal documents. Hence, every judgment of a court is based exclusively on the analysis of the legal documents relevant for the judged case [3, p. 41]. We analyzed, how judges and lawyers are supposed to analyze a law, based upon legal literature research. These insights lead to a basic structure of laws which we used to create law patterns.

First of all a law is a textual document. This law document is structured into *sections*. Each section defines a legal aspect of the law and contains several statements. These statements are *dictates of justice*, so-called *legal rules* [4, p. 240]. There are different types of dictates of justice. Complete and self-containing dictates of justice are one type. This type is the fundamental building block of every law [4, p. 241]. We derived the following structure of complete and self-containing dictates of justice. A * next to an element of the structure means the element is optional.

Addressee(s) describe(s) actions that an addressee has to follow or avoid
Facts of the case
    Activity(ies) describe(s) actions that an addressee has to follow or avoid to be compliant.
    Target subject(s)* describes impersonal subjects that are objectives of the activity(ies).Subjects can be material, such as a product, or immaterial, such as information.
    Target person(s)* are directly influenced by the activity(ies) of an addressee, or have a relation to the target subject(s).

Legal consequence defines the consequence for an addressee, e.g. the punishment when violating the section.

A dictate of justice is divided into the *facts of the case*, the setting which is regulated, and the *legal consequence*, the resulting implications of the setting [5, p. 7]. Furthermore, a dictate of justice has also an *addressee(s)*. The reason is that every complete dictate of justice is an *imperative*, or can be transformed into an imperative [4, p. 243-44], and an imperative has to be directed towards an addressee(s) [3, p. 3-4].

The facts of the case need to be further refined to be useful for a pattern. The legal method called *subsumption* contains a further refinement of the facts of the case [4, p. 260-64]. This refinement results in the basic elements *activities*, *target subjects*, and *target persons* [5, p. 23-31]. Lawyers use the subsumption to analyze if a dictate of justice is applicable to a specific case. The case is described in terms and notions. Lawyers map these to the notions and terms describing the basic elements [3, p. 52-53]. If not all terms and notions of the case can be mapped to basic elements, the dictate of justice is not relevant for the case.

A mapping between all terms and notions of the case and the basic elements is not sufficient to prove the relevance of a dictate of justice for a case. The reason is that the facts of the case of the dictate of justice can contain an element that has no mapping to a term or notion of the specific case. The subsumption solely considers a mapping from the term or notion of the specific case to the dictate of justice. The other direction is not considered. Moreover, such an element has the potential to prove that the law is not relevant for the specific case. The subsumption provides this gap intentionally, because the mapping of specific cases to laws is based upon human interpretation.

Besides the complete, self-containing dictates there are [4, p. 247-251] *definition dictates* that describe and refine terms and other basic elements, *restricting dictates*, which add exceptions to a complete dictate, *directing dictates*, which reference one or more other dictates, and *fiction dictates*, which equate different facts of the case.

These dictates cannot be analyzed in isolation. All of them have relations to other dictates (or even laws). The types of relation between these dictates are *refinement*, *addition*, and *constraint*. This implies that all of resulting dictates and laws, and the relations between them, have to be considered when analyzing laws. A *regulation* is the set of rules applicable to a specific case [4, p. 254].

Thus, relations between laws, sections and dictates of justice are of fundamental importance. They are arranged in a hierarchy, which is not always free of conflicts [4, p. 255]. A special part of these relations is the terminology used within a jurisdiction. This terminology is organized as hierarchical tree where the terms and notions of the more general dictates of justices are refined by subsequent dictates of justice.

2.2   A Process for Identifying Relevant Laws

Our general process for identifying relevant laws consists of five steps. For this process law experts and software engineers have to work together for the necessary knowledge transfer. Step one can be done alone by legal experts and for step two only software engineers are needed. But in step three and four both groups are needed to bridge the gap between legal and technical world. The last step can be accomplished alone by legal experts.

Step 1: Law Pattern. Based on the previously discussed structure of laws, we define a *law pattern* shown on the upper left-hand side of Fig. 1. The pattern consists of three parts: the dark grey part represents the Law Structure, the light gray part depicts the Classification to consider the specialization of the elements contained in the Law Structure in related laws or sections, and the white part considers the Context. We organize the mentioned hierarchies by Person Classifier, Activity Classifier, and Subject Classifier using *hierarchies*. Figure 2 shows example instances for all three hierarchies according to BDSG. The Context part of the law pattern contains the Legislator(s) defining the jurisdiction, and the Domain(s) clarifying for which domain the law was established.

As it is necessary to know in which context and relation a law is used, we introduce Regulation(s), which are Related To the section at hand. Regulation(s), Legislator(s), and Domain(s) can be ordered in hierarchies, similar to classifiers. For instance, Germany is part of the EU and consists of several states.

We now describe the instantiation process for our law pattern using Section 4b BDSG as an example. We explained the importance of this particular law in Sect. 1. Section 4b BDSG regulates the abroad transfer of data. The resulting instance is shown on the right-hand side of Fig. 1. Our process starts based on the first sections of the law to be analyzed. These sections are self-contained, i.e. they define all necessary elements of our Law Structure. Additionally, the Legislator(s) and Domain(s) can be instantiated according to the considered law (e.g. Germany and General Public in the Context part). Given a section of a law not yet captured by our law pattern, we identify and document the related laws and sections referred to by the given section (e.g. BDSG Sec. 1 in the Context part). Then, we search for the Law Structure directly defined in this section. In Section 4b BDSG, we find Abroad Transfer, and we use it to instantiate Activity(ies). Addressee(s), Target Subject(s), and Target Person(s) are not defined in Section 4b

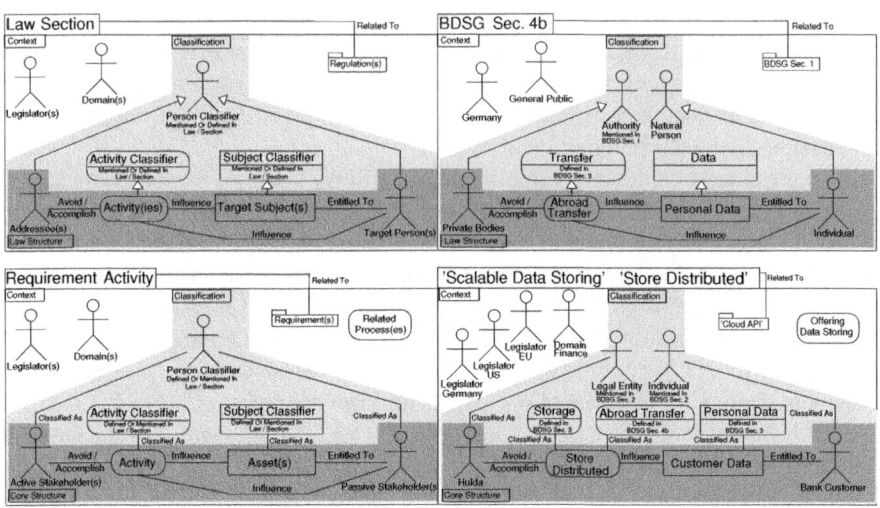

Fig. 1. Law Pattern (upper left) and Instance (upper right), Law Identification Pattern (lower left) and Instance (lower right)

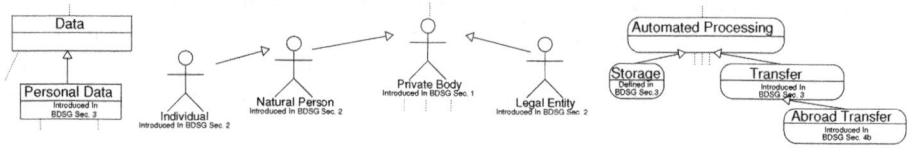

Fig. 2. Examples for Person (left), Subject (middle), and Activity (right) Hierarchies

BDSG. Therefore, related sections defining these terms have to be discovered. In our example, we find Private Bodies for the Addressee(s), Personal Data for the Target Subject(s), and Individual for the Target Person(s) in Section 1 BDSG (according to BDSG Sec. 1 in the Context part). We arrange these specializations in the appropriate parts of the hierarchies in Fig. 2. The classifier is instantiated with the parent node of the corresponding hierarchy, which is for instance Transfer for Abroad Transfer.

Step 2: Law Identification Pattern. Identifying relevant laws based on functional requirements is difficult, because functional requirements are usually too imprecise, they contain important information only implicitly and use a different wording than in laws. To bridge between gap of the wording and to facilitate the discussion between requirements engineers and legal experts, we define a *law identification pattern* to support identifying relevant laws

Figure 1 shows on the lower left-hand side our law identification pattern. The structure is similar to the law pattern on the upper left side of Fig. 1 to allow a matching of instances of both patterns. In contrast to the legal vocabulary used in the Law Structure of our law pattern, the wording for the elements in the dark gray colored Core Structure of our law identification pattern is based on terms known from requirements engineering. For example, the element Asset(s) in our law identification pattern represents the element Target Subject(s) in our law pattern.

Our law identification pattern takes into account that requirements are often interdependent (Requirement(s) in the Context part). Given a law relevant to a requirement, the same law might be relevant to the dependent requirements, too. Furthermore, the pattern helps to document similar dependencies for a given Activity using the Related Process(es) in the Context part.

As our example on the lower right-hand side of Fig. 1 shows, we select Hulda as the cloud provider, then we choose the functional requirement Scalable Data Storing. One of the activities associated with this requirement is the activity Store Distributed , which refers to the asset Customer Data of the Bank Customer. Moreover, we instantiate the elements Legislator(s) and Domain(s). In our example on the lower right side of Fig. 1, we include the legislators Germany, US, EU, and the domain Finance. In addition, we discover the related requirement Cloud API and the process Offering Data Storing, and document them in the instance of our law identification pattern.

Step 3: Establishing the Relation between Laws and Requirements. To instantiate the Classification part, legal expertise is necessary. According to the Core Structure of the instance of our law identification pattern and the hierarchies built when instantiating our law pattern, legal experts classify the elements of the Core Structure. For example, the activity Store Distributed is classified as Abroad Transfer based on a discussion between the legal experts and software engineers.

Step 4: Deriving Relevant Laws. The identification of relevant laws is based on matching the classification part of the law identification pattern instance (light gray part) with the law structure and classification part of the law pattern instance (light and dark gray parts), and thereby considering the previously documented hierarchies. If all elements match, the law is identified as relevant. For example, we find direct matches in the law pattern instance depicted on right side of Fig. 1 for the elements Abroad Transfer, Personal Data, and Individual contained in the law identification pattern instance shown on the lower right side of Fig. 1. Hulda is classified as Legal Entity and the only element that does not directly match with Private Bodies in the law structure of Section 4b BDSG. In this case, the hierarchy in Fig. 2 helps to identify that Legal Entity is a specialization of Private Bodies, and thus, we identify Section 4b BDSG as relevant.

Finally, we check for all laws identified to be relevant if Legislator(s) and Domain(s) are mutually exclusive. In our example, the legislator Germany contained in Context of the law pattern instance depicted on lower right side of Fig. 1 can be found in Context of the law identification pattern instance shown on the lower right side of Fig. 1. The domain General Public in the law pattern instance can be considered as a generalization of the domain Finance in the law identification pattern instance. The resulting set of laws relevant for the given development problem serves as an input for the next step.

Step 5: This last step covers the identification and specification of requirements based on laws identified to be relevant by our approach, e.g. using existing approaches such as the one from Breaux et al. [6].

3   Related Work

Breaux et al. [6] present a framework that covers analyzing the structure of laws using a natural language pattern. This pattern helps to translate laws into a more structured The approach has some drawbacks of formal logic analysis of laws we will discuss later.

Siena et al. [7] describe the differences between legal concepts and requirements. The resulting process to align legal concepts to requirements and the given concepts are quite high level and cannot directly be applied to a scenario. In contrast to our approach they do not identify relevant laws and do not intertwine compliance regulations with already elicited requirements.

Álvarez et al. [8] describe reusable legal requirements in natural language. We believe that the work by Álvarez et al. complements our work, i.e., applying our law identification method can precede using their security requirements templates.

4   Conclusions

We presented a *pattern-based method for identifying and analyzing laws*, which can be embedded in common system and software development processes. The novelty about our approach is that we analyzed common methods lawyers use to identify and analyze laws. We captured this knowledge in patterns. We derived this pattern-based approach from the subsumption method, while other approaches use formal logic to formalize and analyze laws. Logic-based approaches seem to be more precise. However, legislators formulate laws imprecise by design [4,3,5, p. 298-99, p. 36-39, p. 32-33]. Hence, we decided to capture the modus operandi from lawyers in a pattern-based method. Biagioli et al. investigated Italian law and derived also a structure of dictates of justice, which is very similar to the structure presented in this work. [1, p. 247]. Thus, it is likely that the pattern is also applicable to further laws in the tradition of the Roman jurisdiction. The case law system, in the US or Great Britain, is another important legal system. We plan to adapt our method for the case law system, via case patterns that extend law patterns. We also aim to work on tool support for our approach, e.g. to store, load, and search for laws once they have been fitted to our law patterns. The tool support will be used for validation of our method. We are planning to use our approach on the entire BDSG, which has 48 sections.About 40 of them have to be modeled, as some sections were invalidated or definition sections. We estimate that around 6 pattern are required per section on average, making 240 instances in total. On the other hand we will make use of a small real life example with about 50 requirements. So about 50 law identification pattern will be instantiated and matched.

Acknowledgements. We thank Maritta Heisel and Christoph Sorge for their extensive and valuable feedback on our work.

References

1. Biagioli, C., Mariani, P., Tiscornia, D.: Esplex: A rule and conceptual model for representing statutes. In: Proceedings of the 1st International Conference on Artificial Intelligence and Law, ICAIL 1987, pp. 240–251. ACM (1987)
2. Otto, P.N., Antón, A.I.: Addressing legal requirements in requirements engineering. In: Proceedings of the International Conference on Requirements Engineering (RE), pp. 5–14. IEEE Computer Society (2007)
3. Schwacke, P.: Juristische Methodik mit Technik der Fallbearbeitung, 4th edn. Kohlhammer Deutscher, Gemeindeverlag (2003)
4. Larenz, K.: Methodenlehre der Rechtswissenschaft, 5th edn. Springer, Heidelberg (1983)
5. Beaucamp, G., Treder, L.: Methoden und Techniken der Rechtsanwendung, 2nd edn. C.F.Müller (2011)
6. Breaux, T.D., Antón, A.I.: Analyzing regulatory rules for privacy and security requirements. IEEE Transactions on Software Engineering 34(1), 5–20 (2008)
7. Siena, A., Perini, A., Susi, A.: From laws to requirements. In: Proceedings of the International Workshop on Requirements Engineering and Law (RELAW), pp. 6–10. IEEE Computer Society (2008)
8. Álvarez, J.A.T., Olmos, A., Piattini, M.: Legal requirements reuse: A critical success factor for requirements quality and personal data protection. In: Proceedings of the International Conference on Requirements Engineering (RE), pp. 95–103. IEEE Computer Society (2002)

Towards a Requirements Modeling Language for Self-Adaptive Systems

Nauman A. Qureshi[1], Ivan J. Jureta[2], and Anna Perini[1]

[1] Fondazione Bruno Kessler - CIT, Software Engineering Research Group
Via Sommarive, 18, 38050 Trento, Italy
{qureshi,perini}@fbk.eu
[2] FNRS & Louvain School of Management,
University of Namur, Belgium
ivan.jureta@fundp.ac.be

Abstract. **[Context and motivation]** Self-adaptive systems (SAS) monitor and adapt to changing end-user requirements, operating context conditions, and resource availability. Specifying requirements for such dynamic systems is not trivial. Most of the research on self-adaptive systems (SAS) focuses on finding solutions to the requirements that SAS is built for. However, elicitation and representation of requirements for SAS has received less attention at early stages of requirements engineering (RE). **[Question/problem]** How to represent requirements for SAS in a way which can be read by non-engineering stakeholders? **[Principal ideas/results]** A requirements modeling language with a diagrammatic syntax to be used to elicit and represent requirements for SAS and perform analysis based on our recently proposed core ontology to perform RE for SAS. **[Contribution]** A modeling language, called Adaptive RML, for the representation of early requirements for Self-adaptive systems (SAS). The language has graphical primitives in line with classical goal modeling languages and is formalized via a mapping to Techne. Early validation is performed by modeling the same case study in an established goal modeling language and in Adaptive RML. The results suggest that context and resource concepts, as well as relegation and influence relations should be part of graphical modeling languages used to make early requirements models for SAS and to perform analysis over them.

Keywords: Requirements Engineering, Requirements Modeling, Self-Adaptive Systems.

1 Introduction

A self-adaptive system (SAS) can change its behavior in response to anticipated and unanticipated variations in its operating context, its users' requirements, and the availability of its resources. Requirements engineering (RE) for SAS is receiving increasing attention in research and has been recognized as one of the key areas where progress is needed in order to enable the engineering of SAS [1].

Initial work on high-variability design in [2] models variability in user's goals and alternatives for goal achievement, which is reflected in the design and coding of Belief-Desire-Intention (BDI) agents. This work provided a basis to extend *Tropos* for adaptive

B. Regnell and D. Damian (Eds.): REFSQ 2012, LNCS 7195, pp. 263–279, 2012.

systems [3], where design abstraction like goal-conditions and environment modeling are added to *Tropos* goal models and correspondingly a mapping is provided to Jadex BDI architecture. This approach is confined to the design of adaptive BDI agents and requires fine grained knowledge about the domain to specify the alternative solutions and goal achievement conditions enabling the agent to switch its behavior in a given environment.

In [4], Whittle et al. proposed a language to represent uncertainty in requirements via fuzzy operators and using Fuzzy Branching Temporal logic as the underlying framework. In the context of KAOS [5], mitigation strategies are proposed to accommodate uncertainty and failures with obstacle analysis [6]. We proposed to engineer *adaptive requirements* using goal models and ontologies to make explicit the domain assumptions and requirements for feedback loop functions (i.e. monitoring, evaluation criteria, and adaptation alternative) [7]. Similar ideas were adopted by Baresi et al. [8] to extend KAOS goal models. The concept of *adaptive goals* has been introduced to specify adaptation strategies, while qualitative goals are relaxed by being replaced with fuzzy goals, the satisfaction of the former being binary, while the latter are associated to a continuous fuzzy membership function, the value of which is interpreted as the level of satisfaction of the fuzzy goal.

Ongoing research has also recognized the need to ensure that SAS have a runtime representation of their own requirements, i.e., that requirements should become artifact used, processed, and changed at runtime [7–10]. Considerable part of current research into the RE for SAS focuses on the specification of requirements for SAS, while there is comparatively less interest in what information should be part of *early* requirements models for SAS. In particular, how should early requirements models reflect (i) that there is uncertainty in the behavior and properties of the operating context and of the SAS, (ii) that the context of the SAS can vary and that this should influence the behavior of the SAS, and (iii) that resources of the SAS may vary, and that the SAS should adapt to those variables.

In our view, this requirements problem in case of SAS should be treated as a *dynamic RE problem*, where changes in requirements, contexts and resources lead to a new requirements problem – finding new candidate solutions to the changed requirements [11]. To fulfill this aim, we build on the core ontology for RE [12] and introduce two new concepts i.e. context and resource as well as two new relations, relegation and influence, formalized using Techne expressions [13] that are helpful in the early phases of RE to formulate the requirements problem for a SAS.

Based on this, we introduce here a new modeling language for early requirements for SAS, called *Adaptive RML*, to model the dynamic RE problem and perform analysis by finding candidate solutions. The aim of this paper is to introduce Adaptive RML, its concepts, relations, modeling guidelines and analysis features needed for early RE for SAS. This is a first attempt to provide a concrete RML for early RE that provides the necessary concepts and relations to model requirements for SAS and enables the analyst to perform analysis about the candidate solutions as function of contexts, where not only the conditions or resource demand changes but also the requirements problem changes. We motivate the need for Adaptive RML to model requirements for SAS using an example from a travel domain. As a preliminary validation, we model the example

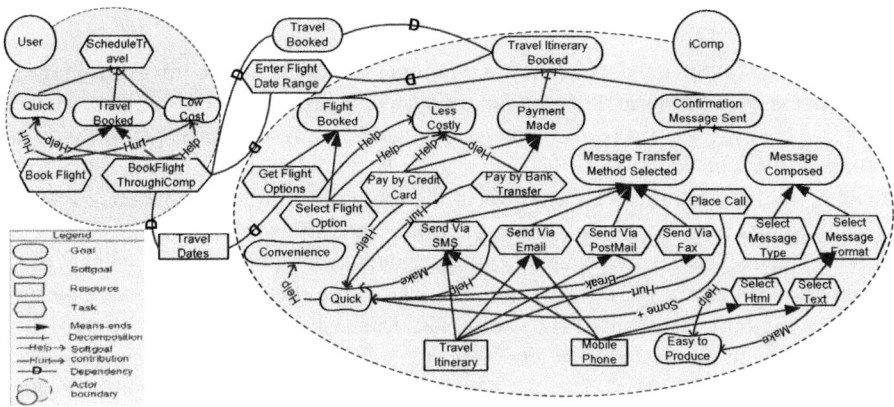

Fig. 1. Requirements Modeling using iStar Concepts and Relations only

first with *i** [14], identify the information needed for early RE of SAS and that cannot be modeled in *i**, then introduce Adaptive RML. In fact, we adopt *i** at this stage of the work due to its wide adoption in requirements modeling and to make Adaptive RML accessible to researchers using *i**.

The rest of the paper is organized as follows. Section 2 introduces the example modeled with *i**, and compares it with the same example in Adaptive RML. Section 3 presents Adaptive RML. Section 4 discusses Adaptive RML in light of related work. Section 5 summarizes conclusions and directions for future work.

2   Modeling the Requirements of *iComp*

In this section, we focus on a simple scenario for a travel booking application. We model it with the *i** requirements modeling language and identify key elements that are missing in this language for modeling requirements for SAS. We describe an excerpt of a scenario from a travel companion case study introduced in our prior work [7], in which self-adaptive properties of the system are illustrated.

Scenario: *The iComp application is a self-adaptive system that aids business travelers while on the move. It supports them in booking their travels, making payment and receiving timely updated information about their booking confirmation (e.g., confirmed, canceled, in progress). The booking confirmation messages must be sent to the user (customer) via Email or SMS instantly (in less than an hour or maximum less than 1 day) on their device (i.e. laptop or mobile) and depending on their context (e.g. home). Payment must be ensured before iComp sends the message (i.e. composing the message) by selecting a suitable message format (e.g., size, scaling, format) to adapt to the device from which they will be read. Finally, in case there are some problems (i.e. user is not accessible) and the message cannot be delivered to the user then iComp must send the message to an alternative recipient (e.g., the customer's secretary).*

2.1   Requirements Modeling with i*

Fig. 1 shows *i** strategic dependency and rationales models for the travel booking scenario. In the main scenario, the user and the system are represented by circles, whereby
the content of the dashed ovals (strategic rationales) represents their goals, tasks, and
resources. We can see in this model that what leads the user to chose the iComp for
travel booking results from the analysis of the root task of Schedule Travel, which
is decomposed into the goal of Travel Booked and the softgoals of Low Cost and
Quick. These softgoals are negatively influenced (shown with contribution links) by the
subtask of BookFlight. The task Book Flight through iComp, however, partially
satisfices the Low Cost and Quick softgoals. This task in turn depends on the iComp
Actor, since the associated goal Travel Itinerary Booked has been assigned to
the system.

The strategic rationale model of iComp reveals a decomposition of goal Travel
Itinerary Booked into three main goals Flight Booked, Payment Made -
and Confirmation Message Sent. For example, we can now reason about
Confirmation Message Sent, which is decomposed into two goals i.e. goals:
Message Transfer Method Selected and Message Composed. Along their subsequent means of accomplishing tasks, and assess their contributions towards softgoals
Quick and Easy to produce, which helps in ranking a particular solution. For example, tasks: Send via SMS and Send via Email with means to use resources:
Travel Itinerary and Mobile Phone contributes fully and partially to the softgoal Quick, which in turn satisfices softgoal Convenience. The aim of this analysis
is to identify one particular solution that satisfies the high level goals and optimally
satisfies the softgoals.

Modeling iComp in *i** lead us to identify some limitations of the language when
used for SAS. *i** does not provide concepts for the modeling of alternative solutions
to the requirements problem, which are feasible in different contexts. For instance,
in context (e.g. Home) the candidate solution should be *Send Message via Email* and
in another context, e.g. Market, *Send message via SMS* should be more appropriate in
case no 3G or no smartphone is available for the user, and so on. That is we were not
able to model the fact that the context of the user may change as well as resources
availability, and ultimately to capture monitoring conditions and evaluation criteria that
should characterize the dynamically adaptive behavior of the system. Moreover, in *i**,
it is not possible to model quality constraints, such as *send the message within one
hour after the payment*, and domain assumptions that need to be made explicit during
the analysis as they contribute to the definition of the requirement problem, such as
standard Credit Card Options must be Displayed.

Efforts has been made to capture requirements for SAS by extending *i**/*Tropos*
[3, 15]. The main idea behind these extensions is to annotate goal models. For instance,
in [3] goal achievements conditions and environment modeling (using UML class diagrams) is used to annotate the *i**/*Tropos* goal model, and transform them for use with
an implementation architecture (e.g. BDI). Similarly in [15] location abstraction is used
to formalize context and annotating the variation point (e.g. AND/OR decomposition)
within a goal model. This approach provides a systematic design-time approach to build
context models based on locations concepts (e.g. using UML class diagrams). Common

to both approaches is the use of UML notation to formalize the concept of environment and context hierarchies. Both approaches are focused on finding a single best solution in case of adaptation. Moreover, both of the approaches are limited to show how the system can move across contexts (with changing domain assumptions, resource availability) by altering the requirements problem with respect to the variety of candidate solutions.

2.2   Requirements Modeling with Adaptive RML

Differently from the previously mentioned extensions of goal-oriented modeling languages for SAS, we rest on Techne [13], an abstract modeling language for early requirements, which adopts the core ontology for RE [12]. This core ontology extends the goal-oriented perspective allowing to model optional requirements, preferences, and to treat non-functional requirements in terms of approximations and quality constraints. The basic elements of Techne models are requirements, modeled as natural language propositions that are labeled as domain assumptions, goals, quality constraints, or tasks. A requirement can be mandatory or optional. Links between model elements are used to represent how the satisfaction of an element may impact the satisfaction of the other, through inference and conflict. Preferences are used to compare requirements in terms of desirability. Performing the analysis of a requirements problem specified in Techne, results in finding candidate solutions in terms of tasks and quality constraints that together satisfy all mandatory goals and cover, as much as possible, optional ones.

The proposed modeling language for SAS, called Adaptive RML, builds on Techne by adding two new concepts, namely, context and resource, and two relations, i.e. relegation and influence. Adaptive RML has its own visual notation. In the rest of this section we illustrate an Adaptive RML model of iComp with the aim to provide a preliminary qualitative evidence about its support in overcoming the limits mentioned above in modeling requirements for SAS. A detailed account of Adaptive RML will be given in the following sections.

Fig.2, shows a requirements model for iComp in Adaptive RML (in form of a Techne r-net). Its root level goal Travel Itinerary Booked is modeled as a mandatory node (*modeled as M node, a unary relationship*). It is decomposed via an a binary inference relation (*modeled as black I node with a arrow*) into the other mandatory goals: Flight Booked, Payment Made and Confirmation Message Sent, to represent the fact that it will be satisfied through the joint satisfaction of these three goals.

Let's focus on the goal: Confirmation Message Sent (i.e. the shaded part of the model), which is decomposed into two goals: Message Transfer Method Selected and Message Composed via inference relation. We can add here information that were missing in *i** model, i.e. the domain assumption Booking Confirmation is sent after the payment is assured (*modeled as rounded rectangle*) and the quality constraint Message sent in < 1 hour after the payment (*modeled as diamond shape*) connecting them through the same inference node.

An influence relation is added among the two decomposed goals: Message Transfer Method Selected and Message Composed (*modeled as dotted green line with arrowhead*) to account for the prevailing context conditions and resource

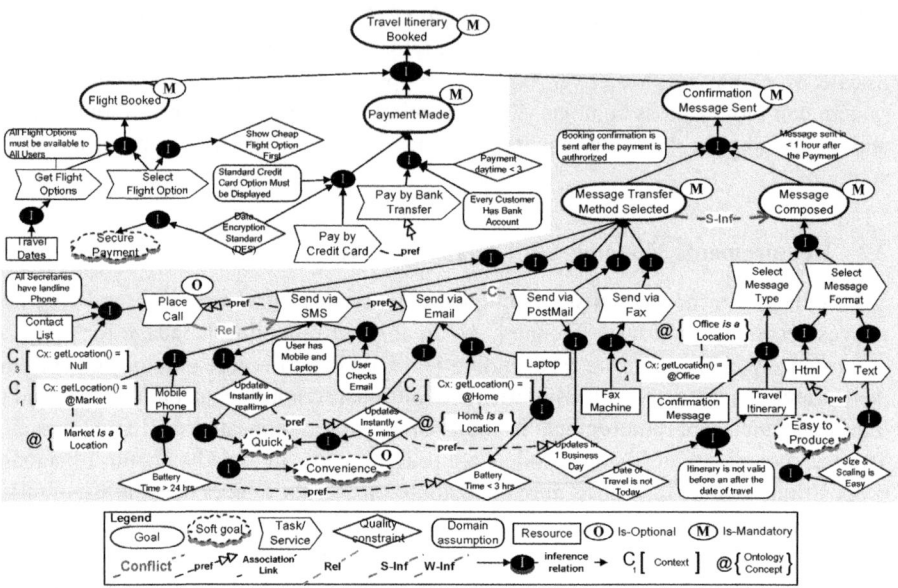

Fig. 2. Modeling using Adaptive RML Concepts and Relations

availability that influences the achievement of goal: `Message Composed`. For example, if the context conditions support to choose Email as a candidate transfer method, the ways to satisfy goal:`Message Composed` is by selection a correct format that is either text or html.

The analysis of the `Message Transfer Method Selected` proceeds by linking via inference nodes task-rooted subgraphs, which defines candidate solutions. Besides tasks e.g. `Send via SMS` (*modeled as hollow motion arrow*), each candidate solution includes domain assumptions e.g. `User has mobile and laptop`, context e.g. `Market`, `Home` (*labeled as C with its number, associated to @ symbol*[1]), and resources e.g. `Mobile Phone` (*modeled as a rectangle*). Preferences (*dotted line with doubled empty arrow heads*) are used to compare requirements in candidate solutions, and thereby compare candidate solutions; e.g., `Send via SMS` is preferred over `Send via Email`. Requirements can be in conflict (e.g. `Send via Email` is in conflict with `Send via PostMail`. *Conflict is shown as a dotted line with C in the middle with red color*). Here, conflict exist due to the difference in the quality constraints e.g. `email updates in < 5 mins`, whereas `post mail updates in 1 business day`. Notice that it was not possible to model these information with *i**.

Optional solutions, in case of problems (e.g. user is not accessible, as mentioned in the scenario) can be identified via a relegation relation (*drawn as dotted light red line with arrowhead* between two possible candidate solutions). For instance, `Place Call` relegates `Send via SMS`. This allows to take into account the situation in which a user's context changed resulting in being not accessible

---

[1] @ labels a concept defined in domain ontology e.g. travel.

(e.g. C3 [Cx:getLocation()= Null]), and to describe as preferred the solution to make the user able to access the resources Confirmation Message and Ticket Itinerary, via contacting her secretary. The Place Call task is inferred via a domain assumption (e.g. All secretaries has landline phone) and a resource (e.g. contact list) and the context (e.g. C3 [Cx:getLocation()= Null]).

Summary. Gain in expressiveness of Adaptive RML with respect to *i** models are summarized below:

- we can model information about context, resources and domain assumptions that need to be monitored by the SAS in order to enable adaptation;
- softgoals evaluation in *i** is subjective and provides no clear evidence to rank a solution. In Adaptive RML, candidate solutions can be ranked and evaluated via quality constraints over measurements that may be collected by the SAS;
- candidate solutions can be associated with contexts and requires resource.

3   Definition of Adaptive RML

3.1   Concepts and Relations

We define the concepts and relationships in order to formulate the requirements problem for SAS. Addition of these concepts and relations leads us to an ontology for requirements in SAS and the formulation of the *runtime requirements adaptation problem* as a dynamic problem of changing (e.g. switching, re-configuring, optimizing) the SAS from one requirements problem to another requirements problem, whereby the changing is due to change in requirements, context conditions, and/or resource availability [11]. We add two new concepts, Context and Resource as well as relations Relegation and Influence that enhance the tool set for the proposed Adaptive RML to model and analyze requirements for SAS.

Context: This concept allows modeling information that the stakeholders assume to hold when they communicate particular requirements. We say that every requirement depends on one or more contexts to express the fact that the requirement would not be retracted by the stakeholders in every one of these contexts. This information needs to be made explicit in the early requirements model for SAS. For instance, in our example we modeled "context" as information about location (e.g. Office or Market), which are defined as concepts in a specific domain ontology (e.g. travel), and we linked them to tasks via an inference relation. In Fig.2, context is shown as e.g. "C1 [Cx:getLocation()= @Market]" where "@Market" is an instance of a concept term (i.e. Location) defined in a domain ontology. Combining requirements and context reveals interesting cases, where we can see requirements maybe in conflict.

Resource: The concept of resource has been well supported in RE methods such as in goal-oriented approaches [2, 5, 14]. In our case, we define it as an entity that is referred to by the requirements, e.g., physical/tangible entities such as mobile phone, ticket itinerary; e.g., intangible entities, such as user assets (social relations or contacts). In order to introduce resources in the definition of the requirements adaptation problem for SAS, we need to elicit a resource availability function that tells us which resources

Visual Notation	Concepts & Relations
Goal	**Definition:** A **Goal** represents a desired state of affairs, the achievement of which can be measured and is definitively concluded. **Example:** *"Meeting to be Scheduled"*
Soft goal	**Definition:** A **Soft goal** represents a desired state of affairs, the achievement of which can only be estimated, not definitively concluded. **Example:** *"Convenience"*, *"Easy"*
Task/ service	**Definition:** A **Task** corresponds to an activity, an action whose achievement leads to the definitive conclusion of its means. **Example:** *"Download music"*, *"Show song listed as most viewed"*
Quality constraint	**Definition:** A **Quality constraint** is desired value of non-binary measurable properties of the system-to-be that constrains a goal or a soft goal. **Example:** *"Music download speed must not be less than 128kbps/sec"*
Domain assumption	**Definition:** A **Domain assumption** is a condition within which the system-to-be will be performing tasks in order to achieve the goals, quality constraints, and satisfy as best as feasible the soft goals. **Example:** *"Subscribers can download the music from the online database"*
inference relation	**Definition:** An **<Inference> relation** stands between a requirement that is the immediate consequence of another set of requirements, the former is called the conclusion, the latter the premises. Alternatively, inference relation can be used to connect the refined requirement to the requirements that refine it. **Example:** *"Generate revenue from the audio player"* has <inference> relation with two requirements: *"Music is available to subscribers"*, *"Display ads in the player"*.
---Conflict---	**Definition:** A **<Conflict> relation** stands between all members (two or more) of a minimally inconsistent set of requirements. **Example:** *"Req1: Music is available to subscribers"* is in <Conflict> with *"Req2: Music is available to users"*
---pref--⟫	**Definition:** A **<Preference>** is a binary relation that exists between two requirements and it defines the stakeholder evaluations of requirements that determine the desirability of a requirement. **Example:** *"The bitrate of music delivered via the online audio player should be at least 256kb/s"* is <Preferred> over *"the bitrate of music delivered via the online audio player should be at least 128kb/s"*
(O) Is-Optional	**Definition:** An **<is-Optional> relation** is unary that states the evaluation of stakeholder of requirement, which may be desirable. Functional requirements, which are "nice to have". **Example:** *"Color printing of a meeting schedule"* <is-Optional>.
(M) Is-Mandatory	**Definition:** An **<is-Mandatory> relation** is unary that states the evaluation of stakeholder of requirement, which must be satisfied. Functional requirements. **Example:** *"Each Participant must have meeting schedule available"* <is-Mandatory>.
Association Link	**Definition:** An **<Association> link** is used to define a link between two elements. **Example:** *"High level Context (e.g. Outdoor)"* is <associated> to *"an ontology concept (e.g. place)"*.
Relegation Relation	**Definition:** A **<Relegation> relation** is n-array relation that stands between one or more requirements, to relax or to suspend conditions imposed over them. A mandatory requirement can have a <relegation> relation with an optional requirement. **Example:** *"download the music"* has <Relegation> relation with the *"stream the song online"*.
—Weak-Influence— —Strong-Influence—	**Definition:** An **<Influence> relation** is said to exist between a set of requirements, where satisfaction of one requirement warrants the satisfaction of the other. This determines the satisfaction of the requirements set. There are two types, weak-influence (where partial satisfaction is possible) and strong-influence (when there is no way to satisfy the requirement). **Example:** *"subscribe and pay"* have <Strong-Influence> over the *"download the music"*. *"subscribe and make payment"* have <weak-Influence> over the *"listen music online"*
Resource	**Definition:** A **Resource** is an entity either tangible or intangible referred to by one or more instances of the information communicated during elicitation by the stakeholder. **Example:** Tangible Resource: *"Physical e.g. Mobile phone"* Intangible Resource: *"Data e.g. Agenda"*
—Requires→	**Definition:** A **<Requires> relation** is a binary relation that exists between a task and a resource. **Example:** *"Task: Download song"* <requires> *"Resource: internet connection"*
C_1 [Context]	**Definition:** A **Context** is defined as a set of information (condition) that is presupposed (or believed to be true) by the stakeholders to hold when they communicate a particular requirements. **Example:** *"System states (e.g. searching a song)"*, *"User states (e.g. Listening to music)"*, *"User Location (e.g. at home)"*, *"Device Status (e.g. Battery is low)"*
@ { Ontology Concept }	**Definition:** An **Ontology Concept** defines an entity and its characteristics or essential features in a particular domain of discourse. **Example:** *"Frame rate in Music Ontology"*

Fig. 3. Visual guide for concepts and relations in Adaptive RML

are available and used in some way, in order to ensure that the relevant domain assumptions and context propositions hold, and that the tasks can be executed. Here again we may exploit ontology definitions of user-assets and asset modifiers that represents tasks effects on their resources, as proposed in [16]. In the modeled example shown in Fig.2, we introduced "Mobile Phone" and "Laptop" as resources available in different contexts.

Relegation Relation: The purpose of the Relegation relation (Rel for short) is twofold. First, it facilitates engineer at design-time to analyze requirements (including goals, quality constraints, preferences) and relegate their associated conditions (e.g. pre/post, achievement, trigger conditions) by anticipating runtime change scenarios. Secondly, it enables SAS at runtime to analyze requirements problem in case of changes that can occur dynamically e.g. change in user's context, violation of domain assumption, resource usage or change in user's need or preference, either through sensing the operational environment or explicitly given by the end-user.

A Rel is applied to manage unanticipated events, by flexibly relegating some of the requirements, with the aim to avoid failure in achieving the critical ones. In this case by applying Rel, either the solution that operationalizes a goal needs to be replaced, or an instance of the same goal with revised conditions is linked using Rel with the original goal e.g. in Fig.2, candidate solution "Send via SMS" is relegated by "Place Call", when context conditions changes. In this example, the instance of the original goal is not compromised rather relegation is considered by replacing the preferred solution with an optional solution.

Influence Relation: An influence relation (Inf) is introduced to analyze the impact of changes in model elements that define different, mutual dependent requirements. This means, if change in the operational environment or in end-user requirements happens at runtime it might cause a change in another requirement. This chain of dependency needs to be identified, since along them we may identify changes consequences such as violation of a goal or a invalid solutions. For example, in Fig.2, if no candidate solution is possible to achieve the goal "Message Transfer Method Selected" due to invalid context and domain conditions, then this goal will fail, which causes a violation in satisfying the corresponding goal i.e. "Message Composed". Similar dependencies can be collected and subsequent consequences are determined by analyzing the impact of changed solution.

3.2 Adaptive RML Visual Notations

The Adaptive RML language provides a graphical notation, which is in line with classical goal modeling languages and is formalized via a mapping to Techne. A detailed guide on visual elements is presented in the Table shown in Fig. 3: each row contains a graphical symbol and a short description of it's intended meaning. For the elements that map the Techne core ontology, the corresponding semantics is given in [13], while the formal semantic of the additional concepts is defined in [11].

Worth to be mentioned is that recent research evaluated weaknesses of widely used goal-oriented modeling notations with respect to principles for cognitively effective visual notations [17]. The proposed visual notation considers two among the principles discussed in [17]. The first is visual expressiveness: notation must comprise of color, shape and brightness instead of shape only. Second is Semiotic clarity, which postulates that each graphical symbol must have a 1:1 correspondence with its semantic definition. Our proposed notation takes as much as possible these principles into account, but further effort is needed to fit with the proposed recommendation for improving usability and communicative effectiveness of visual notations in RE modeling.

3.3   Modeling in Adaptive RML

Modeling requirements in Adaptive RML enables the analyst to construct the requirements model by recording and structuring relevant information obtained through elicitation. As a result, the runtime requirements adaptation problem is formulated for the SAS-to-be. New pieces of information are gathered during modeling time to refine the problem iteratively. At analysis time, all candidate solutions to that problem are sought along with their differences to each other and are compared with respect to varying context situations and resource availability.

The modeling process develops by performing iterations of the following activities.

1- Modeling Mandatory and Optional Goals:

We start modeling goals, optative statements that defines the desired properties of the SAS-to-be, via inference relation (i.e. symbol (I)). We use (I) node to depict refinements (e.g. AND/OR decomposition, or means-end relation). Each (I) node connects the model element to be refined to simpler or more concrete elements that refine it. In this way it is concluded that if the requirements defined by the concrete elements are satisfied then the more abstract one will be achieved. Further, we add softgoals vague properties of SAS-to-be, which are approximated in terms of quality constraints that determines the criteria to measure them. Goals can be either mandatory or optional (i.e. (M)) or (O) respectively), we model this by adding these unary relation over goals.

2- Modeling Domain Assumptions:

While modeling goals we discover domain assumptions that are statements in the domain which are assumed to be always true. We add them via (I) node and add (if any) to each goals. Subsequently, during refinement, quality constraints can be inferred. We add criteria to measure the goal satisfaction via (I) node. During this, new pieces of information are discovered such as conflicts and preferences among the goals.

3- Modeling Conflicts and Preference Relations:

Conflicts and preferences are identified during refinement. We discover conflicts between inconsistent / contradictory requirements or tasks node between conflicting set of requirements / tasks. Further, we identify preferences taking into account stakeholder's evaluations about different requirements. We add preference relation between requirements where satisfying one is strictly more desirable than satisfying the other.

4- Modeling Mandatory or Optional Tasks:

Likewise, we model tasks as further refinement of goals. Task modeling can be seen as an analysis activity, where we add tasks via (I) node to operationalize goal. This means, if the tasks will be successfully completed, the goal will be achieved.

5- Modeling Context and Resources:

Once the requirements model is constructed, we further anticipate the various situations in which requirements or tasks can be either achieved or not. We add *context* node to each requirement/task. Context refers to any information, which is presupposed by the stakeholder and we make it explicit, e.g. a location etc.. A domain ontology compliments this context information by precisely defining the terms (instances of context). We link context with an ontology annotation (shown as @) via an association link.

While discovering tasks and context that can satisfy requirements, we may also identify **resources** that the tasks need to use. We add *resource* node via (I) node with each task. Note that resource concept is also available in other RML, however, we distinguish it as not only tangible e.g. mobile phone, Fax machine, but also intangible e.g. assets such as money, time, agenda. In our model, each resource may have domain assumptions or quality constraint attached to it via (I) node.

6- Modeling Influence and Relegation Relations:

Finally, identify during refinement requirements/tasks may have influence on the achievement of each other. *Influence relation* is added between a set of requirements/task, where the achievement of the former becomes critical due to the achievement of others (strong influence i.e. s-inf). If achievement of the latter is not critical, it will be modeled as weak (w-inf). However, it becomes interesting in case of tasks, where execution of one tasks may have influence of other tasks.

Finally, we look for conflicting context conditions, resource availabilities, quality criteria which may helps to determine requirements/tasks whose achievement can be delayed or relaxed. We add *relegation relation* between requirements/task that are less critical to the requirements/task more critical/preferred to in corporate uncertainty about changes in context or resource availability.

3.4 Towards Detailed Specification Analysis

Analysis in Adaptive RML suggests which candidate solutions are relevant in the prevailing context conditions and resource availability. A requirements model defines the requirements problem for a SAS-to-be, along with candidate solutions. This model is used by the analyst to discover *adaptive requirements* by looking at differences between candidates solutions that are modeled.

Adaptive requirements are requirements that not only hold the definition of functional or non-functional requirements but encompass the notion of variability, by having monitoring specification, evaluation criteria and adaptation alternatives. To discover them detailed analysis is performed on the available information represented in the early requirements model. We analyze the candidate solutions that remain valid in a particular situation. We look at the context nodes and domain assumptions, we anticipate changes as we move to a different context and this leads to different resource availability requirements. Alternative solutions can be inferred during this process.

Adaptive requirements help specifying alternative ways to adapt to context and resource changes via a pattern, details of which are out of the scope of this paper. Consider, while monitoring runtime changes, SAS moves across different contexts by altering the requirements problem that leads to change in candidate solutions. At runtime, several solutions get activated based on context and based on resource availability. Mechanisms for adaptation are triggered, therefore, reasoning over the adaptive requirement leads SAS moves (i.e. enact adaptation) to the candidate solution which is appropriate to the new current context.

For example, an adaptive requirement can be defined as **AR1:** *Message must be composed by selecting an appropriate format*. From this we determine that appropriate format i.e. HTML or Text, needs to be selected as modeled in Fig.2. But to select the candidate solution, we need to *monitor* the user's context (e.g. Office, Home) and resources (e.g. Mobile phone or Laptop) and domain assumptions with quality preferences. Along monitoring specification, we need also to specify *evaluation criteria* to check the difference between two tasks. Based on this criteria, among the possible candidate solutions that are adaptation actions *e.g. tasks and domain assumptions in a context*, a possible candidate solution will be selected. For instance, while monitoring the user context, resource, any change can lead to change the selected format, i.e. either html or text format.

So far, we argued on the need of a requirements modeling language (RML) for SAS that enable the analyst to capture and analyze requirements for SAS by incorporating the above core properties of SAS at early stages of RE. Below we present how the SAS at runtime tries to resolve a runtime requirements adaptation problem, by finding and comparing a candidate solution in response to changing context, resource variability using its own requirements model and detailed specification i.e. adaptive requirements.

3.5 Detailed Specification at Runtime

We recognize that in case of SAS, not all information can be collected, defined during requirements- or at design-time, but that this will depend at runtime when the system exploits its solutions implemented using different technologies (e.g. exploiting available services or agents). For example, any variation in the context and resource availability can be monitored or recorded by gathering the data through sensors, then matching patterns of data provides implications on the satisfaction of the goals. However, regardless of the technologies used, the SAS still needs to be designed to ensure the general conditions and relations that the requirements problem states: e.g., that the SAS needs an internal representation of information pertaining to contexts, domain assumptions, tasks, goals, and so on.

To give an intuition about how the adaptive requirements specification can support runtime adaptation, in Fig.4, an adaptation sequence is shown along the time dimension, where the SAS operates as per the candidate solution (S1) selected to satisfy the particular context and resource variation. At this time (t1) the SAS, while monitoring, evaluates the user's current situation and attempts to satisfy a given set of goals (e.g. *Confirmation Message Sent, Message Transfer Format Selected*) and quality constraints via its candidate solution. A candidate solution is composed of tasks, domain assumptions that hold valid for a context and available resources to achieve such tasks. E.g., candidate solution **S1**: *Context: (@Market), Resource: (Mobile Phone), Task: (Send via SMS), Domain Assumption: (All Users have Mobile Phone & Laptop)* was selected, but due to traveling, the context is not recognized anymore. Therefore the SAS has to reason about this change at time (t2) by looking at the difference in candidate solutions with respect to context conditions, resource availabilities and user preferences.

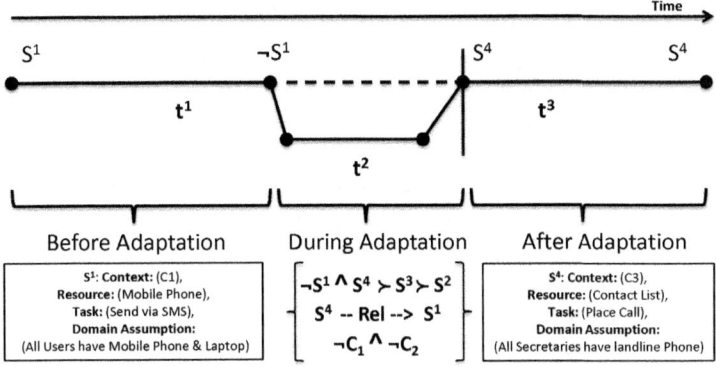

Fig. 4. Runtime Adaptation Sequence of SAS

SAS performs the reasoning based on the differences among the alternative candidate solutions, which states a comparison and ranking of the solutions based on criteria e.g. (S1) Send via SMS is not valid, (S2) Send via Email is not feasible as user's context is not recognized. Thus the change in requirements problem, changes the candidate solution in different contexts and with different resources. The adaptive requirements play critical role here, as they operationalize the mechanisms for adaptation i.e. monitor and evaluating the difference between candidate solutions and provides criteria to compare and rank them. To reason on adaptive requirements, automated reasoning techniques (e.g. AI Planning) can be employed. Discussion on such techniques is out of the scope of this paper.

Finally SAS selects a candidate solution e.g. "Place Call" by evaluating the relegation relation, specified earlier in the adaptive RML model and detailed in adaptive requirements e.g. $S4 \succ S3 \succ S2$. The new candidate solution **S4**: *Context: (Null), Resource: (Contact List), Task: (Place Call), Domain Assumption: (All Secretaries have landline Phone)*.

4   Discussion and Related Work

Advantages and open aspects of the proposed language are discussed with respect to state-of-art work and along well recognized issues in requirements modeling for SAS, which includes uncertainty about environment conditions and resource availability, context awareness and monitoring, requirements reflection and runtime reasoning. Adaptive RML provides visual notations to the concepts defined in the revised core ontology of RE for SAS. On the correctness of the concepts used to model requirements, we refer to the definitions in [11].

Systems that operate in an open environment, need to be able to manage uncertainty about environment conditions and resource availability. So for instance our system has to be designed in a way that it can communicate through SMS if the cell phone is on and connection is available, and if not, choose a different way to communicate. An attempt to address this problem at requirements time has been proposed within the RELAX framework [4], through the use of a language that provides three types of operators to handle uncertainty: temporal (e.g. eventually, until, as early as), ordinal (e.g. as close, as many), and modal (i.e. shall, may / or). The RELAX language semantics is formalized in Fuzzy Branching Temporal Logic. In [6], a set of analysis methods are then provided to support goal modeling refinement towards detailed design, which exploit mitigation strategies based on obstacle analysis, and lead eventually to relax constraining conditions (i.e. our quality conditions). Analogously, the approaches proposed in [3] and [8] propose interesting methods to deal with uncertainty at detailed design.

In Adaptive RML, we provide, the Relegate relation, which is more general than the RELAX operators [4], since we do not commit to fuzzy logic: we only ask for a way to represent alternatives and to compare them. In this sense, RELAX can be seen as a particular way to implement the Relegate relation, and obtains a straightforward interpretation in the language we used here. There are other ways to handle uncertainty and relaxation of requirements, and our aim in this paper was to remain independent of particular approaches.

Concerning the knowledge about the *resources*, which are needed to achieve specific behavior while the SAS is operating, this notion of resource has been implicit in the requirements modeling languages like KAOS and *i*/Tropos*. In case of requirements for SAS, we believe that it is necessary to model resources in a more explicit way, not only to express their variability, but also to include dynamic lifecycles that might describe their availability.

Along the dimension of *context*, in RE, context has been defined as *An abstraction of location, an event, environment or as a set of conditions that may change overtime* in [15, 18, 19]. Another common and well accepted definition of context to date is by Dey in [20], i.e., *Context is any information that can be used to characterize the situation of an entity.*

Specifically, in RE for SAS, it has been argued that alternative behaviors must be supplied to the system, which can be switched to meet the changes in the environment by monitoring the context [18]. To capture the contextual variability, explicit knowledge about the domain is required. In [15], variation points are used to annotate the goal models, for representing pre-defined contexts and alternative behaviors to be exploited while reasoning over them. To use this approach, a requirements driven reconfiguration architecture is proposed in [21], which leverages the concept of context and monitor-diagnosis-compensate loop. Moreover, our Adaptive requirements, follow similar ideas, but go beyond the above mentioned approaches by making explicit domain assumptions and requirements for feedback loops [7]. However, the notion of context is trickier and brings newer requirements to be analyzed while specifying requirements for SAS. In Adaptive RML, we provided an explicit graphical notation, where context properties can be modeled exploiting specific domain ontology, which defines the domain concepts and their instances.

On the basis of recent works, we recognized issues in requirements modeling for SAS that provide premise to the proposal of Adaptive RML. For instance *requirements monitoring* [22–24], where the running systems must be monitored during its execution as per its own requirements model. Any runtime deviation or violation leads to needs for the system to reconcile its behavior to its requirements. In case of SAS this is critical, as it operates in an open environment where changes can occur dynamically in the operating context, availability of resources and end-user needs can change over time. In Adaptive RML, we propose modeling concepts so as to model early requirements for SAS, which then guides the detailed specification, which will eventually include monitoring specification. However, implementation of monitoring and linking early models with runtime events is nontrivial.

Requirements reflection is another issue, where ideas from computational reflection has been borrowed to provide SAS the capability to be aware of its own requirements [10]. Similarly, online goal refinement [25] is of prime importance considering the underline architecture of the intended SAS. To support runtime reasoning of requirement by SAS itself, in [9, 26, 27], we proposed a Continuous Adaptive RE (Care) framework and architecture for continuous online refinement of requirements by the system itself. This work describes different types of runtime adaptation, which are realized by exploiting incremental reasoning over adaptive requirements represented as runtime artifact. The main aim of this framework is to provide continuous refinement of requirements and provide solutions (i.e. leveraging available services) by the system at runtime involving the end-user.

Adaptive RML models and their support in deriving detailed specification in terms of adaptive requirements, represents a relevant contribution towards realizing continuous adaptive requirements engineering.

5   Conclusion and Future Work

This paper introduced Adaptive RML, a visual language for the modeling of early requirements for SAS. In contrast to previous proposals [3, 6–8] that rest on well established goal-oriented modeling languages (i.e. *i**, Tropos, Kaos), Adaptive RML builds on the abstract requirements modeling language Techne [13], which provides a richer set of concepts, along the CORE ontology for RE defined in [12], and supports requirements analysis leading to sets of candidate solutions for the stated requirements problem. A few additional concepts and relationships are used in Adaptive RML (i.e. context, resource, relegation and influence) to model and represent the runtime requirements adaptation problem and perform analysis.

The motivations for Adaptive RML were first introduced by contrasting requirements modeling of an example of SAS, made with *i** and with Adaptive RML, providing also an early qualitative validation of its advantages. A detailed account of Adaptive RML was then given in terms of concepts, visual notation, modeling and analysis guidelines. Finally, novel features of Adaptive RML were discussed along the research challenges, which have been recently identified in RE for SAS [1, 10] and open points were highlighted.

As future work on Adaptive RML, we will focus on investigating easier-to-use visual syntax, tool support for modeling and automated reasoning methods for the analyst to find candidate solutions in the model. To further consolidate the approach, a systematic process to guide the detailed specification in terms of adaptive requirements should also be provided. A survey is also planned to acquire feedback on the effectiveness of the proposed visual modeling notions and their adequacy for early requirements modeling of SAS involving subjects.

References

1. Cheng, B.H.C., de Lemos, R., Giese, H., Inverardi, P., Magee, J., Andersson, J., Becker, B., Bencomo, N., Brun, Y., Cukic, B., Di Marzo Serugendo, G., Dustdar, S., Finkelstein, A., Gacek, C., Geihs, K., Grassi, V., Karsai, G., Kienle, H.M., Kramer, J., Litoiu, M., Malek, S., Mirandola, R., Müller, H.A., Park, S., Shaw, M., Tichy, M., Tivoli, M., Weyns, D., Whittle, J.: Software Engineering for Self-Adaptive Systems: A Research Roadmap. In: Cheng, B.H.C., de Lemos, R., Giese, H., Inverardi, P., Magee, J. (eds.) Self-Adaptive Systems. LNCS, vol. 5525, pp. 1–26. Springer, Heidelberg (2009)
2. Penserini, L., Perini, A., Susi, A., Mylopoulos, J.: High variability design for software agents: Extending Tropos. TAAS 2(4) (2007)
3. Morandini, M., Penserini, L., Perini, A.: Towards goal-oriented development of self-adaptive systems. In: ICSE Workshop on Software Engineering for Adaptive and Self-Managing Systems (SEAMS 2008), pp. 9–16 (2008)
4. Whittle, J., Sawyer, P., Bencomo, N., Cheng, B.H.C., Bruel, J.-M.: RELAX: Incorporating Uncertainty into the Specification of Self-Adaptive Systems. In: 17th IEEE Int. Requirements Eng. Conf., Atlanta, pp. 79–88 (2009)
5. Dardenne, A., van Lamsweerde, A., Fickas, S.: Goal-directed requirements acquisition. Sci. Comput. Program. 20(1-2), 3–50 (1993)
6. Cheng, B.H.C., Sawyer, P., Bencomo, N., Whittle, J.: A Goal-Based Modeling Approach to Develop Requirements of an Adaptive System with Environmental Uncertainty. In: Schürr, A., Selic, B. (eds.) MODELS 2009. LNCS, vol. 5795, pp. 468–483. Springer, Heidelberg (2009)
7. Qureshi, N.A., Perini, A.: Engineering adaptive requirements. In: ICSE Workshop on Software Engineering for Adaptive and Self-Managing Systems (SEAMS 2009), pp. 126–131 (2009)
8. Baresi, L., Pasquale, L., Spoletini, P.: Fuzzy goals for requirements-driven adaptation. In: 18th IEEE Int. Requirements Eng. Conf., pp. 125–134 (2010)
9. Qureshi, N.A., Perini, A.: Requirements engineering for adaptive service based applications. In: 18th IEEE Int. Requirements Eng. Conf., pp. 108–111 (2010)
10. Sawyer, P., Bencomo, N., Whittle, J., Letier, E., Finkelstein, A.: Requirements-aware systems a research agenda for re for self-adaptive systems. In: 18th IEEE Int. Requirements Eng. Conf., pp. 95–103 (2010)
11. Qureshi, N.A., Jureta, I., Perini, A.: Requirements Engineering for Self-Adaptive Systems: Core Ontology and Problem Statement. In: Mouratidis, H., Rolland, C. (eds.) CAiSE 2011. LNCS, vol. 6741, pp. 33–47. Springer, Heidelberg (2011)
12. Jureta, I.J., Mylopoulos, J., Faulkner, S.: Revisiting the core ontology and problem in requirements engineering. In: 16th IEEE Int. Requirements Eng. Conf., pp. 71–80 (2008)
13. Jureta, I.J., Borgida, A., Ernst, N.A., Mylopoulos, J.: Techne: Towards a new generation of requirements modeling languages with goals, preferences, and inconsistency handling. In: 18th IEEE Int. Requirements Eng. Conf., pp. 115–124 (2010)
14. Yu, E.: Towards modeling and reasoning support for early requirements engineering. In: Proc. 3rd IEEE Int. Symp. on Requirements Eng., pp. 226–235 (1997)
15. Ali, R., Dalpiaz, F., Giorgini, P.: A Goal Modeling Framework for Self-contextualizable Software. In: Halpin, T., Krogstie, J., Nurcan, S., Proper, E., Schmidt, R., Soffer, P., Ukor, R. (eds.) BPMDS 2009 and EMMSAD 2009. LNBIP, vol. 29, pp. 326–338. Springer, Heidelberg (2009)
16. Marchetto, A., Nguyen, C.D., Di Francescomarino, C., Qureshi, N.A., Perini, A., Tonella, P.: A design methodology for real services. In: Proceedings of the 2nd International Workshop on Principles of Engineering Service-Oriented Systems, PESOS 2010, pp. 15–21. ACM (2010)

17. Moody, D.L., Heymans, P., Matulevicius, R.: Improving the effectiveness of visual representations in requirements engineering: An evaluation of i* visual syntax. In: 17th IEEE Int. Requirements Eng. Conf., pp. 171–180 (2009)
18. Salifu, M., Yu, Y., Nuseibeh, B.: Specifying monitoring and switching problems in context. In: 15th IEEE Int. Requirements Eng. Conf., pp. 211–220 (2007)
19. Finkelstein, A., Savigni, A.: A framework for requirements engineering for context-aware services. In: Proc. of 1st International Workshop From Software Requirements to Architectures (STRAW 2001), pp. 200–201 (2001)
20. Dey, A.K.: Understanding and using context. Personal Ubiquitous Comput. 5(1), 4–7 (2001)
21. Dalpiaz, F., Giorgini, P., Mylopoulos, J.: An Architecture for Requirements-Driven Self-reconfiguration. In: van Eck, P., Gordijn, J., Wieringa, R. (eds.) CAiSE 2009. LNCS, vol. 5565, pp. 246–260. Springer, Heidelberg (2009)
22. Fickas, S., Feather, M.S.: Requirements monitoring in dynamic environments. In: RE 1995: Proceedings of the Second IEEE Intl. Symp. on Reqs. Eng., p. 140. IEEE CS (1995)
23. Feather, M.S., Fickas, S., Lamsweerde, A.V., Ponsard, C.: Reconciling system requirements and runtime behavior. In: IWSSD 1998: Proceedings of the 9th International Workshop on Software Specification and Design, p. 50. IEEE CS (1998)
24. Robinson, W.: A Roadmap for Comprehensive Requirements Monitoring. Computer 43(5), 64–72 (2009)
25. Kramer, J., Magee, J.: Self-managed systems: an architectural challenge. In: Future of Software Engineering, FOSE 2007, pp. 259–268 (May 2007)
26. Qureshi, N.A., Perini, A., Ernst, N.A., Mylopoulos, J.: Towards a continuous requirements engineering framework for self-adaptive systems. In: RE 2010 Workshops, First International Workshop on Requirements@Run.Time (RE@RunTime), pp. 9–16 (2010)
27. Qureshi, N.A., Perini, A.: Continuous adaptive requirements engineering: An architecture for self-adaptive service-based applications. In: First IEEE International Workshop on Requirements@Run.Time (RE@RunTime), pp. 17–24 (2010)

Requirements Monitoring
for Adaptive Service-Based Applications

Marc Oriol[1], Nauman A. Qureshi[2], Xavier Franch[1], Anna Perini[2], and Jordi Marco[1]

[1] Universitat Politècnica de Catalunya, Barcelona, Spain
{moriol,jmarco}@lsi.upc.edu, franch@essi.upc.edu
[2] Fondazione Bruno Kessler - CIT, Trento, Italy
{qureshi,perini}@fbk.eu

Abstract. **[Context and motivation]** Adaptive Service Based Applications (SBAs) need to cope with continuously changing environments. Monitoring becomes a key requirement for engineering Adaptive SBAs. **[Question/problem]** Ongoing research on Requirements Engineering (RE) for Adaptive SBAs strives to answer challenging questions such as how to monitor changes affecting user's requirements? and how the monitored information helps in adapting to the candidate solutions? **[Principal ideas/results]** Existing approaches and techniques to specify requirements monitoring for Adaptive SBAs are either formal or specialized to a particular domain. A convenient and easy approach to specify requirements monitoring for Adaptive SBAs is still missing. In this paper, we focus on this issue. **[Contribution]** We describe a systematic approach for deriving requirements monitoring specifications for the running Adaptive SBA. We use a running example from a travel domain case study to elaborate our approach.

Keywords: Requirements Monitoring, Self-Adaptive Systems, Services-Based Application.

1 Introduction

Service-Based Applications (SBA, hereafter) reply on third party services while operating in an open environment (such as the Internet) [1]. In such a dynamic environment, SBAs must adapt in response to changing end-user's needs and preferences (e.g. book travel using different services), changes in context (e.g. wifi service is available in downtown, but is not available in a mall nearby) or variation in the availability of resources to exploit such solutions (e.g. mobile battery went down) or the availability of the service (e.g. travel service is not available due to server maintenance). Research on self-adaptive systems has started to gain considerable attention from the research community [2]. However, research on Requirements Engineering (RE) for Adaptive SBAs has received less attention.

Existing works in the field of service-oriented computing aims at architectural aspects when focusing on service monitoring and discovery [3]. In the context of RE, requirements monitoring has been tackled as a way to observe the deviations in the running system by instrumenting the code [4,5,6]. However, these approaches anticipate changes that might occur at runtime, which makes them limited in the case of adaptive

B. Regnell and D. Damian (Eds.): REFSQ 2012, LNCS 7195, pp. 280–287, 2012.

SBAs. Recently it has been pointed out that to cope with unanticipated changes that can occur dynamically at runtime, self-adaptive systems need to be aware of their own requirements and end-user's needs at runtime [7]. Taking this vision to adaptive SBAs, in several cases, the decision on how to adapt in response to changes and what to monitor can be postponed to runtime as well with respect to the real environment involving the end-user. In the context of Self Adaptive Systems, there are many instances where adaptation decisions cannot be determined at design time. For instance, if a flight is delayed (unanticipated event) the Self Adaptive System may choose to rebook a similar flight, cancel the flight and hotel booking or explicitly involving the end-user asking for what to look for (e.g. travel by train, rent a car, etc). Such decision cannot be pre-fixed, as dynamic changes may occur at run-time.

In this work, we consider changes that pertain to end-user requirements, operational contexts and variability in resource's availability posing challenging questions to the field of RE. In particular, we aim to address the following research questions: (1) how to systematically obtain and configure monitors from end-user's requirements? (2) how to configure an adaptive SBA to adapt at runtime in response to changes in operating context, availability of resources and by involving the end-user if needed?

To address these questions, we envision a novel approach to systematically derive monitoring specifications from the user's requirements for a running adaptive SBA. We adopt an operational pattern based on Event-Condition-Action to configure adaptive SBAs to monitor changes and adapt at runtime.

The paper is organized as follows. Section 2 describes the related work and high-lights the challenges. Section 3 briefly recalls the baseline of our proposed work [8,9] and describes our envisioned approach on requirements monitoring for adaptive SBAs. Section 4 summarizes the next steps.

2   Related Work and Baseline

Relevant works on requirements monitoring are briefly recalled here below. In [4,5] a formal language (Formal Language for Expressing Assumptions - FLEA) is proposed to express the assumptions about the environment that has to be monitored as prerequisite in order to apply remedial actions if the related requirements are violated. Similarly, in [10] a monitoring framework, named ReqMon, is proposed for monitoring web service requirements expressed using a goal-oriented language (KAOS). KAOS model of requirements is used to analyze obstacles for specifying monitors. Another framework to monitor and diagnose failures of software requirements has been proposed in [11]. The framework logs the execution of the system, and a diagnostic component identifies if there has been any violation of the requirements by means of propositional formula in CNF and using SAT solvers. In [12] an approach to deal with self-adaptation of BPEL compositions by means of adaptive goals, which are responsible for the evolution/adaptation of the goal model, is presented. Using the KAOS goal model they transform the obstacles and additional conditions into the languages of two monitoring systems: ALBERT, Dynamo which are used to evaluate properties of a BPEL process.

A comparison between these works and our envisioned approached is shown in table 1.

Table 1. Comparison with the related work

Framework	Usage of a Goal Model	Adaptation support	Different Monitoring Configurations	Goal reasoning (bottom-up)	General / Service Based
Fickas et al. [4,5]	Yes: *KAOS*	No	No	Partially *based on activities*	General
Robinson[10]	Yes: *KAOS*	No	Partially *Implemented by the designer*	-	Service
Wang et al.[11]	Yes	No	Partially *Testing not supported*	No	Service
Baresi et al.[12]	Yes: *KAOS*	Yes	No	-	Service
Our approach	Yes: *ARML*	Yes	Yes	*Future work*	Service

These works on requirements monitoring tend to consider only changes that can be anticipated at design-time. This limits their applicability in case of adaptive SBAs. Many decisions need to be postponed to runtime while engineering adaptive SBAs. In context of RE for adaptive SBA, requirements monitoring demands a flexible approach to derive and configure application monitoring with respect to the changes in the requirements or in the environment. An easy and convenient approach to support the analysts at design-time to derive and configure application monitoring with respect to the requirements and later provide the support to the running adaptive SBA at runtime to automate it monitoring and adaptation with respect to the changes. To address this target, we envision a convenient and systematic approach that enables the analyst to express monitoring specification from requirements (without obfuscating the requirements specification using a complex formal language), and provide supporting features to re-configure at runtime.

The baseline of our envisioned approach is our ongoing works on the Continuous Adaptive Requirements Engineering (CARE) [8] Framework and the SALmon Framework for Monitoring SLA [9].

The CARE framework attempts at bridging the gap between design-time and runtime RE. At design-time requirements model is constructed using the concepts (i.e. goals, tasks, context, resources etc.) defined in the revised core ontology of RE for self-adaptive systems in [13]. The resulting instances of the requirements specification (i.e. candidate solutions to the requirements problem) are stored in the requirements database. At run-time, the CARE is instantiated by a running adaptive SBA, performing RE by itself. It exploits the requirements specification instances for runtime refinement of requirements by involving the end-users, if needed, to satisfy their needs exploiting the available services.

SALMon is a framework focused on monitoring the quality of service (QoS) of web services, evaluate them accordingly to stated conditions, and notify violations to the interested parties. For this project, SALMon has been extended with new measurement capabilities, such as monitoring the change of status of a service, which goes beyond QoS. SALMon is able to combine both passive monitoring and testing approaches accordingly to the preferences of the user. The framework has been implemented as a

SBA itself, providing hence easy integration with other frameworks. It provides the following two services: the Monitor, responsible to retrieve the data of the target services; and the Analyzer, responsible for the evaluation of conditions.

3 Requirements Monitoring Framework

In this section, we elaborate our overall envisioned approach to derive monitors from the requirements, as well as the rules that guides the system adaptation in response to changes detected from the monitoring data. We exploit a Event-Condition-Action pattern to operationalize the requirements as a monitoring specification which is used to configure the running adaptive SBA with respect to the requirements.

3.1 Scenario

We elaborate our approach exploiting a scenario from a Travel Companion exemplar case study (adopted from [8]). Travel Companion is an adaptive SBA, responsible for managing users' travel booking by maintaining users' goals. In this scenario, the user must be notified about changes about her flight itinerary i.e. flight booking status (e.g. flight status changes to delayed or canceled). The notification message about her flight booking status must be sent on her device (e.g. mobile phone) instantly (e.g. with in less than 5 mins) exploiting the available services (e.g. the Internet wifi, flight booking service, SMS service etc.), keeping in view her preference (e.g. send email on a corporate mail account while in office) and context (e.g. location: outdoor, indoor).

3.2 The Framework at Design-Time

We describe our envisioned approach that supports the analyst at design-time to conveniently specify requirements and derive monitoring specification that is used to configure the components of the running adaptive SBA as shown in Fig. 1. We use the above scenario to help to clarify the elements of our approach.

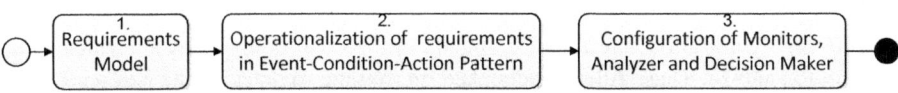

Fig. 1. Design-time process for deriving and configuring Monitor, Analyzer and Decision Maker

1. Requirements Model: The requirements model is defined by exploiting the concepts and relations defined in the revised core ontology of requirements for self-adaptive systems in [13]. Concepts includes: goals, softgoals, tasks, resources, domain assumptions (i.e. conditions considered to be true for the correct behavior of the system), quality constraints (i.e. requirements that expresses conditions over the expected quality of service), context (i.e. information that defines the system state, user's presupposed information about a requirement etc.) and relations includes: preferences (i.e. defining priorities over mandatory or optional requirements), conflicts (i.e. inconsistent set of requirements), inference (i.e. a generalized relation over decomposition such as AND/OR in goal models). The resulting model describes the requirements specification, which not only the mandatory requirements but also encompass monitoring specification, evaluation criteria and alternative candidate solutions for the intended Travel companion SBA.

2. Operationalization: To operationalize the given requirements, there exist several alternatives, such as using the Object Constraint Language (OCL) [14], Event-Condition-Action (ECA) [15] or Temporal Logics [5] [16], beyond others. We adopt a convenient Event-Condition-Action (ECA) pattern that helps expressing the adaptive requirements specification. Although, ECA pattern for expressing requirements is not the most compact and only form. We chose this pattern to provide a straight forward operationalization of adaptive requirement, thereby capturing the feedback loop functions (i.e. monitoring specification, evaluation criteria and adaptation/trigger actions, making them explicit using ECA rules). The operationalization of these requirements is as follows:

Specifying Events: The analyst can include either goals or tasks to monitor. The framework navigates through the given defined element in the requirements model until it reaches the leaf tasks that implement the functionality and generate the events to observe. For instance, from a high-level goal 'changes over the flight itinerary being monitored', the framework reaches the task 'invoke flight status' and monitor the events of this task. The current framework supports the generation of monitors for web services. In order to automate the generation of monitors, the analyst annotates these tasks with the required information (i.e. endpoint, WSDL and SOAP action). The invocation of these tasks are the events to monitor. The concrete properties to monitor on each event are obtained from the Quality Constraints defined in the requirements model that applies over the task. The requirements model includes also a set of preferences i.e. Preference Requirements (PRs). PRs specify preferences regarding how the monitoring should be performed (i.e. actively invoking the service every time-interval or passively observing the interaction between the system and the end-user). This information is used to automatically generate a Monitoring Specification, an XML file that describes what is to be monitored, and is used in order to generate the monitors accordingly.

Specifying Conditions: The list of elements in the condition specify the rules of the system to analyze. These rules are checked on runtime to detect if the behavior of the system fulfills the expected functionality with the desired performance. The given elements involved in the Condition section are the Quality Constraints (QCs) that specify the conditions to check, and the runtime data obtained as Resources (i.e. the results of the monitored events). This information is used to automatically generate of the Condition Specification, which specifies the conditions to be checked at runtime.

Specifying Actions: This part consist on the execution of an action over the defined elements in the model. There are several kind of actions that can be performed in order to correct or mitigate the malfunction of the system. Currently we have focused on two kind of actions to perform over the requirements model. Namely, SELECT and INVOKE. Operationalizing the SELECT(task): the element included as a parameter in the SELECT function is a composite task that can be met by several alternatives. This action defines the preferred alternative to execute at runtime. For instance, in the given scenario, there is a task 'NotifyUser' composed of several alternatives (e.g. Notify-ByEmail, NotifyBySMS,etc). When a condition over these tasks is not met, the action SELECT(NotifyUser) is triggered, which updates the selection of the most convenient device to notify the user. INVOKE(task): the element included in the INVOKE function is a task that is executed by the system as a result of the failure of the condition. For instance, if the flight has been delayed, INVOKE(NotifyUser) notifies the user to his most convenient device that the flight has been delayed. The set of defined actions are used to generate the actions specification.

3. Configuration: From each generated specification using the ECA rules, the components of the running adaptive SBA i.e. Monitor, Analyzer and the Decision Maker are configured. Here we exploit monitor of SALMon framework, which is configured from the Monitoring Specification, providing hence at runtime the monitored information of the target services to the Analyzer. The Analyzer, which is configured from the Condition Specification, checks if the rules are fulfilled or not and notifies any violation to the Decision Maker (i.e. part of the adaptive SBA itself, which instantiate CARE framework). The Decision Maker is configured by means of the Action Specification, which triggers the defined actions.

3.3   The Framework at Run-Time

In this section, we describe our runtime architecture that combines both CARE's runtime process (instantiated by Travel Companion) and SALMon that provides runtime monitoring information to Travel Companion.

Monitoring the Events: The resulting Monitor Specification is used as the input to configure the monitor of SALMon accordingly. The monitor can be configure in either passive or active way (i.e. by passively observing the invocation over the defined services or by invoking systematically the target services in different time intervals). Once the service is invoked, the monitor retrieves the desired information, which can be the value of a quality metric or the result of the invocation.

Analyzing the Conditions: The Analyzer is configured to check the conditions stated in the Condition Specification. During execution, the analyzer is subscribed to the new values that the monitor retrieve. That is, for each new monitored value, the analyzer checks the fulfillment of the conditions. Currently the conditions are stated as a tuple of $< property, operand, value >$. If the conditions are not met, the Analyzer notifies the violation to the Decision Maker.

Triggering the Actions: The Decision Maker retrieves the failure of a condition, and triggers the defined actions. The Decision Maker is composed of several decisions modules, each one responsible for a concrete kind of action to perform. As stated previously, we have defined two kind of actions, namely SELECT(task) and INVOKE(task). The SELECT action is achieved by means of updating the model with the preferred concrete task that will realize the composed task. The trigger action is achieved by means of invoking the specified task. To this aim, the given task is implemented as a service, and the invocation is performed as a SOAP-based message invocation. In the given scenario, the status of the flight is monitored actively by the monitor through a web service interface. For each invocation, the analyzer checks if the status of the flight is 'OK'. In case the status is 'Delayed' or 'Canceled' the Analyzer triggers the Decision Maker, which performs the action INVOKE(NotifyUser).

4   Conclusions and Future Work

In this paper, we have proposed a systematic tool-supported approach for deriving monitoring specifications from the users requirements for a running Adaptive SBA. Our proposal provides a tool set that allows linking requirements models with more concrete operational artifacts, i.e. adaptive requirements expressed as ECA rules, and deriving monitoring specifications from requirements model elements. Such specifications are used to implement and configure our monitoring framework, which is flexible enough to accommodate changes (e.g. changes in monitoring specification), and to configure an adaptive SBA to adapt in response to observed runtime changes. We adopted Event-Condition-Action pattern in order to operationalize the requirements specification. ECA rules are then used to specify and configure automatically the different components of the adaptive SBA presented in the framework at design-time. At runtime, the monitors provides observed data to analyze the execution of the adaptive SBA. Realizing this framework will help bridging the gap between the design-time and run-time, which exists in the current approaches. To implement monitors and analyzer we exploited SALMon (for monitoring the events and evaluation the conditions) and for decision maker, we exploited Companion SBA, which instantiate CARE (for triggering the defined actions).

Currently we have implemented the generation of monitors from the requirements model. As an ongoing work, we plan to validate the overall process by realizing and evaluating our envisioned framework. We aim to conduct empirical studies which demonstrate the suitability of our envisioned approach. By one hand, we will conduct tests to assess the performance of the implemented framework, by the other, we plan to perform an evaluation of the usability by means ofstudents using the framework.

Acknowledgments. This work has been supported by the research project ADICT, TIN2007-64753, MCyT, Spain. Marc Oriol has a FPI grant bound to the project TIN2007-64753.

References

1. Di Nitto, E., Ghezzi, C., Metzger, A., Papazoglou, M., Pohl, K.: A journey to highly dynamic, self-adaptive service-based applications. Automated Soft. Eng. 15(3-4), 313–341 (2008)
2. Cheng, B.H.C., de Lemos, R., Giese, H., Inverardi, P., Magee, J., Andersson, J., Becker, B., Bencomo, N., Brun, Y., Cukic, B., Di Marzo Serugendo, G., Dustdar, S., Finkelstein, A., Gacek, C., Geihs, K., Grassi, V., Karsai, G., Kienle, H.M., Kramer, J., Litoiu, M., Malek, S., Mirandola, R., Müller, H.A., Park, S., Shaw, M., Tichy, M., Tivoli, M., Weyns, D., Whittle, J.: Software Engineering for Self-Adaptive Systems: A Research Roadmap. In: Cheng, B.H.C., de Lemos, R., Giese, H., Inverardi, P., Magee, J. (eds.) Self-Adaptive Systems. LNCS, vol. 5525, pp. 1–26. Springer, Heidelberg (2009)

3. Baresi, L., Ghezzi, C., Guinea, S.: Smart monitors for composed services. In: ICSOC 2004: Proceedings of the 2nd International Conference on Service Oriented Computing, pp. 193–202. ACM, New York (2004)
4. Fickas, S., Feather, M.S.: Requirements monitoring in dynamic environments. In: RE 1995: Proceedings of the Second IEEE Intl. Symp. on Req. Eng., p. 140. IEEE CS (1995)
5. Feather, M.S., Fickas, S., Lamsweerde, A.V., Ponsard, C.: Reconciling system requirements and runtime behavior. In: IWSSD 1998: Proceedings of the 9th Intl. Workshop on Software Specification and Design, p. 50. IEEE CS (1998)
6. Robinson, W.: Monitoring web service requirements. In: Proceedings of 11th IEEE International Requirements Engineering Conference, pp. 65–74 (September 2003)
7. Sawyer, P., Bencomo, N., Whittle, J., Letier, E., Finkelstein, A.: Requirements-aware systems a research agenda for re for self-adaptive systems. In: 18th IEEE Intl. Requirements Eng. Conf., Sydney, Australia, pp. 95–103 (2010)
8. Qureshi, N.A., Perini, A.: Requirements engineering for adaptive service based applications. In: 18th IEEE Intl. Requirements Eng. Conf., Sydney, Australia, pp. 108–111 (2010)
9. Oriol, M., Franch, X., Marco, J., Ameller, D.: Monitoring adaptable soa-systems using salmon. In: Workshop on Service Monitoring, Adaptation and Beyond (Mona+), pp. 19–28 (2008)
10. Robinson, W.N.: A requirements monitoring framework for enterprise systems. Requirements Engineering Journal 11(1), 17–41 (2006)
11. Wang, Y., McIlraith, S.A., Yu, Y., Mylopoulos, J.: Monitoring and diagnosing software requirements. Autom. Softw. Eng. 16(1), 3–35 (2009)
12. Baresi, L., Pasquale, L.: Live goals for adaptive service compositions. In: ICSE Workshop on Software Engineering for Adaptive and Self-Managing Systems, SEAMS 2010 (2010)
13. Qureshi, N.A., Jureta, I., Perini, A.: Requirements Engineering for Self-Adaptive Systems: Core Ontology and Problem Statement. In: Mouratidis, H., Rolland, C. (eds.) CAiSE 2011. LNCS, vol. 6741, pp. 33–47. Springer, Heidelberg (2011)
14. Souza, V.E.S., Lapouchnian, A., Robinson, W.N., Mylopoulos, J.: Awareness requirements for adaptive systems, Technical Report DISI-10-049, DISI, Universit'a di Trento, Italy (2010)
15. Knolmayer, G., Endl, R., Pfahrer, M.: Modeling processes and workflows by business rules. In: Business Process Management, pp. 16–29 (2000)
16. Baresi, L., Pasquale, L., Spoletini, P.: Fuzzy goals for requirements-driven adaptation. In: 18th IEEE Intl. Requirements Eng. Conf., pp. 125–134 (2010)

Release Planning with Feature Trees: Industrial Case

Samuel Fricker[1] and Susanne Schumacher[2]

[1] Blekinge Institute of Technology, School of Computing
Campus Gräsvik, 371 79 Karlskrona, Sweden
`samuel.fricker@bth.se`
[2] Zurich University of the Arts
Ausstellungsstrasse 60, 8005 Zurich, Switzerland
`susanne.schumacher@zhdk.ch`

Abstract. [Context and motivation] Requirements catalogues for software release planning are often not complete and homogeneous. Current release planning approaches, however, assume such commitment to detail – at least implicitly. [Question/problem] We evaluate how to relax these expectations, while at the same time reducing release planning effort and increasing decision-making flexibility. [Principal ideas/results] Feature trees capture AND, OR, and REQUIRES relationships between requirements. Such requirements structuring can be used to hide incompleteness and to support abstraction. [Contribution] The paper describes how to utilize feature trees for planning the releases of an evolving software solution and evaluates the effects of the approach on effort, decision-making, and trust with an industrial case.

Keywords: features, abstraction, release planning, roadmapping, case study.

1 Introduction

Software releases are planned by allocating requirements to development projects [1]. A strategic release plan aligns the development of an evolving software solution with market and stakeholder needs, company objectives, and constraints such as time and resources. Release planning is a central concern in iterative development, where multiple iterations, rather than a single project, are defined [2].

Release planning involves the following steps [3]. Requirements are elicited and specified. Criteria [4] are defined to evaluate and prioritize requirements [5]. Releases are then scoped by allocating the prioritized requirements to development projects. The resulting release plans are implemented, delivered, and analyzed with post-release reflections [6].

Requirements that enter release planning are often of low quality [7]. Their homogeneity [8], completeness, and understanding [9] are hard to ensure due to the limited effort invested before a development project is funded. This situation contradicts with the assumptions of release planning approaches that scope projects simply by prioritizing and allocating available requirements. Consequently, the results are not trusted and not used for guiding ensuing development steps [10].

B. Regnell and D. Damian (Eds.): REFSQ 2012, LNCS 7195, pp. 288–305, 2012.

This paper describes in detail how to hide the requirements-related problems by structuring the release planning inputs. The approach, whose initial ideas were introduced in an earlier position paper [11], is based on variability modeling [12] that allows abstracting from requirements with AND, OR, and REQUIRES relationships [13]. Variability is here used to structure decision options [14] for product evolution. This paper then introduces an industrial case [15] to understand how to use variability modeling in a real-world context of continuous agile product management [16]. Evaluated were feasibility of the approach and its effects on effort, decision-making, and trust were evaluated.

The paper is structured as follows. Section 2 describes background and motivation. Section 3 introduces variability-based release planning. Section 4 describes, analyzes, and interprets the industrial case. Section 5 discusses and concludes.

2   Background and Motivation

Release planning for software products is a key practice of software product management [17]. Software releases are planned to answer a stream of requirements that approach the product development organization [18]. The requirements are first homogenized [8] and pass triage [19] before they enter release planning [3]. Release planning then involves evaluation and selection of requirements to scope development projects [4]. The requirements that are closest to implementation are those that are detailed most [16].

Current release planning approaches fit well into this context of continuous requirements inflow. They require a complete catalogue of comparable requirements that are evaluated, prioritized, and selected for implementation [20]. Known prioritization approaches include manual techniques such as top ten, numerical assignment, ranking, and 100$-test [5], and computer-based techniques such as Integer Linear Programming [21, 22] and the Analytical Hierarchy Process [23].

Prioritization allows evaluating requirements in a controlled way and leads to requirements ordering that suits development projects [10]. However, scalability is limited; and the results are mistrusted and perceived inadequate to guide how to act [10]. Post-release reflections help improving decision-making over time [6].

We investigated release planning in an organization that developed innovative software as a service for managing media such as text, sound, pictures, and movies. The solution provided first-of-its-kind features, was in an early stage of its evolution, and had a small, but rapidly growing user base.

Responsible for the development was a product manager, a project manager, and a team of up to five developers. They reported to a company-internal steering committee with management of the development organization, of the product-owning organization, and of departments that used the solution. A product reference team was used to coordinated development with important stakeholder groups.

Surprisingly, there was no stream of requirements that the product organization was confronted with. No homogenization and triage of incoming requirements was necessary. Instead the requirements were based on ideas that originated from the product manager who was an expert in the product's application domain and on feedback from pilot users. Ideas were made explicit during product planning and specified in detail when communicating with the development team.

The requirements catalogue was managed in a word processor document and used as a basis for release planning. It contained 108 requirements. The requirements were grouped into 12 sections and 19 subsections or themes. In average, a group contained 3.6 requirements and was allocated to 1.93 releases. The grouping, however, did not show a relationship with requirements allocation to development releases.

The requirements were not prepared and analyzed in a form that was expected by current release planning approaches. A key concern to the practitioners was development efficiency. Effort was only put into requirements when the return of such an investment was obvious.

Requirements that were not likely to be implemented in near future were not specified. Some requirements were specified with descriptions of up to 245 words, others only with a few words in a declarative manner, again others were completely omitted because not relevant within a practical planning horizon. Many requirements were discovered while development progressed.

Requirements were not evaluated. Isolating a requirement from its context would have increased the risk of misunderstandings. For example, the requirement *thumbnails of variable sizes* would have carried the following ambiguities: *When would thumbnails be shown? For what purpose? Which sizes? What (photos, videos, documents, etc.) would be depicted by these thumbnails?* The many potential interpretations of such a requirement would have led to different interpretation of importance, dependencies, implementation cost, and risk.

Requirements were not prioritized. The product organization avoided to compare requirements. For example, questions like "is the requirement *thumbnails of variable sizes* more important than the requirement *storage of search results?*" have not been posed. Such comparison would have led to detailed evaluation results. However, details irrelevant at the given product evolution stage would have been sub-optimized.

The organization wanted to transition from implementing the whole solution with a single large project to incrementally evolving the solution with short development iterations. They considered improvements in their release planning capabilities as a key enabler and asked *how release planning can be implemented by abstracting from the detailed requirements and by focusing on the key product evolution decisions*. The desired approach had to support decision-making, maintain flexibility of how the solution evolves, and keep effort to be invested at a low level.

3   Feature Trees for Release Planning

The lacking stream of requirements and the tendency of not specifying and evaluating individual requirements motivated us to identify alternatives to current release planning approaches. The alternative had to fit the described organization with the innovative product and the strong leadership of the product manager. Release planning should remain a low-effort activity, however with improved decision-making support and flexibility.

Feature diagrams are a widespread approach to document and analyze variability of software products [12]. They are used to specify how features vary for the products of a product line (variability in space). Applied to release planning, variability models can be used for defining the evolution of software (variability in time) [24]. How feature trees are utilized for release planning, has been proposed in this line of research for the first time [1, 11].

We use AND, OR, and REQUIRE dependencies [13] to structure a solution's requirements as a feature tree. Figure 1 illustrates the feature tree of a solution, *Online Shop Sales*. A feature is a named group of requirements that are implemented in the same development increment (AND dependencies). E.g. the *Sales* feature in Figure 1 refers to six such requirements. To enable acceptable implementation of the feature, the feature's requirements are elicited [25] and refined until they comply with the solution's environment and design [26].

Sub-features extend a feature. They can only be implemented after their super-feature has been implemented (REQUIRES dependency). E.g. *Enhanced Cart Display* is such a sub-feature to the super-feature *Sales*. A chain of REQUIRES dependencies that connects the root with a leaf is called a feature vector [27]. Such a vector captures the foreseen levels of implementing a functional or non-functional concern of the software solution. E.g. the *OnlineShop Sales* solution may support just *Sales* or support both *Sales* and *Enhanced Cart Display*.

The implementation order of a feature's sub-features is not constrained a-priori (OR dependency). E.g. the root's eight sub-features can be implemented in any order.

OnlineShop Sales Solution

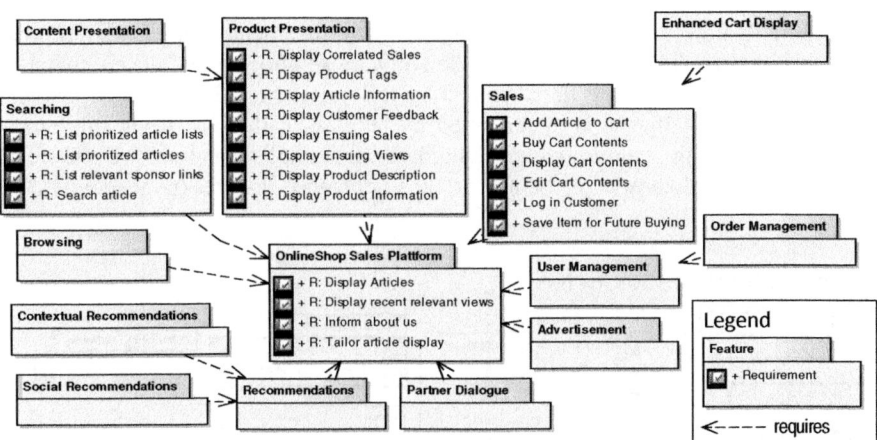

Fig. 1. Example of requirements structuring with a feature tree. The tree's root is *OnlineShop Sales Platform* in the middle of the diagram.

Figure 2 shows how we construct a feature tree, starting at the root. Initially, requirements and constraints related to architecture and infrastructure of the solution are allocated to the root. Then, feature vectors are built iteratively. For each feature, relevant requirements are identified and allocated to that feature. Feature-extending sub-features are identified and related to that feature. Requirements whose implementation can be postponed are extracted from the feature into these extending sub-features [28]. The requirements extraction process stops when no requirement can be extracted without making the concerned feature useless.

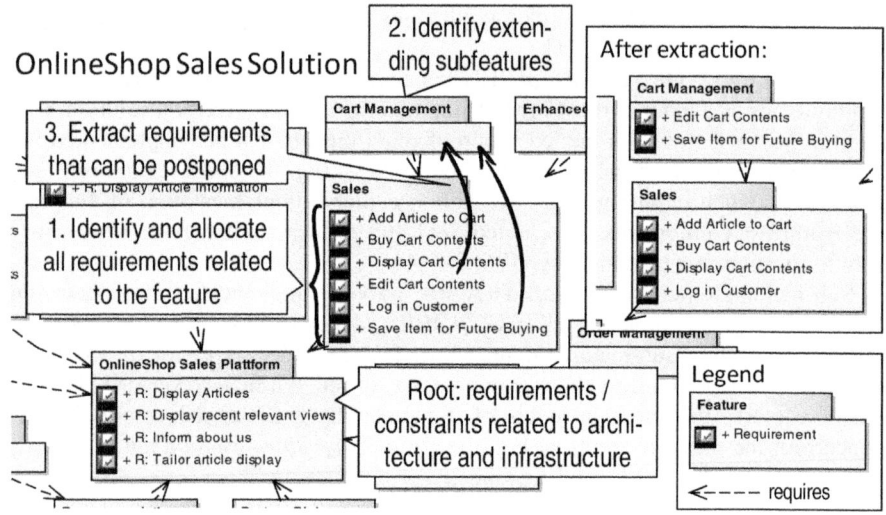

Fig. 2. Iterative feature tree construction process: repeat steps 1 to 3 for each feature until that feature contains just the minimal set of requirements to be useful. Progress from root to leafs

Figure 3 shows how we use the feature tree to document implementation progress and to visualize options for evolving the software solution. Initial development starts with the root. Features are implemented by following the REQUIRES dependencies. Implementation progress is documented by tagging features as being implemented, for example with a color code. Candidates for implementation are the features connected with already implemented or already planned features (connectivity rule).

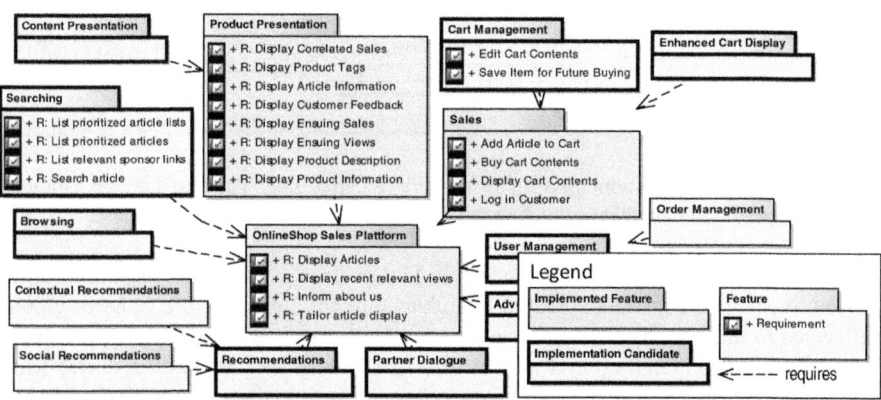

Fig. 3. Progress tracking and visualization of options for software evolution

A feature tree simplifies the handling of a requirements specification in a release planning context. Features abstract from detail by grouping AND-related requirements. Allocating features instead of requirements to software releases reduces the number of release planning decisions. A feature tree hides incompleteness by handling non-specified features the same way as specified ones. Figure 1 shows ten features that can be used for feature-level release planning, even-though they do not contain requirements yet. Feature trees with information about development progress can be used to focus requirements analysis. Implementation candidates need to be of higher quality than other features.

A feature tree also captures requirements changes. Emerging requirements, e.g. discovered during elicitation or development, are added based on the product manager's judgment to existing non-implemented features or as new leaf features to the tree. Urgent changes are introduced as changes to active features according to a release project's change management process. Changes to already implemented features are introduced as part of the solution's maintenance process. The allocation of changes to features increases transparency for root-cause analysis and subsequent process and competence improvements.

4   Industrial Case Study

4.1   Study Definition, Planning, and Operation

Study Definition. Case study research was used to evaluate feature trees for release planning and to compare the approach with the backlog-oriented practice of using a flat list of requirements. The study aimed at understanding feasibility and impact of the approach in a real-world practical context from the perspective of the product manager responsible for release planning.

We asked the following research questions. RQ1: *How are feature trees used for planning software releases?* RQ2: *How do feature trees affect effort, decisions-making, and trust?* RQ1 focuses on the documentation of product features and the use of that documentation. It provides a rich picture of variability-based release planning and the context in which it is used. RQ2 describes the effects of the approach. It reports lessons-learned from the practitioner that has performed variability-based release planning. The answers help implementing the practice and deciding when to adopt the approach.

Case study research is adequate when *how* or *why* questions are asked and when the focus is on a contemporary phenomenon within a real-life context [15]. Case study research deals with many more variables of interest than data points. Hence, obtained results cannot be generalized statistically. However, they provide insights for building theories that are explored and evaluated with ensuing research.

Study Planning. The case study was performed in the organization described in section 2. This organization is characterized with a software product that is novel, but already has an initial user base. The product implemented the vision of a product manager who is an expert in the application domain. Corresponding to the product's development stage, the organization was small with many responsibilities bundled on a few professionals.

The organization desired to enhance its project-centered development approach by strengthening the product perspective. It decided to introduce short- and long-term planning to increase the impact that it could generate with the limited resources it had available. It decided to pilot feature-driven release planning and complemented it with roadmapping to cover timing and resource aspects [29].

The first author of this paper introduced the basic methodology to the organization and performed the case study research. The second author was the product manager who tailored and implemented the approach together with stakeholders. Over a period of a year, work results and experiences were reviewed repeatedly to collect lessons-learned and to fine-tune the implementation.

Study Operation. The authors obtained data by collecting work results created by the practitioners during release planning, by performing interviews with the project leader and steering committee members, and by reflecting on the release planning experiences. The use of multiple data sources enabled triangulation for reducing validity threats of the study results.

The collected work results included a description of product stakeholders, the feature tree, feature specifications, a detailed roadmap, and a project backlog. The collected data represented the state of the organization after the feature tree-based practice had been introduced and its use calibrated. Calibration balanced efficiency and effectiveness with the organization's needs. The data allows answering RQ1 with a multi-faceted view of how feature tree-based release planning was implemented.

The interviews surfaced the product manager's stance towards feature tree-based release planning and experiences from applying the practice. The interviews were performed on multiple occasions during and after implementing the approach. The interviews helped interpreting the work results and allowed answering RQ2.

4.2   Threats to Validity

Every empirical study has limitations. Typical threats to validity were addressed in this case study as follows.

Conclusion validity: is there a true relationship between the treatment and the outcome? Triangulation over multiple empirical data sources, accompaniment of the organization over a year, and review of the research results by the practitioners reduced threats to conclusion validity. The use of multiple views for describing how the approach was implemented provides transparency.

Internal validity: does the treatment and not something else cause the outcome? Particular threats are that second author's involvement in the release planning affects researcher bias and that already the awareness of being observed affects the behavior of practitioners [30]. The former threat was a conscious decision to increase the accuracy and completeness of the description as practiced in action research [31]. Researcher bias was controlled by triangulating data sources. The latter threat was reduced through the long-term collaboration and the repeated interviews about why the practitioner believed that the described effects were achieved.

Construct validity: do the treatment and outcome measurements adequately represent the theory? The study controlled proper feature tree use by analyzing how well the feature tree construction rules were adhered to and by letting the practitioner reflect on the technique's strengths and limitations. Effort, decision-making, and trust were evaluated by comparing the subjective practitioner views with the results of artifact analysis.

External validity: can the results of the study be generalized? The study was performed in a real-world industrial context. Such contexts differ, however, for example in terms of how innovative and how large the developed products are. It is likely that the same results can be achieved in organizations that develop new product features incrementally.

The obtained results should be further tested in follow up studies. Positive and negative replications in other contexts can corroborate or refute the results. Experiments that compare feature tree-based and backlog-oriented release planning can test whether the results generalize statistically.

4.3   Use of Feature Trees for Release Planning

Feature trees were a central element for planning software releases. They acted as pivotal point for integrating analyses of user groups and of design options, for planning product development in the form of detailed roadmaps, for steering development iterations with backlogs, and for capturing progress. This integration of the core idea, the feature trees, with related practices, the user group analysis and roadmapping, was not planned, but emerged naturally in the context of the company. The features and their traces to these other views became a basis for coordinating stakeholder involvement with product development.

User Groups. The organization desired to address the needs of important stakeholders groups with the software solution. The product manager refined these groups by defining personas [32] and by appointing representatives. The needs of these personas affected the scope of the solution and the supported use scenarios [33]. The availability of the personas' representatives for pilot projects affected the timing of corresponding feature development.

To support such analysis the product manager developed and maintained the stakeholder tree shown in Figure 4. The tree implemented the VORD viewpoint structuring concepts [34]. The needs of a given high-level group were valid for refined groups, but not vice-versa. For example the need *finding publishable media* of *ZHdK* was also valid for *Publicity* and of *Lecturer*. The need *understand frequency and sources of site visits* of *Publicity* was not applicable *ZHdK* in general.

The product manager felt too much uncertainty to draw sharp boundaries between user groups and their needs. As a consequence, the stakeholder tree was used to build a vocabulary of stakeholders and to guide analysis, but not for formally defining traceability to features. Concrete needs were elicited, and feature development re-planned if necessary, during pilot projects performed with the stakeholder representatives. The total support of a persona was documented with a bar chart.

Media Archive of the Arts Stakeholder Tree

April 1, 2011 / Number 2

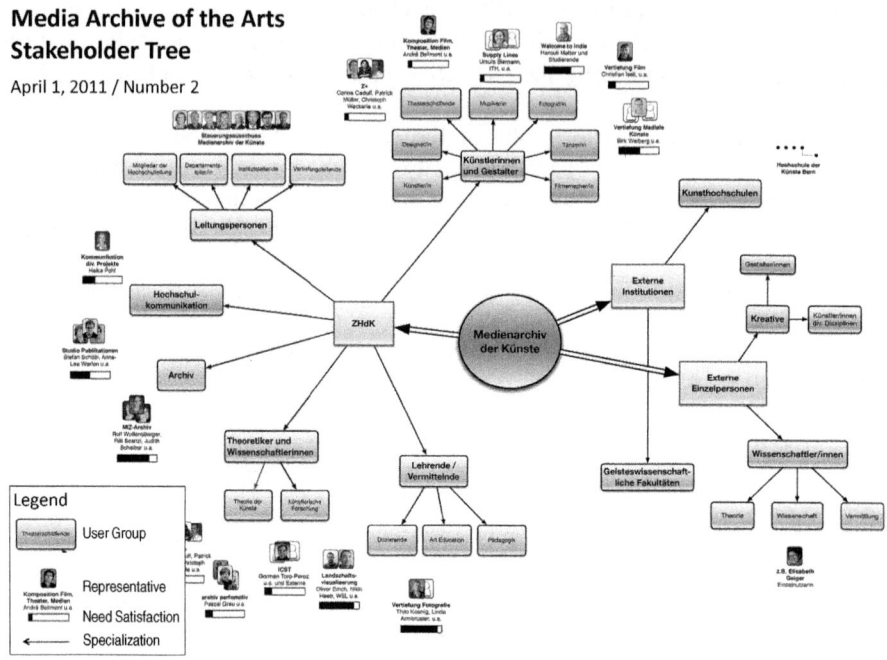

Fig. 4. Structure of the stakeholder tree. Geometric form: user groups. Photographs: user group representatives. Arrows: refinement of a generic user group to a special group. No need to read the feature names for understanding the case study.

Product Features. The feature tree provided an overview on the software solution by abstracting from requirements to features and by showing the fullest possible scope of the solution. It supported release planning by grouping requirements into cohesive units of implementation. The dependencies between these groups affected their order of implementation.

To support such analysis the product manager developed and maintained the feature tree shown in Figure 5. The tree captured the AND, OR, and REQUIRE requirements dependencies described in section 3. For example, the feature *Indexing* could not be developed before *Media Entry* and not after *Project-Oriented Indexing*. Not such dependency was defined between the features *Indexing* and *Basic Administration Interface*. The tree structure was not completely adhered to, however: some sub-features depended on more than one super-feature. The intention of these features was to combine these super-features. For example *Project-Oriented Filtering and Browsing* integrates *Filtering* and *Browsing*.

The feature tree captured the product manager's understanding of how the product should evolve. The initial tree was constructed by analyzing the originally available requirements specification based on the product manager's experience and gut feeling. The tree then was continuously evolved based on inputs from analyzing inputs elicited in stakeholder interviews and analysis of interfacing systems.

At the moment of analysis, the tree consisted of 91 features. It contained five branches with 57 functional features, one branch with 7 usability-related features, and one branch with 27 features that referred to supported media formats. The three types of branches interacted with each other. For example, adding a media format such as *Text* implied adjusting already implemented functional features. The necessary changes were planned before the implementation of the concerned media feature.

The product manager used the feature tree for reviewing progress and planned evolution with the steering committee, the reference team, and the pilot users. Color codes captured development progress, cooperation with company-external groups, and long-term scoping decisions. When planning the support of a pilot project, non-implemented but needed features were identified and integrated into the product's development sequence. The pilot projects were chosen so that the solution's key features could be implemented and validated as part of the public version 1.0 release.

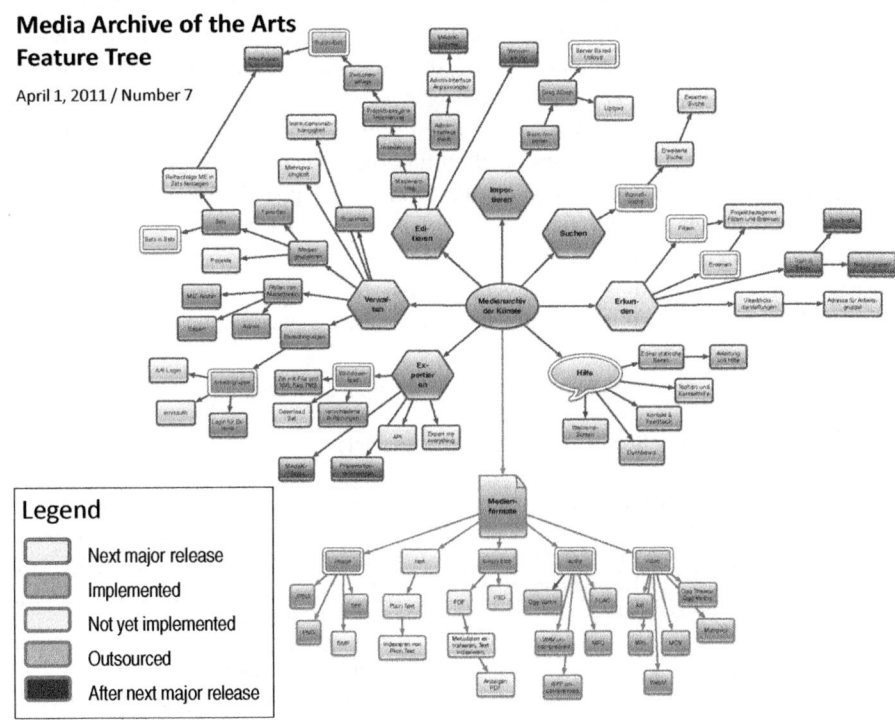

Fig. 5. Structure of the feature tree. Each geometric form represents a feature. Each arrows points from a base feature to enhancing features. No need to read the feature names for understanding the case study.

Feature Specification. The product manager used the features to align the developed solution with stakeholder needs. A feature was specified with 0 to 39 requirements. The progress of feature elaboration and development affected how far a feature was specified.

This practice allowed investing effort into those features that were implemented in near future.

No formal process was used to group known requirements into features, hence to define AND dependencies between the requirements. Instead, the product manager used her experience and gut feeling. Candidate features were then refined by removing requirements until they contained no optional requirements. The removed requirements were allocated to already known or ad-hoc defined sub-features, hence establishing REQUIRES dependencies. Alternatives, the OR dependencies, were captured by defining multiple sub-features.

Further refinement was done by considering each feature acted as a bridge between requirements and solution design [9]. The exploration of how a given feature would be implemented helped the product manager to set the right requirements and the development team to improve effort estimates. This dialogue also resolved situations where the requirements were fragmentary or specified at the wrong abstraction level.

To support the dialogue between the product manager and the development team the features were specified with the attributes shown in Table 1. The feature attributes were filled incrementally as specification and development progressed. Each feature was identified with its *name*. The product manager regularly discussed the features with the project leader and architect, leading to a *description* of the chosen of implementation alternative, early *effort* estimates, and initial *requirements*. The requirements were completed and important design aspects specified just before the feature was implemented. At the moment of feature implementation, the requirements were used to form the project backlog. A *comments* attribute provided a discussion forum for clarifications and coordinating implementation. *Bugs* and *future requirements* were placeholders for documenting maintenance and future enhancement needs.

Table 1. Feature specification attributes

Attribute	Description	Example
Name	Identifier	*Indexing*
Description	Feature's key ideas: concept describing the chosen implementation alternative	*Capture as much meta data as possible with input assistance, resp. an editor. Formalized metadata can be used for filtering and browsing.*
Effort	Estimated implementation effort	*35 points*
Requirements	Project backlog	*18 concluded requirements:* *- Keyword field* *- Standardized thesaurus* *- Visualize geo data with google maps widget...*
Attachments	Specification of important design aspects	*(examples of GUI elements)*
Comments	Discussions related to clarifications and open issues	*We can close Indexing if we close the ticket [...].*
Bugs	Problems with the implemented solution	*20 resolved, 2 pending bugs such as* *- Auto complete does not work...*
Future Requirements	List of potential enhancements of the feature	*12 not implemented requirements:* *- New media files for already existing meta data Icons...*

Formal feature specification in the context of software product lines expects specification of requirements, domain assumptions, and solution [26]. This specification practice was calibrated to increase work efficiency and flexibility and to support depending activities, while accepting dependency on the involved practitioners for interpreting the documentation. Information used to steer and track development was specified: the explicit list of requirements, enhanced with effort estimates and lists of bugs and future requirements. Knowledge related to understanding the features was kept implicit. Domain assumptions that would relate the feature to its use scenarios and the users' personas were not documented. The solution that would describe how to implement the feature was only fragmentarily documented. Lack of such information was compensated with the discussion thread.

Roadmap. The product manager planned a hierarchy of development iterations. Full version releases, for example version 1.0, had to address all key needs of selected stakeholder groups, for example the *ZHdK* stakeholders. Such a version release was split into feature releases that supported the needs of selected pilot projects. The development project then had bi-weekly releases to provide transparency and feedback to the product manager.

The feature trees lacked timing information. To define the feature's development timing the product manager decided to use a detailed, layered product roadmap [35] with a time horizon of two years. Figure 6 shows an extract of the detailed first-year plan. The second year was more fragmentary. The layer *features* defined when given features would be implemented. A feature's spacing corresponded to its development duration that was computed based on estimated effort, available *resources*, and availability of *technologies*. For example, *Authorization* was dependent on AAI and required roughly one calendar month. The availability of a feature enabled *use scenarios* that were needed by the *pilot projects*. For example, *Authorization*, *Login for Externals*, *Work Groups*, and *Download of Different Resolutions* enabled the *Production* scenario that was first evaluated in the *Z+* and *Studio Publications* pilots. The top-most layer referred to milestones such as external events and own releases.

The roadmap provided the context for release planning. It allowed exploring planning options together with stakeholders to agree on the implementation sequence. Time-to-market of version 1.0 was expected to be minimized and piloting aligned with development activities. The critical path was represented by the sequence of double-edged key features. Availability of pilot projects was documented by defining their start and end points. Surprises that affected the planning were discussed with the steering committee. For example, development staff was increased to account for development delays. The roadmap simplified release planning to allocating imminent features, for example *Filter* and *Extended Search* to imminent development iterations.

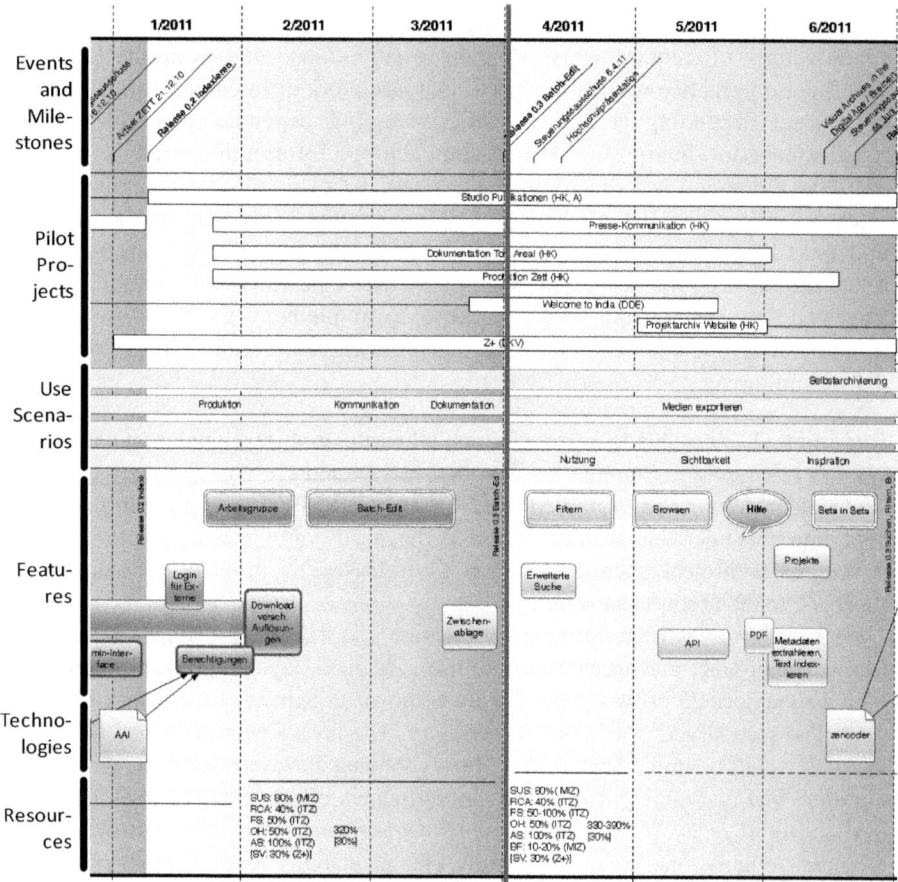

Fig. 6. Product roadmap (extract). Red bar: moment when the snapshot was taken. No need to read the detailed contents for understanding the case study.

Impact of Feature Trees

Effort. The feature tree, in comparison with a flat backlog of requirements, reduced complexity of release planning. The abstraction from requirements to features reduced the total number of elements to be considered by a factor 10.3. Table 2 evaluates the situation at April 2011. Row 1 describes the effect of the AND grouping. Row 2 describes the effect of adding the REQUIRES dependencies. Row 3 shows the complexity of prioritizing the implementation candidates, row 4 of the roadmap, and row 5 of the feature release project where the focus shifted from features to requirements.

Table 2. Comparison of list-based and feature tree-based approach

*: The feature-tree based requirements catalogue was intentionally incomplete. The estimate is extrapolated from the statistics of fully specified features.	Flat Backlog: Requirements	Feature Tree: Features
1 Total number of elements	937*	91
2 Number of implementation candidates	453*	23
3 Number of comparisons, efficient algorithm: $O(n \log_2 n)$	3997*	104
4 Number of elements in backlog of major release	206	20
5 Average number of elements in backlog of feature release	21	2

The product manager perceived planning of about twenty items fine-grained enough and feasible. Still discussions often centered on an even smaller set of features and did not need as much detail information about context as the tree provided.

Decision-Making. The feature tree and the roadmap were the key instruments used for deciding what to implement and when to implement. The feature tree provided a basis to discuss the scope of pilot projects with the stakeholders identified in the stakeholder tree. Stakeholder needs that could not directly be addressed led to discovering new potential features.

The roadmap was used for aligning the timing of feature implementation with the pilot project. The product manager had to ensure that needed features were available to the pilot users at the right moment in time and that no unnecessary feature was implemented. The roadmap was useful to check these rules together with the concerned stakeholders.

A number of criteria are known to evaluate product evolution options [4]. They include management concerns like development cost-benefit, business concerns like stakeholder priority and satisfaction, and system concerns like evolvability. Such information that is typically part of a business case [36] was not specified explicitly. Instead, the impact of these concerns was discussed in terms of product evolution scenarios. The agreement on which scenario to pursue was documented in the form of features in the feature tree and as timing information in the roadmap.

Traceability between features, use scenarios, and pilot projects was difficult to maintain, however. This difficulty now motivated the product manager to evaluate how specification of use scenarios, for example in terms of supported user groups and supporting features, could be used to bundle traceability. This approach could reduce the number of traces between stakeholders and features by a factor ten to hundred.

Development and use of the so far implemented solution led to massive learning about the real user needs and about what an effective media management solution is. Hence, even-though the product manager accepted a feature to be finished, new non-implemented requirements were added to the feature. These requirements are planned to be structured as features and enter development through enhancements of the feature tree shown in Figure 5.

Trust. In comparison to a flat list of requirements, the feature tree allowed building a mental model of the solution. The reduced number of features allowed building a shared vocabulary with stakeholders, the color coding visualizing growth of the solution, and AND-OR feature dependencies understanding design options. This focused discussions and communication with stakeholders on aspects that were essential for planning. Decisions could be taken together with these stakeholders, which led to trust in the plans and in the product organization.

Surprises and problems emerged despite the common decision making. For example, the feature tree only captured usability-related quality requirements. The pilot projects discovered that the solution's performance was too low. The resolution of that problem led to changes in technologies and architecture and required significant amount of unplanned time. The product manager now started to specify and plan quality with dedicated feature vectors [37].

5   Discussion and Conclusions

This paper has explained how feature trees [38] can be used to structure requirements and simplify release planning, hence to support release planning [20], i.e. the planning of variability over time [24]. AND relationships [13] can be exploited to group requirements into features. Feature vectors [27] can be built by exploiting REQUIRES dependencies. Features that have the same super-feature stand in an OR relationship. The resulting tree can be used for planning the development of the specified software and for controlling development progress.

The paper has shown a revelatory industrial case to evaluate feasibility and impact of the approach. The practitioners integrated the feature tree into stakeholder and need analysis, adapted the feature specification to communicate requirements and to manage the development project, and integrated the features into a roadmap that aligned the timing of pilot projects and development.

The approach reduced complexity of release planning that before would have been made with flat requirements lists [16]. The feature tree, combined with a roadmap, was a key instrument to plan development that allowed the product manager to make decision together with stakeholders. The visualization of the requirements as a feature tree allowed them building a mental model and a shared vocabulary. As a consequence, the stakeholders developed trust in the decision-making and in the product organization.

As any other approach, feature-tree based release planning had limitations, however. Documentation was based on office tools and traceability often kept implicit. Decisions, even though made together with the concerned stakeholders, turned out to be wrong because of omissions and rarely perfect estimates. These two issues made analysis of dependencies and coordination of stakeholders difficult.

The presented work has relations to other research beyond feature trees and release planning. The described feature trees are a new kind of AND/OR trees that differs from AND/OR goal trees [39]. The feature trees do not represent means-ends relationship, but dependencies in the implementation order. The documentation of a single feature, however, can be made with a goal tree. For example, the feature specification attributes *requirements* and *description* corresponded to two abstraction levels and were used to capture means-ends relationships [8]. Such feature-oriented goal trees specification is narrow in scope and can be developed incrementally. It hence has the potential to improve the scalability of goal modeling.

The case shows how feature trees can integrate roadmapping [35] and software specification. It has extended a the layered form of product roadmaps encountered in small companies [40] with explicit traceability to product feature. Such traceability allows understanding the impact of changes, for example changed effort estimates, to the other aspects of release planning, such as stakeholder support, and piloting.

Future research should replicate the study in different contexts to better understand when and how feature tree-based release planning should be used. Experimentation that compares the feature tree-based approach with the use of flat requirements backlogs provide statistical analysis of effort reduction and eliminate the potential presence of the Hawthorne effect.

Future research should enhance the presented approach with an understanding of how traceability, for example between features and stakeholders, can be structured to enhance understanding of these traces and effort for handling traceability. Also tool support can greatly simplify consistency management between the feature tree and related views and ease what-if analyses for exploring software development planning options.

References

1. Svahnberg, M., Gorschek, T., Feldt, R., Torkar, R., Bin Saleem, S., Usman Shafique, M.: A Systematic Review on Strategic Release Planning Models. Information and Software Technology 52, 237–248 (2009)
2. Cohn, M.: Agile Estimating and Planning. Prentice Hall (2006)
3. Amandeep, N.F.N.G., Ruhe, G., Stanford, M.: Intelligent Support for Software Release Planning. In: Bomarius, F., Iida, H. (eds.) PROFES 2004. LNCS, vol. 3009, pp. 248–262. Springer, Heidelberg (2004)
4. Wohlin, C., Aurum, A.: What is Important when Deciding to Include a Sotware Requirement into a Project or Release. In: International Symposium on Empiricial Software Engineering (2005)
5. Berander, P., Andrews, A.: Requirements Prioritization. In: Aurum, A., Wohlin, C. (eds.) Engineering and Managing Software Requirements. Springer, Heidelberg (2005)
6. Karlsson, L., Regnell, B., Karlsson, J., Olsson, S.: Post-Release Analysis of Requirements Selection Quality - An Industrial Case Study. In: 9th International Workshop on Requirements Engineering: Foundation for Software Quality, RefsQ 2003 (2003)
7. Karlsson, L., Dahlstedt, Å., Regnell, B., Natt och Dag, J., Persson, A.: Requirements Engineering Challenges in Market-Driven Software Development - An Interview Study with Practitioners. Information and Software Technology 49, 588–604 (2007)
8. Gorschek, T., Wohlin, C.: Requirements Abstraction Model. Requirements Engineering 11, 79–101 (2006)
9. Fricker, S., Gorschek, T., Byman, C., Schmidle, A.: Handshaking with Implementation Proposals: Negotiating Requirements Understanding. IEEE Software 27, 72–80 (2010)
10. Lehtola, L., Kauppinen, M.: Suitability of Requirements Prioritization Methods for Market-driven Software Product Development. Software Process Improvement and Practice 11, 7–19 (2006)
11. Fricker, S., Schumacher, S.: Variability-Based Release Planning. In: Regnell, B., van de Weerd, I., De Troyer, O. (eds.) ICSOB 2011. LNBIP, vol. 80, pp. 181–186. Springer, Heidelberg (2011)

12. Schobbens, P.-Y., Heymans, P., Trigaux, J.-C., Bontemps, Y.: Generic Semantics of Feature Diagrams. Computer Networks 51(207), 456–479
13. Carlshamre, P., Sandahl, K., Lindvall, M., Regnell, B., Natt och Dag, J.: An Industrial Survey of Requirements Interdependencies in Software Product Release Planning. In: 5th IEEE International Symposium on Requirements Engineering (2001)
14. Haberfellner, R., Nagel, P., Becker, M., Büchel, A., von Massow, H.: Systems Engineering: Methodik und Praxis. Verlag Industrielle Organisation (2002)
15. Yin, R.: Case Study Research: Design and Methods. SAGE Publications (2009)
16. Vlaanderen, K., Jansen, S., Brinkkemper, S., Jaspers, E.: The Agile Requirements Refinery: Applying Scrum Principles to Software Product Management. Information and Software Technology 53, 58–70 (2011)
17. Bekkers, W., van de Weed, I.: SPM Maturity Matrix. Utrecht University (2010)
18. Regnell, B., Beremark, P., Eklundh, O.: A Market-Driven Requirements Engineering Process: Results from an Industrial Process Improvement Programme. Requirements Engineering 3, 121–129 (1998)
19. Davis, A.: Just Enough Requirements Management. Dorset House Publishing (2005)
20. Carlshamre, P.: Release Planning in Market-Driven Software Product Development: Provoking an Understanding. Requirements Engineering 7, 139–151 (2002)
21. Ruhe, G., Saliu, M.O.: The Art and Science of Software Release Planning. IEEE Software 22, 47–53 (2005)
22. Li, C., van den Akker, M., Brinkkemper, S., Diepen, G.: An Integrated Approach for Requirements Selection and Scheduling in Software Release Planning. Requirements Engineering 15, 375–396 (2010)
23. Karlsson, J., Ryan, K.: A Cost-Value Approach for Prioritizing Requirements. IEEE Software 14, 67–74 (1997)
24. Pohl, K., Böckle, G., van der Linden, F.: Software Product Line Engineering: Foundations, Principles and Techniques. Springer, Heidelberg (2005)
25. Zowghi, D., Coulin, C.: Requirements Elicitation: A Survey of Techniques. In: Aurum, A., Wohlin, C. (eds.) Engineering and Managing Software Requirements. Springer, Heidelberg (2005)
26. Classen, A., Heymans, P., Schobbens, P.-Y.: What's in a Feature: A Requirements Engineering Perspective. In: 11th International Conference on Fundamental Approaches to Software Engineering, Budapest, Hungary (2008)
27. Nejmeh, B., Thomas, I.: Business-Driven Product Planning Using Feature Vectors and Increments. IEEE Software 19, 34–42 (2002)
28. Stoiber, R., Glinz, M.: Feature Unweaving: Efficient Variability Extraction and Specification for Emerging Software Product Lines. In: 4th International Workshop on Software Product Management (IWSPM 2010), Sydney, Australia (2010)
29. Phaal, R., Farrukh, C., Probert, D.: Strategic Roadmapping: A Workshop-Based Approach for Identifying and Exploring Strategic Issues and Opportunities. Engineering Management Journal 19, 3–12 (2007)
30. Draper, S.: The Hawthorne, Pygmalion, Placebo and Other Effects of Expectation: Some Notes, vol. 2011 (2010)
31. Davison, R., Martinsons, M., Kock, N.: Principles of Canonical Action Research. Information Systems Journal 14, 65–86 (2004)
32. Pruitt, J., Grudin, J.: Personas: Practice and Theory. In: 2003 Conference on Designing for User Experience (DUX 2003), New York, NY, USA (2003)

33. Carroll, J. (ed.): Scenario-Based Design: Envisioning Work and Technology in System Development: Envisioning Work and Technology in Systems Development. John Wiley & Sons (1995)
34. Kotonya, G., Sommerville, I.: Requirements Engineering with Viewpoints. Software Engineering Journal 11, 5–18 (1996)
35. Phaal, R., Farrukh, C., Probert, D.: Technology Roadmapping - A Planning Framework for Evolution and Revolution. Technological Forecasting and Social Change 71, 5–26 (2003)
36. Schmidt, M.: The Business Case Guide. Solution Matrix (2002)
37. Regnell, B., Berntsson Svensson, R., Olsson, S.: Supporting Roadmapping of Quality Requirements. IEEE Software 25, 42–47 (2008)
38. Schobbens, P.-Y., Heymans, P., Trigaux, J.-C., Bontemps, Y.: Generic Semantics of Feature Diagrams. Computer Networks 51, 456–479 (2007)
39. van Lamsweerde, A.: Goal-Oriented Requirements Engineering: A Guided Tour. In: 5th IEEE International Symposium on Requirements Engineering (RE 2001), Toronto, Canada (2001)
40. Vähäniitty, J., Lassenius, C., Rautiainen, K.: An Approach to Product Roadmapping in Small Software Product Businesses. In: 7th International Conference on Software Quality (ECSQ 2002), Helsinki, Finland (2002)

Goal-Oriented Requirements Engineering and Enterprise Architecture: Two Case Studies and Some Lessons Learned

Wilco Engelsman[1,2] and Roel Wieringa[2]

[1] BiZZdesign
`w.engelsman@bizzdesign.nl`
[2] University of Twente
`roelw@cs.utwente.nl`

Abstract. An enterprise-architecture (EA) is a high-level representation of the enterprise, used for managing the relation between business and IT. [**Problem**] Ideally, all elements of an enterprise architecture can be traced to business goals ad vice versa, but in practice, this is not the case. In this experience paper we explore the use of goal-oriented requirements engineering (GORE) techniques to improve this bidirectional traceability. [**Principal ideas/results**] We collected GORE techniques from KAOS, i*, Tropos, BMM and TOGAF and integrated them in a language called ARMOR. This was used by enterprise architects in case study. It turned out that the language was too complex for the architects to understand as intended. Based on this we redefined ARMOR to contain only a minimum number of goal-oriented concepts, and this was tested in a second case study. This second case study suggests that the minimal version is still useful for traceability management in practice. [**Contribution**] We have identified a core set of concepts of goal-oriented requirements engineering, that can be used in the practice of enterprise architecture. Our analysis provides hypotheses into GORE that will be tested in future case studies.

1 Introduction

In large companies the gap between business and IT is usually bridged by designing and maintaining a so-called *enterprise architecture* (EA), which is a high-level representation of the enterprise, used for managing the relation between business and IT. A full-scale EA consists (i) an architecture of the business, in terms of products, services and processes, (ii) an application architecture in terms of of application components, functions and services, (iii) an infrastructure architecture in terms of servers, mainframes, network, and (iv) the relationships between these different architectures [19].

Enterprise architectures are typically modelled in larger organizations (say starting from 500 employees) and are used to coordinate IT projects and to manage the cost of IT. Increasingly, they are also used to increase flexibility of

B. Regnell and D. Damian (Eds.): REFSQ 2012, LNCS 7195, pp. 306–320, 2012.
© Springer-Verlag Berlin Heidelberg 2012

the organization and to justify the contribution of IT to business goals. This requires traceability of business goals to IT architecture (to quickly identify the impact on IT of changes in business goals) and of IT architecture to business goals (to justify the contribution of an IT component to a business goal). This requires a goal-oriented addition to the current crop of EA modelling languages. In this experience paper, we explore the addition of goal-oriented requirements engineering (GORE) to enterprise architecture modelling in order to realize this bidirectional traceability. An important constraint is that we want the resulting language to be usable and useful for enterprise architects in practice. Usability means at least tool support and understandability for the architects; utility means that the resulting language and tool can indeed be used to realize traceability in practical cases.

2   Related Work

The Business Rules Group has published a model that relates the business goals and EA, called the *Business Motivation Model* (BMM),[1] which is now an OMG standard. The Open Group TOGAF standard also assume a close link between EA and business goals [19].

However, little research has been done to date to extend architecture modelling with goal modelling. Clements & Bass [4] extend software architecture modelling with GORE, but abolish all notational conventions of GORE techniques and return to the basics of bulleted lists of possible goals and possible stakeholders. Stirna et al. [16] describe a participative approach to enterprise modelling that includes relating goals to enterprise models. Jureta & Faulkner [9] sketch a goal-oriented language, that links goals and a number of other intentional structures to actors, but not to enterprise architecture models. Horkhoff & Yu [8] present a method to evaluate achievement of goals by enterprise models, all represented in i*. None of these methods presents a technique to relate business goals to EA validated in practice with enterprise architects.

An important obstacle to applying GORE in practice is the complexity of the notation. Matulevičius and Heymans [11] concluded that i* and KAOS contain constructs not used in practice and contain different constructs representing the same thing. After an ontological analysis they concluded that the i* goal and soft goal are essentially the same concept, just as the means-end relation and the contribution relation [12]. Moody et al. [13,14] identified many opportunities for clarification and simplification of the i* notation. Carvallo et al [3] recommended that practitioners should not and need not learn the entire syntax of i*. Our paper is not about notations but about usability and utility of GORE concepts in EA practice; the Archimate 1.0 language on top of which ARMOR is defined, was already understood and used by the architects who participated in our case studies.

---

[1] http://www.businessrulesgroup.org/bmm.shtml

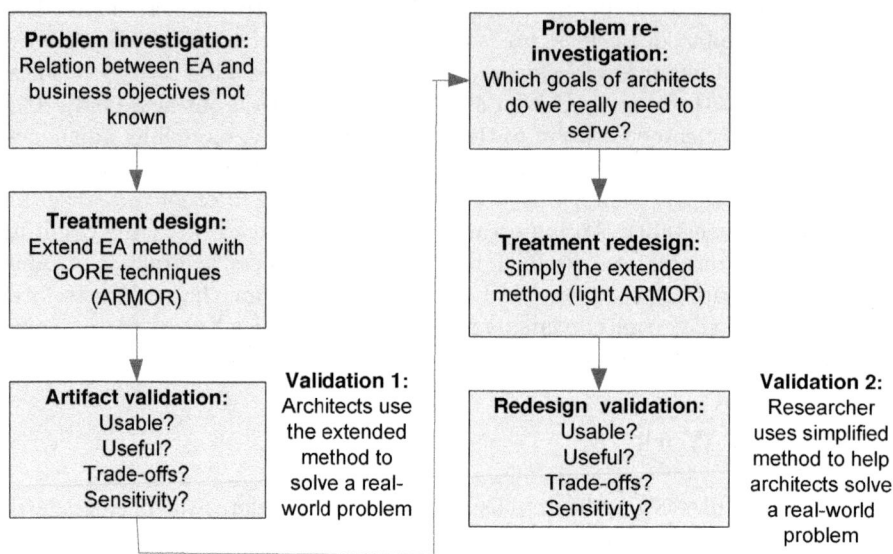

Fig. 1. Design research methodology of this paper

3 Research Methodology

We used a design research methodology in which we alternate over an engineering cycle, where we design an artifact, and a research cycle, where we investigate the properties of this artifact and of the problems it is intended to solve [7,20] Figure 1 shows that we executed the engineering cycle twice. In the first iteration, we investigated the problem to be solved, designed a method called ARMOR to treat the problem (section 4), supported by a tool for editing and traceability analysis[2] and validated the artifact (section 5). In the second, we stripped ARMOR to its essentials, called Light ARMOR (section 6), and validated this lightweight version and supporting tool (section 7).

ARMOR is an extension of an EA modelling language called Archimate 1.0 [18] with goal-oriented requirements engineering (GORE) techniques [5]. We call this a *treatment* rather than a solution because it would be simplistic to assume that any real-world problem can be totally solved, just as it would be simplistic to assume that any medical problem could be totally eliminated by a medicine.

ARMOR combined concepts from all well-known GORE languages, which is why this research also provides insights into GORE concepts in general. To validate ARMOR, the first author taught the method to enterprise architects of a large government organization, who then used it to perform an EA design project. This is a form of *technical action research* (TAR), in which an artifact is validated by actually using it to solve a real-world problem. This TAR project itself has the structure of an engineering cycle performed by the enterprise architects (figure 2).

---

[2] http://www.bizzdesign.nl/download/downloads-trial-software

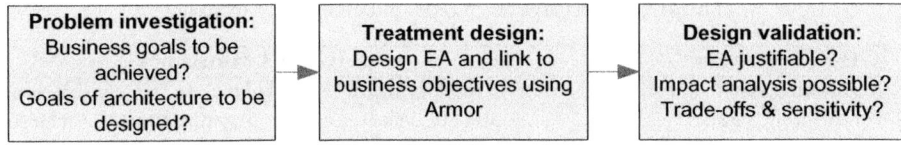

Fig. 2. Structure of validations 1 and 2

These insights from case study 1 led to an improved problem understanding and in a second engineering cycle we simplified ARMOR in the light of the lessons learned. Light ARMOR was then used by the first author to design an EA for another client, acting as consultant. This is validation 2 in figure 1. This is a second TAR project, but this time with the researcher (Engelsman) as actor, rather than the client itself, as in validation 1.

The lessons learned from validation 2 were used to answer the researchers' validation questions about Light ARMOR. These answers were then generalized to GORE concepts in general, when used in similar contexts (section 8).

4   Definition of ARMOR

Table 1 lists the major GORE concepts and shows how we have used them in ARMOR. The following list summarizes the motivation for the construction of ARMOR. More detail is provided elsewhere [5].

- Goals belong to *stakeholders,* and different stakeholders may have conflicting goals. This is important in practice but is left undefined in most GORE languages, although the i* concept of intentional actor has some similarity with our stakeholder concept. We have adopted the stakeholder concept of TOGAF [19].
- BMM, i*, and KAOS all define a *goal* as an end (or desire or intention) of a stakeholder but differ in defining this goal as a property of the system or of its environment. We define goal as some end a stakeholder desires to achieve and leave open what it is a property of.
- We follow i* in distinguishing *hard* and *soft* goals but make the requirement "clear satisfaction criteria" explicit by requiring measurability.
- Goal *decomposition* is in terms of conjunction of subgoals. It is called "refinement" in KAOS. Tropos uses the concept of satisficing. i* and BMM have rather vague definitions.
- The *contribution* relation is defined most clearly in Tropos and is taken to mean influence, positive or negative.
- The *means-end* relation is used in i* to identify tasks to realize goals and in KAOS to identify operations to realize goals. In ARMOR we define it as relating a goal (the end) to some artifact (the means) that realizes the goal. This artefact can be anything, such as a goal, requirement or an element from the architecture.

Table 1. Overview of GORE and ARMOR constructs

GORE construct	ARMOR construct
"Organizational actors are viewed as having intentional properties such as goals, beliefs, abilities, and commitments" i* [21].	A *stakeholder* is an individual, team, or organization (or classes thereof) with interests in, or concerns relative to, the outcome of the architecture ARMOR [5]. adopted from TOGAF [19].
"Goals are desired system properties that have been expressed by some stakeholder(s)" KAOS [10]. 'Goals are the intentions of a stakeholder" i* [21].	A *goal* is some end that a stakeholder wants to achieve [5].
"Hard Goals are the intentions of a stakeholder" i* [21].	A *hard goal* is a goal with measurable indicators [5].
"Soft Goals are goals without clear satisfaction criteria" i* [21].	A *soft goal* is a goal without measurable indicators [5].
"An element that is linked to its component nodes" i* [21]. "An end that includes an other end" BMM [2]. "The parent is satisficed if all of the offspring are satisficed" Tropos [1]. "The conjunction of all the subgoals must be a sufficient condition entailing the goal" KAOS [10].	A goal can be *decomposed* into two or more concrete sub-goals, such that the goal is achieved if and only if all its sub-goals are achieved.
"The contribution of a design on a qualitative goal ..." KAOS [10]. "Link elements to a soft goal to analyze its contribution" i* [21]. "Contribution analysis identifies goals that can contribute positively or negatively in the fulfillment of the goal to be analyzed..." Tropos [1].	A goal G1 *contributes* to another goal G2 if satisfaction of G1 influences the satisfaction of G2 positively or negatively [5].
"These links indicate a relationship between an end, and a means for attaining it i* [21]". "Relationship linking a requirement to operations KAOS [10]".	A *means-end* relation relates a goal (the end) to some artefact (the means) that realizes the goal [5].
"Goals are conflicting if under some boundary condition the goals cannot be achieved altogether" KAOS [10]".	A *conflict* relation exists between two goals if under some boundary conditions they cannot be achieved together [5].
"Goal assigned to an agent of the software being studied. KAOS [10]". "A quantitative statement of business need that must be met by a particular architecture or work package" TOGAF [19] .	A *requirement* is some end that must be realized by a single component of the architecture [5].
"Concerns are the key interests that are crucially important to the stakeholders in the system, and determine the acceptability of the system" TOGAF [19].	A *concern* is some key interest that is crucially important to certain stakeholders in a system, and determines the acceptability of the system [5].
"An Assessment is a judgment about some Influencer that affects the organization's ability to employ its Means or achieve its Ends BMM [2]".	An *assessment* is the outcome of the analysis of some concern [5].

- Only KAOS defines the *conflict* relation. However we believe it to be so different from the contribution relation that we include it, adopting the KAOS definition.
- KAOS is also the only GORE language that explicitly defines the *requirement* concept. It is defined as a concrete goal that has been assigned to a single actor. TOGAF defines requirement as a business need allocated to an architecture. The ARMOR definition combines these two definitions.
- The concepts of *concern* and *assessment* are not part of GORE but of the EA literature. We therefore included these concepts, taking our clues from BMM and TOGAF.

ARMOR has a notation that extends the EA language Archimate 1.0 [18], and tool support in the form of an editor. The editor supports the creation of integrated goal models and EA models. The tool also provides functionality to trace requirements to EA and vice versa. The resulting language is called ArchiMate 2.0. ArchiMate 1.0 is an Open Group Standard[3]. ArchiMate 2.0 is currently under review by The Open Group for acceptance to update ArchiMate 1.0. The notation is described and motivated elsewhere [5,15] and does not concern us here.

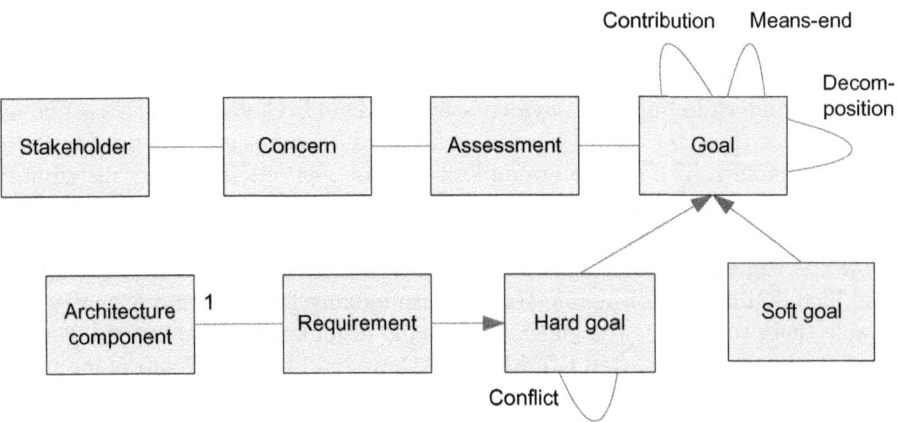

Fig. 3. ARMOR's metamodel. The arrow represents specialization. Cardinalities are not shown in the figure.

Figure 3 shows the core part of ARMOR's metamodel. Cardinalities are not shown so as not to clutter up the diagram, except the cardinality from requirement to architecture component, which is many-one. The diagram shows that stakeholders have concerns, that they assess in a certain way, which leads to goals, that are hard or soft; hard goals can be requirements, and each requirement is allocated to exactly one architecture component. Goals can be decomposed, can have contribution and means-end relations, and they can conflict. The complete meta-model of ARMOR has been described elsewhere [5].

---

[3] http://www3.opengroup.org/subjectareas/enterprise/archimate

5   Case Study 1

To validate ARMOR we first wanted to test usability by enterprise architects. The further question of utility can only be answered once we have a usable language. However, we did want to know whether ARMOR misses potentially useful constructs. We therefore identified the following research questions.

Q1. What constructs of ARMOR do enterprise architects use in practice?
Q2. Why (for which purpose) do they use these concepts and relations?
Q3. Is this the intended use of the constructs?
Q4. Which construct not in ARMOR are considered by architects useful additions to ARMOR?

The only way to answer these questions is to have practicing enterprise architects use ARMOR and observe how they do it. Since ARMOR will not be transferred to a practical context unless we do the transfer, we needed to perform an action case study, where we first transferred knowledge of ARMOR to a company and then observed ARMOR use.

5.1   Case Description and Research Design

The case study took place at a large governmental organization in the Netherlands that we will call Organization 1. The organization is responsible for state pensions and child support payments by the Dutch Government. The budget available for these payments is around thirty billion euros, consisting entirely of taxpayer money. The company employs around 3000 civil servants distributed over several locations in the country. Relevant stakeholders include enterprise architects and information analysts, who are looking for a technique that can show the value of their designs to business stakeholders. Relevant stakeholders also include information managers, who are looking for a technique that would enable them to analyze the effect of changing organization goals on the EA.

Organization 1 contacted BiZZdesign if they could help with improving traceability between the business objectives and the enterprise-architecture. BiZZdesign offered to provide ARMOR with tool support, which the organization accepted.

The first author (Engelsman) provided a one-day training on ARMOR to six enterprise architects of Organization 1. The architects of Organization 1 then proceeded to create ARMOR models of business goals and their links to the existing EA. They did this on their own, by investigating business documents of Organization 1 and by conducting workshops. No help was provided. However, the first author visited Organization 1 every two weeks to review the models made by the architects and to provide advice. On those occasions the first author also made notes of discussions among the architects.

To summarize, the treatment applied to the case consisted of (1) a one-day training and (2) bi-weekly advice. Data collection took place by collecting documents produced by the architects and by making notes during discussions among architects. There was no possibility to collect observations by other means, such as questionnaires or interviews, as the enterprise architects were too busy for that.

5.2 Observations and Explanations

We extracted the following observations from the data.

– The architects used the *stakeholder* concept as intended, to record the existence of some entity that has a stake in the development of the organization. The (obvious) explanation is that the stakeholder concept is widely known in businesses, and has a meaning well-captured by the TOGAF definition that we adopted.
– The architects also used the *goal* concept as intended. This too is a concept well-known in the practice and theory of business management. However, they did not see why the distinction between soft goals and hard goals would be relevant in their models. This is explained by their way of working: The architects started out identifying relevant business goals and then proceeded, later on in their work, to decompose these into key performance indicators (KPIs). So initially, all goals are soft; eventually, all goals are decomposed into hard goals. For example, the soft goal to maintain quality of service was decomposed into the goals to maintain timeliness of service requests and to maintain legality of service, which are hard goals because measurement procedures were defined for them: the maximum amount of time for a service request, and for every decision a reference to the law on which the decision is based, must be documented. They did not see the point of making this transition explicit by using a different symbol for soft and hard goals.
– The *decomposition* relation was used as intended: to refine a goal into more concrete sub-goals, in such a way that achievement of the conjunction of the sub-goals implies the achievement of the higher level goal. For example, the goal to decrease cost was decomposed into the sub-goals to decrease cost of internal services, to decrease cost of external services and to decrease cost of IT.
– The *contribution* relation was used by the architects as intended, namely to indicate that achievement of one goal influences the achievement of another goal. For example, the goal to increase automatic service delivery contributed positively to the goal of decreasing cost of external services.
– The *means-end* relation is constrained in the ARMOR tool to be an influence relation from a system requirement to a goal. This was understood by the architects and they used it in this way. But they did not understand why a separate means-end relation was included to represent this, where a contribution relation expresses in their view exactly the same thing: Influence.
– The *conflict* relation was not used by the architects in this case. The architects explained that in this case there simply were no conflicts between different stakeholder goals. In addition, they did not see any difference between a conflict and a negative contribution.

- In ARMOR, a *requirement* is a goal that must be achieved by a single component of the architecture. This definition was not quite understood by the architects, and they often formulated requirements that were not goals of a single architecture component. An example of this is the "requirement" that the use of marketing techniques must be improved. This is a business goal, not a system requirement.
- The architects had difficulty understanding the difference between *concerns* and goals. The intention of the concept is that it be used for areas of concern for the stakeholder, such as sales, cost or profit. Instead, architects in our case used it to denote stable goal-like statements, such as the goal to achieve excellent service delivery, or to achieve a result-oriented working environment. Even after explaining the difference in one of our bi-weekly meetings, they kept using it the same way. An explanation of this could be that the concern concept is too general to be of use. What concerned the architects in our case was goals; so they used it to express goal-related concerns.
- The architects found it difficult to understand the difference between concern, goal and *assessment*. They sometimes used the assessment concept to store the contextual reasons for having a goal. For example, the goal of cost-reduction was annotated with an "assessment", that is a contextual reason, namely that the Dutch government faces the need for large budget cuts due to the financial crisis and the aging population.

5.3   Answers to Research Questions

Q1. *What constructs were used?* All constructs except the *conflict* relation were used by the architects in this case. The conflict relation was not used because the architects stated that there were no conflicting goals in this case. There is not much we can conclude from this: Surely there are some cases where there are no conflicting goals, and we believe this is one of them; but there are other cases where there *are* conflicting goals. At the very least we can conclude that the idea of conflicting goals (goals that cannot always be all satisfied at the same time) was understood by the architects.

Q2. *Why (for which purpose) do they use these concepts and relations?*

Q3. *Is this the intended use of the constructs?* The constructs of *stakeholder, goal, decomposition* and *contribution* were used as intended. The concept of *requirement* was not used as intended, but rather was used as if it were the same concept as that of a goal. That is, requirements were not always allocated to one architecture component.

The *means-end* relationship was used as intended, namely as relation from requirement to goal, because the tool did not allow any other use. The architects did not see a relevant difference with the contribution relation.

Finally, the concepts of *concern* and *assessment* were not understood by the architects.

Q4. *Which potentially useful constructs do architects miss in ARMOR?* The architects found it useful to express contextual reasons for a goal, and used the *assessment* construct to do this.

5.4   Validity

Our observations may have been influenced by the fact that the first author also designed the language; this may have impacted the training positively (exceptionally inspiring explanations) or negatively (too much knowledge taken for granted). It may also have motivated the architects to have a socially desirable opinion about ARMOR. However, the architects had to do a real-world project with limited resources and as they are paying for this consultancy in money, and spending time on using ARMOR, they have no reason to present their experiences more favorably to the designer of ARMOR than they are.

Also, the observer (Engelsman) may have let his desire to design a usable and useful language influence his observations. This may have impacted the observations where architects where observed to use the ARMOR constructs as intended, but not the observations where the architects were observed to misunderstand the constructs of ARMOR. We regard at least those latter observations as credible.

Finally, could we generalize from this case to other cases? Generalization from case studies cannot use statistical inference but can use reasoning by analogy [6,17]. This means that we should explain our observations in terms of some general characteristics of the case, and provide a plausible argument that in cases with the same general characteristics, the same observations will be made.

Our observations all relate to understandability, and this relates to the cognitive competencies of the enterprise architects in Organization 1. The architects in Organization 1 had to be able to design and understand a distributed enterprise architecture for an organization of 3000 employees. Each of them had at least 2 years of experience as enterprise architect, and the organization operated its EA process at a maturity level comparable with level 2 of the US Department of Comments Architecture Capability Maturity Model[4]. All of this may explain why they used the constructs of stakeholder, goal, decomposition and contribution as intended, and we expect that in other organizations, similar to Organization 1 in the aspects just mentioned, architects will understand and use these constructs as intended too. But we also expect that in many of those organizations, the constructs of hard and soft goal, requirement (as defined in ARMOR), concern and assessment will not be understood and be used in a way not intended by the designers of ARMOR, that the means-end relation will be considered superfluous and that negative contribution will not be distinguished from conflicts. This generalization is a hypothesis that must be validated in replications of this case study. We do not claim that it will be found to be true for all future case studies. However we do expect to encounter in the future cases similar to this one. This was a sufficiently strong reason for us to redesign the language.

---

[4] http://ocio.os.doc.gov/ITPolicyandPrograms/Enterprise_Architecture/
PROD01_004935

6 Redesign

Figure 4 shows the metamodel of a stripped down version of ARMOR that we call Light ARMOR. We dropped the constructs of concern, assessment, hard and soft goal and means-end from the language as these were not understood, or the relevance not understood, by the architects. To facilitate recording contextual reasons for a goal (the construct missed by the architects in Organization 1), the *Goal* construct was extended with a text attribute in which this reason could be recorded in free text.

The construct of *Contribution* was replaced by that of *Influence* so that we can avoid the locution "negative contribution", which we ourselves find as confusing as the concept of negative income. A goal G1 *influences* another goal G2 if satisfaction of G1 has an effect on the satisfaction of G2. So influence is a causal relation.

We did keep the notion of *Conflict* as the inability to satisfy two goals simultaneously can be a case of causal prevention ("negative contribution") but it may also be a case of logical inconsistency, legal exclusion, ethical incompatibility, or plain monetary conflict (satisfying the goals jointly exceeds the budget). The concept of conflict is complex and awaits future exploration; but we find it too important to drop from the language just because it has not been used in one case.

Finally, requirements are a special case of goals, just as before, but we dropped the idea that we require a separate modeling concept for it. A requirement is just a goal assigned to a component of the architecture.

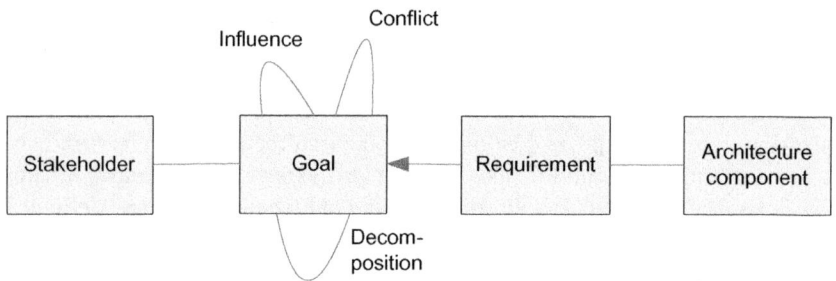

Fig. 4. Meta-model of Light ARMOR

7 Case Study 2

In addition to learning about the understandability of Light ARMOR, we would now like to learn about the utility of the language. Did our drastic reduction in the number of constructs impact the ability of enterprise architects to use the language (and supporting tool) to trace business goals to architecture components and vice versa?

The best way to find an answer to this question is to have enterprise architects use Light ARMOR to model the goals of an enterprise architecture, and then actually let them do the backward and forward tracing. This turned out not to be possible on short notice, and so we chose another form of action research, namely one in which the researchers themselves use their technique to solve a customer problem. In case study 2, the first author used Light ARMOR to solve an organizational problem following the engineering cycle of figure 2 and then used this experience to answer some validation questions about the design of Light ARMOR (figure 1). The research questions of case study 2 are, then:

- Q1 Is Light ARMOR understandable to architects?
- Q2 Can Light ARMOR be used to trace back and forth between business goals and enterprise architecture components?

7.1 Case Description and Research Design

The case company, called Organization 2 henceforth, is at a drinking water production facility in the Netherlands. The company is responsible for the production and delivery of fresh drinking water to 1.2 million people and transports 73 billion liters of drinking water each year. It has about 500 employees divided over three divisions, viz. Production, Sales and Environment.

Enterprise-architects and information analysts in Organization 2 are facing rapid change and shrinking budgets and are looking for a technique that will enable them to assess the impact of changing business goals (forward tracing) and to determine the value of the architecture (backward tracing). We were given the opportunity to use Light ARMOR to link business goals to their current enterprise architecture model in a no-fee small consultancy project. This would allow them to see if they would want to use this technique in the future, and gave us the opportunity to perform a first test of Light ARMOR.

We planned and performed the following interactions with Organization 2. The first author interviewed the architect responsible for the EA of Organization 1, and studied primary documents documenting the EA and business goals. He designed a Light ARMOR model of the links with the two, and then interviewed the enterprise architect a second time, asking her, without providing training in Light ARMOR, (1) to explain the Light ARMOR model and (2) to assess whether she could use this model to solve her traceability problem. This provided the enterprise architect with sufficient information to conclude her problem solving cycle (figure 2) and provided the researcher with information to find initial answers to his validation questions (validation 2 in figure 1). The researcher kept a diary of his own modelling process and made a transcript of the interview to be able to answer his own research questions.We emphasize that in this case we interacted with only one enterprise architect of the organization.

7.2 Observations and Explanations

- The major observation recorded in the researcher's diary is that it was often difficult to identify the stakeholders responsible for the goals from the primary documents or from the first interview with the enterprise architect. There are several possible explanations of this, such as that there is so much agreement about goals in Organization 2 that there is no need to record the goal owner; or that there is so much disagreement among the stakeholders that it is too dangerous to record a goal owner.

- The influence relation in this case is truly a causal relationship; including it in a model is an empirical statement that must be true about the world. For example, the goal to perform water filtering influences the goal to achieve clean drinking water. A second example is that the goal to achieve lower operating cost is influenced by the goal to achieve economics of scale with collaborative buying. Like all empirical statements, these influence statements could turn out to be falsified by events in the real world.

- The decomposition relation by contrast is not empirical, but definitional. It was used to create a definition of a term that the stakeholders agreed on. It only expresses an agreement between those stakeholders and not necessarily between other stakeholders. For example, the goal to achieve excellent drinking water quality was decomposed into the goals of sufficient pressure, safe drinking water, odorless drinking water and visually clean drinking water. This is a definition that turns a soft goal into a hard goal.

- The architect judged that Light ARMOR could be used to link business goals to architecture components to realize forward traceability (assessing impact of goal change) and backward traceability (justifying an architecture component). She suggested that this would also be useful to link project goals to business goals, providing a way to scope projects.

- In the opinion of the architect, the conflict relation would be useful in the assessment of project risks. This would however also require a way to document the resolution of these risks.For example record that one of the goals was dropped or that an other way was found to resolve the conflict.

- To test understandability of Light ARMOR we asked the architect to explain the model to us. The architect did not have prior training on GORE or Light ARMOR, but she could readily identify what the models meant.

7.3   Answers to Research Questions

The last observation provides support for the claim that Light ARMOR is understandable for practicing enterprise architects, which answers Q1 for this case.

The positive opinion of the architect about forward and backward traceability provides support for the claim of utility of Light ARMOR, answering Q2. In addition to the use for (1) estimating impact of change and (2) justifying the presence of an architecture component, the enterprise architect suggested using the model for (3) setting project goals and (4) documenting project risks and their mitigation. We will include these possible uses of Light ARMOR in our future research.

7.4   Validity

The major threat to internal validity is that the architect answered our questions in a socially desirable way. There is in this case nothing we can do to mitigate these risks, but in this case too we note that Organization 2 is looking for a way to exercise tighter control over its enterprise architecture in order to respond to changes in goals and a decreasing budget, and, doing so, has little reason to please the researchers. A *negative* response of the architect would have been really informative (and disastrous for the designers of Light ARMOR); the positive response that we actually received is less informative but is still encouraging.

The observations in this case make it plausible that if we were to repeat such a project in a similar organization (similar size, maturity of EA, experience of enterprise architect, dynamics of changing goals and shrinking budgets), we are likely to get similar results (positive opinion of the architect). This is a hypothesis to be tested in future case studies.

8   Lessons Learned and Further Work

In line with the evaluations reported in related work (section 2), we found that GORE concepts such as means-end relations and the distinction between hard and soft goals could not be used in our two case studies; and the concepts of concern and assessment taken from BMM and TOGAF could not be used either in our two cases. Also, the idea that a requirement exists as a separate modeling concept puzzled the practitioners in case 1. They had difficulty distinguishing between the two.

Stripping these elements away and including the results from case study 2, we conclude that our case studies provide support to the claim that the GORE concepts of *stakeholder, goal, decomposition, influence* and *conflict* are usable in practice and potentially useful for the practitioner. The particular syntax of the language that we used in our case studies did not play a role in these evaluations.

A third lesson we draw from these two case studies is that a stripped down language adding only these elements to an EA language can be useful for maintaining traceability between business goals and enterprise architecture. This is a hypothesis to be tested and possibly further qualified in future case studies.

A fourth and final lesson is that the conflict relation can be confused with the negative contribution relation, but still can be useful to keep because it allows representing project risks and their mitigation. This final hypothesis will be a topic of future case studies.

References

1. Bresciani, P., Perini, A., Giorgini, P., Giunchiglia, F., Mylopoulos, J.: Tropos: An agent-oriented software development methodology. Autonomous Agents and Multi-Agent Systems 8(3), 203–236 (2004)
2. Business Motivation Model: Business motivation model version 1.0. Standard document (2007), http://www.omg.org/spec/BMM/1.0/PDF (22.09. 2009)

3. Carvallo, J.P., Franch, X.: On the use of i* for architecting hybrid systems: A method and an evaluation report. In: The Practice of Enterprise Modeling, pp. 38–53 (2009)
4. Clements, P., Bass, L.: Using Business Goals to Inform a Software Architecture. In: 18th IEEE International Requirements Engineering Conference, pp. 69–78. IEEE Computer Society Press (2010)
5. Engelsman, W., Quartel, D.A.C., Jonkers, H., van Sinderen, M.J.: Extending enterprise architecture modelling with business goals and requirements. Enterprise Information Systems 5(1), 9–36 (2011)
6. Forrester, J.: If p, then what? thinking in cases. History of the Human Sciences 9(3) (1996)
7. Hevner, A.R., March, S.T., Park, J., Ram, S.: Design science in information system research. MIS Quarterly 28(1), 75–105 (2004)
8. Horkoff, J., Yu, E.: Evaluating Goal Achievement in Enterprise Modeling – An Interactive Procedure and Experiences. In: Persson, A., Stirna, J. (eds.) PoEM 2009. LNBIP, vol. 39, pp. 145–160. Springer, Heidelberg (2009)
9. Jureta, I., Faulkner, S.: An Agent-Oriented Meta-model for Enterprise Modelling. In: Akoka, J., Liddle, S.W., Song, I.-Y., Bertolotto, M., Comyn-Wattiau, I., van den Heuvel, W.-J., Kolp, M., Trujillo, J., Kop, C., Mayr, H.C. (eds.) ER Workshops 2005. LNCS, vol. 3770, pp. 151–161. Springer, Heidelberg (2005)
10. Lamsweerde, A.: Kaos tutorial. Cediti, September 5 (2003)
11. Matulevičius, R., Heymans, P.: Comparing Goal Modelling Languages: An Experiment. In: Sawyer, P., Heymans, P. (eds.) REFSQ 2007. LNCS, vol. 4542, pp. 18–32. Springer, Heidelberg (2007)
12. Matulevičius, R., Heymans, P., Opdahl, A.: Comparing grl and kaos using the ueml approach. In: Enterprise Interoperability II, pp. 77–88 (2007)
13. Moody, D.: The physics of notations: Improving the usability and communicability of visual notations in requirements engineering. In: 2009 Fourth International Workshop on Requirements Engineering Visualization (REV), pp. 56–57 (September 2009)
14. Moody, D., Heymans, P., Matulevicius, R.: Improving the Effectiveness of Visual Representations in Requirements Engineering: An Evaluation of i* Visual Syntax. In: 17th IEEE International Requirements Engineering Conference, RE 2009, pp. 171–180. IEEE Computer Society Press (2009)
15. Quartel, D.A.C., Engelsman, W., Jonkers, H., van Sinderen, M.J.: A goal-oriented requirements modelling language for enterprise architecture. In: Proceedings of the Thirteenth IEEE International EDOC Enterprise Computing Conference, EDOC 2009, Auckland, New Zealand, pp. 3–13. IEEE Computer Society Press, Los Alamitos (2009)
16. Stirna, J., Persson, A., Sandkuhl, K.: Participative Enterprise Modeling: Experiences and Recommendations. In: Krogstie, J., Opdahl, A.L., Sindre, G. (eds.) CAiSE 2007 and WES 2007. LNCS, vol. 4495, pp. 546–560. Springer, Heidelberg (2007)
17. Sunstein, C.R.: On analogical reasoning. Harvard Law Review 106, 741–790 (1993)
18. The Open Group: ArchiMate 1.0 Specification. Van Haren Publishing (2009)
19. The Open Group: TOGAF Version 9. Van Haren Publishing (2009)
20. Wieringa, R.J.: Design science as nested problem solving. In: Proceedings of the 4th International Conference on Design Science Research in Information Systems and Technology, Philadelphia, pp. 1–12. ACM, New York (2009)
21. Yu, E.: Towards modelling and reasoning support for early-phase requirements engineering. In: Proceedings of the Third IEEE International Symposium on Requirements Engineering, pp. 226–235. IEEE Computer Society Press (2002)

Author Index